HTML, CSS & JavaScript® Mobile Development

FOR DUMMIES®

by William Harrel

WILEY

John Wiley & Sons, Inc.

HTML, CSS & JavaScript® Mobile Development For Dummies®

Published by
John Wiley & Sons, Inc.
111 River Street
Hoboken, NJ 07030-5774

www.wiley.com

About the Author

William Harrel has nearly 25 years of digital design experience. He was one of the pioneers of publishing on desktop computers, starting with the very first digital design and graphics programs, PageMaker and Photoshop. Like so many of the early "desktop publishers," with the emergence of the World Wide Web, he found that making the transition to web design was the next logical step. His design firm has designed hundreds of websites, Flash websites, and electronic documents. His earlier books on Photoshop, PageMaker, and digital media in general were some of the first publications on these topics.

William Harrel has authored or coauthored 19 books on designing both print media and electronic documents, such as websites, PDFs, Flash sites and Flash applications, slide and multimedia presentations, on computers. These include titles on Photoshop, Acrobat *(Acrobat For Dummies)*, PageMaker, Flash, Director, and several other graphics and publishing packages.

His latest online courses, Introduction to Adobe Flash CS4, Introduction to Adobe Flash CS5, Intermediate Adobe Flash CS4, and Intermediate Adobe Flash CS5, are currently offered at more than 2,500 colleges and universities. These are fully accredited courses offering in-depth instruction on Flash, including lessons on developing Flash applications for handheld devices.

He has also written hundreds of magazine articles, ranging in subject matter from Mac, PC, and other hardware reviews to all types of software packages — including page layout, graphics, web design, Flash, multimedia, and word processing — in such notable magazines as *PC World, Home Office Computing, Compute, Windows Magazine, Publish, Entrepreneur, Home Office,* and many, many others. He currently reviews printers, notebook computers, and tablets for *Computer Shopper.*

Harrel's blog, Communications Technology Watch (`http://comm techwatch.com`), is a well-respected source for information related to media designed for and on computers. Communications Technology Watch contains volumes of material on using Flash and other applications, including most programs in the Adobe Creative Suite.

William Harrel was also the owner-operator of a nationwide Internet Service Provider (ISP) for 14 years. In addition to hosting thousands of wWebsites, his ISP firm designed and maintained websites for hundreds of clients. The firm also specialized in Voice over IP (VoIP) telecommunications technology, which entailed (in part) designing web apps for integrating mobile devices into their customers' VoIP phone systems.

Harrel has managed and been the chief designer at his design firm for well over two decades. The firm has designed websites and other marketing material for such notable firms as the California Spine Institute, local Red Cross chapters, local chapters of Narcotics Anonymous, and scores of others. Nowadays, designing mobile versions of his clients' websites is part of the normal course of his firm's business.

Dedication

To my lovely 13-year-old daughter, Samantha, who puts up with my long and inconveniently timed hours sitting in front of a computer.

Author's Acknowledgments

If it weren't for the fine folks at Wiley Publishing, including Katie Feltman, Christopher Morris, Barry Childs-Helton, Debbye Butler, Brian Walls, and Ronald Norman, this book would not have been possible. These projects require a herculean effort on everybody's part. Thank you for the hard work in turning this into a top-notch publication.

Thanks also to Bill Sanders of sunlight.com for his tremendous help in developing the JavaScript sections of this book. Without his contributions, this book would not be nearly as complete a work on mobile website development. Bill stepped in and helped on a moment's notice, and I'm truly grateful.

My family, also, deserves a heartfelt *thank-you* for putting up with the long and ridiculous hours it takes to complete a project of this scale. They've done this with me 19 times now. I hope they understand how sincerely thankful I am.

Finally, thank you to all the authors of all the books — so many of them Wiley publications — I've read over the years. These books allow self-taught designers like me to learn what it takes to make a living in this high-tech information-technology age. I'm proud to be among their ranks. I can attest firsthand that this hard work — the toil involved in writing these long, highly technical publications — really does make a valuable contribution to the advancement of information technology, as well as to the careers of many design professionals. Thank you.

Publisher's Acknowledgments

We're proud of this book; please send us your comments at http://dummies.custhelp.com. For other comments, please contact our Customer Care Department within the U.S. at 877-762-2974, outside the U.S. at 317-572-3993, or fax 317-572-4002.

Some of the people who helped bring this book to market include the following:

Acquisitions, Editorial, and Vertical Websites

Sr. Project Editor: Christopher Morris

Sr. Acquisitions Editor: Katie Feltman

Copy Editors: Barry Childs-Helton, Debbye Butler, Brian Walls

Technical Editor: Ronald Norman

Editorial Manager: Kevin Kirschner

Vertical Websites Project Managers: Laura Moss-Hollister, Jenny Swisher

Supervising Producer: Rich Graves

Vertical Websites Associate Producers: Josh Frank, Marilyn Hummel, Douglas Kuhn, Shawn Patrick

Editorial Assistant: Amanda Graham

Sr. Editorial Assistant: Cherie Case

Cover Photos: © istockphoto.com / Ali Mazraie Shadi; © istockphoto.com / David Humphrey

Cartoons: Rich Tennant (www.the5thwave.com)

Composition Services

Project Coordinator: Kristie Rees

Layout and Graphics: Lavonne Roberts, Corrie Socolovitch

Proofreader: ConText Editorial Services, Inc.

Indexer: Potomac Indexing, LLC

Publishing and Editorial for Technology Dummies

 Richard Swadley, Vice President and Executive Group Publisher

 Andy Cummings, Vice President and Publisher

 Mary Bednarek, Executive Acquisitions Director

 Mary C. Corder, Editorial Director

Publishing for Consumer Dummies

 Kathy Nebenhaus, Vice President and Executive Publisher

Composition Services

 Debbie Stailey, Director of Composition Services

Contents at a Glance

Table of Contents

Part V: The Part of Tens *367*

Introduction

When I first started writing about and designing websites, one of the major design concerns was compensating for low bandwidth and low-resolution displays. Creating websites was a balancing act between visual content — images, sound, and video — and the overall size of the files that made up my web pages. Gradually, though, computer screen resolutions got higher and higher. and high-speed Internet connections became increasingly more common. Web designers were set free to create highly visual websites, complete with digital video, Flash content, and lots of images.

Along come web-enabled cellphones and other mobile devices — with even smaller, low-resolution screens, lower bandwidth, and puny processors. Now, the design restrictions became even greater than when the Web first came into existence. Media files had to be even smaller, and very few of the features we had come used to deploying — big, nice-looking images, digital video, Flash content — were supported on these small devices.

The good news is that mobile technology is advancing very rapidly. The latest round of smartphones and handheld computers — tablets — have nice, high-resolution screens. The processors get faster every day. The latest round of iPhones, iPads, Android smartphones, and tablets support nearly every web feature supported by desktop computers. They also support Wi-Fi and 3G and 4G data networks. Designing for these devices is no longer an exercise in restraint.

Not every mobile user has jumped into the latest round of handheld devices, though. That's why this book looks backward and forward. To allow as many mobile users as possible to view your website, you really do need to create pages that take advantage of the latest technologies and compensate for earlier technologies. It's important to create mobile websites that meet the expectations of the users of the newer devices, and, at the same time, counterbalance the limitations of the older devices.

About This Book

I have designed *HTML, CSS & JavaScript Mobile Development For Dummies* to cover the 10-year spectrum of web-enabled handheld devices — everything from the early feature phones that barely supported the web at all, to the latest, lightning-fast smartphones and tablets. This encompasses a wide range of technologies. The book is designed to teach you how to design and develop websites and web applications for all of them.

Even though this book is designed with the basic stuff up front, and then moves, section by section, into the more advanced topics, each section stands alone — you don't have to read the book from cover to cover to find the solutions you're looking for. If, say, you want to create a contact form for your mobile site, you can jump to Chapter 9. Do you want to learn the basics of JavaScript? Turn to Chapter 3.

Would you rather learn web development step by step, from the basic concepts to the more complicated — like a web design course? This book's organization will let you do that, too. Simply start at Chapter 1.

What You Are Not to Read

The real question is why did you buy this book? It contains several task-oriented chapters designed to help create specific web applications for handhelds. If you don't plan to sell anything on your mobile site, then don't bother with Chapter 17. If you don't have the time or desire to create multiple versions of your mobile site, don't bother with Chapters 5 and 6.

In other words, use the Table of Contents and the "How This Book Is Organized" section of this Introduction to determine what chapters will help you accomplish what you want to do. Don't read the rest, if you don't want to. I won't know.

Conventions Used in This Book

Conventions is a term meaning *practices* or *standards*. Since it is a term, I have chosen to define it (because I thought maybe you don't know the term), in italics. Using italics for introducing new terms is one of the conventions of this book. Here are some others:

- ✔ URLs (web addresses), code, filenames, computer folder names, links, menu commands, and e-mail addresses appear in `this fixed space font`, so that you can recognize and find them easily.

- ✔ When I show you how to do something in a step-by-step demonstration, these instructions are in **bold** type; as are words, phrases, URLs, and other things I ask you to type.

- ✔ When I teach procedures in a step-by-step fashion, I use numbered lists, to make it easier for you to follow along.

Foolish Assumptions

Many of the web pages on the Internet do not display well on some handheld devices. However, as mobile devices become more capable, and websites become more mobile-device friendly, this situation — like everything else in the Internet technology world — is rapidly changing.

This book assumes you have little-to-no web design experience. As long as you know how to turn on your computer, and have a basic understanding of how computers store and arrange files, you should be able to use this book.

However, web design does not happen in a vacuum. Creating web pages often requires contributions from many other technologies, or programs, such as graphics editors, digital video editors, and Flash applications. A huge percentage of designers design their sites in Adobe Dreamweaver (as do I). If you are not familiar with these applications and the types of files they create, you're in luck. There's a slew of Dummies books available to help you.

This book introduces several highly involved web technologies, such as HTML, CSS, and JavaScript. This book is not a manual or complete reference on any of them. Instead, it is a task-oriented reference, providing you with the information you need to complete the tasks. I do, however, provide you with several links to pages describing these technologies. If you are interested in learning any or all of these technologies in depth, you may find books such as _HTML, XHTML, & CSS All-in-One For Dummies_ by Ed Tittel and Jeff Noble helpful.

How This Book Is Organized

HTML, CSS & JavaScript Mobile Development For Dummies, is a complete reference, designed so that you can achieve specific web development tasks without reading the entire book. You may, however, if you don't have experience with the topic at hand, find yourself referring to previous sections to help fill in your knowledge of the concept under discussion. When I think you may need additional information, I provide you with references to the sections containing that info.

This section provides an overview of the five sections and what you can find in each section. Each chapter begins with an introduction to the material covered in the chapter. Some chapters have step-by-step instructions for completing tasks, and some chapters describe completing tasks from a multiple-option, what-do-you-want-to-achieve approach.

Part I: In the Beginning, There Were No Mobile Devices . . .

Part 1 begins by introducing you to the average mobile device user and how their web-surfing habits differ from the average desktop or notebook computer user. Then you get overviews of HTML, CSS, and JavaScript — what these three technologies do and how they work together to create websites. The part ends with an introduction of the design software, utilities, and many other tools available to help you become a web developer.

Part II: Creating a Mobile Site

In Part 2, you dive right in and create a mobile website. You start by exploring how designing for handhelds differs from designing for standard computers. Then you learn how to direct mobile traffic to your mobile pages, and how to create separate sets of pages based on types of mobile devices and their capabilities. This part ends with exercises in creating your site's home page — the first page of the site — and how to design a template system for completing the rest of the site and modifying and adding content in the future.

Part III: Enhancing Your Site with Advanced Interactivity and Multimedia

In this part, you learn how to make your mobile site sing and breakdance. You start by creating a contact form your site visitors can use to request information about the site or your organization. Then you get a crash course on using digital media — images, digital video, sound, and Flash. This part ends with a look at the latest mobile web technologies, HTML5, CSS3 and WebKit extensions. You learn how using the latest and greatest design tools help you create great-looking sites and interactive web effects.

Part IV: Building Real-World Applications

Now we're talking advanced mobile site development — real-world applications that actually do things, such as validating HTML form fields with JavaScript and writing scripts that store data and make decisions based on user input. You learn how to create a JavaScript quiz, how to make your site search-engine friendly so that people can find it, and how to build a search page for your site so that people can find information on it. Do you want to sell things on your site? In this part, I also show you how to create a mobile shopping cart. This part ends with discussion of how to create a blog mobile interface.

Part V: The Part of Tens

This part provides links to a bunch of stuff you should find useful. Chapter 18 shows you where to find 10 different mobile emulators, which are small applications that allow you to see what your site will look like on specific devices. Chapter 19 contains links to several sites that have multiple mobile web templates — some are free; some are for sale. In Chapter 20, you'll find links to 10 widgets, which are small snippets of code you can use to create page elements, such as menus, Google Maps, 3D product viewers, and several other useful web page features.

Icons Used in This Book

Like other *For Dummies* books, this one uses several icons, or small pictures, in the margins that indicate useful or important information.

 The Tip icon indicates that I am giving you a tip — telling you something about the current topic or procedure that should make the process easier or save you time and money.

 This seems obvious, doesn't it? When you see this icon, read it! I'm telling you something that will help you avoid problems, or telling you not to do something to keep you out trouble.

 Okay. So most of this book is, in one way or another, technical. When you see this icon, I'm pointing to something ultra geeky, such as how something works, or elaborating on a highly technical process. Don't worry, though, they're short and to the point. I have tried not to use them too much, because I know they are a lot like hitting the Snooze button.

 This icon points out what I consider critical information, a point or two that deserves your special attention. In other words, I think it's important enough for you to know about and not forget.

Where to Go from Here

What do you want to do? Do you want to learn the basics of using HTML, CSS, and JavaScript? Well, then start with Chapter 1 and read it and the next two chapters. Would you rather dive right in and create a mobile web page? If so, turn to Chapter 7. Are you getting the idea? Check out the "How This Book Is Organized" section of this introduction and decide what you want to do. Then, go to that chapter.

You can also obtain code samples from this book at the *HTML, CSS & JavaScript Mobile Development For Dummies* companion website at www. wiley.com/go/htmlcssjscriptmobiledev.

Part I
In the Beginning, There Were No Mobile Devices . . .

The 5th Wave   By Rich Tennant

"Good news—we found PCs that consume less energy."

In this part . . .

Few things better represent the 21st century than mobile technology — all of mankind's knowledge delivered to you instantly via that little gadget in your back pocket. As a mobile designer, it's your job to create the websites that make that happen.

In this part, you meet and become familiar with the critical players involved in designing content for handheld devices. First, you meet the key player — the mobile web user — and discover how he or she differs from the desktop computer user. Then you meet and get to know the HTML, CSS, and JavaScript technologies — what they are and how they work together. This part ends with an introduction to the design programs, utilities, and other software available to help you become a successful web developer.

Chapter 1

Designing Websites for Big and Small Screens

*T*alk to nearly anybody who's been designing web pages for a while. The one thing most of them agree on is that creating websites for handheld devices is a giant step backward. Mobile users, on the other hand, consider the ability to get web content delivered to their smartphones, PDAs, and mobile tablets cutting-edge technology. For them, few things (on this planet, anyway), are more advanced than whipping a small gadget out of their pockets, pressing a few buttons, and voilá: You have the answers to nearly every question, access to almost any solution, information on just about every product, access to all of mankind's accumulated knowledge — the part of it parked on the web, anyway — at your fingertips.

So which is it? Is the mobile web the bleeding edge of information technology or a trip back in time to the medieval days of the Internet?

In the early days of the Internet, all but a select few users "surfed the Net" from very slow computers (by today's standards) connected to the Internet via agonizingly sluggish and unreliable dial-up modems. Not only did Internet users wait interminably for content to download and appear on-screen, they contended with frequent dropped connections, overloaded Plain Old Telephone System (POTS) networks, busy signals, and a host of other annoying inadequacies.

Web design in those days was a balancing act. Designers often had to quell their desire to deliver attractive, rich content with more practical considerations, such as file size and download times. Until, that is, the advent of affordable broadband — relatively fast and reliable DSL and cable Internet connections — along with advancements in web browsers and content compression.

These advancements set the design spirit free. No longer was it as necessary to compensate for technical limitations. Web content went from moderate pages consisting of small images and text to rich, multimedia-laden extravaganzas. Then along came mobile devices, with their small screens, slow processors, and low-bandwidth cellphone networks — bringing web page design back nearly full circle. Once again, web designers find themselves confined to delivering content in small, manageable chunks, compensating for familiar limitations.

In this chapter, I introduce you to the average mobile user and show you why designing for him or her is different from designing for the average user who accesses the Internet with a desktop or notebook computer. Then I introduce you to the most basic web-page design tool — HTML — what it is and how it works.

A word about HTML: It started out as, and remains, a very basic web-page design language. Without enhancements, such as XHTML and CSS, it really isn't suitable for mobile web design. This chapter also briefly discusses HTML5, the future of web design, and how the evolution of HTML affects mobile web design.

Introducing the Mobile Internet User

In some ways, it's hard to believe that the Internet has been around long enough to discuss it in terms of generations, or in terms of groups of users categorized by *when* they started using the Internet. Granted, it's always risky (especially when talking about people) to categorize and generalize, but sometimes it's necessary. Before I get started, though, I should let you know that I know that the stereotypic distinctions I'm about to make are just that — stereotypes, or generalizations. Generalizations (the ones used here, anyway) demonstrate commonality, but in no way do they actually *define* members of the category.

With that said, let me step way out on a limb here. There are two types of mobile Internet users:

✔ **Old schoolers:** For the sake of this discussion, *old schoolers* have been around for a while. They started using the Internet before handheld devices came onto the scene. They're used to information coming to them in large doses, on big screens with lots of leg room to stretch out and get comfortable. And they like it that way. To them, viewing the Internet on a mobile device seems, well, unnatural.

✔ **New schoolers:** *New schoolers* — often the offspring of old schoolers — grew up mobile. For them, accessing the Internet — the web, e-mail, text messaging, the entire shebang — on their mobile devices is part of the natural order of things. They haven't experienced life without the mobile web and don't really get that it hasn't always been this way.

Old-schooling it

Old schoolers, or pre–mobile Internet users, have several habits and attitudes in common. The most important thing to remember about them is that even though they're appreciative of mobile technology (even somewhat awed by it), it's not their main way to use the web: Although they're accessing the web on their handheld devices, they're really wishing they were sitting in front of their big, comfortable desktop or notebook computers.

As convenient as the mobile web is, when you're used to having volumes of information delivered to your computer screen, getting it spoon-fed to you in little pieces that fit on a three- or four-inch-screen can be annoying. Many pre–mobile web users simply don't like the short-and-sweet, just-the-facts, piecemeal way that the mobile web disseminates content.

Like it or not, there's really no denying that as humans get older they get set in their ways. The older we are, the less we like change. Most pre–mobile Internet users have been on planet Earth for a little while. Going from a roomy 15- 17-, or even 24-inch (or bigger) monitor — with a nice, comfortable keyboard and oh-so-easy-to-use mouse — to a tiny handheld is jarring; it's a culture-shock experience. It's kind of like trading in your SUV for a Smart Car.

Many old schoolers use their mobile devices to access the web reluctantly. Although they appreciate quick access to information, no matter where they are, they'd rather not squint at the small screen and fumble with the small buttons, keys, and navigation wheels. It's a love-hate relationship — convenient and frustrating all at once.

Is mobile web technology truly a time warp?

There's a lot a talk in this chapter (and any other book about designing for mobile devices) about designing for the mobile web being a step backward in time. Granted, right now mobile web technology as a whole is fraught with limitations — small screens, small memory allocations, small processors, low bandwidth, and so on. However, just as information technology itself advances, so does mobile technology.

For example, recent improvements in hardware, such as some of the new Android phones and tablets, and the iPhone 4 and iPad, are bringing larger, higher-resolution screens, much faster processors, and bigger memory banks to the mobile market. Some mobile devices can now use standard HTML and Cascading Style Sheets (CSS) formatting, as well as enhanced Flash and digital video playback — rivaling modest desktop and notebook computer performance.

We've also seen significant improvements to the Internet delivery networks, such as the expansion of much faster 4G cell networks and the creation of a lot more Wi-Fi–enabled hot spots. Accessing the mobile web on mobile devices might seem like a step backward now, but the technology itself is on a fast track to becoming just as capable as traditional computers. The compensations we're forced to make today probably won't be necessary a year or two from now.

Growing up mobile

Nowadays, most people take for granted the speed at which technology advances. But stop a minute. Think about the diversity of these two groups of users. The current generation, for the most part, has never seen a long-playing vinyl record, or perhaps even a cassette tape. This, the iPod generation, has never heard of a Walkman CD player. They have not experienced life without the mobile web. For them, text messaging is not a novelty or a convenience. It's a part of life as they know it.

Getting information and communicating in short, rapid-fire bursts is a major part of their life experience. They think in sound bites. Say *hello* to the new schooler or post–mobile web Internet user. Say *hello* to the future.

New-school mobile users are young, nimble, and on the move. They can broadcast a text message to 20 acquaintances in the time it takes an old schooler to dial a phone number. The new schooler's cellphone is not a convenience; it's an appendage, an implant; using it is second nature, akin to walking, talking, and eating. They use their handhelds in the same way they approach life: Get it done and move on.

If they're not already, new schoolers will soon be the largest of our two mobile Internet groups. Considering the demographics (young versus mature), the newer group will, without question, be the longest lasting.

Companies, other entities, and even web designers themselves who ignore this ever-expanding group of Internet users do so at their own peril. By virtue of their sheer numbers alone, the mobile web users are a force to contend with — they deserve web content tailored for them.

Inherent in the young-and-on-the-go character is a lack of patience. These Internet users don't like waiting. Faced with a website full of huge, cumbersome pages that take forever to download — or aren't mobile-device-friendly when they do load — the mobile web user moves on. (When comes to waiting for content to download, nobody likes that. New schoolers *and* old schoolers alike have that in common.)

Your job, then, as a web designer, is to give those nomadic web users what they want — the way they want it — quick. My job, in addition to teaching you how to use HTML, CSS, and JavaScript to create mobile-friendly web pages, is to show you how to create sites that mobile web users will actually stick around to use.

Designing for Mobile Devices

Although the mobile web user often has needs different from users who access the web from desktop and laptop computers, there really is only one web. The advent of so many mobile devices, of so many types, all accessing the web certainly does change the game. It reminds me of the days when most of the world accessed the Internet through dialup telephone connections.

In those days, we often designed two or more versions of the same website and then provided users with links that took them to versions of the site optimized for their connection speeds. (See Figure 1-1.)

Although designing for mobile devices doesn't set web design back quite that far, two of the design concerns from those days have come back to visit us again: Designing for the mobile web forces us to balance and compromise content and zero in on the intended message.

Figure 1-1:
Allowing
users to
choose a
site that
works best
for them.

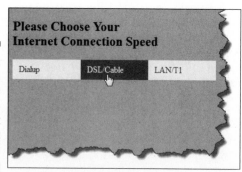

Please Choose Your
Internet Connection Speed

Dialup   DSL/Cable   LAN/T1

Balancing and compromising

Recently I read an interview with a famous fiction writer in which the interviewer asked, while discussing the story line of the author's most recent novel, "So what made you decide to turn this story into a novel?"

The author replied, "I didn't have time to write a short story."

On the surface, this answer seems nonsensical. How could a few-thousand-word short story take more time to write than a several-hundred-thousand-word novel? The author was being facetious, of course, but the point was that a short story requires much more attention to story-crafting and detail. Word for word, the short story is more work.

This is also true of designing for the mobile web. Balancing and compromising — providing the most important information as succinctly as possible — is a much higher priority when you're designing for the small screen. Often, deciding what *not* to include — which images, Flash content, digital video, and so on to leave out — entails painstaking evaluation, and a an unemotional willingness to slash all but the most pertinent information.

Zeroing in on the message

Does this seem redundant? Isn't balancing and compromising the same as zeroing in on the message? Well, sort of. What I mean by *zeroing in on the message* is deciding what the message — the most important point, or the conclusion — is, and then providing that information first.

Newspaper articles are good examples. They're written with the understanding that many readers will not read the entire article, just as the mobile web user is very likely not to read (or pay attention to) all the information on your mobile website — or even all the material on the home page, for that matter. Professional reporters structure their stories so that the essence of the story — the point of the article and the conclusion — is spelled out in the first couple of paragraphs. The remaining information fleshes out or supports the conclusions drawn in the opening paragraphs.

This technique — *Tell 'em what you're going to tell them. Tell 'em, and then tell 'em you told 'em,* as one of my composition teachers used to say — is a very practical way to approach not only mobile website design but also all website design. Of course, when you consider the confined space of the typical mobile website, and the just-the-facts mindset of the mobile web user, it's worth disciplining yourself to pay close attention to *how* you present the site's message can determine the success or failure of your designs.

Many new designers (and not just web designers, but all types of document designers) overload their work with all kinds of impressive images, Flash special effects, and a bunch of other design elements that show off their newly learned abilities. And hey, why not? It's exciting to put what you've learned into practice. But if you *really* want to show off your abilities as a mobile web designer, make focusing on presentation and information flow a priority.

Introducing HTML

HTML stands for *HyperText Markup Language.* Although there are several web page markup languages, HTML, or some variation or extension of HTML, is by far the predominant markup language on the Internet.

Before I start talking about HTML, what it is and what it does, I should first clear up a common misconception: HTML is not a programming language. In fact, it's not really a "language" at all; it can't tell your computer what to do. (Yeah. I know what I said in the introduction to this chapter. I won't say it again. But we're stuck with the term, okay?) Instead, HTML is a *page markup language*, also called a *page description language:* Instead of issuing orders, HTML describes the page for web browsers. The browser interprets the description and displays that interpretation onscreen for the computer or mobile device.

Describing pages for browsers

Even this definition — *describing pages for web browsers* — is oversimplified. Quite literally, HTML tells the browser everything about the page, from what type of HTML, or extensions of HTML, such as XHTML and CSS, the page uses, to how to format and display individual elements, such as text and images, on the page. (Yes, I know I'm throwing a bunch of initials and terms at you all at once. I'll define them as we go — and soon, I promise.)

Structuring the basic HTML page

No matter how simple or how complicated your HTML web pages, they all start with the same basic structure — four basic *tags* (tags are discussed a little later in this chapter), as shown in Listing 1-1.

Listing 1-1: The basic HTML page

```
<!DOCTYPE html PUBLIC "-//WAPFORUM//DTD XHTML Mobile 1.0//EN" "http://wapforum.
          org/DTD/xhtml-mobile10.dtd">                              →1

<html xmlns="http://www.w3.org/1999/hxtml">                          →3

<head>                                                               →5
<meta http-equiv="Content-Type" content="text/html charset=utf-8: />
<title>The World's Best Mobile Site</title>
```

(continued)

Listing 1-1 *(continued)*

```
<link href="/styles.css" rel="stylesheet" type="text/css" media="handheld" />
</head>                                                                    →9

<body>                                                                     →11

</body>                                                                    →13

</html>                                                                    →15
```

✔ **Line 1 (doctype):** The `doctype` tag, discussed in Chapter 7, describes the type of HTML the page uses.

✔ **Lines 3 and 15 (`<html></html>`):** The `<html>` tag pair, discussed in Chapter 7, does several things, but its most important function is to mark the beginning and ending of the page. You put all information about this page — as well as all elements on the page, such as text, graphics, and other media — in between these two tags.

✔ **Lines 5 and 9 (`<head></head>`):** The `<head>` tag pair, discussed in Chapters 7 and 12 (and a couple of others), holds information *about* the page, including the page title, meta data to help search engines index the site, and much, much more. (This is probably the most simplistic definition ever, though.) Although there are exceptions, for the most part the `<head>` tags hold non-displaying page data.

✔ **Lines 11 and 13 (`<body></body>`):** The `<body>` tag pair marks the beginning and ending of the page content, or the elements that display on the page. Although there are exceptions (aren't there always?), most of the graphics, photos, videos, and text that display on your pages go between the (`<body>` tag pair, as shown in Figure 1-2.

A rose by any other name

So far, you've seen me refer to the content — the objects such as text and graphics, videos, and so on — that appear on web pages as *elements, objects,* and *content*. And I'm just getting started! So what are they really called?

There really is no technical catchall term for the objects that display on your web pages. I thought I should clear that up before getting into this next discussion of HTML tags.

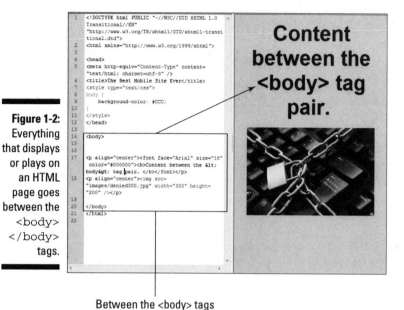

Figure 1-2: Everything that displays or plays on an HTML page goes between the `<body>` `</body>` tags.

Between the <body> tags

Describing page objects for browsers

Not only does HTML describe the web page for browsers; it also describes, or formats, the objects, or content on the page. For example, in Figure 1-3, the `<b></b>` and `<i></i>` tags tell the browser to display the text as bold italic.

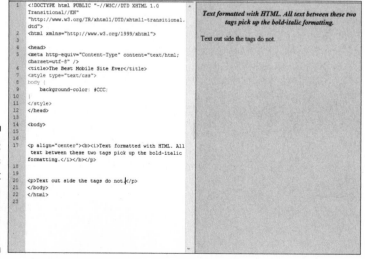

Figure 1-3: Examples of text formatting described for the web browser.

Understanding HTML Tags

HTML, as discussed earlier in this chapter, describes web pages for web browsers, such as Internet Explorer (IE) and Firefox. HTML is written in HTML *elements* that consist of *tags* enclosed in angle brackets, or greater-than and less-than symbols, like this: `<tag>`.

The paragraph tag, `<p>`, for example, indicates the beginning of new paragraph, like this:

```
<p>Paragraph text.</p>
```

Nothing happens on an HTML page without a tag or two. HTML tags do all the heavy lifting — everything, including setting up the page (discussed earlier in this chapter), describing the type of HTML used to format the page, where to find supporting files (such as CSS style sheet files, discussed in Chapters 2, 4, and 7), and the formatting of individual page objects (see Figure 1-4).

Anatomy of the HTML tag

Many tags support properties, or *attributes*. Attributes provide additional information, such as how to format an object, where to find a file, or where to display an object on the page. The following paragraph tag, for example, contains the `"center"` attribute, which tells the browser to center the paragraph:

```
<p align="center">Paragraph text.</p>
```

Although there are infrequent variations, attributes are usually written as shown in the preceding example, as *name-value pairs* separated by an equal sign, (=). In the example, `align` is the *name* and `"center"` is the *value*.

Formatting text with tags

As is the case with most methods for formatting text on computers, HTML starts with default settings — everything has to start somewhere, right? In computer-speak, *default* means: *Do this unless you're told to do something else*. Browsers, unless told to do otherwise, display all text as body text, or as text formatted with the paragraph tag `<p>`.

The default attributes of the `<p>` tag, such as font, size, color, and so on are determined by the browser. Out of the box, unless the user changes it, in most Windows browsers the default font, or typeface, is Times New Roman; on a Mac, it's Times. In each case, the font size and color are the base (default) font. Any time you format text with a tag you are, in effect, modifying or overriding the base font. In the following `<font>` tag, for example, the three attributes, `face`, `size`, and `color`, override all the base settings and change the text to white, 18-point Arial:

```
<font face="Arial" size="18" color="#FFFFFF">Paragraph text.</font>
```

A little bit about HTML standards

HTML began as a very simple, very loose markup language. For example, when you use basic HTML formatting without XHTML (discussed a little later in this chapter) or some other extension or enhancement, tags can be written with "loose" formatting. XHTML, on the other hand, forces you to write your tags in lowercase. Basic HTML supports upper- and lowercase, even combinations, such as <P></p>.

HTML also doesn't force you to close tags. You can, for example, start new paragraphs with a single <p> tag, and you don't need to close the paragraph (</p>) before starting a new one. But there's a catch: Very few web pages are written in basic HTML nowadays, primarily because, on its own, HTML isn't robust (doesn't do) enough, and to avoid these loose standards.

Formatting text is, of course, a very important part of creating web pages, and we revisit this topic several places throughout this book.

Tags that tag other tags that tag other tags

Not only do tags modify and override default settings; they can also modify and influence the behavior of each other. Tags format objects in a top-down, hierarchical, or building block manner. Depending on where and how they're placed on the page, browsers read and use them differently. (Chapter 2 describes how browsers read and apply tags to format a page.) Understanding this dynamic relationship between tags becomes increasingly significant as your web pages become more sophisticated.

Here's a simple example. In this example, the <p> tag and its attributes set up the default paragraph text, and then the <font> and its attributes override the default settings:

```
<p align="center"><font face="Arial" size="18" color="#FFFFFF">Text formatted
            with HTML.</font></p>
```

Figure 1-4 shows how the second tag and its attributes modify the first tag.

Media formatting tags

Media — now there's a word that gets bandied around in the computer world. Depending on the context, it means different things to different people. In this context — web page content — *media* refers to specific types of computer files that load into and display on (or play in) HMTL pages. The most common media file types are images (or graphics); Flash movies and animations; as well as digital videos, 3D animations, and sound files.

Unlike text, which you type directly into your HTML pages so it becomes part of the HTML file itself, media files live elsewhere: You use tags to link your page to them; if they're embedded, you use tags to format them. They're saved as separate files on the web server and downloaded at runtime, or when the user's browser loads a web page and reads the tags. When the browser comes across a set of tags relating to a media file, it requests the file from the server and displays (or plays) it on the page, formatted as designated within the tags.

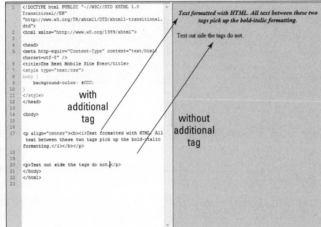

Figure 1-4:
Example
of tags
modifying
other tags.

The media type dictates the tags you use. To embed an image into your pages, for example, you use the `<img src>` tag, like this:

```
<img src="img02.jpg" width="800" height="200" />
```

The name-value pair is, of course, `img src="img02.jpg"`. The `width=` and `height=` attributes set the image width and height. In this particular configuration, for example, you could resize the image on the page by changing the value of those attributes, like this:

```
<img src="img02.jpg" width="400" height="100" />
```

Figure 1-5 shows how adjusting the attributes can change how an image displays.

Using tag attributes to resize media, especially when you're designing for mobile devices (which we discuss in Chapter 10), is a handy technique. However, whenever practical, it's always preferable to embed your media at a 1-to-1 display-size ratio. In other words, resize the image, Flash movie, digital video, or whatever — in the application in which you created it — to fit the mobile device you have in mind, and *then* display the embedded media in your web page at that size. Why go to the trouble? Well, allowing the user's browser to resize embedded media can sometimes produce unexpected results, usually not happy ones. Also, when you're resizing large media files to display on small screens, keep in mind that the file itself is the same size as before: No matter what size you impose on the media file when you display it, the browser must still download the entire file if it has to resize the image. Displaying a 640x480 image on a 320x240 screen, for example, forces the mobile device to download twice the amount data it needs to display the image. Figure 1-6 demonstrates what I mean.

800 x 200

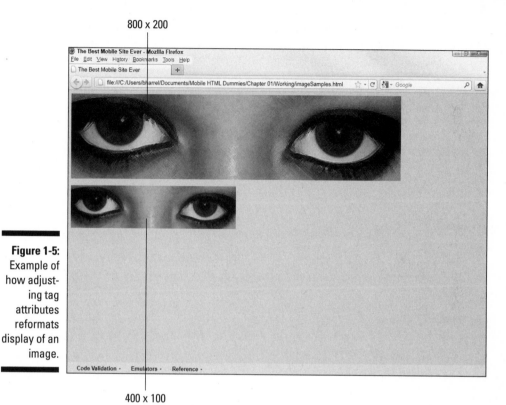

Figure 1-5:
Example of
how adjust-
ing tag
attributes
reformats
display of an
image.

400 x 100

Figure 1-6:
Allowing
your
browser to
reformat
oversized
images
can force
your mobile
device to
download
far more
data than
it needs to
display the
media.

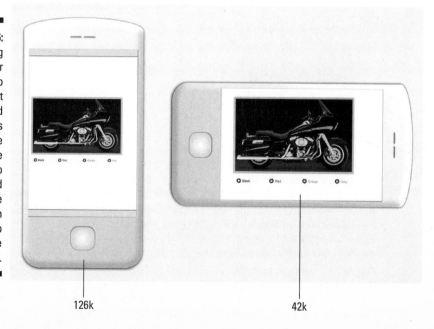

126k   42k

Linking to other pages and URLs

The web wouldn't be the web if it weren't for its support for *links*. Links are, of course, the menus, buttons and strings of text we click on to navigate to other pages on the Internet. As with everything else on HTML web pages, links are created with tags — more specifically, the <a href> </a> tag pair. The data between these two tags becomes the clickable link, like this:

```
<a href="http://www.anyURLonTheInternet.com">The clickable text</a>
```

To turn a graphic into a button, you simply place the tag that embeds the graphics file, as discussed in the previous section, between the <a href> </a> tags, like this:

```
<a href="http://www.anyURLonTheInternet.com"><img src="globe.png" width="40"
                height="50" /></a>
```

Of course, there's a whole lot more to this linking thing, and it's covered in several chapters throughout this book, including Chapters 7, and 10.

Limitations of HTML — Everything on the Table

Believe it or not, at one time the basic HTML elements described in the previous section were about all there was to creating web pages. In fact, the past few pages describe all you really need to know to create a basic web page. Furthermore, any page you create using the information in the previous section would most likely display on any mobile device that supports web browsing. Whether it would look good or not, that's a different issue.

Easy, right? It's also quite limiting. This simple set of formatting tags gives you very little control over the layout and functionality of your pages. Early web pages consisted of one object after another placed vertically down the page — they were often quite boring and unattractive. Fortunately, time marches on, and so did HTML.

One of the early updates to HTML was the addition of the HTML table. You know what tables are. You've probably used them in Word or Excel to display tabular data or create spreadsheets. Initially, that capability — displaying tabular data — was the whole reason for adding <table> tags to the HTML markup language. But innovative designers figured out how to use those same humble tags to arrange the objects on their pages to create more sophisticated, attractive layouts.

More tables and tables inside tables inside tables

If you're familiar at all with HTML tables, or any program's tables feature for that matter, then the concept of placing different objects inside table cells to anchor them to positions on the page might seem simple. Although the concept itself is quite simple, HTML's ability to nest tables inside tables and the designer's unwavering dedication to artistic freedom transformed laying out pages this way into a fine art.

Designers began creating entire graphical interfaces, dismantling them piece by piece and reassembling them with HTML tables. Photoshop, Illustrator, and other media applications (such as Flash) began supporting 9-slice scaling, which basically lets you slice up images or artwork in one program and then save them all in intricately related HTML table cells.

The web page shown in Figure 1-7 shows a web page cut up and saved in sections in table cells. All of the beveled boxes represent table cells. Notice that some of the objects are in cells four or five tables deep.

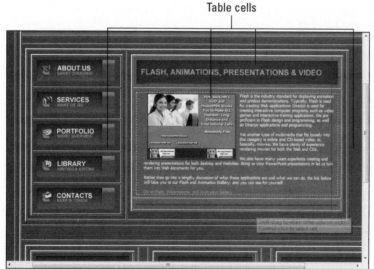

Figure 1-7: Tables inside tables inside tables.

Too many tables, but not enough

Although designing layouts in tables does work, it can be time-consuming and tedious. It also requires far too much code and has some severe limitations, such as the inability to precisely control cell padding and margins.

This practice has been replaced with CSS <div> tag containers (discussed in general in Chapter 2 and in detail in Chapter 7). CSS containers are desirable over tables for several reasons. The CSS <div> container, for example, lets you write one set of formatting instructions that you can use in several locations on one page or across several pages. This allows you to make changes to multiple pages by editing only one set of instructions, which is one of the major attractions of CSS.

CSS, or Cascading Style Sheets, discussed in Chapter 2, is not HTML. It is an add-on, or extension of HTML that allows you to perform additional formatting to your HTML pages and their content. CSS substantially expands your page- and content-formatting options. It also provides several other huge advantages over standard HTML, as discussed in Chapters 2 and 7.

Introducing XHTML and HTML5

Technically, HTML is outdated. Nowadays, XHTML, which stands for *eXtensible HyperText Markup Language*, is the Recommended (see the enlightening sidebar) and most widely used page markup language on the web. XHTML derives from *XML*, a much stricter and more robust extension of HTML. Not only does XHTML extend the design possibilities of HTML but its support for CSS (discussed in Chapter 2) also greatly enhances the possibilities of web page design. XHTML's adherence to stricter, "well-formed," tag construction also ensures greater compatibility with various devices — especially *mobile* devices.

Designing websites based on device profiles

In a word, we use XHTML instead of HTML today because it's *better*. Its stricter standards assure a higher level of compatibility across device types, and its support for CSS greatly extends web page and website design possibilities. One example of how XHTML is more powerful, especially in mobile web design, is its support for device profiles.

Designing for specific devices

Much of this book covers how to create web pages designed to work optimally on different types of mobile devices. Part of this process entails designing different versions of the same website. There are several ways to do this; the techniques range from fairly easy — catchall methods that work for many mobile devices — to elaborate device-profiling systems that refer to databases and decide which device "profile" to use for displaying a specific version of the website.

Evaluating devices, determining their capabilities, and designing websites based on device profiles is covered in detail in Chapters 5 and 6.

How does a markup language get "Recommended"?

When you hear a teacher, writer, or techno-pundit of some sort make a sweeping statement like, "Nowadays, XHTML. . . is the Recommended and most widely used web page markup language," do you stop and wonder who makes those recommendations? I do. How does one markup language get *Recommended* over another? Is there some sort of all-knowing, web markup language higher power passing down edicts from on high?

Well, not exactly. When it comes to oversee-ing and developing web markup languages, the ultimate authority, if you will, is the World Wide Web Consortium, or *W3C*. The W3C is a committee of a few hundred (mostly) volun-teers who analyze and develop standards for the web. Way back in January of 2000, they Recommended that we all start using XHTML 1.0. Then, in June of 2001, they Recommended XHTML 1.1.

To some, especially new web designers, this hodgepodge of different versions and types of markup languages — XML, HTML, XHTML, CSS, XHTML-MP (Mobile Profile), and so on — make web development seem the like the cha-otic Wild West all over again. Frankly, without the guidance of the W3C, web page develop-ment for all the different devices available today would be even more of a moving target. W3C's oversight does keep the beast under control.

Furthermore, its ongoing development of the latest standard, HTML5 (discussed a little later in this chapter), which folds HTML, XHTML, and CSS into a robust and comprehensive web-authoring markup language, promises to further standardize web design — especially mobile web design — and bring significant design prow-ess to the web. If you want to learn more about the W3C, get a look at how standards are devel-oped, participate in the discussions, or perhaps become a member or the Consortium, you can do so at the W3C's website (www.w3c.org).

XHTML MP

XHTML MP stands for XHTML Mobile Profile, a markup language designed specifically for mobile phones. It is an HTML document type, or doctype, defined by the Open Mobile Alliance (OMA). Somewhat similar the W3C, the OMA was founded in June 2002 tests by a group of companies with interests in the mobile market — everything from providers (such as AT&T, Verizon, and Sprint) to cellphone manufacturers (such as Nokia, Samsung, Ericsson and so on) to mobile software vendors (such as Microsoft, Apple, and Google).

The goal of the OMA is standardization of XHTML for all mobile devices. As you can imagine, the OMA is playing important role in the development of websites for mobile phones and other mobile devices. XHTML MP is dis-cussed in Chapters 2 and 6.

Introducing HTML5

If you're starting to suspect that creating websites for mobile devices is a moving target, well, you're right. In many ways it is. With so many different devices with widely varying capabilities, and so many page markup standards and versions, it might seem amazing that we get them to work at all on more than just a couple devices. What's with all this bouncing around? Why can we just settle on one good HTML markup standard, develop it, and go with that?

Everybody involved in web design has been all too aware of the inconsistencies and challenges brought on by all these different standards; granted, it's an overly fragmented approach to modern web design. The advent of the mobile web — especially the diversity of mobile devices — made these flaws even more glaring.

A while back, the W3C realized that veering off into all these splintered variations wasn't working, and responded with the announcement of a plan to develop a universal markup language that works for everybody — HTML5. A huge endeavor, HTML5 will standardize how designers write their tags and how browsers interpret them.HTML5 is discussed in detail in Chapter 11.

The development of HTML 5 has been going on for a while — since about 2004. Although a few more years will probably roll by before the completion and adoption of this new standard, many parts of HTML5 have been completed, declared stable, and adopted — they're already in use. Several smartphones, such as the iPhone, Droid, most of the new tablets, and several others already support some HTML5 specifications.

As I write this, speculation is that HTML5 will reach Candidate Recommendation (CR) status sometime in 2012. A CR status is similar to a beta-test version of a software application: HTML5 will be released to the development community — who will, in turn, assess whether the candidate is ready for implementation. During the CR period (which can be several years), more and more of the standard will become commonplace.

As we work our way through using HTML and CSS in this book, I'll point out when and where you can use HTML5, and brief you on how and why that new standard is better than XHTML standards in use today. Again, you can find a detailed discussion of HTML5 in Chapter 11.

Chapter 2

Bringing More to HTML with Cascading Style Sheets (CSS)

C ascading style sheets, cascading style sheets — such a fancy-sounding term for a page markup language (or, more precisely, a style-sheet language). It sounds more like some kind of art form, or perhaps a classical music term, such as *crescendo, resonance, intonation,* or one of those other impressive, pleasant-sounding terms from a music appreciation class. It's the imagery it evokes: a cascade of style sheets tumbling gently over . . . . (Oops. Sorry about that. I got carried away.)

Instead, a cascading style sheet is a list of rules, each one triggering the next — *cascading* rules for formatting web pages. The "cascade" is essentially a priority scheme that determines how the rules are applied, and in what order. If, for example, more than one rule is assigned to a page element, the browser calculates a cascade of priorities, or weights, to determine which rule to apply: Higher priority means a heavier weight; think of a high priority as leaning on you harder.

The point of all this cascading, then, is reliability — or, better yet, predict-ability. What all this means to you — the web designer — is that CSS is a much more dependable (and flexible) way to create web pages than plain old HTML.

Although there are many reasons why CSS is preferable over standard HTML, one of the more compelling is that, unlike HTML tables (discussed in Chapter 1), CSS allows you to keep the content separated from the tags and the other code that formats it, as well as from the page it resides on. This chapter shows you how this arrangement works — and why it's preferable over standard HTML. We also look at creating CSS containers, which are similar to HTML table cells, but much more flexible. And we talk about the different versions of CSS, including some evolving mobile standards, as well as the different types of style sheets.

Understanding CSS

Simply put, CSS is a style sheet language that describes the appearance and formatting of a document written in a markup language — usually HTML or XHTML. It also works with pages written in XML (eXtensible Markup Language), and you can use CSS to format text in Flash movies, as well as many other applications. Cascading style sheets aid in the layout pages, all types of pages, but most often web pages. Style sheets contain styles, and styles are lists of instructions, such as size, color, placement, font, and so on, for formatting page elements.

This concept, creating and saving formatting instructions to apply to multiple objects, often across multiple pages or documents, is neither new nor exclusive to web design. If you use a word processor, such as Microsoft Word or Apple Pages, you are probably familiar with word-processing's version of styles. Page layout software, such as Adobe Indesign or Microsoft Publisher, also use styles. Other programs you may be familiar with, such as Photoshop or Flash, use a ready-made form of styles called *presets*.

A style by any other name

A *style* is a set of text-formatting instructions, such as font, color, size, and so on. Cascading style sheets can also format pages and containers (that is, page sections or boxes such as sidebars, discussed a little later in this chapter); such instructions include background color and margins. Typically, in much the same way they work in your word processor, styles perform their magic globally; you can then override some or all of the formatting instructions locally.

Huh? Here's what I mean: Say, for example, you create a style to set all of your body (`<body></body>`) or paragraph (`<p></p>`) text to Arial, 12 point, regular. Inevitably, some words or phrases will need further formatting, such as bold or italics. Just as you would in your word processor, you can apply these more specific changes — overriding the style — directly to the text you want to make bold or italicize. The huge difference, though (unless you're using Dreamweaver or some other web design software that supports CSS, as I discuss in Chapter 4) is that you apply the formatting with XHTML and CSS tags, and not by simply selecting the text string and clicking a button.

CSS styles go far beyond word-processor styles in what they can do. You can also use them to format other content, such as images, Flash content, and digital videos. When I say *format*, I don't mean that CSS can make an image bold or italicize it, of course, but that you can use CSS styles to resize an item of media content, place borders and padding around it, and so on. And, as I discuss in Chapter 11 (and a few other places in this book), you can use the yet-to-be-released (but already widely used and supported), latest version of CSS, CSS3, to add special effects — such as drop shadows or boxes with rounded corners, and even simple animations such as fade-in and fade-out transitions.

In fact, CSS3 is poised to revolutionize web design, making this an exciting time to be a web designer.

After reading this introduction to CSS, you might be thinking that since HTML and CSS both format elements on Web pages, they are the same thing. Not really. Similar to software application plug-ins, CSS is an add-on to HTML. CSS enhances the capabilities of HTML. It works in conjunction with HTML. Although they work together, the two markup languages have separate sets of rules, tags, attributes, and properties. HTML, in effect, takes formatting instructions from CSS and applies them to page elements. Together, HTML and CSS provide a much wider range of formatting capabilities than HTML can do on its own.

Global formatting

There's much more to this global formatting thing, though. You can set up your cascading style sheets so that they format one page, 10 pages, or 10,000 pages. Say you're the lucky designer and webmaster for that 10,000-page site. Finally, after months of work, your client comes to you and says, "Great work. You've done a nice job. We're ready to go live tomorrow, but we need to change all the headings from red to blue."

(Yes, I know. If you have any web design experience at all, you know that nobody in his or her right mind would create a 10,000-page website one static page at a time, but that's not the point of this story. Bear with me.)

If you've set up your style sheets up properly, you can change the headings on all 10,000-pages by changing just one tag.

Not only can you use the same style sheet for every page in your website, you can use the same style sheet for more than one website. You could, if somehow the need arose, format 10,000 or more websites with just one style sheet! And, on the other hand, you can also use multiple style sheets to format the same web page. This versatility, as demonstrated throughout this book (and explained in the accompanying sidebar), makes CSS a seriously useful tool for creating mobile websites.

One page, many style sheets; one page, many pages

Many web pages are made up of several sections, such as headers, sidebars, multiple columns, footers. Not only can you create all of these "containers," and more, with style sheets, you can do so with multiple style sheets. You can, for example, have a separate style sheet for each of your two- or three-column pages, another style sheet for your footers, one for, say, an information box or rotating banners, and yet another for your sidebars.

Why is this important? For a number of reasons. For instance, on large, multiple-page sites, it can get monotonous to use the same layout page after page — not only for you but for the site's visitors, too. By creating separate style sheets for the various sections or features of your site's pages, you can easily vary the layouts by mixing and matching style sheets. With this method, you can, in effect, create a library of page features. (Creating and using style sheets is covered in many chapters in this book, depending on the type of page element in question. Style sheets for creating and formatting form fields, for instance, are covered in Chapter 9. Style sheets for formatting and working with digital video and Flash movies are discussed in Chapter 10, and so on.)

Your web pages can also consist of more than one page. (I hear you thinking: *How can a page be more than one page?*) Just as web pages call to and embed external media content (such as images and videos, as discussed in Chapter 1 and in more detail in Chapter 10), they can also call to and embed other HTML pages — an operation known as an *include*.

Why would you want to *include* other pages in your web pages? Well, for the same reason you would use style sheets: to make the process of updating your content and formatting easier. Say, for example, your pages have a running footer with your contact information — e-mail, phone numbers, fax, and so on — across the bottom of each page. If you keep this data in an include, if you ever need to change it, you can change it for every page in the site by simply editing the include.

For example, one of my websites has across the bottom of every page a running footer with copyright information. The site consists of 20 or so pages. Every January I have to update the copyrighted year. To keep from having to edit every page each year, I use an include. Figure 2-1 demonstrates how this works.

Using includes in your pages often entails a bit of basic programming, such as JavaScript or some sort of *server-side scripts* (scripts that run on the server hosting the page, rather than in the user's browser). This isn't as complicated as it sounds. I show you how to do it in Chapter 8.

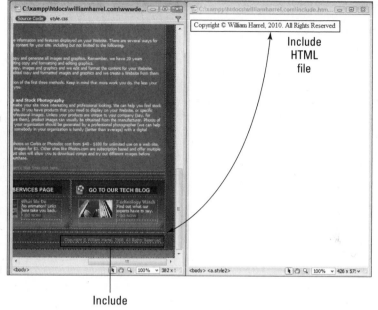

Figure 2-1:
Editing this include file each year updates the copyright information automatically.

Include

Types of styles, or style rules

CSS supports three types of styles, often referred to as *rules*: inline, internal, and external. You can use just one style type or a combination of two or more in each page in your site, and each page can use a different combination. And, as discussed in the preceding sidebar, you can use (or *attach*) several different external style sheets to format the same document.

Inline styles

You can use an inline style to format a single element, such as, say, a heading you want to be different from the other headings on the page. Overall — except for a wider range of formatting options — inline styles don't provide a significant benefit over using basic XHTML or HTML tags. You attach them directly to the objects themselves, and they apply only to the object to which you attach them, so inline styles don't provide the ability to format, and then quickly change the formatting, to multiple objects, as do the other types of CSS styles.

Also, since an inline style attaches directly to a single object, there is no need to reference it (discussed in a moment under the other two style types), and, since it doesn't require referencing, it doesn't need a unique name. As shown in Figure 2-2, inline styles use the <span></span> tags.

Usually all attributes (such as font, color, size, and so on) are included as part of the opening tag.

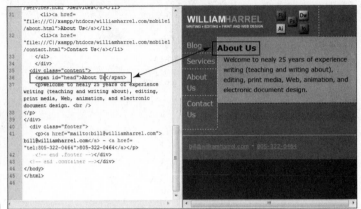

Figure 2-2:
Example of
inline style
formatting a
heading.

At this point, most authors would warn you against using inline styles unless you're absolutely positive that you won't need to attach the style's formatting to other elements on the page or to objects on other pages in your site. My experience is that you just don't know what the future will bring — situations change. So my advice is that you should just not use inline styles at all. This type of style is also the easiest to create and use, and you'll be tempted at times to get this little bit of formatting done quickly, just this once. But don't do it. You'll thank yourself later.

Internal styles

Unlike inline styles, you set up internal styles separate from your content. In other words, internal styles allow you to format multiple objects with same style, which in turn allows you to make global formatting changes by simply editing a single style. Because internal styles are, however, internal — that is, included in the document containing the objects they format — they are rather limiting. You'd use them for websites that consist of just one page each (not many of those around) or for pages with formatting different from that of the other pages in your document. Internal styles go between the <head></head> tags, as shown in Listing 2-1. The <head></head> tags are discussed in Chapters 1, 7, and a couple of others where they are relevant to the topic at hand.

Listing 2-1: Internal style sheet

```
<style type="text/css">
<!--
body {
    font: 100%/1.4 Verdana, Arial, Helvetica, sans-serif;
    background: #42413C;
    margin: 0;
    padding: 0;
    color: #000;
}
```

```
ul, ol, dl {
    padding: 0;
    margin: 0;
}
h1, h2, h3, h4, h5, h6, p {
    margin-top: 0;
    padding-right: 15px;
    padding-left: 15px;
    font-size: small;
}
a img {
    border: none;
}

a:link {
    color: #42413C;
    text-decoration: underline;
}
.container {
    width: 960px;
    background: #FFF;
    margin: 0 auto;
    overflow: hidden;
}

.sidebar1 {
    float: left;
    width: 180px;
    background: #EADCAE;
    padding-bottom: 10px;
}
-->
</style></head>
```

 Although internal styles are not as powerful as external styles, they are preferable in some situations. Say, for example, you decide to use includes, discussed in the preceding sidebar and in Chapter 8, for the headers and footers in your pages. Internal styles are perfect for formatting the actual include HTML pages themselves, making each one a self-contained, easy-to-keep-track of and easy-to-edit module.

External styles

Of the three style types, external styles are by far the most versatile. As the name suggests, they are external, or separate files. Style sheet files have a .css extension.

One of the primary benefits of this arrangement is the ability to format multiple pages with the same style sheet. On the surface, this may sound a bit anticlimactic — ho hum — until, that is, you stop and think about it. Furthermore, these benefits become even more advantageous when designing for mobile devices. Let's do that — think about it, I mean. Here's a list of some of the more important benefits:

- ✔ **Global formatting and reformatting:** In computer-speak, *global formatting* simply means formatting multiple objects, usually on multiple pages, with the same style. This advantage itself is huge, for some obvious reasons and some not-so-obvious reasons. Having a set of external style sheets in place as you create the pages in your site eliminates the need to format every object as you go. All you do is reference the style. You don't re-create it, which on sites with multiple pages saves a lot of time, work, and tedium. (In web design, especially freelance web design, time really is money!) But where this really becomes a time- and money-saver is when you need to make formatting changes. Just change one style to change all of the elements on each page attached to the style.

- ✔ **Maintain consistency:** As you work on your website, adding pages, text, and other elements to your pages, and so on, it doesn't take long before the site gets too big to keep intact in your sorely inefficient biological memory. I can't tell how many times — before CSS — when, after making a simple format change, I had to go back over big sites, page by page, and make the same changes, instance by instance and page by page. Not only is this time-consuming, it's woefully inefficient and hardly foolproof. Even when you use the most painstaking care, it's far too easy to miss important details inadvertently. When your style sheets are in place and functioning properly, such snafus become a lot less likely.

  Using CSS can also help ensure that your mobile site looks more like your regular, or non-mobile site (providing it too is formatted with CSS). Why is this important? Hey, I'm just a geeky design guy, but ask any marketing expert and she'll tell you that it's important for an organization's marketing materials to have the same look and feel — for name recognition and establishing a consistent identity.

- ✔ **Reduced code:** In mobile web design, anything you can do to make file sizes smaller is a huge boon. It doesn't take long at all before applying the same set of tags and attributes over and over on the same page starts degrading the performance of the average pea-brained mobile device. All along the web-content delivery path — from limited bandwidth, to miniscule memory banks, to tiny processors — smaller is better.

- ✔ **Increased workgroup, or team, efficiency:** Many websites are created in team environments, with various members of the team working on individual sections. Distributing external style sheets to team members ensures consistency and cuts down much of the work load. Along the same lines, as a freelancer, I often find I need to subcontract to other freelancers to meet my deadlines. Providing the subcontractors with style sheets helps ensure the pages I have them work on look like the rest of the site.

- ✔ **Standards compliance:** In order for any industry or technology to work optimally for everybody — or for as many people as possible — the participants, or manufacturers, must adhere to established standards. If you, for example, manufacture and distribute a widget that has different connectors than all the other widgets in the same industry, chances are nobody will be able to use your product. Web designers manufacture web pages, websites, and web applications. Adhering to W3C standards, discussed in Chapter 1, ensures that the greatest number of browsers and devices can use your product.

✔ **Different style sheets for different users and devices**: In Chapter 6, I show you how to detect specific devices and switch to the appropriate layout based on device type. CSS allows you to create different style sheets based on device types. In other words, you can use the same content and use style sheets to format it to display optimally for various devices.

For example, you can create one style sheet for desktop and notebook computers; another for iPhones, Droids, and other high-end mobile devices; and another for iPads and other tablet mobile devices.

These are just a few of the most significant advantages to external style sheets. I'm sure you'll realize many others as you use this book. Figure 2-3 shows an external style sheet and the resulting page.

Listing 2-2:   External style sheet

```
@charset "utf-8";
body {
    font: 100%/1.4 Verdana, Arial, Helvetica, sans-serif;
    background: #000000;
    margin: 0;
    padding: 0;
    color: #333333;
}
ul, ol, dl {
    padding: 0;
    margin: 0;
}
h1, h2, h3, h4, h5, h6, p {
    margin-top: 0;
    padding-right: 5px;
    padding-left: 15px;
    color: #CCC;
    text-align: left;
}
a img {
    border: none;
}
a:link {
    color:#6aa3a0;
    text-decoration: underline;
}
```

(continued)

Listing 2-2 *(continued)*

```css
.container {
    width: 100%;
    max-width: 800px;
    min-width: 320px;
    background: #000000;
}
.header {
    background: #000000;
}
.sidebar1 {
    float: left;
    width: 25%;
    background: #000000;
    padding-bottom: 10px;
}
.content {
    padding: 10px 0;
    width: 75%;
    background: #333333;
    float: left;
```

Using XHTML with CSS

CSS, as a style sheet language, is not a standalone language; if you try to use it by itself — without combining it with a markup language such as HTML or XHTML — you won't get very far. CSS is designed to work with, or inside, a markup language. XHTML (discussed in Chapter 1) is the latest "Recommended" version of HTML, or the standard that the W3C (also discussed in Chapter 1) suggests we all use.

XHTML has its own set of base, or default, tags, many of which are determined by the web browser unless you add some sort of modifying or overriding tags. XHTML, for example, has its own heading — <h1>, <h2>, and so on — and body text, or paragraph, <p>, tags, as well as default tags for formatting images and other media types.

One of the most common and simplest approaches to web page design is to use CSS classes and rules to *override* XHTML's built-in tags or create variations of them. You might, for instance, use CSS to change your headings instances from a serif to a sans-serif typeface (see the accompanying sidebar), or change the size, placement, and color of your headings, and so on.

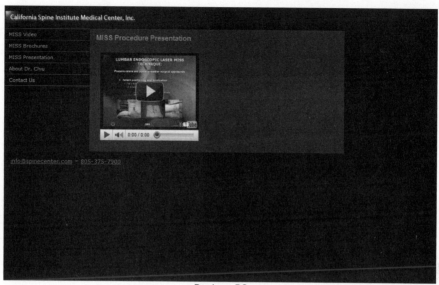

Desktop PC

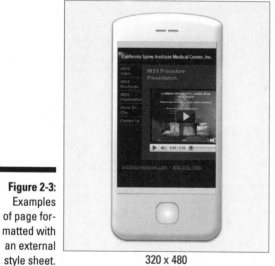

320 x 480
smartphone

800 x 480
smartphone

Figure 2-3:
Examples
of page for-
matted with
an external
style sheet.

Serif versus sans-serif — the patter of little feet

In the grand scheme of how long humans have communicated with the written word, displaying text on electronic devices is brand new. Typesetting — arranging text mechanically in a readable format (usually on paper) — is not new. Today's technology, though, would make typesetters—people who arrange type for printing on paper and other media—such as Benjamin Franklin (the world's most famous typesetter), green with envy. Here's a quick rundown on some typesetting terms you need to know, even today . . .

Excluding *display*, or decorative, fonts (such as Stamp or Broadway), the typefaces used to create English text are all variations of the Latin character set. As such, they come in two flavors: *serif* and *sans-serif* — meaning, respectively, with or without serifs (see following figure). Serifs, also known as *feet,* are the small strokes that complete the ends of *characters* (letters and numbers). A consistent design for a complete set of characters is a typeface, or *font*. Serif typefaces, which include Times, Times New Roman, and Garamond (and a few thousand others), have these little feet, *sans-serif* fonts (*sans* means *without*) do not.

In typesetting, there are all kinds of theories about which types of fonts work best for certain types of text. It's thought, for example, that serifs help guide the reader's eyes from word to word in dense, large blocks of small text, such as *body text*, an example of which you're reading now. Sans-serif fonts are thought to work best for larger type, such as banners, headlines, and subheads.

Nowadays, though, especially when it comes to computer and mobile device displays, the whole serif versus sans-serif issue has become a matter of taste — mostly. There is a school of thought that sans-serif fonts work best for body text on electronic displays, simply because they show up better at low resolutions. I prefer using them on web pages, especially mobile web pages, because I think they look better — period.

In any case, there are times, especially when designing for tiny screens, when you should be mindful of the typefaces you use. Seldom should your opinion as to whether a certain font is more attractive carry more weight than the overall readability of the text. Curiously, though, most browsers set serif typefaces as their default fonts, for both headlines and body text. (You can find a discussion of how to override the default font in Chapter 7.)

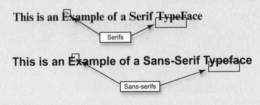

Using CSS to layout XHTML pages

Unless you're using inline styles (discussed earlier in this chapter), you need a way to tell the browser which styles to associate, or attach, to the page elements you want to format. In addition to styles to format text strings and media content, you can also use XHTML tags to create containers, or boxes, to hold your content, and then use CSS to format them.

Similar, in concept, anyway, to HTML tables, discussed in Chapter 1, XHTML containers section off your pages. When combined with CSS, XHTML boxes are infinitely more flexible and adjustable than HTML tables. They allow you a much wider range of control, not only over the container itself, in terms of position, size, alignment, borders, margins and padding, but you also have a much more diverse set of options for formatting the content — the stuff that's in the container.

Creating the container

To create the XHTML container, you use the `<div></div>` tag pair, with the CSS container name, or *selector* (discussed next) as an attribute, like this:

```
<div class="header">
Your content
</div>
```

Creating containers and formatting them is discussed and put into action in Chapter 7, and used again and again in several other chapters as required to create specific types of content. In the meantime, Figure 2-4 should give you an idea how all this works.

Formatting the container

To tell the browser which CSS styles to use to format your containers, you use *style selectors*. The selector is followed by the formatting instructions. Check out the following example:

```
container {
        width: 100%;
        max-width: 800px;
        min-width: 320px;
        background: #000000;

}
```

As you can see, the nice thing about CSS is that you don't usually need a translator to figure out what a style says. It's written in plain ol' everyday English. The example just given says, "Create a container named for every container of type `container`; size it 100 percent of the browser window, but no larger than 800 pixels wide and no smaller than 320 pixels wide; and set the background to the hexadecimal value to #000000, or black." (If hexadecimal colors are unfamiliar, see in Chapter 7.)

Containers   Sidebar   Header   Content   Footer

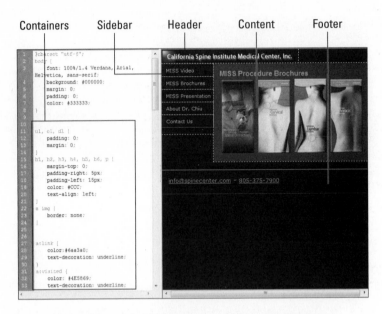

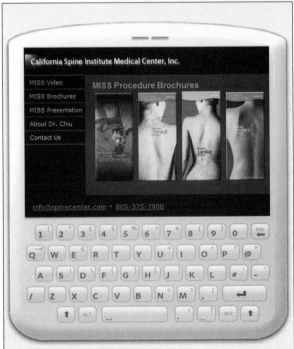

Figure 2-4:
Using container tags and style selectors to create page sections.

One of the exciting aspects of web design is that it's an ever-evolving discipline. You can do it every day for many years and never learn it all, or even close to all of it. For me, analyzing the work of other designers has always been helpful. The nice thing about HTML, XHTML, and sometimes even CSS styles (when pages are designed with internal styles) is that they're just hanging out there on the Internet waiting for my scrutiny. When you come across a page with features you find interesting and you want to know how the effects were achieved, you can often do so right from your browser. All popular web browsers have a feature that lets you view the source code behind a web page. In Firefox, for example, you simply right-click the page and choose View Page Source. In Internet Explorer (IE), it's View Source.

CSS Standards and Versions

Like just about every aspect of information and computer technology, CSS — and web design itself — is in a constant state of flux, ever-changing and constantly evolving. Currently there are three versions of CSS — yep, you guessed it: CSS1, CSS2, and CSS3. Oh yeah, and the currently "Recommended" version of CSS2, CSS 2 revision 1, or CSS 2.1, which fixes some bugs and removes some poorly supported features of the original CSS2. (If you're wondering about how and why a markup or style sheet language becomes Recommended, it's explained in Chapter 1.)

The process for developing and deploying markup and style sheet languages is at best fuzzy and can be highly confusing. Often the new version of a language gets put to work piecemeal; the design community and the makers of web browsers start implementing parts of the new version almost immediately after the W3C announces that they've begun working on it. Take HTML5, for example. It's still a ways away from becoming a candidate for Recommendation, but parts of it are already widely used. Most of the popular web browsers, such as Internet Explorer, Firefox, Apple's Safari, and Google's Chrome — along with many mobile device browsers — support much of HTML5. The same is true of CSS. Although version 2.1 is the Recommendation, CSS3 is already widely supported.

Deciding when to use which version might seem like aiming at a moving target — and often it is, especially when you're designing for the widely diverse mobile device market. That's why (as discussed in detail in Chapter 4 and 5), it's important to know what devices you're designing for and what they're capable of.

CSS1

CSS has been around for quite some time. In fact, CSS1 reached Recommendation level back in December of 1996, which means it began development some time before that. Compared to what designers do with CSS today, CSS1 is quite simple and somewhat limited. But it started web design on its way to using CSS to do some vital positioning and formatting tasks, especially for

- ✔ Backgrounds, margins, borders, and the padding of containers
- ✔ Element attributes such as text color, typefaces, word, letter and line spacing
- ✔ Many other features unsupported (or sorely lacking) in simple HTML and its cumbersome reliance on tables

Although it took some time to catch on, CSS1 brought a lot of options, if you will, to the HTML table. But we really didn't start to see a major shift to CSS until CSS2. In fact, it wasn't until the release of IE 5.0 for Mac in March of 2000 that any browser supported better than 99 percent of the CSS1 specification, which was almost two years after the W3C published the Recommendation of CSS2.

If you're interested in checking out the CSS1 Recommendation, which includes the entire specification itself — something of a CSS1 manual — you can see it on the W3.org website at www.w3.org/TR/REC-CSS1/.

CSS2 (CSS 2.1)

CSS2 is a superset of (that is, it contains) CSS1; the W3C published CSS2 as a Recommendation in May of 1998. Among its most important enhancements are the inclusion of media-specific style sheets, which allows designers to create pages and sites tailored to various devices, such as special access visual browsers, aural devices for the hearing impaired, Braille devices, and mobile handhelds.

CSS2 also provides greater control over the positioning of elements than CSS1. Version 2.1 is the current Recommendation and is widely supported among many smartphones and other mobile devices. See Chapter 5 for the word on how to determine which devices support what CSS versions and to what degree.

You can see the entire CSS 2.1, complete with full documentation, specification at www.w3.org/TR/CSS2/.

CSS3

CSS3, discussed in some detail in Chapter 11, is such a major enhancement that it's difficult to decide what to talk about first. It makes possible many effects that we now use other programs for — such as drop shadows on text, simple animations, rotating text and other objects, and so much more. This CSS level is truly a maturation of web design technology that's akin to advancements reached by the desktop publishing industry at the turn of the 21st century.

I'm not saying that designers won't need Photoshop or Flash anymore, but they won't find themselves having to create separate files for each simple little effect as often.

Regarding mobile devices, expect to see CSS3 show up in many of the newer smartphones, such as the iPhone, Droid, and some others (though not Windows Phone 7, at least not as I write this). The mobile world, though, does not consist solely of advanced smartphone users. You can't ignore the users of the millions of not-so-smart phone. It isn't (*ahem*) smart.

One of the more exciting features is CSS3, especially for mobile web designers, is a feature called Media Queries. Typically (as discussed in Chapters 4 and 5), when you're designing for mobile devices in CSS1 and CSS2, you design your style sheets based on device profiles. The result is a static version of the web page based on what's built into the profile. Instead of working from a profile of what's known about the device, Media Queries just go ask the device itself about its capabilities. For example: What is your screen size, orientation, and resolution? Are you in portrait (upright) or landscape (rotated) mode? The answers, along with a whole bunch of other useful info, come back. The style sheet then formats the page accordingly. Chapter 11 looks at some of CSS3's more exciting features. You can see the CSS3 specification at www.w3.org/TR/css3-roadmap.

If you really want to get a feel for the power behind CSS3, do a search for "CSS3 features" and see what the design community has to say about it. Designers are truly excited and chomping at the bit to use it. For example, check out "22 Handy HTML5 and CSS3 Tools, Resources, and Guides" at www.1stwebdesigner.com/freebies/22-handy-html5-css3-tools-resources-and-guides.

Figure 2-5 shows a couple of simple text boxes formatted with solely with CSS3.

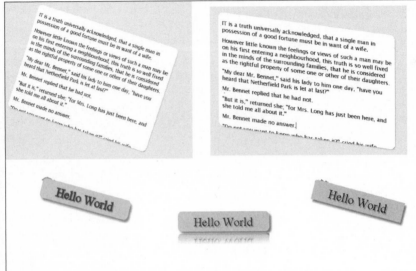

Figure 2-5:
Examples of
text boxes
skewed and
transformed
with CSS3.

A bright future

This is exciting stuff. But keep in mind that all the CSS3 magic is performed by the mobile device — or, more specifically, by the device's browser. If the device doesn't support CSS3, Media Queries don't work. While smartphones are flying off the shelves, relying solely on CSS3 for your mobile device design would make your site unavailable to a huge number of mobile web users. But cheer up: You can bet that CSS3 is going to revolutionize mobile web design in the not-too-distant future.

Combining CSS3 with HTML5 — speaking of the future — will more than likely revolutionize web design in mid-revolution. Many browsers, and many mobile browsers, already support many CSS3 and HTML 5 features. Your job as a mobile designer is to provide the best mobile web experience for as many of your site's mobile visitors as possible. That means you can't rely on one standard — and you can't, for that matter, rely solely on CSS. You can see some of most useful CSS3 formatting options for mobile devices in Chapter 11.

You have a bunch of tools at your disposal, including XHTML and CSS, but you'll accommodate many more mobile users if you throw in spatterings of other technologies, such JavaScript and server-side PHP scripts (which run on the server, instead of the device), and a few other techniques covered throughout this book.

Chapter 3

Introducing JavaScript for Building Mobile Web Pages

• •

In This Chapter

▶ Using JavaScript with mobile browsers

▶ Integrating HTML with JavaScript

▶ Using the head section to add JavaScript code

▶ Creating automatically launched JavaScript files

▶ Giving the user dynamic controls of page content

▶ Dynamically changing graphics with JavaScript and the Document Object Model

• •

*T*he good thing about JavaScript is that a little goes a long way. You can add a little script in your HTML code and use it and reuse it again and again. JavaScript helps you make your website look just right for your big computer with a 27-inch screen, your laptop, your tablet computer, and your smartphone — all with the same HTML page. Just let JavaScript do all the work figuring out the type and size of the device you're using.

You can write JavaScript using any application you write HTML with. That includes web development programs like Adobe Dreamweaver or text editors like NotePad and TextEdit. As the song goes, *Do it your way*. Any way you want, you'll find writing JavaScript code a snap. More importantly, though, you'll find that it will exponentially increase what you can do with your web pages, especially on your mobile device.

JavaScript works with *most* browsers — whether on your computer or mobile device. All the work of interpreting the code is done by the browser, not your operating system, your hardware, or the little mouse who lives in your computer and types really fast. It is considered *interpreted* because you don't have to compile it into binary code. Just like HTML, JavaScript depends wholly on the browser, and because both HTML and JavaScript (along with CSS) all live and work together, you can enter JavaScript right in the middle of an HTML page.

So what does JavaScript do besides making adjustments to web pages viewed on a mobile device? In a word, it increases the interactivity of your web pages. With HTML alone, the only reaction that occurs when a user taps a link is to bring up a different page. With JavaScript, you can make the page respond in many different ways without changing pages. For example, JavaScript can bring up an alert window to bring the user's attention to timely information, a friendly greeting, or a reminder to take out the cat.

Getting Mobile with JavaScript

On both mobile and non-mobile devices, JavaScript runs in the browser— not the operating system. Like HTML, not all JavaScript implementations are exactly alike despite the existence of standards (known as ECMAScript). Further, users can turn their JavaScript on or off, and if turned off, the JavaScript will not launch. At this writing, JavaScript is implemented in several common mobile browsers and is in wide use within HTML applications designed for mobile devices, so you're not going to have a difficult time finding browsers that support JavaScript. However, you should be prepared for different implementations. For example, the most widely used smartphone platform in the world is Symbian S60 — one you may have never heard of. The newer version of the browser called the "S60v3 browser" supports JavaScript, but the older S60 browser does not. Likewise, most of the newer and widely used mobile browsers support JavaScript; so don't think that only a few mobile browsers support it. Most do.

When you create your mobile application with JavaScript, be sure to test it on different mobile browsers. Then you won't be surprised if it works in unexpected ways on some browsers — or it doesn't work at all.

Where to Put JavaScript in Your HTML Script

In general, the code for your JavaScript programs is placed in an area of your script known as the *head*. You can easily spot the *head container* by its surrounding tags — it's the region between the opening head tag <head> and the closing head tag </head>. For example, you may have seen a snippet of code that looks like the following:

```
<head>
<style type="text/css">
body {
    background-color:#fbf7e4;
    font-family:Verdana, Geneva, sans-serif;
    margin-left:20px;
    color:#8e001c;
}
</style>
<title>My Mobile Page</title>
<meta http-equiv="Content-Type" content="text/html; charset=UTF-8">
</head>
```

Common tags you'll find in the head include the following:

- ✔ **Style sheets:** Your CSS style sheets are found here.
- ✔ **Title:** The title appears at the top of the web page.
- ✔ **Meta tags:** These are the tags that give information about the page to the web server.
- ✔ **Scripts:** These tags embed JavaScript (or some other scripting languages) in an HTML page.

The head region of an HTML page can either have lots of material or just a little. So now let's see what we need to do to add JavaScript.

The JavaScript script

Before you write your first JavaScript program, look at the tags used to indicate that the script is JavaScript and not something else. The following shows the `<script>` container inside of the `<head>` container:

```
<script type="text/javascript">
    //This is where the JavaScript goes
</script>
```

All the code in the `<script>` container is treated as a full program.

The important feature about the head region of your web page is that all materials in the head load first. In that way, your JavaScript (or CSS style sheet) is all ready to go when the rest of the page loads. Think of the head area as being first in line.

Sometimes you want to make sure that your JavaScript *does not* launch until after your page is loaded. Because all the materials in the <head> container launch first, you can just put your script within the <body> container. The general format is shown in the following:

```
<body>
<h1>My Big Page</h1>
<script type="text/javascript">
    //JavaScript
</script>
<p/>This is more interesting material..
</body>
```

Adding the little pieces of JavaScript in the text will not disrupt what the viewer sees. The JavaScript within the <script> tags is invisible.

If you have some JavaScript that you find yourself reusing a lot, you can place it in an external text file instead of placing it in the HTML script. Then, whenever you want to use it, just call the name of the file and your JavaScript acts like it's part of the HTML. You can place the JavaScript reference in the same places, the head or body, as you would enter it directly. For example, the following might be a greeting that you place in all your HTML pages:

```
<head>
    <script src="welcome.js"></script>
</head>
```

The JavaScript in the text file named welcome.js is just straight JavaScript with no HTML tags. You could place the same kind of tags in the body as well. For instance, you may have a notice you place at the bottom of every page:

```
<body>
    ...all the rest of your HTML
    <script src="welcome.js"></script>
</body>
```

So just remember that JavaScript tries to be as accommodating as possible! Add JavaScript *your* way.

Your first JavaScript program

To get started, take a look at a built-in JavaScript function named alert(), which pops up an alert box over your HTML page. To set up this function, open a new HTML page in Dreamweaver or in your favorite text or HTML editor, enter the code in Listing 3-1, and then save the file as alert1.html.

Listing 3-1:   A JavaScript alert box

```
<!DOCTYPE HTML>
<html>
<head>
<script type="text/javascript">
alert("Hello from your mobile!");
</script>
<meta http-equiv="Content-Type" content="text/html; charset=UTF-8">
<title>Alert!</title>
</head>
<body>
</body>
</html>
```

If you test this file using the Google Chrome browser, you'll see an alert box as shown in Figure 3-1. (Other browsers will show different results.)

Figure 3-1:
JavaScript alert box shown in Chrome browser on desktop computer.

Now that you have an example to work with, you can check out how it looks on a mobile device. Unlike a desktop or laptop computer — where you can test HTML and JavaScript directly from the computer using a browser — a mobile device requires you to place your script on a server and then use your mobile browser to view it as you would any remote website on your computer.

Before you can place your HTML file on a web server, you need to have a hosting service or access to a web server on your computer. If you have a hosting service (which you may have through your work or school), the system administrator has instructions available for placing your HTML file on the web server. If your computer has a web server on it (and most do!) you need to have access to the IP address that you can access through the Internet to your computer. If you have a Local Area Network (LAN) set up, you can use it to access your file. A common LAN IP address begins with 192.168 . . . . For example, my computer's LAN address is 196.168.1.26. I've placed my `alert1.html` file in a folder named `js` — right at the root of my web server. Whenever I want to look at the appearance of a website on my mobile device, I can type in `196.168.1.26/js/alert1.html`. For details, see these sites:

> ✔ **For Windows**: `http://windows.microsoft.com/en-US/windows-vista/Setting-up-a-home-network`
>
> ✔ **For Mac**: `www.apple.com/support/`

Another method for testing your mobile pages is installing a full-featured Apache emulator as test server. Apache is the web server application popular on Linux servers, which most of the Web is hosted on. For a description of how to install and use a test server, see Chapter 4.

The mobile view

Now that you have an actual JavaScript function in an HTML page, you need to look at it on your mobile browser. Figure 3-2 shows the alert window opening on a mobile device using a Safari mobile browser.

Figure 3-2:
JavaScript
alert box
shown in
a Safari
mobile
browser.

As you can see in Figure 3-2, the pop-up alert window is different from what you see on the desktop, but it's just a minor matter of style. The Safari mobile browser does not have a graphic icon, and it displays the URL of the web page. In Figure 3-2, a LAN IP address appears instead of a descriptive domain name address. In any event, there's not too much difference between the desktop and mobile browser views. When we try a different mobile browser, however, we get a much different look. Figure 3-3 shows an Opera mobile browser displaying the same page hosted on a remote server.

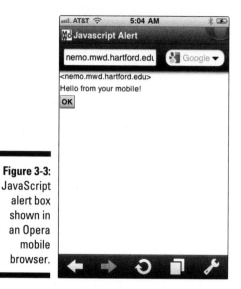

Figure 3-3:
JavaScript
alert box
shown in
an Opera
mobile
browser.

As you can see in Figure 3-3, a wholly different view appears in the Opera mobile browser. It doesn't look anything like the other alert boxes. Will users recognize it as an alert window? That probably depends on what you're using it for — and on the general context of its use. Further, how well the alert box does its job will depend on the look and feel of the web page design. Don't assume that just because it looks the way you like on your computer that you'll get the same look on your mobile device.

Functions: Wait Until You're Called!

JavaScript in the head container will execute as soon as you load a web page. Alternatively, you can create a function that waits until it's called — an event occurs that tells the function, "Hey you! Your services are needed!" A *function* is really just a collection of JavaScript statements packaged together to run as soon as a certain event occurs. Before you get too far into working with functions, the first order of business is to understand how to *call* (request) a function with events and event handlers.

Events, listeners, and their handlers

When you look at your web page, you may not think it is doing much, but take my word for it; your page is a huge party animal! When you open a web page, that's an event. When you play or stop a video (in HTML5, discussed in Chapter 11), that's an event. When you click the mouse or tap the mobile display, that's an event. At last count, there were 71 events that your HTML5 page recognizes! (XHTML recognizes fewer.) Events can be found in the following categories:

- ✓ **Window events:** These events occur in your computer's window. When a web page has loaded, that's an event detected by the `onload` event listener.

- ✓ **Form events:** Any event within a form container. For example, when you click a Submit button that sends form data, the `onsubmit` event listener detects that event.

- ✓ **Keyboard events:** Banging away on your keyboard certainly is an event — and it can be caught by `onkeypress` and other keyboard listeners.

- ✓ **Mouse events:** On a mobile device, your finger takes the place of the mouse; when you tap, the device hears `onclick` as well as several other mouse-like actions.

- ✓ **Media events:** The media events on your mobile don't involve reporters and the paparazzi, but rather events of audio and video — such as `onplay` when a media process starts and `onended` when it's over.

JavaScript lets you enter event listeners in a few different ways. You can use the `onload`, `onclick` options discussed here, or the `addEventListener` method discussed later in this chapter and in Chapter 15. Which option you should use depends on the script and context.

An *event handler* is nothing more than a function that does something when a specified event occurs. JavaScript can create event handlers in the form of `functions`. A function has the following format:

```
function myFunction()
{
    //do something
}
```

JavaScript functions are generally written in the page head, just like any other JavaScript. To try one, open a new HTML page in Dreamweaver or your favorite text or HTML editor, enter the code in Listing 3-2, and then save the file as `WriteFunction.html`.

Listing 3-2: A JavaScript function

```
<!DOCTYPE HTML>
<html>
<head>
<script type="text/javascript">
function sayHello()
{
    var greetVar="This greeting... ";
    var lineBreak="<br/>";
```

```
    var moreGreet="...is brought to you by a function.";
    document.write(greetVar);
    document.write(lineBreak);
    document.write(moreGreet);
    document.write(lineBreak);
}

</script>
<meta http-equiv="Content-Type" content="text/html; charset=UTF-8">
<title>Greeting Function</title>
</head>
<body onLoad="sayHello()">
</body>
</html>
```

Place this file on a web server, open a browser on your mobile device, and then locate the URL with the `WriteFunction.html` and select it in your browser. On your mobile device, you'll see something like the image in Figure 3-4, depending on your device and mobile browser.

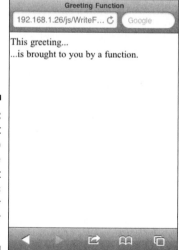

Figure 3-4: JavaScript writes to your mobile screen just as it does to your computer screen.

You might be thinking, *That's no different from just having the JavaScript outside the function and firing when the page loads!* The difference is subtle. Using the `onload` event waits until the page has loaded and *then* fires the function. What you've been seeing before is the JavaScript in action *before* the page has loaded — the head loads first.

Not all events are handled the same way on all mobile devices and browsers. The technical differences between a "tap" and a "click" on the screen, for example, can be quite significant. Likewise, not all mobile devices respond well to other mouse events such as *mouseovers, mouseouts,* or *double-clicks.* Keyboards on mobile devices only appear in certain contexts — so you need to check any keyboard events in your JavaScript to see whether their contexts are correct. If you test your programs using JavaScript event handlers with as many different devices as possible, you'll find the most commonly accepted events — as well as some that just don't work with mobile devices at all.

Making functions with variables and a little DOM

JavaScript uses `variables` to store information for future use. A *variable* is a property that stores information. Some of that information is text — called *strings* — and most of the rest is numbers. So if I write

```
var sayHi="Hello there!";
```

the variable named `sayHi` stores the text (called a *string*). When that stored text is needed, it is placed into a function that displays it on the screen.

In the example, we used the Document Object Model (DOM) in HTML5, discussed in Chapter 11. The DOM is a way of organizing HTML properties (attributes) and methods (functions — elements that cause an action to take place) that treat an HTML page as an object called a `document`. Using JavaScript allows you to use the DOM to specify values and issue commands through available DOM functions. For example, the DOM includes a function called `write()`. So all that is required is this statement:

```
document.write(sayHi);
```

Whatever is stored in the variable (`sayHi`) appears on the screen as soon as the function is called by the `onload` event listener. To learn more about what is in the DOM, the official word can be found at www.w3.org/DOM/.

Wait until I tell you!

Now, if you don't want anything to happen until you say so, you'll need some way to type or tap your intentions. The `onload` event is fine, along with other event listeners, but not when the user has to directly communicate with the page.

To make the function wait for the user, you can use `onclick`. On mobile devices, your finger does the clickin' and so you might think of `onclick` as `ontap`. The following script shows a very simple example. To experiment with it, open a new HTML page in Dreamweaver or your favorite text or HTML editor, enter the code in Listing 3-3, and then save the file as `tap-Function.html`.

Listing 3-3: Tap versus click

```
<!DOCTYPE HTML>
<html>
<head>
<script type="text/javascript">
function headTap()
{
   var elTappo="I just got tapped in the head(er)";
   alert(elTappo);
}
</script>
<meta http-equiv="Content-Type" content="text/html; charset=UTF-8">
<title>Function On Tap</title>
</head>
<body>
<header onclick="headTap()">
  <h1>Tap Me!</h1>
</header>
</body>
</html>
```

Place this file on a web server, open a browser on your mobile device, and then locate the URL with the `tapFunction.html` and select it in your browser. When the page opens, you'll see the words `Tap Me!` Tap those words with your finger — think of your fingertip as a mouse button. As soon as you tap the text with your finger, the alert window shown in Figure 3-5 appears. (Tap OK when you're finished.)

As you can see, you were able to fire off the JavaScript alert window, and you didn't need a button or a mouse — just call your finger "squeaky." In HTML5, discussed in Chapter 11, you can add structural tags like `<header>` and place the event listener (`onclick`) and assign it a JavaScript event handler (a function). Your mobile device thinks your finger tap is a click.

Make and break your own event handlers

You can get very fancy with events and event handlers. Keeping in mind that only some of the mouse and keyboard events work with mobile devices at this time, you can combine functions and add or remove event handlers.

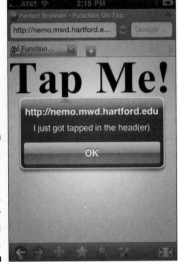

Figure 3-5:
Tapping the
text in the
<header>
container
launched
the function.

First, you need something that you can exercise an event with — something to tap, kick, or tickle. Because your mobile device doesn't recognize kicks or tickles, let's see how to add a tap to an HTML button and then remove the tap capacity. The ingredients include

✔ Two buttons

✔ A function to add events to both buttons when the page loads

✔ Two more functions to do something when each button is clicked

To add an event listener to an object, you have to set up a variable name with the name of the object. Then you add an event listener to the object as shown in the following snippet:

```
var tapper = document.getElementById ("tapButton");
tapper.addEventListener("click",Tapped,false);
```

To remove an event listener, you do essentially the same thing, except you use the operation to remove the event listener, as follows:

```
var tapper = document.getElementById ("tapButton");
tapper.removeEventListener("click",Tapped,false);
```

After *either* adding or removing an event listener, you enter the type of event, enter the name of the function it jumps to (leaving out the parentheses), and add `false` to the last parameter. The `false` means that you want the event handler to launch in the "bubbling" phase. A `true` would launch the event in the "capturing" stage. The correct answer is "either," but if you're not sure, use `false`.

To try this, open a new HTML page in Dreamweaver or your favorite text or HTML editor, enter the code in Listing 3-4, and then save the file as `tapButton.html`.

Listing 3-4:   Adding and removing event listeners

```
<!DOCTYPE HTML>
<html>
<head>
<script type="text/javascript">
function Tapped()
{
    alert("I just got tapped");
}
function Remover()
{
    var tapper = document.getElementById ("tapButton");
    tapper.removeEventListener("click",Tapped,false);
    tapper.style.background='black';
    tapper.style.color='white';
    alert("Tap Man is broken!");
}

function setUp()
{
    var tapper = document.getElementById ("tapButton");
    tapper.addEventListener("click",Tapped,false);
    var killer = document.getElementById ("spoiler");
    killer.addEventListener("click",Remover,false);
}

</script>
<meta http-equiv="Content-Type" content="text/html; charset=UTF-8">
<title>Tap Button</title>
</head>

<body onload="setUp()">
    <button id="tapButton">Tap Man</button>
    <button id="spoiler">Killer</button>
</body>
</html>
```

Place this file on a web server, open a browser on your mobile device, and then locate the URL with the `tapButton.html` and select it in your browser. When the page opens, you'll see two buttons — one named `Tap Man` and the other named `Killer`. Tap the Tap Man button, and an alert message informs you that you just got tapped. Now tap the Killer button, and an alert message informs you that you just broke the Tap Man button. What you've really done is to remove the event listener from Tap Man; now it will no longer be able to launch the function. Also the black and white colors on the Tap Man button have reversed.

Tap the Tap Man button again. Nothing happens; however, the Killer button is still working — and you can tap it to bring up the alert message.

Figure 3-6 shows the different events and changes that occur when adding and removing events.

Figure 3-6:
Using and removing an event handler.

Let JavaScript Do the Thinking!

You may have heard that computers can think. Well, you heard right. So can web pages using JavaScript. All you need is a problem for them to figure out. Need to figure out how to add sales tax? Let JavaScript do the work.

For example, you can have a web page calculate your sales tax for you. That particular problem breaks down into these simple steps:

1. Input amount of purchase: 14.95

2. Input sales tax rate: 5%

3. Compute sales tax on purchase: 14.95 times .05, which is 75¢

4. Compute total: Amount of purchase plus sales tax: $15.70 (rounded up)

All JavaScript needs now are some basic arithmetic operators to take care of the calculations and here they are:

+	Addition
–	Subtraction
*	Multiplication
/	Division

To use an operator, all you need to do is to place it between two variables or actual numbers, as in these examples:

```
9 / 3 = 3
10 * 5 = 50
```

Using variables, you'd type

```
var alpha = 15;
var beta = 10;
alpha + beta = 25
```

Putting an expression inside a JavaScript listing is just as easy. To create a function that figures out your total cost based on a sales tax rate and amount of a purchase, here's the drill: Open a new HTML page in Dreamweaver or your favorite text or HTML editor, enter the code in Listing 3-5, and then save the file as `salesTax.html`.

Listing 3-5:   Calculating total cost

```
<!DOCTYPE HTML>
<html>
<head>
<style type="text/css">
section
    {
    font-family:"Comic Sans MS", cursive;
    color:#900;
    }
</style>
<script type="text/javascript">
function salesClerk()
{
    var purchasePrice=14.95;
    var taxRate=.05;
    var taxOnPrice=purchasePrice * taxRate;
    var total=purchasePrice +taxOnPrice;
    alert("Your bill is $" + total);
}
</script>
<meta http-equiv="Content-Type" content="text/html; charset=UTF-8">
<title>The Thinker</title>
</head>
<body>
<article>
<section onClick="salesClerk()">
  <h1>Your total is...(tap me)</h1>
</section>
</article>
</body>
</html>
```

Place this file on a web server, open a browser on your mobile device, and then locate the URL with the `salesTax.html` and select it in your browser.

You may have noticed that we added a little CSS (discussed in Chapter 2) to spice it up a bit. Figure 3-7 shows what you can expect to see when you view the file.

Figure 3-7:
Tapping the text displays the total cost in the alert window.

If you're familiar with the comic sans font, you may wonder what the cursive script is doing in the mobile browser display. That's just a reminder that mobile devices still have a limited font set.

You also may be curious to know why the value of the total price has not been rounded off. It's because we didn't tell JavaScript to handle that detail. Now we will. While we're at it, let's change the tax rate from five to four percent. Just change the following two lines:

First change

```
var taxRate=.05;
```

to

```
var taxRate=.04;
```

And then change

```
alert("Your bill is $" + total);
```

to

```
alert("Your bill is $" + Math.round(total*Math.pow(10,2))/Math.pow(10,2));
```

Save your program and run it again. This time, the outcome is different, and it has only two integers after the decimal point — just like real money! (By the way, the new tax rate is helpful. Just look at Figure 3-8 — the mobile device fainted and displays the results on its side.)

Figure 3-8:
The adjust-
ment shows
a two-dec-
imal-point
result.

The `math` statement to handle two decimal points may be a little much to grasp, but it's just a fancy way of writing:

```
Math.round(total*100)/100
```

Even better, just save the formula (*algorithm* in geek-speak) somewhere handy on your computer and pull it out when you need to round off a value to two decimal places. If you use Dreamweaver, you can save it that program's Snippets panel and insert into your documents whenever you want.

Graphic Magic with JavaScript

Maybe you don't like math, but JavaScript just loves it! However, what about the more artistic side of JavaScript? Does JavaScript have an artistic temperament as well? Yes it does! In this section, you'll see how JavaScript handles graphics using the Document Object Model (DOM).

The DOM and graphics

If you think of the HTML DOM as a big object (document) that has lots of properties, you'll find it easier to understand. In many respects, the DOM is just another representation of your web page — it just expresses it differently. In HTML, you load a graphic file with the following format:

```
<img src="myGraphic.png" name="graphicLand">
```

To express the same line in the DOM, using JavaScript, you write

```
var mygr = new Image();
mygr.src="myGraphic.png"
document.graphicLand.src=mygr.src
```

You might be thinking that the JavaScript method looks a bit more convoluted, but the logic is the same. The name of the graphic "holder" is `graphicLand` in both the HTML and DOM versions. The name of the graphic file is assigned to an `src` attribute in both HTML and DOM coding, but in the DOM version an image object named `mygr` is created to hold the reference to the actual graphic file.

Be still my heart

In plain-vanilla HTML, your graphics stay put. By adding some JavaScript, you can move them into and out of the DOM location defined by JavaScript. To see an example of what you can do, consider two heart graphics — a thumbnail and large size — created as PNG files. The thumbnail is the original; when the user clicks the thumbnail, a big heart image appears. By using the `onclick` event listener, you can replace the thumbnail heart with the big heart. To do so, open a new HTML page in Dreamweaver or your favorite text or HTML editor, enter the code in Listing 3-6, and then save the file as `imageSwap.html`.

Listing 3-6:   Converting thumbnails to larger graphics

```
<!DOCTYPE HTML>
<html>
<head>
<script language="Javascript">
var bigHeart= new Image()
bigHeart.src="bigHeart.png"
function goBig()
{
    document.heart.src=bigHeart.src
}
</script>
<meta http-equiv="Content-Type" content="text/html; charset=UTF-8">
<title>Big Heart</title>
</head>
<body>
<header onclick="goBig()"> <img id="heart" src="littleHeart.png" border=0></
               header>
</body>
</html>
```

Place this file on a web server, open a browser on your mobile device, and then locate the URL with the imageSwap.html and select it in your browser. When the program loads, you see a small heart image. When you tap the heart image, a large heart appears onscreen. In Figure 3-9, you can see the original image on the left and the larger image after the tap.

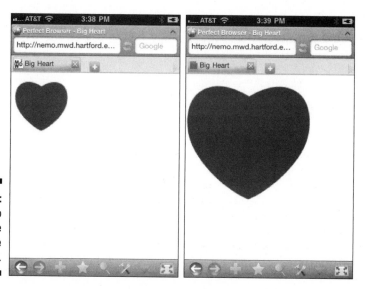

Figure 3-9: Tapping to make the image bigger.

Mobile browsers seem to have a mind of their own. If you double-click the big heart, it gets bigger! Double-click it again, and it gets smaller. As you can see in the code — and experience when you click the thumbnail — only a single click is required. However, the double-click — whether a function of the particular browser or due to the mobile device's operating system — is a different story; on some mobile browsers, nothing happens! So be sure to first test your HTML app on the mobile browser that you expect it to be used on.

As you've seen, you can open a whole new realm of possibilities in mobile web applications with JavaScript, and this chapter has just scratched the surface. JavaScript can be as simple or complex as your app's needs require — but make no mistake about it: there's a great deal more that you can do with HTML *with* JavaScript than without it!

Chapter 4

Mobile Web Design Software and Utilities

*I*n the world of professional web design, there are essentially two disciplines, or schools of thought, or camps — or whatever you want to call them. On the one hand, there are the purists — usually *hand-coders* who type in the code that creates web pages "by hand," without the aid of WYSIWYG (pronounced *wih-zee-wig*, for What You See Is What You Get) software. Which brings us to the second type of professional web designers: You guessed it — those professionals who *do* use WYSIWYG design software to create web pages.

At one time there were somewhere in the neighborhood of 20 or so web design applications. Nowadays, though, there are only a handful, and they can easily be separated into two categories: High-end, professional web design packages and low-end, beginner software. (Then, too, there are the scores of other programs, such as Microsoft Word and PowerPoint — clearly intended to do something *other* than web design — that allow you to export the documents you create in them to HTML or some other type of web-ready format. Word, for example, also lets you import your word processor files to XML, a somewhat sophisticated cousin of HTML.)

Nowadays, the only industrial-strength, professional WYSIWYG web design program left is Adobe's Dreamweaver. Hand-coders, on the other hand, tend to use *source code editors* — programs designed for typing in and editing source code — and they have all kinds of programs and utilities at their disposal to help out, including a couple of popular web browsers — Firefox and Google's Chrome. These free and readily available programs allow you to install add-ons (also free) that turn a common web browser into a fairly sophisticated hand-coding and testing environment.

In this chapter, I compare the two approaches — hand-coding and using Dreamweaver. There are significant advantages and disadvantages to each method. This chapter also discusses what HTML- and CSS-specific features to look for in source code editors, as well as some popular browser add-ons for producing and testing mobile sites. If you haven't already set up your mobile site creation and test environment, the information in this chapter should help make your choices easier.

Hand-Coding versus Web Design Programs

If you're new to web design and considering hand-coding, the huge number of applications, utilities, and techniques available can seem daunting. After many years of teaching web design and designing sites for my clients, I've noticed that for the most part, new designers tend to stick with the methods they start with — or the applications and utilities of their teachers and mentors. Then, too, there are the self-taught, who learn from scouring the web and self-help books, especially *Dummies* books. These professionals seem to learn and create from a whatever-works, task-oriented mentality — the shortest path to getting the job done.

There are many ways to create a website. Let's take a closer look and compare the tools available to help you create mobile websites.

And the nominees are:

- **Text editors:** You can use simple text editors, such as Windows Notepad or Mac OS TextEdit, or your word processor to code your pages by hand. This is the most spartan approach, especially if you use your operating system's built-in text editor. This method provides no help, leaving you to rely solely on your knowledge of HTML and CSS coding. Choose this method and become a hand-coding gladiator.

- **Source code editors:** You can use one of the many HTML/CSS source code editors — such as UltraEdit or Aptana — to help you hand-code your pages. Source code editors are text editors with added features for writing code.

- **Browser Add-ons:** You can use a browser, such as Firefox or Chrome, with third-party add-ons that increase the browser's functionality, to hand-code and test your web pages.

✔ **Adobe Dreamweaver:** You can use the sole remaining industrial strength WYSIWYG site design and web application development program — Adobe Dreamweaver — to create your site and design your pages. Figure 4-1 shows a web page in Design view, Dreamweaver's WYSIWYG editing mode. Dreamweaver is a very powerful program, as discussed a little later in this chapter.

✔ **Adobe Creative Suite:** You can make the ultimate commitment to web design and invest in Adobe's web design suite — Creative Suite Web Premium — to create all the supporting content, style sheets, and scripts; and to design and lay out your site and supporting pages and files. This option is discussed later in this chapter.

You can, as many professional designers and developers do, choose one of these options, learn it well and stick with it; or you can use a combination of two or more of these methods, as many other designers do. Each method has its own set of advantages and drawbacks. Nothing's perfect, as the saying goes, and some web design tools and utilities are less perfect than others. But that shouldn't stop you from trying to find the perfect design tools — or at least the best tools for you and the way you work.

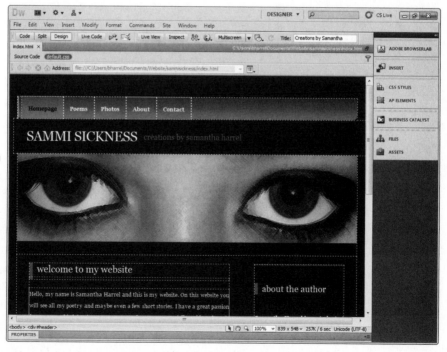

Figure 4-1: Using Dream-weaver's WYSIWYG interface to create and see your new web page in real time.

Coding by Hand (or Shaving with Glass)

As you might have guessed by now, I am not a big fan of hand-coding. To me, coding web pages by hand is far too close to programming — which I think requires a special kind of mindset that I don't have. I have the utmost respect for programmers. In this line of work — website and web application design — though, to become a good, state-of-the-art, cutting-edge designer, sometimes you just can't avoid hand-coding and programming.

Some hand-coders are quite adamant about not using WYSIWYG software for creating their sites. It's not unusual, for example, to find help-wanted ads for web designers that read something like this: "Web Designer Needed. If you use Dreamweaver, don't apply."

So why, then, do these designers find hand-coding superior to web design software?

Most of the WYSIWYG design programs available — other than Adobe Dreamweaver, that is — are really aimed at beginners and small business owners who care more about getting their sites up quickly and with as little fuss as possible than about learning the intricacies of HTML and CSS. For the sake of this discussion, let's assume the only professional WYSIWYG editor left is Dreamweaver. From here on, when I refer to web design software, I mean Dreamweaver.

So let's look at the primary reasons hand-coders state for preferring hand-coding over using Dreamweaver.

More control over the code

The hand-coders I've talked to over the years (and collaborate with on projects frequently) say that working directly in the code, rather than letting the design software create the code for them, provides a higher level of control, thereby allowing them to create superior documents. The obvious question here is, superior how? Here are some of the more common responses:

- **Hand-coding lets you get at features and refinements unsupported by graphical editors**. In other words, you can do things by hand-coding that you can't do with Dreamweaver.

- **Hand-coding provides better control over the syntax of the code.** You are probably familiar with the term *syntax* from your high-school and college composition classes. (And no, I'm not talking about government levies on drinking and gambling.) *Syntax* refers to the overall construction — the way it's put together — of the code. Just as this is important in writing, it's also important in page markup and programming languages.

> ✔ **Hand-coded documents are more likely to meet W3C standards.** This sort of speaks for itself. It implies that Dreamweaver does not produce standards-compliant code. W3C standards are discussed in Chapters 1 and 2.
>
> ✔ **Hand-coding produces leaner and meaner "machine-ready" code.** Along the same lines as the preceding point, this suggests that Dreamweaver produces inferior code and that machines — computers and mobile devices — have more difficulty interpreting and executing it than hand-coded code.

These sound like some pretty good reasons to stay away from Dreamweaver, don't they? At the risk of sounding like a major Adobe stockholder, let me say this: They are very good reasons to hand-code — if they were true. At one time, some time back, all of these complaints were valid, not only of Dreamweaver, but all other web design packages. Since purchasing Dreamweaver from Macromedia several years ago, though, Adobe has done an excellent job of correcting these shortcomings. These are no longer applicable reasons to avoid Dreamweaver.

Hand-coding is less expensive

Is this true? If we're talking initial investment — avoiding the purchase price of web design software — well, then, yes hand-coding is less expensive. After all, whether you use a Windows machine or a Mac, you already have a text editor you can use to hand-code, right? And you probably already have Word or some other word processor. So, no, you don't have to buy anything else if you're going to hand-code.

But you really can't measure expense solely in terms of initial outlay. Whether you are a freelance designer or the designated web designer for your company, *time* is a significant and immensely relevant variable when assessing cost. When it comes to web design, the old cliché, "time is money," is, without question, oh-so-true. Dreamweaver costs less than $200. The average professional designer charges upwards of $50 per hour (with many charging $100 per hour or more). If using Dreamweaver saves you just a few hours on one project, hand-coding is no longer less expensive.

In order to become effective at hand-coding, you'll need to develop a high level of expertise. Professional designers who hand-code web sites must know the program or markup languages they design in very well. And if this is the approach you choose, so will you. Otherwise you'll find yourself constantly researching, referencing, trying this, trying that — spending far too much time to get things right.

When deciding whether to code by hand or use a web design program, keep in mind that the time you spend learning, researching, and testing your pages adds up quickly. It doesn't take long for the extra hours spent hand-coding to take your projects well beyond budgets and deadlines.

Dreamweaver is a crutch

Many hand-coders say that Dreamweaver's users become too reliant on the WYSIWYG interface and other automation tools. They don't really learn how (or they forget how) to use HTML and CSS code. Of the reasons listed here, this one has the most validity. You can become too dependent on the program and thereby stunt your growth in terms of learning how HTML, XHTML, CSS, and any other markup or programming language, for that matter, actually work.

But few things — and this is especially true of web design — are that cut and dried. This argument neglects to consider a very important component: human nature. Although we might all be created equal, in terms of ability and temperament, we are not all the same. After many years of designing websites, working with many, many professionals, and teaching design, I have a different take.

Generally, professionals who prefer hand-coding approach creating websites from a left-brain, more logical, *development* or *programming* perspective. They find it easier to break projects down into small, analytical pieces and to stitch all those pieces together with code. Professionals who use WYSIWYG software, on the other hand, typically tend to work from a more right-brain, visual, *design* point of view. Like nearly everything else in the world, the web design world needs both types of professionals.

Can't we all just get along? Of course we can. We do it all the time. For example, large design firms and the design departments in large corporations usually employ both types of web designers, and they work together. The WYSIWYG designers concentrate on the actual look and feel of the site, the visual aspect, such as theme, layout, buttons, information flow, and so on. These elements of a website are often referred to as the site's *frontend*. Hand-coders (often programmers) work on the site's behind-the-scenes, or *backend*, functionality, such as database integration, shopping carts, and other applications.

Lots of programs export or convert their native document formats to HTML and XHTML. The programs in the Microsoft Office suite, for example — in particular, Word, PowerPoint, and Excel — all have a Save-As-HTML option. These, and most other programs that aren't really web design programs, usually play havoc with HTML tags and Cascading Style Sheets (CSS). The convoluted style sheets and other code these programs produce can drive mobile browsers crazy. (Word's HTML output is notoriously dirty, so much so that

Dreamweaver comes with a special import option dedicated to picking the junk tags out of HTML files exported from Word.) So do yourself a favor: Don't even think about using programs that try to turn their native content into HTML for creating mobile web content.

A long-term advantage of hand-coding is that — if you force yourself to hand-code — after a while, you'll know HTML and CSS well. Very well. Maybe much better than you ever would if you relied solely on Dreamweaver — which, when you work in WYSIWYG mode, writes most of the code for you. I find switching back and forth between hand-coding and WYSIWYG editing the most effective approach (in terms of efficiency, that is).

Many of the dedicated hand-coders I know say hand-coding is easier. I believe that *for them* it's easier. But I also believe that it takes a special kind of mind and a tremendous amount of patience to hand-code entire websites from beginning to end. Many people find it too tedious and time-consuming — why shave with a dull piece of glass when it's so much easier (and less painful) to use a soothing and elegant electric razor?

Most of the examples in this book are hand-coded — not because it's the way I work or because it's the way I think you should work, but instead because this book is about learning to use HTML and CSS, not using Dreamweaver. Still, as demonstrated later in this chapter, Dreamweaver is a powerful web design tool well worth your consideration. If you want to learn Dreamweaver, I suggest you check out *Dreamweaver CS5 For Dummies* by Janine Warner.

Does Dreamweaver have a bum rap?

A common complaint of the dedicated hand-coder is that Dreamweaver has its own way of doing things and often doesn't comply with the accepted W3C HTML, XHTML, and CSS standards discussed in Chapters 1 and 2. The complaint is that Adobe's WYSIWG editor doesn't always use the W3C-preferred tags and tag properties, and often uses too many tags or the wrong syntax to achieve specific tasks.

At one time, W3C standards noncompliance was a somewhat serious problem for Dreamweaver — but that was several versions ago. In those days, hand-coders had a valid complaint. Since acquiring the program from Macromedia several years ago, Adobe has done a good job of turning the program around; now Dreamweaver's code is pretty clean.

When designing for mobile devices, where precision is critical, noncompliant code can be troublesome. Whether you decide to hand-code, use Dreamweaver, or combine the two methods, you have good reason — as a mobile web designer — to be concerned about compliance with standards. However, in my humble opinion, noncompliance is no longer a valid reason *not* to use Dreamweaver. In fact, Adobe is and always has been a major player in developing design standards — on many fronts.

Hand-Coding with Source Code Editors

Source code editors are programs designed for writing and editing code. They are, essentially, text editors with additional features specific to programming. Hand-coders — even the most hardcore — use them to write computer programs and to create websites and web applications. Source code editors come in all shapes and sizes. Most of them specialize in one or a few languages. Several (and there are many available) specialize in HTML, XHTML and CSS, as well as other web page markup and web-specific programming languages.

Of the literally hundreds of source code editors available, most range in price from free to well over $100. Most have been around for quite some time. (Many are not-so-well-supported freeware and shareware that no longer get upgraded regularly — rendering them too long in the tooth and less than ideal for hand-coding those ever-changing markup languages. So shop carefully.)

Source code editors range widely in features and the languages they support. Figure 4-2 shows a popular HTML-friendly source code editor, UltraEdit, in action. Most, however, have a standard fare of features in common:

- ✔ **Line numbering:** Each line is numbered, making it easier to locate and correct problems. When reporting errors, program compilers, test environments, or even some web browsers usually identify errors based on the line in which the problematic code appears.

- ✔ **Color coding:** Different colors identify different characteristics of a program or HTML document. In web pages, different types of tags, tag properties, comments, body text, and all other parts of the page appear onscreen as individual colors, making them easier to find, identify, and distinguish from one another.

- ✔ **Automated tagging:** The capability to select a line or block of text and apply tags with a single click.

- ✔ **Tag lists:** A complete list of tags assignable from the list.

- ✔ **Error reporting:** The capability to find and highlight errors in the code.

- ✔ **Code hinting:** Sometimes called *code completion,* the code hinting feature available in some code editors watches as you type code and tries to figure out what you're typing. The program displays "hints," which at any time you can accept (usually by pressing Enter), and the code is completed for you. Some source editors also close code pairs automatically. When you type </, the program looks for the last open tag and enters the corresponding closing tag. (This doesn't sound like a lot of help, simply entering a few characters for you. But if you're writing hundreds, even thousands of lines of code, it adds up.)

Numbered lines

HTML tag list

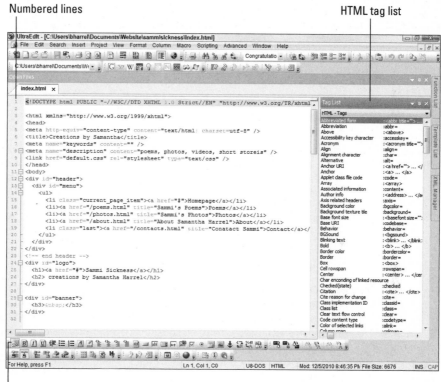

Figure 4-2:
HTML-
friendly
UltraEdit
source code
editor.

HTML tag bar

Looking at HTML/CSS source code editing features

One of more popular HTML source code editors is UltraEdit. It's a share-ware program that has done a great job of keeping up with web technology, changes to HTML and CSS, and advances in other web-specific programming and markup languages. UltraEdit has a bunch of features that make hand-coding easier.

UltraEdit and programs like it ease right up to the edge of WYSIWYG, coming as close as possible without actually making that final leap — letting you edit the actual page file itself while it's in WYSIWYG view. At that point, the program itself starts making decisions about which tags to use, and you're no longer hand-coding.

With that in mind, here's a list of features you should look for in a source code editor for creating and editing HTML and CSS web pages:

- ✓ **Tag and code syntax checking**: A good source code editor automatically checks how and where you place your tags, and points out when you haven't used them correctly. A common example is pointing out when you don't close tags (</p>) tags properly.

- ✓ **Support for JavaScript and other popular web scripting languages:** Often, much of the functionality of a website goes on beyond simple HTML and CSS coding. Animated drop-down menus, collapsible (accordion) and tabbed sections, for example, often rely on JavaScript. (JavaScript is introduced in Chapter 3 and discussed in several places throughout this book. Chapters 13 and 14 cover creating specific applications with JavaScript.) Mobile device detection and switching to the appropriate device profile, discussed in Chapter 5, often depends on JavaScript (discussed in Chapter 13), PHP, or CGI scripting. Your source code editor should have basic support for these languages, just so you don't have to use multiple editors.

- ✓ **Macros for automating lengthy or repetitive tasks**: Many programs support macros, even if they sometimes call them something else. Photoshop, for example, calls them *actions*; Microsoft Word calls them *macros.* By any name, they're simply scripts containing sequential program commands and tasks. You create them by recording the tasks one after the other, and you play them back with a mouse click or keyboard shortcut.

- ✓ **Frequent upgrades**: Make sure the source code editor you choose is still well supported and upgraded regularly to comply with recent HTML and CSS standards.

- ✓ **Browser previews:** Your source code editor should have a built-in previewer so you can easily see what your pages look like, or at least jump quickly to a browser on your system and preview the file there.

- ✓ **Project or file groups:** The capability to define groups of files as projects, which is helpful for creating entire sites.

The ultimate source code editor

The best source code editor I know of (and no, I swear I don't work for Adobe) is Dreamweaver. As shown in Figure 4-3, you can work in the program's Code or Split modes without ever having to do anything in the Design mode WYSIWIG editor. In addition to supporting all the features in the preceding section, it has *many* other features that make hand-coding easier, such as automatic tag closing and code hinting — which suggests and enters tags and other code for you.

Code hinting

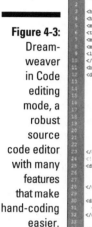

Figure 4-3:
Dream-
weaver
in Code
editing
mode, a
robust
source
code editor
with many
features
that make
hand-coding
easier.

One is never enough

Most source code editors are not very expensive (UltraEdit is about 60 bucks after a 30-day trial period). Even if you do use WYSIWYG web design software, you'll find the right source code editor useful. For example, UltraEdit's spell checker is much better than Dreamweaver's spell checker at weaving in and out of tags and program code to check the spelling of your page content.

No program is perfect. In Dreamweaver, you can set up your source code editor as a secondary editor, which allows you to quickly jump over to it for making specific kinds of edits, such as spell checking. Simply go to Dreamweaver's Preferences dialog box, shown in Figure 4-4 (Edit⇨Preferences in Windows and Dreamweaver⇨Preferences on a Mac); select File Types/ Editors in the Category list; type the types of files you want to edit in the Open in Code View field; and then click the Browse button next to the External Code Editor field and browse to and choose the source code editor's executable program file.

You never know when having a good source code editor (and knowing how to use it) will come in handy. More than once — when consulting or working with other designers — I've been asked not to work on their files in Dreamweaver. I learned a long time ago that sometimes it's better to just let sleeping dogs lie.

When looking at source code editors, keep this in mind: A good source code editor makes no changes to your files except those that you manually enter yourself. Period.

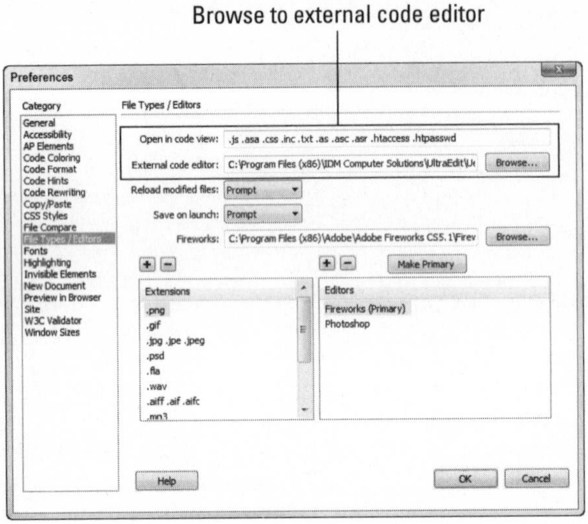

Browse to external code editor

Figure 4-4:
Setting up
a source
code editor
as an
alternate
code
editor in
Dream-
weaver.

Advantages of Design Software

The most obvious advantage of web design software is that you see your edits in real time, as you make them. The software rewrites the HTML and updates your CSS rules for you. As discussed earlier in this chapter, not everybody considers this an advantage. The point of using design software is, of course, to make your design projects easier, thereby saving your time (and your sanity). Most web design programs — such as Back to the Beach Software's Web Studio or Virtual Machine's SiteSpinner, for example — rely heavily on built-in templates and predesigned page modules, insulating the designer (usually beginners or people who do occasional work on websites) from the actual code.

The problem with this approach, especially from a mobile design perspective, is that, while they're easy to use, the code they produce is seldom clean or lean enough for mobile devices. Making matters worse, getting to the code at all in some of these programs is often a challenge. They really are designed around a single concept — ease of use — and not conducive to creating or repurposing websites for mobile devices. Besides, using them does little or nothing toward advancing your HTML or CSS skills.

Using Adobe Dreamweaver

Then there's Dreamweaver, the application of choice for most web design professionals. Looking at Dreamweaver from an ease-of-use perspective is not really relevant. How you chose to use it determines the level of difficulty. This program does nearly everything, and then some. It's also the only high-end web design program left — and, because it's an Adobe product, it's well integrated with Adobe's popular graphics editors, Photoshop and Illustrator — as well as with Flash, the immensely popular platform for creating animations and application content.

Not only is Dreamweaver a WYSIWYG page editor; it's also a source code editor on steroids. You can choose to work in Design mode, allowing you to make edits in a WYSIWYG view of the page, or you can hand-code exclusively in Code view. Dreamweaver even has a Split view that allows you to work in WYSIWYG and code views of your pages at the same time, as shown in Figure 4-5.

Dreamweaver and CSS

In addition to its intuitive coding and layout tools — such as a Tag Inspector that checks for errors in your code and a Live View that displays and plays back Flash and other media files without leaving the design environment — Dreamweaver's support for CSS styles is superb. It allows you to easily create site-wide style sheets and templates, adapt your pages for multiple devices, and easily apply JavaScript and other supporting code. When you open a page formatted with CSS, Dreamweaver references all corresponding style sheets, rendering the page in Design view. As you make changes to different objects, the program displays the corresponding code, offering you a choice of creating a new CSS rule or modifying the existing one, as shown in Figure 4-6.

Figure 4-5:
In Dreamweaver, you choose whether to hand-code or work in Design view — or both at the same time.

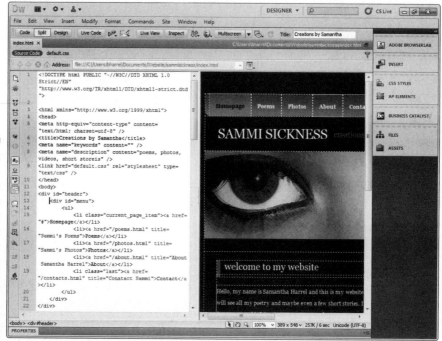

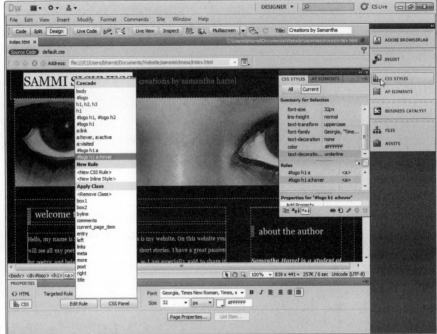

Figure 4-6:
Dream-
weaver
makes it
easy to
edit existing
styles or
create new
ones.

Source code editor on steroids

The program has a Live Code option that, when working in Split view, high-lights the changes made in the Design window and updates the Code window on the fly, providing you with valuable feedback as you work. There's also a code-hinting option: When you're hand-coding in either Split or Code view, the program tries to figure out what tags you're typing, and continuously updates as it offers available code options. At any time, you can choose to have the program finish the code for you.

You can step through the file in Inspect view, selecting various objects in the Design window, and Dreamweaver displays the corresponding CSS code in the Code window, simultaneously checking it for errors and standards compliance. Each time you save the file, the program alerts you to code errors or inconsistencies.

As you can see, in addition to making the design process easy, if you're willing, the program can also help you learn HTML, CSS, and a bunch of other languages. And this list is a very small sampling of how Dreamweaver can help you create and maintain your CSS pages and websites. It really does automate a lot of the processes — and it keeps track of things for you.

Dreamweaver extensions, widgets, and code snippets

Again, the primary reason to use Dreamweaver instead of hand-coding is to save time (and aggravation, even though learning a program this powerful has its own inherent frustrations). Although hand-coding your pages is a noble, even admirable endeavor, there's a lot to be said for getting your projects done within budget while meeting your deadlines. The previous sub-heads of this section look at how the program's built-in features can help you do that, but Dreamweaver also supports several third-party add-ons, known as *extensions,* that can help tremendously in creating professional quality pages and page elements in record time.

Dreamweaver also provides several ways to deploy prebuilt content into your pages; these include *widgets* and *code snippets.* Widgets are, in effect, customizable mini-applications, and code snippets are just what they sound like — little blocks of code you can save and use whenever you need them.

Extensions

Like most Adobe programs, Dreamweaver supports third-party extensions. Extensions are little applets that you install into Dreamweaver via the Extensions Manager. You can find Extensions at the Dreamweaver Exchange (Choose Dreamweaver Exchange from the Help menu) or at several other places on the Internet. Some are free, and others are third-party products ranging in price from just a few dollars to a few hundred dollars and beyond. Simply search for *Dreamweaver extensions.*

You'll find extensions that do almost everything — from creating search engines for your site and inserting Google maps to creating complete CSS page templates. There are hundreds, perhaps thousands, of CSS template extensions for creating customizable page elements such as drop-down menus, forms, headers and footers, and so on. Extensions can save you all kinds of time, and the resulting code provides an excellent opportunity for learning how to create and customize specific CSS page elements and effects. Figure 4-7 shows an extension for creating CSS menus.

Widgets

Widgets are premade, customizable page elements, typically consisting of CSS styles and JavaScript. Dreamweaver comes with a set of built-in widgets for creating menus, collapsible sections, user authentication fields, and many other objects. You can also import several third-party widgets from Dreamweaver Exchange. (Widgets are created and made available by Dreamweaver users and are usually free.) There are widgets for creating menus, live Google Maps, pop-up dialog boxes, charting data, and much more, and new widgets become available regularly. Figure 4-8 shows a widget that creates a Google map and inserts it into a web page automatically.

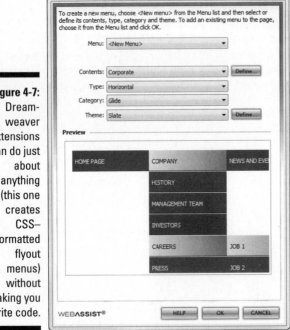

Figure 4-7:
Dream-
weaver
extensions
can do just
about
anything
(this one
creates
CSS–
formatted
flyout
menus)
without
making you
write code.

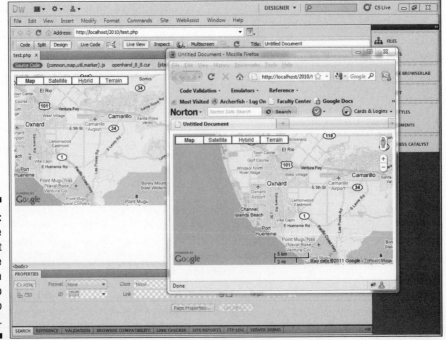

Figure 4-8:
You can use
this widget
to create
and insert a
Google map
into a web
page.

Code snippets

Code snippets are pieces of code you can save and use whenever you need them. Dreamweaver comes with several snippets for common elements, such as drop-down menus, form fields, and several other objects — and you can easily create and save your own snippets. For example, when you create an object you like, or generate an object from a widget or an extension, you can then save that code in the Snippets panel. When you want to use the snippet, simply place the cursor in the document and click the Insert button. Figure 4-9 demonstrates using a snippet for putting a form drop-down on a web page.

Even if you don't use Dreamweaver, you should consider keeping a code-snippet library; that way you don't have to rewrite the code each time you need a commonly used page element. You can save the snippets in static text files, or use a scrapbook program such as Microsoft Notes to save and organize your snippets.

Snippets results   Snippets panel

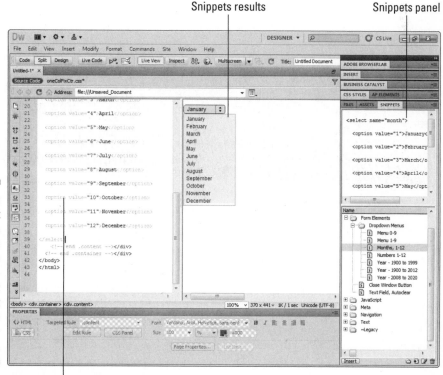

Figure 4-9: Don't reinvent the wheel; save some code as a Dream- weaver Snippet and reuse it whenever you need it.

Inserted snippet code

Using Dreamweaver's Multiscreen views

One of the ways to repurpose the same website for multiple devices is by creating a separate style sheet file for each type of device, as discussed in Chapters 5 and 6. You could, for example, create a style sheet for cellphones, another for tablets, and yet another for computers. Then, to see how your pages will look on all the various devices, you could go out and buy each of the devices. In the tablet category, for example, you could buy a 10-inch iPad and a 7-inch Samsung Galaxy Tab . . . .

Okay. So (obviously) that approach won't work. Can you imagine how many cellphones you'd have to buy? An alternative is Dreamweaver's Multiscreen feature that lets you view different versions of your web page at different screen-display sizes, as shown in Figure 4-10. Not only does Multiscreen show you your page at different resolutions, you can use the Media Queries option in the Multiscreen panel to choose a different CSS style sheet for each display option: Simply set the screen width and the corresponding CSS file.

Figure 4-10: The Dreamweaver Multiscreen option shows your pages at multiple resolutions, each size formatted with its own CSS file.

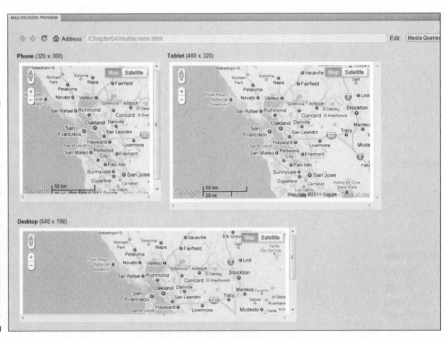

Getting to Know Adobe Device Central

Adobe Device Central is a utility for creating and converting Adobe application content, such as Dreamweaver web pages or Flash movies, to mobile device content. Essentially, the program is one giant mobile device database and device emulator (device emulators are discussed in Chapter 4). It has profiles and crucial information on just about every mobile device ever made, or at least every mobile device with even the slightest Internet capability. Device Central brings together all the critical information about the mobile devices you'll be designing for — display size, memory, supported CSS versions, supported content — under one roof. Plus, you can test your content to see how it will display on any or all of them.

Unfortunately, you can't buy a standalone version of this program. However, Device Central, shown in Figure 4-11, comes with most major Adobe products (version CS4 and later), such as Dreamweaver, Photoshop, Illustrator, Flash Professional, and so on. In my opinion, if you're designing for mobile devices, it's certainly worth the price of Dreamweaver (about $200 retail) just to get Device Central, even if you don't use Dreamweaver to create your web pages. You won't find a source of emulators — and information on the mobile devices you're designing for — that's as comprehensive as Device Central — at least not that you can install on your computer. And, it's updated continuously, by not only Adobe but also Adobe product users and the device manufacturers themselves.

Figure 4-11:
Device
Central lets
you test
your
websites
in emulators
for nearly
every
mobile
device
available.

Chapter 5 discusses creating mobile sites based on classes of mobile devices. (Chapter 5 also covers using Device Central to help you set up mobile device classes.) A highly useful feature of Device Central is that it can create test groups of like devices — or of devices with similar screen sizes and capabilities — and then test your mobile site content in each group.

Using Your Browser as a Testing Environment

The only foolproof way to test your websites for all the various mobile devices available would be to get your hands on each device, and then open the site on each device to see how the site displays and performs. Tools such as Dreamweaver and Device Central (discussed earlier in this chapter) help, but they can't test everything — and they are by no means completely accurate. The truth is, you won't be able to see your site on every mobile device out there, and you can't ever be sure exactly how it will display and perform on every device.

In addition to the Dreamweaver's Multiscreen function and Adobe Device Central, both of which are discussed earlier in this chapter, there are a bunch of other tools at your disposal. The good news is that most of them are free and readily available. You can, for example, use online mobile device emulators. You can also use a web browser as a mobile device emulator and a test environment. All you have to do is install a few browser *add-ons*, also called *extensions*.

As I write this, two popular browsers, the open source Mozilla Firefox and Google's Chrome, have a fairly good collection of add-ons for editing code, emulating mobile devices, and testing HTML and CSS code. Firefox has been around the longest and has a wider range of options, but Chrome isn't that far behind and is catching up quickly.

Let's take a look at some of the add-ons available, how to find and install them, and what they do and how they can help you.

Finding and installing Firefox add-ons

Whether you use Windows or Mac OS, your computer didn't come with Firefox. Before installing add-ons into Firefox, you need to, of course, install Firefox itself. For quite some time now, the latest version of the Firefox installation file has been available at `http://www.mozilla.com/en-US/firefox/new/`.

If, for some reason, the folks at Mozilla decide to move the Firefox file, you can always find it by doing a Google search for *Mozilla Firefox*. Once you get to the download page, simply click the Download Firefox button and follow the installation instructions.

What can browser add-ons do for you?

Did you know you had an agent? Well, actually, it's a *user agent* to be exact — and (to be even more precise) it's your browser. When you browse to a website, your browser introduces itself to the server, telling the server everything it knows about itself, as shown in the first figure.

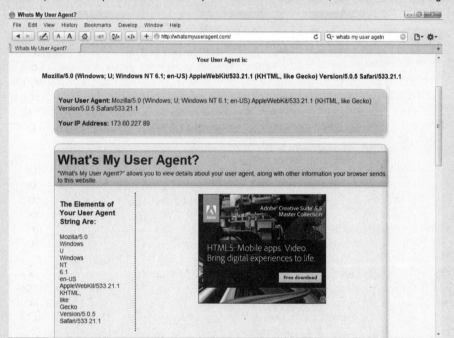

User agents, discussed in Chapters 4 and 6, are very important to you, the mobile web designer. The interaction of the user agent with the web server often, depending on how you design your pages, determines which files and which CSS style sheets are delivered to the browser. One of the more popular browser add-ons is User Agent Switcher — which, as the title suggests, allows you to open websites disguised as a different user agent.

Why? When you combine User Agent Switcher with other browser add-ons, this helps you get an idea how a page will look and behave on mobile devices. In the second figure, for example, I've switched the user agent to iPhone 3.0, enabled another Firefox add-on called Small Screen Renderer, and then enabled yet another plug-in called Firebug. Using Firebug, I can examine all sorts of information about the page, view the CSS files used to format it, and edit the code directly.

(continued)

(continued)

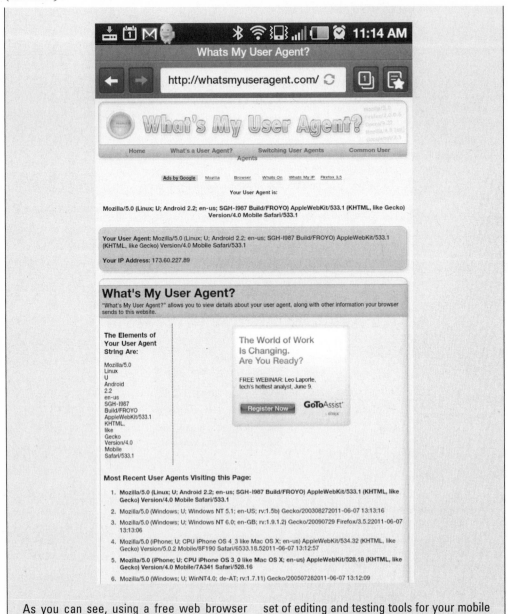

As you can see, using a free web browser and free add-ons can provide a rather handy set of editing and testing tools for your mobile device pages.

When you have Firefox installed, finding add-ons is a breeze. Simply follow these steps:

1. **Launch Firefox, click the Tools menu, and choose Add-ons.**

2. **In the Add-ons dialog box, click Get Add-ons.**

3. **Use the Search field (below the buttons) to search for specific add-ons or click the Browse All Add-ons link to go to a page that lists all the Firefox add-ons.**

After following the previous steps for finding add-ons, you can install them in Firefox like this:

1. **Click the Add to Firefox button.**

2. **In the Software Installation dialog box, click the Install Now button.**

   When the add-on finishes installing itself, Firefox returns you to the Add-ons dialog box. You'll need to restart Firefox to use the new add-on.

3. **Click the Restart Firefox button.**

Finding and installing Google Chrome Add-ons

Regardless of whether you use Windows or Mac OS, your computer didn't come with Chrome. So before you can install Chrome add-ons, you have to (of course) install Chrome itself. You can find the latest version of the Chrome installation file at `www.google.com/chrome/`.

When you get to the download page, simply click the Download Chrome button and follow the installation instructions.

When you've installed Chrome, you can find add-ons (Google calls them *extensions*) by following these steps:

1. **Click Options (the wrench icon) in the upper-right corner of the application window).**

2. **Choose Tools from the flyout menu and then choose Extensions.**

3. **On the Extensions web page, click the Get More Extensions link.**

4. **Use the Search field in the upper-right corner of the Chrome Web Store web page, or choose a category from the Extensions list in the sidebar on the left side of the page.**

   You can try choosing Web Development. Note, however, that as I write this, the list isn't complete. I had to search for many of the add-ons I needed.

After finding an add-on you like, follow these steps to install it:

1. **When you find an extension you want to install, click it.**

   This takes you to a page that describes the add-on. You should pay particular attention to the small yellow box beneath the Install button entitled, `This extension can access`. It tells you about possible security issues arising from installing the add-on.

2. **Click the Install button.**

   That's it. The add-on is installed.

Useful add-ons for web developers

The list of web developers' add-ons for both Firefox and Chrome is extensive and growing. Many of the add-ons do the same things or have overlapping functions. Here's a list of the add-ons I find most useful (most are available for both browsers; I've noted the ones that are not):

- **User Agent Switcher:** This extension allows you to "spoof" specific user agents. If you don't know what a user agent is, see the accompanying sidebar "What can browser add-ons do for you?" Basically, this add-on tells the web server that you are something other than a computer using a standard web browser. You can, for example, switch the user agent to iPhone 3.0.

- **Modify Headers:** When you browse to the website, the browser sends a series of headers to the web server. Headers contain information about the browser, and on mobile devices, about the device itself. Modifying the headers, similarly to User Agent Switcher, tells the web server you are something else. You can, for example, modify the headers to tell the web server you are a specific type of mobile device or mobile browser.

  This add-on is not available for Chrome. However, Chrome comes with a built-in Developer Tools option that allows you to modify headers. To access it, click the wrench icon in the upper-right corner of the application Window, choose Tools, and then choose Developer Tools.

- **Live HTTP Headers:** This add-on simply let you see the exchange of headers between the browser and the server, which can be helpful in telling you which headers to modify with the Modify Headers add-on. This add-on is not available in Chrome. However, Chrome's built-in Developer Tool (discussed in the previous Modify Headers subhead) has a similar feature.

- **Small Screen Renderer:** This add-on simply does what it says. It renders and displays the web page's content in small, mobile-device-like format. This add-on is not available in Chrome.

✔ **Firebug:** Firebug is actually a set of add-ons that allows you to view and analyze several aspects of a web page, including all internal and external style sheets, or formatting of the images, videos, or Flash content — to mention only a few options. Firebug also has an Edit mode that allows you to modify the web pages directly.

✔ **CSS add-ons:** In addition to the add-ons listed here, both browsers have several CSS–specific add-ons for checking and modifying Cascading Style Sheets. Some are quite useful; some are quite useless. To find them, simply search for *CSS* from the browser's built-in web pages for finding add-ons (or extensions), as discussed earlier in this section.

Installing a test web server

Whether you're creating your web pages in Dreamweaver or hand-coding, you'll need to view and test your pages and your site's functionality — often. You can do this by continuously uploading your changed pages and supporting files to a remote web server; however, most designers find it much easier, faster, and more convenient to use a local test server (sometimes called a *test bed*).

If you use Dreamweaver, that program can test most aspects of HTML, XHTML, CSS, embedded video, Flash movies, and several other web page features on its own. However, there are some things, such as server-side PHP scripts that can be crucial to mobile website design, which Dreamweaver can't test. Besides, certain browsers treat certain content differently, and there is no real substitute for seeing the pages as they will actually display in a browser.

There are many shareware webservers available, for both Windows and Mac OS. I, and many of my colleagues, use XAMPP, developed and maintained by apachefriends.org. You can read about it and download it from `www.apachefriends.org/en/xampp.html`.

The online installation and setup instructions are excellent. XAMPP is easy to use, and easy to turn off when you don't need it. If, for some reason, you choose to use something else, do yourself a favor and make sure you choose webserver software than emulates the Apache webserver of UNIX and its descendants (Linux, RedHat, Mandrake, and such). Why? Because that will make you compatible with about 90 percent of the webservers in service today.

You should also make sure the software comes with MySQL, also for compatibility issues, and because we use MySQL in Chapters 16 and 17 of this book for setting up a mobile shopping cart and a mobile blog.

Configuring your test bed

After you install your web server software, you should, from now on, begin creating your websites — those that you want to test as you work on them, anyway — inside the server's public documents folder. On an Apache web server, websites are served up from the *htdocs* folder, as shown in Figure 4-12. Create a separate folder for each site.

Apache web server stores web pages in this folder

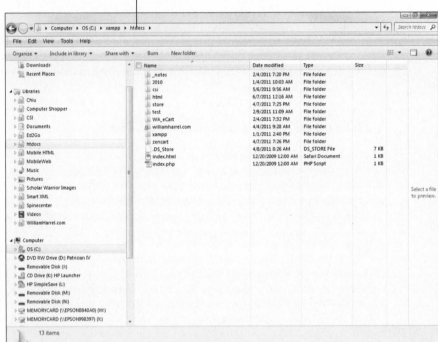

Figure 4-12:
Create all
new web-
sites inside
your new
test server.

Using your web server

To test your pages and your site's functionality on your new test bed, simply open your browser and type in the URL. The URL for a web server on your workstation, or your *local* machine, always starts with *localhost*, which is the root directory of the server. Simply follow *localhost* with the directory containing your local web files, like this:

```
http://localhost/myWebFiles/filename.extension
```

If the file is the home page, or the first page of the site, *index.extension*, you don't need the filename. It looks like this:

```
http://localhost/myWebFiles/
```

How and why the home page is named *index.extension* is discussed in Chapter 6.

Setting up a test sever in Dreamweaver

Not all Dreamweaver websites need a local testing server. If your pages contain only static HTML, CSS, and JavaScript, you can test your pages directly in the program's Live View or with the Preview/Debug in Browser option. Dreamweaver can also display web pages that contain Flash content.

You need a testing server only if you're using a server-side technology, such as ASP or PHP. When designing mobile websites, it's often preferable to use server-side technology to detect and choose the right files to the deliver to the mobile device, as discussed in Chapter 4. The testing server is needed to process the scripts and code and convert them to HTML output that can be displayed in Live View or in a browser. A testing server works just like an ordinary website, except that it's not actually *on* the Internet.

Also, while this book's focus is not server-side scripting, such as PHP, it does explore using simple PHP scripts in several chapters. In Chapter 5, for example, detecting mobile user agents and using PHP to choose the appropriate web files and CSS files is discussed. In Chapter 7, I show you how to use PHP for server-side includes, and using PHP is also touched on for several other solutions in a few other chapters. The point is that it wouldn't hurt to set up a testing server in Dreamweaver for trying some of the techniques discussed in this book.

The procedure for defining a testing server in Dreamweaver varies from version to version, and is somewhat similar to setting up a remote production server. However, rather than reproducing the instructions for each version here, I'll tell you how to find Adobe's instructions for each Dreamweaver version. You ready? Browse to Adobes support site (www.adobe.com/support) and search for *setting up a local testing server in Dreamweaver [version]*.

When you get to the section on choosing a Server Model, choose PHP MySQL.

That's all there is to it.

Part II

Creating a Mobile Site

The 5th Wave   By Rich Tennant

KENNETH BUYS HIS FIRST SMART PHONE

Exercise more.

In this part . . .

This part covers the basics of starting a mobile website. You start by identifying and classifying the devices for which you'll be designing web content — how to create your class, or profile, how to create definitions and how to determine which devices get relegated to what classes.

After you have your mobile class society set up, you'll need a "detect and adapt" system that determines which device your visitors are using and then sends them to the appropriate version of the site for that device. Once that's done, you can start designing your web pages.

The method I prefer is to design the first, or home, page first, so we'll go with that. This allows you to iron out the site's basic look and feel — the overall "design." Once you have that, then you can start creating the various template pages for the site.

Chapter 5

Thinking Small, Smaller, Smallest

. . . .

. . . .

*I*f you're into gadgetry, especially wireless mobile communications and entertainment gadgetry, this is an exciting time to be alive. Apple's recent release of the iPad, and the onslaught of ensuing competing products hitting the market, is rapidly changing the way we think about and use the mobile web. These new tablet devices — and their smaller siblings, the latest round of smartphones — are, in effect, minicomputers, especially when it comes to accessing and using the Internet. These two technologies — full-blown computers (desktops and notebooks) and wireless handheld devices (smartphones and tablets) — are on a fast track to a fusion destined to change the way we use the Internet.

It won't be long before books and courses on creating sites specifically for mobile devices are irrelevant. There just won't be a significant difference in how all these devices use the Internet. The technology is already here. Now, as usual, it's just a matter of waiting for the marketplace, or consumers, to catch up. And if we rely on the recent history of communications technology to help us forecast the future, *that* could take a little time.

Why? Well, in the end, consumers have the greatest influence over how quickly technology becomes mainstream. To reach as many consumers as possible, one of the basic tenants of website creation has always been: Design to the lowest common denominator. For example, designers compensated for low-resolution, 800x600 pixel (VGA) computer display systems for several years — well beyond the time when that technology was considered obsolete by most in the industry (especially by computer manufacturers). Believe it or not, not everybody who uses computers (or cellphones) gets excited or motivated by the latest and greatest advancements in technology. Many — a lot more than you might think — hold on to their devices for a lot longer than you might think. Then, too (and this is even harder for us, the technologically obsessed, to believe), many mobile device users just don't care about whiz-bang advancements. They'd just as soon save a hundred bucks or two and buy a device that doesn't do everything, without any second thoughts or qualms about what their new device can't do or what they might be missing. Imagine that!

If this were not the case — if everybody ran out and bought the next-generation gadget right away — our jobs as designers would be much easier. As a web designer, you *must* consider the huge number of consumers who use *and will continue to use* handhelds that don't support the latest technologies. And that's the focus of this chapter: creating mobile sites that reach the largest possible number of mobile device users. You can't design for handhelds without knowing something about them. So that's where this chapter starts: by telling you what you need to know about mobile devices and where to find that information.

It's also important to consider that handhelds are not computers, at least not in the traditional sense. In addition to tiny screens, small memory allocations, and other limitations, mobile devices don't really support point-and-click technology — no mouse. Instead, they navigate with keys, buttons, and other gizmos such as navigation wheels or Up-, Down-, Right-, and Left-arrow keys. And the newer, smarter mobile devices have touch and multi-touch screens. Bottom line: Although creating websites for mobile devices is, in many ways, the same as designing for computers, in many *other* ways it's not. It's time to get to know the devices for which you'll be creating content.

No Mobile Device Gets Left Behind

As I write this, according to Nielsen (one of the most notable groups who keep track of this kind of stuff), smartphones — including but not limited to Apple's iPhone, some of Google's Android-based devices, several of RIM's Blackberries and Microsoft's Windows Phone (also known as Windows Mobile 7) — make up about 28 percent of the cellphone market in the United States and about 35 percent in Europe. What that means to you as a web designer is that about 72 percent of the devices you'll be designing for don't support all the latest mobile web technology. In other words, if you create a mobile site consisting of HTML5, CSS3, and JavaScript, most mobile devices in use today won't be able to use part or all of the site.

 Another telling statistic in the same market study is that during the last quarter of 2010, of all the handhelds sold, smartphones accounted for only 40 percent of them. So, if you were thinking that you could get away with designing to just the smartphone markets — expecting that consumers would quickly catch up — forget it. Unless you're willing to neglect almost two-thirds of the mobile web audience, resign yourself to compensating for devices that don't take advantage of the latest and greatest mobile technologies. I don't like it either.

What's up with Apple and Flash?

Unless you've been hanging out in a cave, you know that Apple's mobile devices — iPhones, iPods, and iPads — don't support Adobe Flash web content. Instead, Apple has decided to rely on newer, emerging technologies, such as HTML5, CSS3, and the latest mobile enhancements to JavaScript. Although this isn't the place to discuss the motivation and marketing strategies behind Apple's decision, what I will say is that this stance greatly affects not only the mobile website design community but also the web design community as a whole. Users of Apple's mobile devices make up nearly one-third of the user base for "smart" handheld devices. That's a huge number of users — far too big to ignore.

Nobody — not even Apple and Adobe, I suspect — really knows how this spat between these two technology powerhouses will shake out. Recently released Flash-enabled tablet devices, such as Samsung's Android-based Galaxy Tab, as well as soon-to-be-released handheld tablets from other huge players, such

as Motorola, HTC, HP and others, will undoubtedly have a major influence on the future of Flash content on mobile devices. Also, keep in mind that future in-the-works touch and multi-touch enhancements to Flash itself should change the status quo.

Although HTML5, CSS3, and a revamped, handheld-friendly JavaScript all greatly improve what designers can do without Flash, these technologies are not — in my opinion — robust enough to *replace* Flash. The question is how you, as a mobile web designer, should address this issue. I can't answer that for you. But I can tell you what I do. When I think a site will benefit from Flash content, I use it. iPhone and iPad users who visit the sites I design know why they can't see the Flash content. Still, if the information is important enough that I can't logically justify excluding the millions of Apple handhelds out there, then I don't turn the info into Flash content. And, frankly, as a designer, I'm not very happy about that.

Creating your own handheld class society

Everybody knows it's wrong to stereotype, right? When designing for mobile devices it's not. In fact, it's crucial that you do. When you consider that there are hundreds of mobile handheld models in use today, with at least two or three versions of each model, and each of those has several firmware and software revisions . . . I'm sure you get my point: When it comes to which devices support what web content, there are literally thousands of variables. You can't possibly create a separate version of your site for each different type of handheld. Stereotyping in the technical sense — categorizing them according to classes, such as screen size, web formats supported, and so on — is the only way to make sure your content looks good and runs properly on most of them.

Smartphones versus feature phones

Generally, the handheld market consists of four different types of devices: tablets, smartphones, feature phones, and dumb phones. Of the four types, only the first three support web browsing. So, put that fourth type, dumb phones, out of your mind. Their owners use them for making calls and texting; they are not part of your target market. That leaves the other three: tablets, smartphones, and feature phones. And, as you might have guessed, just as the line between smartphones and computers is blurring, so is the line between smartphones and feature phones. Here's how it breaks down:

✔ **Tablets:** Handheld tablets really are exciting technology. As I write this, nearly every manufacturer in both the computer and the cell phone industries are releasing handheld tablets. In a very short time, these devices have become quite sophisticated. Some, for instance, are full-blown computers in the tablet form factor. Some companies, such as HP, have released tablets that run full versions of Windows, and they can do nearly anything a Windows computer can do. Some other companies, such as Samsung, Apple, and Motorola, are selling tablets that run operating systems originally designed for smartphones, such as Android and iPhone OS.

In many ways, creating web content for most of these isn't different from designing for standard computers. Most tablets have fairly large screens, decent processors, and web browsers that support most advanced web content, such as Flash, HTML5, and CSS3. However, not all tablets are created equal. Coby Electronics and a few other manufacturers, for example, sell low-end tablets that don't outperform the average smartphones. Within just a few years since the release of the first iPad, already the tablet playing field, in terms of developing web content, is diverse. To make sure your mobile sites perform well on the majority of tablets, you need to acquaint yourself with the devices in this class and what they're capable of.

✔ **Smartphones:** For the sake of this discussion, let's define smartphones like this: Smartphones support third-party apps and syncing with company e-mail, contacts, and calendars, allowing them to second as personal data assistants (PDAs). What separates smartphones from other phones is that they typically have faster processors, more memory, and they run complete operating systems. This allows application developers to create applications for them. A huge number of devices fit this definition, including iPhones, some Droids and other devices based on the Google Android operating system, some Windows Phone handhelds, some Blackberries, some Palm devices, and many, many others.

Aside from most tablets, this group — our "upper-class, high-society" devices — will have the most robust web support. However, as with any class, there are subclasses; not all smartphones are created equal: Those hitting the market today have much better Internet support than those that hit the market a year ago, and so on. Also, the support for third-party apps allows users to download and install different web browsers, and, usually, the browsers on these devices support plug-ins and other features that expand functionality. In other words, in our quest to relegate smart handhelds to specific classes, we can't really assign all smartphones to one class and forget about it, now, can we?

✔ **Feature phones:** These are low-end mobile phones. They have less computing power and are typically less advanced than smartphones. Although some new feature phones can run simple applications based on scaled-down versions of JavaScript, their operating systems don't support native applications, such as those available for iPhone and Android OS. The feature phone's web browser is typically small and lacks the ability to run advanced web features, such as Flash, CSS3 and HTML5.

You'd think that the inability to use third-party apps would make designing for the feature phone easier. After all, they use the browsers they come with — and the only way to upgrade them is through firmware upgrades. But there are so many different types, with so many versions and features and various screen sizes, that relegating feature phones to specific classes can also be challenging indeed. Before we can start arranging handheld devices in a societal hierarchy, the first order of business is to clarify which devices support what features.

Understanding mobile operating systems and browsers

Handheld device development is a tit-for-tat, okay-now-top-*this* arms race. Each release of an updated mobile operating system (OS) by one developer throws down the gauntlet to competitors. Each time an OS developer such as (say) Apple releases a set of new features, immediately Google, Microsoft, RIM (Blackberry), and other OS developers rush to incorporate equivalents of those new features and to develop new features that move them ahead in the race. And on and on it goes.

A significant result of this arms race is the advancement of mobile browser technology — the part of the war that's pertinent to you, the mobile website developer. When you're setting up your handheld class system, your two most important considerations are device screen size and browser capabilities. Also important are what versions of Flash Player a visiting handheld device supports (if any), as well as which digital video formats it can play. Often the OS itself — not the mobile browser — defines many of these capabilities. Other factors include the mobile service carrier and whether it's had the device's manufacturer build in some service-specific features. Quite a tangled web, actually — an elaborate scheme that seems designed to drive mobile site designers crazy.

Mobile operating systems

A detailed discussion of mobile operating systems — besides being tedious — probably wouldn't really help you in designing mobile websites. Besides, each platform has so many versions, and often the OS is tailored to a specific device. Android running on a feature phone, for example, has different capabilities from Android running on a smartphone. And to make matters even more complicated, Android running on a Samsung Galaxy has different capabilities from those of the same OS running on an HTC Inspire — even though both devices are technically smartphones.

Creating handheld-friendly sites from dynamic content and dynamic mobile device profiles

In mobile web design, as with most things in life, there is more than one way to skin the proverbial cat. This book focuses on using HTML to create conventional *static* mobile websites and pages — the method most web designers use. Another method — highly sophisticated, very complicated, and (when executed properly) ultimately more effective — is to create and deploy dynamic content based on the dynamic profiles of mobile devices: The site is designed to deliver content "on the fly," or on demand.

With this method, you create only one or two pages — and except for the PHP, ASP, or Cold Fusion code (containing references to database files and some formatting information), those pages are *templates*: empty shells, if you will. They don't hold any real content until a user accesses the site. Content is kept in a database; another database holds the device profiles or information about all the various mobile devices. (No, you don't have to accumulate all this information yourself. It's available from several sources, including the open-source Wireless Universal Resource File, or *WURFL*, which is discussed a little later in this chapter.)

When a mobile device visits the site, it introduces itself by announcing its *user agent*. (User agents are discussed in Chapter 3, a little in this chapter, and in Chapter 6.) Then, using the user agent information, a sophisticated set of scripts references the database that contains the device profiles, acquiring information about the device — screen size, what version of HTML and CSS the device supports, whether the device supports Flash and JavaScript, and so on. Armed with this information, another set of sophisticated scripts reference and call the right content from the content database and determine which CSS style sheets and other formatting information to use.

Whew! Sounds a lot like magic, doesn't it?

Although this method delivers much more accurately formatted content to a wider range of handheld devices, it's hard to do. It requires not only a lot of work but also a very talented programmer. Not much HTML and CSS formatting goes into creating this type of dynamic site. Instead, server-side programming (which is not the subject of this book) makes most of the site work. If you're interested in researching this type of mobile site development, you should check out *HTML, XHTML, & CSS All-in-One For Dummies* by Andy Harris.

However, it's difficult and clumsy to create sites for handhelds without some limited *detect-and-adapt programming* that uses either client-side JavaScript (discussed in Chapter 13) or server-side PHP or ASP (as discussed in Chapter 6). The phrase "detect and adapt" refers to a process that determines which pages and style sheets to deliver to the handheld: You use scripts to detect the user agent and other information about the device and another set of scripts to deploy the appropriate pages and formatting data.

I could show you ways to work around this basic programming requirement — but the extra work and convoluted techniques (even the end results, which make for shoddy site quality) would, in my opinion, be a huge disservice. Let's not even go there.

This does not say, however, that the operating system is irrelevant. Handhelds often announce the operating system as the user agent, rather than browser type and version. (As discussed in Chapters 6 and 13, devices announce their user agents to begin negotiation with the web server.) So, instead of beginning the server-device transaction with

"Hello. I'm the Safari Mobile OS. What do you have for me?

the device says, in effect,

"Hi. I'm iPhone 3.0, a specific device. Got anything *especially* for me?"

Sometimes, depending primarily on how you configure your device detect-and-adapt system, the handheld OS, or platform, type is more useful, or provides more information about the device. However, as I discuss in Chapter 6, this usually depends on what you tell the server (or your web pages, when you use client-side detect and adapt) to do with the user agent information.

Mobile browsers

Just as there are several web browsers available on traditional computers, you can download and install several different browsers on most tablet and smartphone-class handhelds. The reasons why users change browsers, of course, are many. I don't use Internet Explorer, for example, because it isn't compatible with the forms I'm required to use at the colleges where I teach digital design online. I have a similar issue with some mobile browsers.

The diversity among mobile browsers is vast and subject to many variables — including, but not limited to, the type of device the browser runs on. Opera Mini running on a feature phone, for instance, often doesn't support the same features it supports on a smartphone. Again, often the type of handheld the browser is used on plays a major role in what the browser can do. Determining the browser and browser version, similar to determining the OS platform is, once again, important in terms of the handheld's user agent. In other words, how does the server, or your detect-and-adapt scripts, identify who (more specifically, *what*) is visiting the site.

Finding Out Which Devices Can Do What

In no way am I advocating that you need to determine what every handheld device in use can and can't do. That would be, well, nuts. You'd become a mobile device expert, all right, but you'd get little else done. Besides, as fast as you learn what one type of device can do, the manufacturers are ramping up to release (say) a new BIOS or browser version, making what you know about any specific device obsolete tomorrow. But, in order to set up your class society, you do need a general idea — a way to categorize the devices your potential user base brings to your website. To do that, you need a general idea what the different types of devices can and can't do.

Any detect-and-adapt system you come up with will depend primarily on user agents, as discussed throughout this chapter, and in Chapters 6 and 13. In other words, whether you use client-side or server-side scripts (also discussed in Chapters 6 and 13) to detect the device type and determine which pages and style sheets to deliver to the device, the *detect* side of the process depends on the user agent. User agents contain information about the type of device and what the device is capable of.

In order to classify your devices, you need to know what they can and can't do. How do you find that out? Well, the good news is that much of that information is readily available.

In this section, I show you how to find the information. In the next chapter, I show how to put that information to use.

Coming up with a classification strategy

When you're designing for traditional computers, designers often use a lowest-common-denominator strategy. In other words, they create their sites so that they will display and function properly on all computers by making sure that the site is compatible with the oldest technology and display sizes. When designing for mobile devices, it's common to use an opposite approach — design the site for the most robust set of features and then start creating new sites by stripping away functionality.

The initial site, for example, might support the largest screen sizes: HTML5, CSS3, JavaScript, Flash Player 10.x, and so on. Then the designer creates a new site for the next class of devices, based on the original design — usually by dumbing down the functionality, adapting the site to smaller screen sizes, eliminating support for the most recent markup languages, and dispensing with JavaScript altogether. Then, depending on how elaborate the class society structure is (and on the time and resources available for the project at hand), the designer might then create yet another set of pages, stripping away even more features and functionality.

Then again, another approach is to start with a very simple set of pages and start working your way upward, adding support for more advanced functionality and features. Either method works. What *doesn't* work in mobile design is the one-size-fits-all approach commonly used when designing for conventional desktop and notebook computers.

Wireless Universal Resource File (WURFL)

One of the most popular resources for finding information on specific devices, operating systems, and mobile browsers is WURFL — an online database containing extensive user agent information. Designers and developers use the WURFL information in various ways. Designers of dynamic detect-and-adapt systems, for example — see the sidebar, "Creating handheld-friendly sites from dynamic content and dynamic mobile device profiles" — use this database (rather than re-create their own) as a source of dynamic mobile device profiles. *You* can use it to gather information about devices in your mobile class society.

An offshoot of WURFL is the Tera-WURFL site (`www.tera-wurfl.com`), where you can enter the name of a user agent and get back extensive information about that user agent or the device itself. In Figure 5-1, for example, I entered *iPhone 3* and got back all kinds of information about this device; far more than I needed to design a website for this phone. I can, however, if I know what I'm looking for, pick through this information to find what I need to know. The Markup section, for instance, shows which versions of HTML the iPhone 3 supports. Another section, Display, shows the device's screen size and whether it supports dual orientation (portrait and landscape) when the user flips the phone on its side.

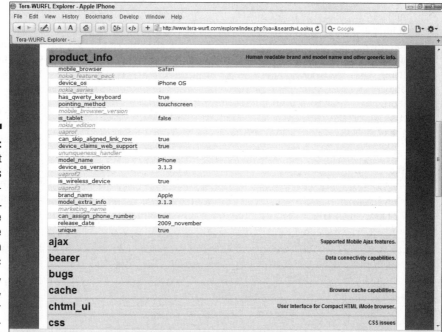

Figure 5-1: User agent queries at Tera-WURFL provide extensive information on specific devices, browsers, and operating systems.

Although WURFL is probably the largest user agent database, it does have some shortcomings. For example, although it has a CSS category, it offers a limited list of supported CSS *features* instead of listing supported CSS *versions* (CSS1, CSS2 or CSS3). This approach forces you to make educated assumptions. If, for instance, a device supports XHTML (listed under Markup), you can assume it also supports CSS1 and CSS2. If it supports HTML5, it's safe to assume it also supports CSS3. Another shortcoming is that WURFL information is not always up to date. It relies heavily on volunteer input. Handheld BIOS and software changes don't always get updated.

Adobe Device Central

Adobe's Device Central (discussed in Chapter 4) is perhaps the most comprehensive and easiest-to-use device profile database. Not only does it provide extensive information about which web features a device supports, it also emulates devices so you can see how your pages will display, which features are available, how digital video, Flash movies, and scripts work on the device, and so much more. You can even test how well your sites will perform by viewing graphical representations of download times and memory and processor usage.

Not only are various devices easy to find and view in Device Central, but you can also sort and list devices by several different criteria, such as screen size or color depth (number of displayable colors) to zero in on what a particular handheld device supports. Figure 5-2 shows the Device Central application window in Device Library view. When you're scrolling this list, pay special attention to the Published column. The dates in this column tell you when the profile was uploaded to the Device Central database, and that gives you a fairly good idea how up-to-date the information is.

However, this highly useful utility is not a standalone product — you'll need to purchase an Adobe design program or graphics editor, such as Dreamweaver, Photoshop, Illustrator, or Flash Professional, to get Device Central. For professional designers, this is seldom an issue. Most designers have at least one Adobe product. Photoshop, for example, is a staple in the web design industry.

Device Central displays information about specific devices organized in a manner very useful to web and content designers. In Figure 5-3, for example, on the General page, you can see the device's screen size, what version of Flash Player it supports, its operating system, and the type of input it accepts. The Device Central web page also displays the user agent and supported web formats, including CSS levels and JavaScript versions.

Figure 5-2:
Device
Central's
extensive
handheld
library
allows you
to sort pro-
files based
on function-
ality.

Screen size   Last updated

As you can see, this utility makes it pretty easy to nail down information on specific devices.

Manufacture specifications

You can always go to a device manufacturer's website to get specs on specific devices. But this is a very tedious, time-consuming, and low-tech approach. I would only use it if I were designing a web application for an organization whose team of employees used all the same (or similar) hand-helds. Of course, that situation is not uncommon. Many organizations create mobile applications for sales and support teams, tailoring the site to specific devices that they then distribute to the team members.

Operating system   Display size

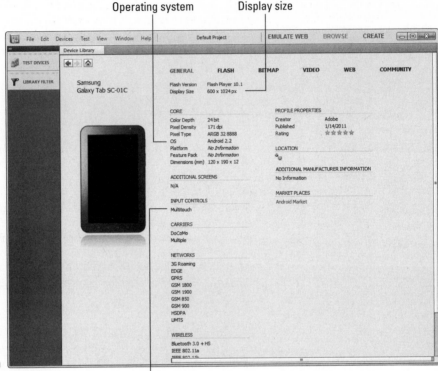

Figure 5-3:
Device
Central's
design-
relevant
informa-
tion in one
easy-to-find
place.

Input type

When Mouse Clicks become Buttons, Touches, and Multi-Touches

When you're designing pages for mobile devices, you have to keep in mind that most handhelds don't interact with web content in quite the same way as traditional computers. Often, instead of point-and-click, it's Tab-and-click. Users of handhelds navigate to hyperlinks and to the fields in forms by using arrows, scroll bars, scroll wheels, or keys. This and other interface differences often affect how you should design your mobile web pages.

A mobile user, it turns out, doesn't have a mouse. Okay, so you're thinking, "Duh. State the obvious, much?" — but this lack is important: Some techniques used in designing sites for computers just don't work on handhelds. For example, on pages designed for traditional computer screens, designers have several significant tools that help users identify hotspots (clickable links) — for example, rollovers and alternate descriptions that depend on the mouse. When users *hover* (place the mouse pointer over and linger on a hyperlink or button), a *rollover* changes the appearance of the hyperlink; *alternate descriptions* provide feedback in tooltip-like boxes (usually a description of what the link does), as shown in Figure 5-4.

Scroll buttons and scroll wheels

On many handhelds, users scroll to links by using arrow keys or some variation of a scroll-and-select wheel, as shown in Figure 5-5. The only feedback the user gets before scrolling to a link is provided by your physical layout — something about the link that makes it obvious that it's a button or hyperlink. After the user has scrolled to the button, you can provide something that functions like a rollover — such as the highlight shown in Figure 5-5, which confirms that the link is indeed a hotspot. While useful, this is not as helpful as the information provided on traditional computers when users hover over the hotspot. It's your job to make sure the hotspot is easily recognizable and provides adequate feedback as to what the link does or where it goes.

Rollover   Alternate description

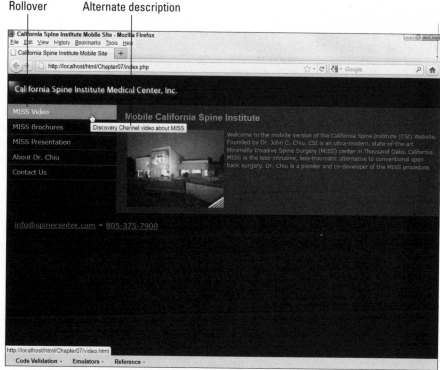

Figure 5-4:
Rollovers and tooltip-like descriptions provide feedback when a mouse cursor hovers over buttons and links. Handhelds don't use them.

Selected link

Figure 5-5:
When users
scroll to hot-
spots, you
can provide
rollover-like
highlights to
help them
identify but-
tons and
links.

Scroll and select

Also, since so many mobile users rely on scroll buttons of some sort, it's also important that you create a logical *tab order* — the order in which the user can select buttons, links, form fields, and other interactive objects with keyboard (the Tab key on standard computers) button actions. In Figure 5-5, for example, you'd want to make sure your tab order moves the cursor down the list of buttons on the left from top to bottom, rather than jumping from object to object randomly. You can control tab order in your markup code with the `tabindex` property, as discussed in Chapter 9.

Touch and multi-touch screens

Some devices, such as iPhones, iPads, Galaxy Tabs, some BlackBerry devices, Droids, and Windows Phone handhelds, don't provide any way to navigate *except* through touch and multi-touch screens. As cool as touch screens are, the only way a user knows for sure if an object is a link is by touching it. Then, if it is a link, a new page loads. The only feedback the user gets about whether a button is a link is the way you design your buttons, as shown in Figure 5-5. When you're designing for these devices, it's especially important that you don't leave your users guessing. Make sure your links are readily recognizable.

Designing for dual-orientation handhelds

Yet another feature you must contend with when designing for handhelds is *dual orientation* — a feature that shows landscape or portrait view, depending on how you turn the device. (See Figure 5-6.) After all, you can't take your computer monitor or your laptop, turn it sideways and have the screen redraw itself to match the new orientation. (It would be nothing but cool if you could.) Technically, you could just ignore this high-end feature, but be assured that many people who come to your site with dual-orientation devices will notice. Chances are, if they own this type of device, dual orientation is one of the features they love about it. And if that's one of the reasons they bought the device, they'll probably *really miss* the feature if you ignore it.

The good news is that compensating for all this back-and-forth-and-to-and-fro-and-back-again isn't that difficult. In fact, some of the measures you take to make sure a site displays attractively on a wide array of screen sizes *also* helps compensate for devices that support both landscape and portrait viewing. I'll show you how to tackle this design issue in Chapters 12 and 13, when we talk about WebKit extensions and JavaScript detect and switch.

Figure 5-6:
Examples of
content in
portrait and
landscape
modes.

Chapter 6

Developing a Mobile Device Detection and Adaption System

During the few short years that handhelds have been displaying web content, somewhere between 6,000 to 8,000 different gadgets have been released onto the mobile device market. Imagine if you had to design a different website for each of one! That, of course, would be silly.

Even so, there are many ways to approach creating content for different types of devices, ranging from the very simple to the extremely complex. No matter which approach you choose, in the long run it comes down to developing two systems: *detection* and *adaptation*. The *device detection system* determines which type of device is visiting the site, and the *adaptation system* delivers the appropriate content for the device.

Most professional designers achieve device detection through server-side scripts, usually written in PHP. *Server-side*, of course, means that the server, rather than the user's browser, interprets and executes the scripts. In most cases, server-side programming cannot be achieved with HTML or CSS markup — therefore it goes far beyond the scope of this book. The good news is that a few open-source (and free) device detection systems are available; this chapter introduces you to a few of them and gives you some advice on how to use them. I also show you a couple of quick-and-dirty detection methods that don't require extensive programming skills and help you deliver mobile content to a significant share of mobile devices.

Most mobile website designers create adaptation systems that consist of creating multiple websites that work with *groups* of device profiles. There are other, more elaborate options — such as dynamic adaptation systems that rely on databases and server-side scripts (discussed in Chapter 4) — but these, too, require programming beyond the scope of the book. This chapter zeros in on the most conventional methods of classifying mobile devices into groups and creating a separate set of pages for each group.

Understanding Mobile Device Detection

Here's a simplistic description of the detection process: When a user browses to a website, the browser and the server have a conversation. At the beginning of the conversation, the browser (or sometimes the handheld itself, depending on how the device handles this function) introduces itself to the server with a string known as the *user agent,* as discussed in Chapter 5; at that point, when the browser says says *hello* to the server, technically, the server has detected the device type. It knows most or all of the following information: what operating system (OS) and OS version the device is using; the type and version of the browser the device is using; the device type and type (bios) version; and which supported extensions, such as WebKit (discussed in Chapter 12), if applicable.

Depending on how you set up your detection system, this opening conversation could be the end of the detection process or just the beginning. Although this may seem like a lot of information, it often doesn't provide enough data to adequately identify what the device is capable of. The scripts in sophisticated device detection systems use the user agent data to discover additional information about the device's attributes, such as screen size and resolution, and features. Does the handheld support multi-touch and dual orientation, for example? Are you getting the idea?

But then again, sometimes, depending on the elaborateness of your detect-and-switch system, the user agent data is more than enough. Sometimes, all the detect-and-switch application needs to know is that the site visitor is using a mobile device. Again, it just really depends on how you want your detection system to work, or, better yet, what you want it to do under which circumstances.

Server-side versus client-side detection

Should you use scripts on the server to detect the device type, or should the browser execute the detection scripts? The answer depends on the range of devices to which you want to deliver optimally formatted versions of your site. Here's why: Nowadays, nearly all client-side scripts are written in JavaScript. Many mobile devices, especially older devices, don't support JavaScript.

Therefore, a detection system based on JavaScript would not detect a rather large segment of handhelds that visit your site. In other words, JavaScript-disabled handhelds would ignore the scripts and try to display the default version of the site — which is usually the desktop computer version.

Truly, though, this is not end of the world. The manufacturers' trend over the past few years, for both smartphones and feature phones, has been to include JavaScript support. Granted, using a JavaScript-based detection system means that some phones won't be able to get to your mobile-optimized pages, but such devices really aren't used much for mobile browsing anyway — and the number of them in use is quickly diminishing. Using server-side scripts is the only reliable way to make sure all web-enabled handhelds can get to your site's mobile pages. Now, in order to create a server-side detection system, the server on which your site is hosted must support PHP (or whatever script type you use). And technically, that means you'd have to create PHP pages rather than HTML. But stay tuned: A little later in this chapter, we show you a way around that. Meanwhile, take a look at the accompanying sidebar for some pointers on using JavaScript for device detection. Also, there is good JavaScript detect-and-switch technique discussed in Chapter 13.

Creating a server-side detection system

Design firms and the web design departments for large companies put a lot of time and effort into developing detection-and-adaptation systems. The most elaborate systems require maintaining a database of devices and a set of sophisticated PHP scripts that detect the user agent and then reference the database. Then, using the information about the device from the database, another set of PHP scripts decides which content to deliver to the device.

Again, this requires significant PHP programming skills that go way beyond the scope of this book. If you're interested in learning how to create this type of system, you'll need to learn PHP. I suggest you check out *HTML, XHTML, & CSS All-in-One For Dummies* by Andy Harris. A couple of free open-source solutions are available — which I tell you about a little later in this section — but even those require some basic PHP programming skills.

Don't worry — I won't just tell you that you have to learn programming to get a detection-and-adaption system and leave it at that. Instead, I show you, step by step, how to use one of the simpler PHP solutions: Andy Moore's detect-and-adapt system from `http://detectmobilebrowsers.mobi`. This system is fairly easy to set up and implement. It works by detecting the device's operating system and then redirecting the browser to the appropriate URL. Using this system, you can create a different site for each OS if you want and a generic catchall site for devices that don't fall into one of the pre-defined OS categories.

Detecting devices with JavaScript

What if you're short on time and resources (or perhaps your client doesn't want to pay for developing content for several different classes of devices), and you can create only one version of the mobile site? Whether you create 1 version or 20, you still need a way to detect the user agent or some other specific information about the device that identifies it as a handheld.

A relatively efficient method I've found is to detect the device's resolution — or, more specifically, its screen width — and then switch to a mobile version of the site based on that information. This simple method works by assuming that if a device's screen is smaller than a specific width (measured in pixels), it's a mobile device. Granted, this is not a very sophisticated system, but it works on every mobile device It works like this:

1. You create a mobile version of your site.

2. You assign a unique URL — a subdomain — to the mobile site, something like mobile. mysite.com.

   If you don't understand subdomains, see the sidebar entitled, "Subdomains or sub-directories," a little later in this chapter.

3. Open the home page HTML file, usually index.html, for the desktop version of the site.

4. Place the following JavaScript at the top of the <body> section of the home page, as shown in the figure.

   Placing the script at the top of the <body> section ensures that the browser executes the script before processing the rest of the page.

```
<script type="text/javascript">
<!--
if (screen.width <= 1024) {
document.location = "http://mobile.
        mysite.html";
}
//-->
</script>
```

This script detects the screen width of the device: if (screen.width <= 1024). If the width is less than 1024 pixels (or whatever width you want to use) the script redirects the browser to the URL for the pages containing the mobile content: document.location = "http://mobile.mysite.html"

Again, in no way is this method foolproof, for two very important reasons: (a) not all handhelds support JavaScript and (b) not all user agents send screen resolution. Still, my educated guess is that this method works for about 70 to 80 percent of mobile devices in use today.

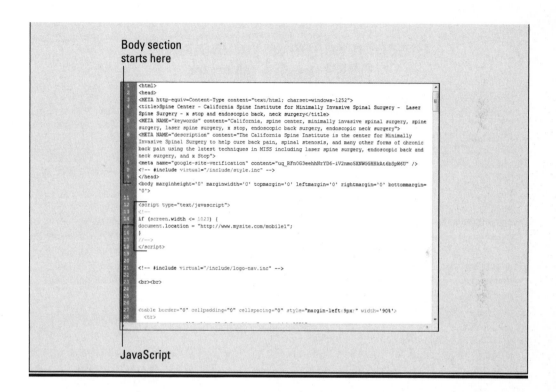

Body section
starts here

```
1   <html>
2   <head>
3   <META http-equiv=Content-Type content="text/html; charset=windows-1252">
4   <title>Spine Center - California Spine Institute for Minimally Invasive Spinal Surgery - Laser
    Spine Surgery - x stop and endoscopic back, neck surgery</title>
5   <META NAME="keywords" content="California, spine center, minimally invasive spinal surgery, spine
    surgery, laser spine surgery, x stop, endoscopic back surgery, endoscopic neck surgery">
6   <META NAME="description" content="The California Spine Institute is the center for Minimally
    Invasive Spinal Surgery to help cure back pain, spinal stenosis, and many other forms of chronic
    back pain using the latest techniques in MISS including laser spine surgery, endoscopic back and
    neck surgery, and x Stop">
7   <meta name="google-site-verification" content="uq_RFn0G3eehhNrYD6-iV2nmo5XNWGGHHkAt6bSpW6U" />
8   <!-- #include virtual="/include/style.inc" -->
9   </head>
    <body marginheight='0' marginwidth='0' topmargin='0' leftmargin='0' rightmargin='0' bottommargin=
    '0'>
11
12  <script type="text/javascript">
13  <!--
14  if (screen.width <= 1023) {
    document.location = "http://www.mysite.com/mobile1";
16  }
17  //-->
18  </script>
19
20
21  <!-- #include virtual="/include/logo-nav.inc" -->
22
23  <br><br>
24
25
26
27  <table border="0" cellpadding="0" cellspacing="0" style="margin-left:9px;" width='90%'>
28   <tr>
```

JavaScript

The system works fairly well, but it doesn't let you detect and adapt on the basis of specific attributes, such as screen size or which version of CSS a device supports. That type of system requires a much more elaborate set of PHP scripts and a device database. A little later in this section, I discuss a few of the more popular solutions and show you how to use Andy Moore's system.

Andy Moore's detect and redirect system

To begin this exercise you need at least two versions of your website — one standard computer version for desktops and notebooks, and one mobile version for handhelds. How to classify and create different mobile versions of a site is discussed later in this chapter and throughout the remainder of this book. Also make sure that your hosting service supports PHP (most do).

This solution allows you to create a different site for several different types of devices, up to seven, based primarily on operating systems. This is overkill. Seldom would you need that many variations. If you just want to try this out, all you need is one mobile version of the site. In fact, for testing purposes, all you need is one simple page. To get started, follow these steps:

Creating adaptive solutions with CSS3 media queries

One of the exciting features of CSS3 on the horizon (and there are many) is the *media query*.

Media queries ask the device for specific attributes, such as screen width and height, orientation (whether the phone is currently being held upright or on its side), and so on. Then, based on the responses from the device, the page is formatted using a style sheet appropriate to the device's attributes. Rather than creating several different versions of the same site, the CSS3 style sheet determines how the page should be formatted, which images and digital media files are loaded, and so on. (Technically, media queries are supported in CSS2, but not many browsers that support only CSS2, and don't support CSS3, have implemented them. This has created a hit-and-miss situation for implementing media queries in CSS2-only browsers that's more trouble than it's worth.)

As I said, this feature will one day be in common use — but not just yet. A prohibitive drawback of deploying them today, however, is that they usually require support for CSS3, which many of today's devices do not have. Users visiting your site with a device that doesn't support CSS3 probably can't use the media queries and won't be directed to the appropriate content. However, once CSS3 is in wider use, they will eliminate the need for maintaining device databases and writing complicated server-side scripts. You would use them today, however, only when creating a site designed specifically for high-end handhelds, such as iPhones, iPads, and other tablets; newer Android-based handhelds; and newer Palm and Blackberry smartphones.

Does this sound like magic? It certainly will eliminate a lot of work and the need to create several versions of the same content. If you're interested in seeing media queries in action and getting some insight into how they work, here are a few links that describe them with examples you can try:

✔ **CSS3 Media Queries and Creating Adaptive Layouts:**

> http://robertnyman.com/2010/09/09/
> css3-media-queries-and-
> creating-adaptive-layouts/

✔ **How to Use CSS3 Media Queries to Create a Mobile Version of Your Website:**

> www.smashingmagazine.com/2010/07/19/
> how-to-use-css3-media-
> queries-to-create-a-mobile-
> version-of-your-website/

✔ **CSS3 Media Queries:**

> www.webdesignerwall.com/tutorials/
> css3-media-queries/

1. **Create subdomains for the mobile versions of your site.**

   A *subdomain* is a second level of a website. You see them all over the place. For your mobile subdomains, you might use naming scheme like this:

   ```
   mobile1.mysite.com

   mobile2.mysite.com

   mobile3.mysite.com
   ```

If you have only one version of the mobile site, of course, you need only one subdomain. If you plan to use a web hosting account, you'll need to set up the subdomain with the hosting provider and create a Domain Name Server (DNS) record for the subdomain. If you don't know how to create subdomains and DNS records, your hosting provider can help you. (If you plan to design mobile websites, this is certainly knowledge you'll need in the future.)

2. **Open your browser and go to** `http://detectmobilebrowsers.mobi`.

   As shown in Figure 6-1, this page allows you to enter the URLs to the different versions of your site. You can enter different URLs for several different types of devices, such as iPhones, iPads, Android devices, Windows devices, and so on. There's also a generic setting to redirect all mobile devices; if you want, you can even redirect desktop browsers (as illustrated in Figure 6-1).

Don't worry about the Buy Now button. Solutions at Detect Mobile Browsers are free, unless you plan on deploying one of them on a commercial site. If that's the case, Andy asks you to buy the code for $50, which is well worth it, considering the amount of time it saves.

Figure 6-1:
Detect
Mobile
Browsers
helps you
create a
set of PHP
scripts for
redirecting
mobile
traffic.

3. **Open the first drop-down menu under Detect iPhones and choose Redirect iPhones to a Specific URL.**

   A new line that says

   ```
   Where do you want iPhone users redirect to: http://
   ```

   appears below the drop-down menu, as shown in Figure 6-2. The last part, the `http//`, is a text field.

4. **Enter the URL to which you want iPhone traffic on your site to be redirected.**

5. **Complete each of the remaining redirects, entering the URL for the alternative content.**

   This script requires you to set criteria for each option. Set the Redirect Desktop Browsers setting to No – Do Not Redirect Visitors – Function Will Return FALSE.

6. **Click the Generate Function button beneath the last drop-down menu.**

   This generates the appropriate PHP function, shown in Figure 6-3, for inserting in your web page. We have a few other things to do first, though.

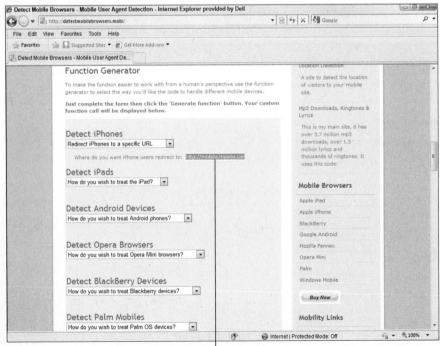

Figure 6-2:
Enter the URL for the new mobile content pages.

Enter mobile URL

Typically, PHP pages have .php, not .html, as an extension; the extension tells the server what to do with the pages. A .html extension tells the server to hand the pages off to the browser. A .php extension, on the other hand, tells the server that the page has scripts that the server must execute. So we work around that little quirk by telling the server to look for and execute PHP code in HTML files. To do that, we create a .htaccess file, otherwise known as a *distributed configuration file*. On Apache web servers (which most hosting companies use, especially on servers that support PHP), distributed configuration files provide a way to make configuration changes on a per-directory basis. Before opening a web page, the server reads the .htaccess file to determine whether the files in a particular directory — or those in a subdirectory of the directory that contains the .htaccess file — require special treatment.

The PHP detect-and-redirect function

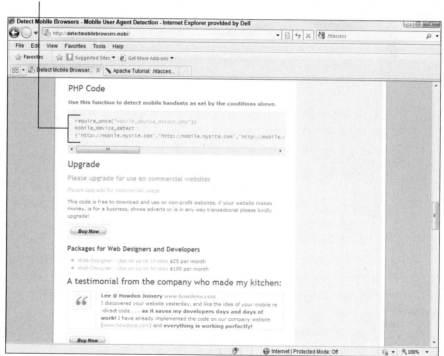

Figure 6-3:
The PHP
function
required
to detect
user agents
and switch
URLs.

7. **Open a text editor and type the following on the first line:**

```
AddHandler php5-cgi .html .htm
```

This line tells the server to run PHP5 scripts in files with HTML and HTM extensions. If your hosting server uses an earlier version of PHP (unlikely), you can use the following lines, rather than the code shown in Step 7:

```
AddType application/x-httpd-php .html
AddType application/x-httpd-php .htm
AddHandler x-httpd-php .html .htm .cgi .php
```

8. **Save the file as** .htaccess **and upload it to the root directory of your website or the directory containing the desktop version of the home page (most likely** index.html**).**

9. **Select and copy all the text in the text field containing the PHP function code.**

10. **Open the home page (most likely** index.html**) for the desktop version of the site in a text editor or whatever program you use to create and edit web pages.**

11. **On the first line of the file (if you're using Dreamweaver, make sure you're in Code View), type:**

```
<?php
```

Paste the function you copied from Detect Mobile Browsers, and then type:

```
?>
```

The top of your index.html file should look similar to Figure 6-4. We've placed this code at the top of the file so it's the first thing the browser and server will see and do. If the user agent that's accessing the page is a mobile device, then the server pushes the alternate URL to the browser instead of continuing to read this page.

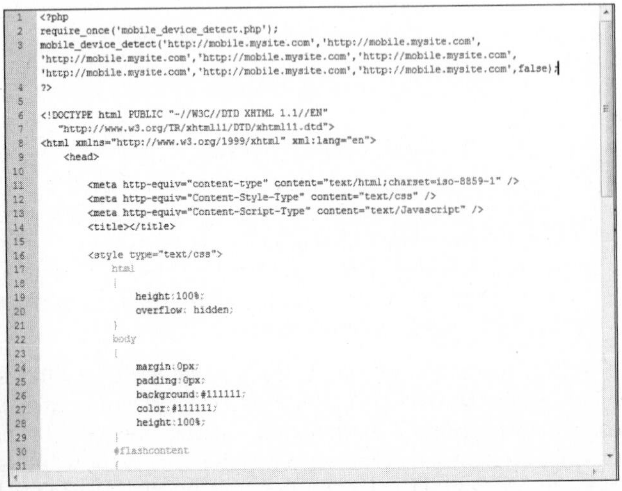

Figure 6-4:
The home
page file
with a
mobile
detect and
adapt PHP
script.

12. **Go to the of the Detect Mobile Browser web page, under the Usage Guide section, and click the orange** `mobile_device_detect.php` **link.**

    After you agree to the terms and follow a few prompts, this link downloads a zipped PHP file to your computer.

13. **Extract** `mobile_device_detect.php` **from the zipped file and upload it to the root directory, or the directory containing the desktop version, of your site.**

That's it. If you browse to the site with a mobile device — or with a desktop browser whose user agent has been changed to a mobile device type — you should be redirected to the mobile version of the site.

Database-driven detect and redirect systems

If the method for detecting user agents and adapting content described in the previous steps doesn't provide the device class system you need, you can always create a database-driven detection system. Because there are already some fairly thorough open-source systems available, I'd advise you not to start from scratch — unless, that is, you have gobs of time and nothing better to do. That's the reason for the upcoming list of three widely used options; because they *are* in wide use, you'll find plenty of information on the Internet describing how to set up and use them.

Not all these solutions are free. Device Atlas, for example, depending on the version you choose, runs between about $100 and a few hundred dollars. When you compare this to the many hours you could spend creating your own system . . . I'm sure you get my point. All things considered — even the solutions that do cost a little something — they're pretty darn close to free.

Here's a short list of some of the most popular open-source, database-driven, detect-and-redirect systems:

- ✔ **Device Atlas (**`http://deviceatlas.com`**):** Device Atlas offers a reasonably complete device database that is updated regularly. And, so you don't have to reinvent the wheel, it offers several different APIs (application programming interfaces) in a few popular languages, such as PHP, Java (a server-side language unrelated to JavaScript), and Windows Server's ASP.NET. Device Atlas also offers a free evaluation license, under which you can download and install all the required files on your server and try out the API components.

- ✔ **WURFL (**`http://wurfl.sourceforge.net`**):** WURFL (Wireless Universal Resource File), discussed in Chapter 5 as a resource for finding information on specific devices, is an XML database of mobile devices. It's maintained by the mobile web design community and it's free. Although this file by itself is not a complete detect-and-adapt system, it provides the biggest and most daunting part of the system — the device database — already done. You'll need some programming skills to put to work, though.

✔ **Tera-WURFL (**www.tera-wurfl.com**):** Tera-WURFL gets its device information from WURFL. It's also discussed in some detail in Chapter 5, in relation to using it for finding attributes for specific devices. A free, open-source solution (they do accept well-deserved donations), this is almost a complete solution as is. All that's missing are the redirection scripts — you'll have to write those yourself. This solution is pretty well documented; however, because it's free, support is handled through user forums and whatever else you can find on the Internet. You'll need to learn some programming, do some research, and spend some time putting this solution together, but if you need an a elaborate by-device detection-and-adaption system, this is a good place to start.

Defining Devices by Classes

Before mobile devices began accessing content on the web, creating websites was a pretty straightforward proposition. The range of capabilities between the computers in use was somewhat diverse. Yet, the differences in what all the various machines could do were not so great that designers had to worry a lot about creating sites that just wouldn't work on some of them. Web designers worry primarily about two things: bandwidth and display sizes, or monitor resolutions. They designed their sites so users with low–bandwidth Internet connections didn't have to sit there growing old while waiting for all the images and other multimedia content to download — and they made sure their pages were not so wide that users with low–resolution display systems were forced into a lot of unnatural back-and-forth scrolling.

Over time, nearly all computer users had broadband Internet connections and very few had low-resolution display systems. Designers took advantage of these technological advancements and began creating content-rich websites capable of delivering high-resolution multimedia images, digital videos, and interactive Flash content. Just as we were getting comfortable with all this new-found freedom, along came web-enabled handhelds — greatly complicating the web design process.

It has taken some time, but mobile web technology is finally reaching the point where designing for handhelds will stop being an exercise in chasing unrelenting moving targets — bringing the craft full circle to where we were when this whole mobile revolution started: designing for the lowest common denominator (which I talk about a little later in this section).

If you decide to create several different sites based on device attributes and capabilities, you'll need a way to classify the device types — a system for relegating them to groups of devices with similar web feature sets and capabilities — in effect, a mobile device class system. To create such groups, you can create a set of profiles, one profile for each group. Each profile represents a version of the site. If, say, you decide you need four separate sites, you'll create four class profiles, and these profiles will consist of feature and capability similarities.

How many site versions do you need? Now there's a loaded question. The answer? How much time do you have? How much money is your employer (in terms of your wages) or client willing to spend? Is the mobile web user an important part of your marketing strategy? How much work do you want to invest in the site? How many other relevant questions can you come up with to help you answer the first question: How many site versions do you need?

Finding the lowest common denominator

Technologically speaking, the lowest common denominator is the point at which something works for every device in the class. In web design, designing to the lowest common denominator simply means finding the most common ground, or the most basic and common standard features, among a range of devices. For example, when designing for desktop computers, if you design your pages no wider than 900 pixels, chances are very good that everybody visiting the site can view it without having to scroll left and right. Nine hundred pixels is a lot of real estate. You have a lot of room to create some nice-looking, easy-to-navigate pages.

Finding the lowest common denominator among *handheld* devices, however, is not nearly that easy. First of all, we're talking screens ranging from about 100 or 200 pixels up to and beyond 1,000 pixels (and screen size is not the only common denominator you need to consider). With this huge variation, you can't really design a one-page-fits-all mobile solution. Figure 6-5, for example, simulates the same website on three vastly different–sized mobile screens. Unless the pages are very bland and uneventful, it's not really possible to come up with one common screen size that would work well for all handhelds — that is, unless you don't mind ignoring all the exciting features you can exploit on higher-end devices. That takes all the fun out website design — and won't entice visitors to come back to your site.

Although screen size is the most important consideration, you'll also need to determine common denominators for a few other capabilities, such as:

✔ Supported HTML and CSS versions

✔ Support for JavaScript

✔ Support for digital video (and what formats)

✔ Support for Flash (and what versions of Flash Player and Flash features)

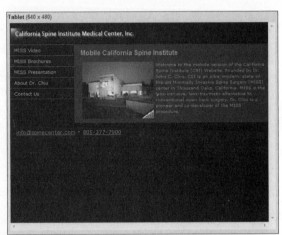
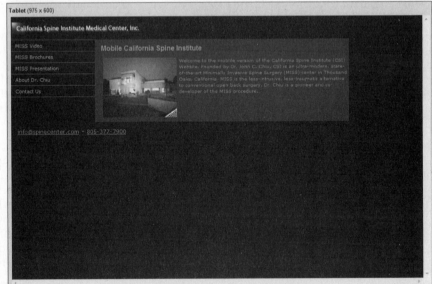

Figure 6-5:
Examples
of the same
website on
vastly dif-
ferent-sized
displays.

Choosing a profiling strategy

As is the case with so many different aspects of web design, there are many viable approaches to creating a set of device profiles. However, the two methods that make the most sense (to me, anyway) are

✔ To begin with profiles that start with a minimal set of features and then add features to create more sophisticated profiles.

✔ To begin at the high end of the feature sets and strip away features to create less sophisticated profiles.

You can choose one of these methods or devise a strategy of your own. To demonstrate how all this profiling works, you might as well start by creating profiles for the newest, most sophisticated devices and then work your way downward to create profiles for handhelds with fewer capabilities. Keep in mind, on the way, that although it's tempting to create a highly versatile class system that includes many profiles, every one of those profiles calls for another version of the site.

To keep track of your profiles, you also need a naming scheme. Because each new profile represents a new version of the site, you also need a separate directory to hold the files for each version. In addition, each version requires a subdomain (or at least a subdirectory) to provide a unique URL for accessing each version. You can call your profiles whatever you want, but you'll find it much easier to keep track of everything if you use the same names for your profiles, subdirectories, and subdomains. In this demonstration of how to create profiles, I use a naming scheme consisting of profile names beginning with *mobile1*, *mobile2*, and so on, as follows:

- ✔ **mobile1:** As I write this, in response to Apple's immensely successful iPad, several manufacturers are releasing handheld tablets. These are, in effect, minicomputers. Most of them support most desktop computer web features, such as HTML5, CSS3, Flash Player 10.x (as opposed to the Flash Player Lite found on most devices) and high-resolution displays of 1024 pixels wide, or wider. (A caveat, of course is that the iPad doesn't support Flash.)

  Considering that these devices are fully web-enabled, it's not necessary to create a separate site to accommodate them. However, they *are* handhelds — they *do not* have a pointing device (mouse), and they *do* support touch and multi-touch. They also support orientation-switching, which greatly increases screen width in landscape mode, and there's a huge difference in screen sizes (as shown in Figure 6-6) between the two orientation modes. For these reasons, it's worth considering including such devices in your mobile class structure. If you do, and you want to provide the best web experience for their owners, they deserve their own class.

- ✔ **mobile2:** The next class meets all the criteria for mobile1, except devices in this profile have much smaller screens. This class would include iPhones, iPods, the latest Android smartphones, the latest Palm OS devices, and many Windows Phone 7 devices. These devices are capable of a lot of fancy tricks, and you can create a feature-rich website for them. Because of their smaller screen sizes (iPhone screens, for example, in landscape orientation, are only 480 pixels wide), a page designed for mobile1 screens would probably not work well on mobile2 devices.

  Keep in mind that this group has a somewhat wide array of screen sizes — loosely, from about 320 up to about 640 pixels wide (with some even a little wider). CSS provides some ways to compensate for this, which are addressed in Chapters 7 and 8.

✔ **mobile3:** This class includes primarily older smartphones that do not support HTML5, CSS3, or JavaScript. For the most part, however, these devices do have screen sizes similar to those in the mobile2 class. The lack of JavaScript support greatly diminishes what the device can do — which curtails your design options. You can't, for example, create forms with self-validating fields (not without server-side scripts, that is). *Form-field validation* makes sure required fields are not left blank and checks what users type into form fields — in particular numerical strings such as credit card and phone numbers — to make sure the entry fits predefined criteria. (Designing mobile forms is discussed in Chapter 9.) In addition, you can't use highly beneficial Ajax calls (discussed in Chapter 16) that would otherwise help you create all kinds of things, such as interactive Google Maps, search pages, or drop-down menus and menu tabs (again, unless you use server-side scripts). Bottom line: In the mobile3 design class, you have to stay mindful of limited features.

✔ **mobile4:** Now we're getting into the not-so-smart feature phones. For the most part, these devices have small screens, about 320 pixels wide and smaller, and they support only the simplest of CSS formatting, if any CSS at all. The sites you create for this class will consist of simple and straightforward HTML — unless you're a pretty skilled programmer. Any fancy functionality built into these sites will come from server-side technology. Support for Flash and digital video is also rather limited. That's not to say you can't use multimedia formats at all, but what you can get by with will be simple (and small).

Figure 6-6:
In portrait mode, the screen width on some tablets is narrow enough to be treated as a mobile device, but not necessarily so in landscape mode.

←————600 pixels————→

←————————1024 pixels————————→

Subdomains or subdirectories?

When you're deploying content to the web from a subdirectory, you have two options for setting up the URL:

✔ Use the subdirectory path as part of the URL, as in `http://www.mysite.com/subdirectory`.

✔ Point to the subdirectory from a DNS subdomain, as in `http://subdomain.mysite.com`.

Either method works fine, but when creating alternate sites, I prefer using subdomains. Why? Well, because they are, after all, separate websites. In my opinion, subdomains just look more polished and more professional. However, they are also somewhat more complicated to set up. With subdirectories, all you have to do is create directories and call them out in your links. There's no additional setup required.

With subdomains, you must create a DNS record for each alternate site. If you use a hosting company that allows you to create your own DNS records and point them to specific directories, this requirement really isn't that much more work — a few extra steps. Some hosting companies, though, require you to request DNS changes (usually via e-mail) and wait for the support team to get around to making the changes. Sometimes this can take a couple of days, which can put a damper on your design schedule. But you can get around that, too — by installing a testing server, as discussed in Chapter 4.

Refining your class system

Are you getting the hang of this? Already you're up to four versions of your site. Fortunately, this set of profiles covers nearly all web-enabled handhelds. Any profiles you add from here would be for refinement, or tweaking, rather than an attempt to include all devices. You could, for example, create subclasses of mobile1 and mobile2 for Apple devices that don't support Flash. You could also create subclasses of mobile4 for very small screens (about 240 pixels wide or smaller).

You can create as many profiles as you need. Again, how far you take this depends on your time, your resources, and your best guess as to whether doing all this work and investing the time makes sense when weighed against a marketing strategy or the purpose of the site. An online store selling mobile accessories, for example, would invest a lot more time in its detect-and-adapt system than, say, an online surf shop. (Hint: Consider the size of the market.)

Letting the User Choose

The simplest — and perhaps the most foolproof — adaptation system is to just let the user choose whether he or she wants to see a mobile version of the site. Simply provide a link to a mobile version of the site — or several links, for that matter, based on device type or screen size. This is a some-what low-tech approach, but not unusual. Some of the biggest websites in the world provide users with this option, as shown in Figure 6-7.

Figure 6-7:
Google
offers users
the option of
viewing the
site in either
Mobile or
Classic
modes.

This option, of course, eliminates the need for creating a server-side detection system. However, unless you're planning a one-version adaptation system, you'll still need to create multiple versions of the site based on device profiles. You see similar presentations for digital video all the time — you know, where you choose which version of a video to watch based on your Internet connection's download speed. It's also not unusual to see sites that allow the user to choose between Flash and non-Flash versions of a site.

If you choose this method, however, you probably should not just automatically present a menu of mobile alternatives to everybody who visits your site. Instead, at least use some detection method, such as Andy Moore's Detect Mobile Browsers solution (discussed earlier in this chapter) to determine that the visitor is indeed using a handheld — and *then* provide a menu of alternate sites. This approach, I think, is much cleaner and appears more professional — perhaps you could just add a setup message such as this:

"We've noticed that you're using a mobile device. To best experience our site, please choose one of the following mobile options."

Chapter 7

Laying Out the Home Page

· ·

In this Chapter

▶ Laying out the home page framework

▶ Using CSS to create headers, footers, and sidebars

▶ Formatting text with CSS

▶ Adding menus and navigation with CSS

▶ Adding images to your layout

· ·

Most designers agree that the most important page of any website is the home page — the first page the user sees when he or she comes to a site. A good home page performs many functions all at once, starting with

✔ Greet the site's visitors.

✔ Announce the site's purpose.

✔ Capture the visitor's attention.

✔ Entice visitors to stay and look around.

✔ Clearly present how to find information.

A Call to Action

Although it's important that all home pages perform the five basic functions listed in this chapter's intro, for mobile sites the effectiveness of the site's first page is essential. Mobile web users are action-oriented. They want their information now, and they want to act on it — now. The page needs to load fast and instantly provide the user with choices. Many of the mobile users who visit your site want to know only two things: what you do and how to get hold of you.

Your job, then, is to provide them with a home page that presents everything clearly (as shown in Figure 7-1), and also makes it easy for the visitor to decide what to do next — whether it's following a link for additional information, clicking a link to send you an e-mail, or even clicking a link to call you from the mobile device from which they're viewing the site. (Read on. I'll show you how to do that a little later in this chapter!)

Menu   Logo and banner   Who you are

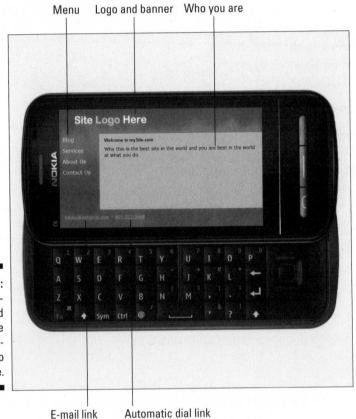

Figure 7-1:
Action-oriented home page with obvious links to everywhere.

E-mail link   Automatic dial link

Laying Out the Framework

Okay. Enough talk. It's time to get your hands dirty. In the following exercises you'll create a quick and easy home page, complete with a banner (often called a *header*), an interactive sidebar menu, and a footer containing easy-to-execute e-mail and phone-number links.

This approach is quick and easy, and the page you create with it will work on a wide variety of mobile devices. I'm aware that many of the concepts introduced might be new to you. With that in mind, I discuss most of them briefly. But keep in mind that the purpose of this chapter is to get your feet wet — to design a workable mobile-friendly page. This is a starting place. The next few chapters take a closer look at many of the tags and techniques used here, and, as you learn to create more sophisticated pages and mobile web applications, I'll go over them in greater detail.

Let's get started.

You can download some files to work with from this book's companion website. These are examples of what you create in this section. Downloading and referring to them will help you better understand this process. Download the file `chapter07.zip`. It contains three files: `index.html`, which is the web page itself; `chapter7.css`, which is the external style sheet; and `logo.png`, which is the logo placeholder. The logo placeholder is a graphics file, and it's located in a subdirectory named `images`. I've also included a Photoshop PSD file of `logo.png`, just in case you want to edit it to create your own logo for this exercise.

Starting the HTML Page

Whether you're using Dreamweaver or hand-coding, you start a mobile HTML page just as you would any other. All HTML pages have the same basic structure. In other words, it's not how you use the tags, but the tags you use that count. Or, is it, it's not how you say it, but what you say that counts? Something like that . . .

Web browsers read tags to determine how to format a page. How browsers interpret and use the tags, though, often depends on the initial tag, or the very first tag at the top of the HTML page, the *doctype*. The doctype introduces the page to the browser and tells the browser what standards the page supports — HTML, XHTML, XML, and so on.

Okay. So, technically, *doctype* is not really a *tag*. In geekSpeak it's a *declaration* or *instruction*. It "declares" the document type to the browser, but doesn't really do any formatting, per se. Granted, it's placed between the less-than (<) and greater-than (>) symbols, which makes it look like a tag. But since it doesn't actually format anything on the page, just because it walks like a duck, it doesn't talk like a duck.

Although there are several doctypes available, only a few are in wide use today, and even fewer are used for mobile sites. Here are two the most common doctypes used for mobile websites and when you should use them:

✔ **XHTML Mobile 1.0:** Known as the *XHTML Mobile Profile*, or *XHTML MP*, this doctype is commonly used for mobile sites. It currently comes in three flavors: Mobile 1.0, Mobile 1.1, and Mobile 1.2. Each version is pretty much the same, except that the newer versions correct technical errors in previous versions. You should use this doctype when designing pages for devices that don't support a lot of the more modern CSS and HTML formatting, such as CSS2, CSS3, and HTML5.

XHTML MP standards are defined by two different alliances. Mobile 1.0 standards, for example, are defined by `wapforum.org`, and Mobile 1.1 and Mobile 1.2 are defined by `openmobilealliance.org`. So, when declaring a doctype for the various versions, you need to refer in your declaration the proper standards compliance URL. The Mobile 1.0 declaration is written like this: <!DOCTYPE html PUBLIC "-//WAPFORUM//DTD XHTML Mobile 1.0//EN"

```
"http://www.wapforum.org/DTD/xhtml-mobile10.dtd">
```

Mobile 1.1 and 1.2 declarations are written like this:

```
<!DOCTYPE html PUBLIC "-//WAPFORUM//DTD XHTML Mobile 1.1//EN"
"http://www.openmobilealliance.org/tech/DTD/xhtml-mobile11.dtd">


<!DOCTYPE html PUBLIC "-//WAPFORUM//DTD XHTML Mobile 1.2//EN"
"http://www.openmobilealliance.org/tech/DTD/xhtml-mobile12.dtd">
```

Notice the that Mobile 1.1 and Mobile 1.2 refer to `openmobile alliannce.org`, not `wapforum.org`.

✔ **XHTML 1.0 Transitional:** Modern devices, such as tablets and the latest smartphones, have browsers that support nearly all CSS and HTML elements supported by desktop computers and notebooks. When creating web pages for these devices, you don't really need a doctype designed specifically for mobile devices. You should use this doctype when designing pages for the latest iPhones, iPads, or Android devices; and other devices that use WebKit extensions, discussed in Chapter 12. The declaration looks like this:

```
<!DOCTYPE html PUBLIC "-//W3C//DTD XHTML 1.0 Transitional//EN"
        "http://www.w3.org/TR/xhtml1/DTD/xhtml1-transitional.dtd">
```

Now that we have all the technical stuff out of the way, let's create a mobile web page. The following steps create the page itself and the accompanying external CSS file:

1. **Begin a new page in Dreamweaver with your source code editor or a text editor.**

2. **Save the page as *index.html*.**

3. **On the first line of the page, type the following tags:**

```
<!DOCTYPE html PUBLIC "-//WAPFORUM//DTD XHTML Mobile 1.0//EN" "http://www.
        wapforum.org/DTD/xhtml-mobile10.dtd">
<html xmlns="http://www.w3.org/1999/xhtml">

</html>
```

The first tag declares the doctype, and the second tag declares the WS3 standard compliance, discussed in Chapter 2. The second tag also the content section the HTML page. All the tags and the content that formats on this page go between the opening `<html>` and closing `</html>` tags.

4. **Save the page.**

Dreamweaver can generate the doctype and some other basic structure HTML tags automatically, as well as link to your style sheets. Simply start your page using the New command on the File menu, which opens the New Document dialog box shown in Figure 7-2. Choosing XHTML Mobile 1.0 from the DocType drop-down in the right pane of the dialog box sets up the page properly for this process. Choosing XHTML Mobile 1.0 in the New Document dialog box completes steps 1–3 for you.

Dreamweaver can automate many of the procedures discussed in this chapter and throughout this book. Throughout this book I try to point out where Dreamweaver can be very helpful or can save you a bunch of time. (However, note that the examples in this book are hand-coded, and so the step-by-step techniques I show you in these exercises are quite different from Dreamweaver's formatting options.)

DocType drop-down

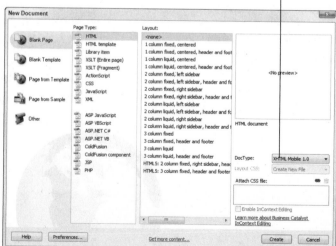

Figure 7-2:
You can use Dreamweaver's New Document wizard to take some of the guesswork out of setting up doctypes.

Good! Now that the HTML page framework is started, it's time to create the style sheet. Chapter 2 discusses the three types of style sheets — external, internal, and inline — and when to use what type and why. Unless your styles are meant to format only one document or web page, you should always use external style sheets.

In the following steps, I show you how to create an external CSS file and reference it in the HTML page, so that the web page uses it to format the page elements.

1. **Start a new text document and save it as *chapter7.css*. (Make sure you save it in the same directory as `index.html`.)**

2. **On the first line of the new document, type the following:**

   ```
   @charset "utf-8";
   ```

   This first line sets up the style sheet by announcing the character set it uses. Nearly all websites, especially those written in HTML, XHTML and CSS, use the utf-8 character set.

   Your new style sheet does little good if you don't tell `index.html` about it: its name, type, and where to find it.

3. **In `index.html`, place your text cursor at the end of the `<html xmlns="http://www.w3.org/1999/xhtml">` tag in index.html, press *Enter* twice.**

   This creates a blank line between this tag and the ones you're about to create. This is not required, and many designers don't write their code this way. The extra white space, which web browsers ignore, is a personal preference and makes it easier for humans, you and me, to read the code.

   For design purposes, HTML pages consist of two sections: The `<head>` section, where you declare the document's style sheets, as well as a lot of other data about the page. The HTML tag `<link href="X">`, tells the browser about the style sheet, providing information such as the document filename, where to find the file, and the CSS type. Whether your page uses one or 20 style sheets, you'll need one `<link href="X">` tag for each CSS file, and they all go between the document's `<head></head>` tags.

4. **Type the following tags:**

   ```
   <head>
   <meta http-equiv="Content-Type" content="text/html; charset=utf-8" />
   <title>My Mobile-Friendly Site</title>
   <link href="chapter7.css" rel="stylesheet" type="text/css" media="screen"
           />
   <meta name="HandheldFriendly" content="True" />
   </head>
   ```

The first <meta> tag in the preceding code sets up the document type — again. Yeah, I know what you're thinking: *How many times do I have to do this?* The short answer is: *As many as it takes.* Not all elements of a web page are formatted from the style sheets. This tag assures that those parts of the document that don't rely on the style sheet get treated correctly, or use the right character set. Keep in mind that making sure your pages appear correctly on as many devices as possible often depends on you covering all your bases.

Yes, here's yet another example of a <meta> tag. These tags provide important information about the document. In the words of somebody famous, "You ain't seen nuttin' yet" — because <meta> tags have many functions. For example, they're also used to set up and provide information for search engines (discussed in Chapter 15) and for calling to includes (discussed in the Chapter 8, which covers creating templates).

The <title> tag names the document. Not only do search engines use the <title> data to help find and index pages but the text between these tags is also the page title that shows up in the browser title bar, as shown in Figure 7-3.

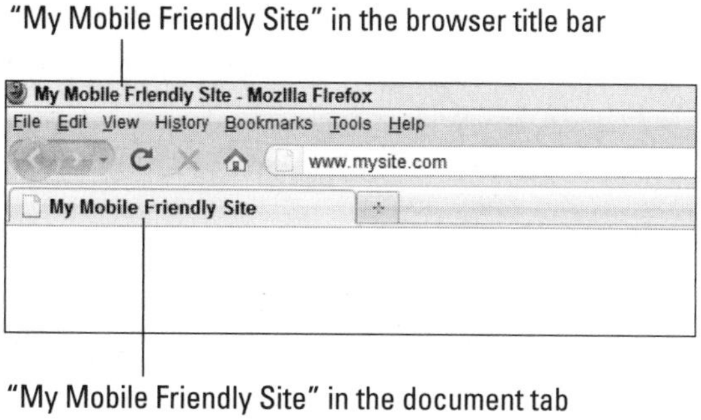

"My Mobile Friendly Site" in the browser title bar

Figure 7-3:
The contents of the
<title>
</title>
tags appear
in the
browser's
title bar and
tab labels.

"My Mobile Friendly Site" in the document tab

The <link href= line declares the style sheet. Notice the media property declaration, "screen". This, of course, tells the browser what type of media, or device, the content is designed for. One of the supported CSS media type options is handheld, but it's very strict and causes browsers to ignore, in my opinion, too much of both the CSS and XHTML formatting, even though nowadays a lot more tags and CSS styles are supported by many of the newer smartphones. The next <meta> tag, <meta name="HandheldFriendly" content="True" /> serves a similar purpose — it tells the browser that index.html is handheld-friendly — without being so draconian.

That's it! Now it's time to start formatting the page elements — what the user sees.

Using CSS for Formatting Columns and Boxes

Style sheets consist of classes and selectors, often referred to as "styles." You define styles in your style sheets and then "call" them out in your HTML pages. Styles can do just about everything, including sectioning off your pages into columns and boxes for holding content, in a way that's similar to (but much more versatile and cleaner than) HTML tables (discussed in Chapter 1). These sections are called "containers," discussed in Chapter 2.

There are a few ways to create containers with styles, including the <div> (divider) tag and the <p> (paragraph) tag. Think of the <div></div> tag pair as a container for setting up page areas, such as headers, sidebars, footers and the body area of your pages. We look at <div> first and <p> a little later in this chapter. Once you've set up a container on the page with <div>, that section becomes subject to all CSS formatting defined for that container in the style sheet — objects in the container automatically assume that CSS formatting.

Keep in mind, though, that you can format page elements further, or override the CSS formatting, within the HTML page itself or with additional CSS styles in the style sheet, as you'll see in a moment.

When setting up your <div> containers, you make associations between the style *selectors* in your style sheet and the containers in your HTML page, as shown in Figure 7-4.

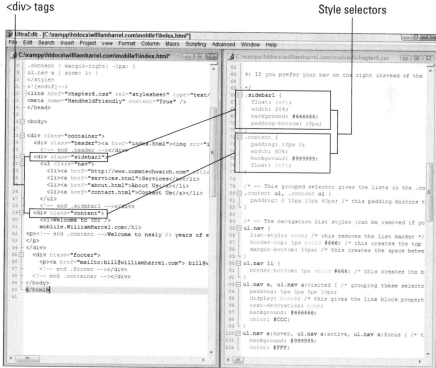

Figure 7-4:
`<div>`
tags and the
associated
style
selectors.

Understanding selectors

Selectors, or style selectors, are the mechanism HTML pages use to associate page elements to styles. There are four basic types of selectors: class selectors, type selectors, id selectors, and compound selectors. Here's a brief description of each type and how and when to use them:

- **Class selectors:** The class style is defined in your style sheet with a period, or dot: `.container`. When you call to it from your document, though, you leave out the dot: `<div class="container">`. Perhaps the most commonly used, the class selector is also the most versatile. You can use it to format more than one object — text, images, or multimedia — on any of your pages, and you can use it as many times on the same page as needed. Keep in mind when creating class selector names that you can't use any spaces or special characters, except dashes and hyphens.

- **Type selectors:** You can use type selectors to modify existing, or built-in, XHTML tags, such as the heading tags, `<h1>`, `<h2>`, and so on. You create them in your style sheet without any predefining characters, like this:

```
h1, h2, h3, h4, h5, h6, p {
    margin-top: 0;
    padding-right: 15px;
    padding-left: 15px;
    color: #CCC;
}
```

When you use one of the preceding tags in your document, the tag automatically assumes this formatting — unless you override it in your document or modify it further later on in your style sheet.

✔ **ID selectors:** Unlike class selectors, you can use an ID selector only once per page. Use it to create unique sections on your pages. The ID selector is identified in the style sheet by a number sign: #header, and you call to it from the HTML page with the <div id=> tag, such as <div id="header">.

✔ **Compound selectors:** Compound selectors, or compound styles, allow you to combine styles. Say, for instance, you want your ordered lists, the <ol> tag, to appear differently in your .content container than in the .sidebar container. You could set up a compound style to accomplish that, like this:

```
.container .content ol {
    font-family: Arial, Helvetica, sans-serif;
    font-size: small;
    color: #000;
}
```

This compound style sets up a distinct ordered list in the sub container *.content,* or the main body container, of the page. Yes, I know I haven't talked much about containers yet. That's next.

Creating containers

Containers, well, contain the elements on your page. Depending on your design, a page can have several containers — one for each element on the page. Or you can design your pages in sections, such as headers, sidebars, footers and a main body, or content, area. While setting up your containers, you can call them whatever you want, but some common standards — which you'll be using here — are in use. It's usually a good idea to adhere to standards, if for no other reason than, just in case somebody else needs to edit your pages.

The <body> tag pair

In general (there are exceptions), just as all elements that do not appear on the page, such as <meta> information, go between the <head></head> tag pair, all elements that *do* appear on the page go between the <body> tags.

So, your container tags need to go inside the opening, <body>, and closing, </body>, tags. You start defining your containers by creating a main, or top-level container, which is, in effect, the page itself.

Follow these steps to create a top-level container:

1. **Go to your** index.html **page, enter a blank line behind the closing** </head> **tag, and enter the following tags:**

   ```
   <body>
   <div class="container">


   <!-- end .container --></div>
   </body>
   ```

   Note the <!-- end .container --> text string before the ending </div> tag. This is known as a *comment*. Just as leaving white space in key locations throughout your code makes the code easier for humans to read, comments also help slow-processor humans to understand the code. Comments are notes, or annotations, and don't do anything but provide information about the code (or anything else you care to put in them, such as, perhaps, questions to other members of the development team?).When browsers see this format, <!--comment-->, they ignore it. As your pages get more complicated, comments come in handy for marking your place in the document or reminding you what the code does or why you did something this particular way, and so on.

2. **Go to** chapter7.css **and enter the following class selector:**

   ```
   .container {
       width: 100%;
       max-width: 800px;
       min-width: 320px;
       background: #FFF;
       margin: 0 auto;
   }
   ```

If you're familiar with programming, you'll recognize this format. The .container is the name of the style (known as a *function* in many programming languages), and everything else — between the two curly brackets — defines, or sets up the properties for, the style. From the top down, this top-level container's format is defined as such:

✔ **width: 100%;** = make this container 100 percent of the page size.

✔ **max-width: 800px;** = don't let the page resize to more than 800 pixels wide.

✔ **min-width: 320p;** = don't let the page resize to smaller than 320 pixels wide. (This forces devices with screens smaller than 320 pixels to scroll sideways, but the alternative is pages with elements that don't fit and overlap each other — the former is certainly the lesser of two evils.)

✔ **background: #666;** = make the background of the container white. This code, #FFF is an abbreviation of the hexadecimal code, #666666. (If you don't know how computers define and pick colors with hexadecimal codes, see the sidebar, "Understanding hexadecimal colors.") If you use Dreamweaver, this is the equivalent of setting the Background option in the Pager Properties (located on the Modify menu). It sets the underlying background color for the entire page.

✔ **margin: 0 auto;** = make the margins zero automatically.

Again, all other containers go inside this top-level container.

Understanding hexadecimal colors

If you've ever wondered how computers pick and define colors, one of the most common methods, especially for web pages, is the *hexadecimal* code system. Hexadecimal notation (in the context of CSS and HTML) is, put simply, a system for defining and calling out colors. When your browser comes across a hexadecimal code, it tells the computer how to colorize the pixels within the defined area. You can find the hexadecimal codes for most colors in nearly any graphics or design program, such as Photoshop or Dreamweaver. Simply look in any of these programs' color definition boxes or panels, as shown in the figure.

Hexadecimal code

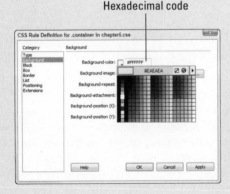

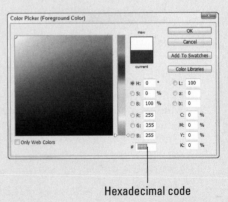

Hexadecimal code

Creating a header

The header usually spans the top of the page and displays information identifying the site itself and the organization the site represents. The header, for example, might hold the company logo and other graphics symbolizing the company and its products or services. A temp office–worker service, for instance, might display an image of people working in an office setting. The header container, like all other containers, goes inside the main, or top-level, container.

To add a header, follow these steps:

1. **Place the** `.header` **container tags, as shown here, in** `index.html`.

```
<body>
<div class="container">

        <div class="header">

<!-- end .header --></div>

<!-- end .container --></div>

</body>
```

2. **Go to** `chapter7.css`, **enter a blank line beneath the** `.container` **style (below the curly bracket), and then enter the following header tags:**

```
.header {
    background: #666;
}
```

As you can see, this container style consists only of a background color. In this case, you don't define size properties for the header container, so the size of the header content — the image you create and import a little later in this chapter — will dictate the size of the header.

Creating a sidebar

On web pages, left sidebars usually contain menus, which is how you'll use this sidebar. Sidebars positioned on the right side of a web page, however, often contain contact information, ads, images, or other content that isn't necessarily part of the main body content. In, say, an e-zine, a right sidebar might contain related or supporting data, similar to the sidebars in this book.

To create a sidebar, follow these steps:

1. **Go to** `index.html` **and enter the following sidebar container tags below the** `.header` **tags, like this:**

```
<body>
<div class="container">

    <div class="header">

    <!-- end .header --></div>

    <div class="sidebar1">

    <!-- end .sidebar1 --></div>

<!-- end .container --></div>

</body>
```

2. **Go to** `chapter7.css`, **insert a blank line beneath the header style and enter the following style:**

```
.sidebar1 {
    float: left;
    width: 25%;
    background: #666666;
    padding-bottom: 10px;
}
```

Notice the `float: left` and `width: 25%` tags in this style. Combined, they make the sidebar column resizable. The `float` option keeps the column size fluid, adjusting it with the size of the page, or as the page resizes. The `width: 25%` property declaration confines the column to 25 percent of the page. Remember the `min width` property you used earlier? When you combine it with `width: 25%` here, you make sure that your sidebar, no matter what device it appears on, never gets smaller than 25 percent of 320 pixels (which figures out to 80 pixels). Restricting the your layout in this way — with tags that limit the effects of other tags — stops the browser from taking this resizing thing too far. In this case, if you were to let your sidebar resize smaller than 80 pixels, it would be too small to hold your buttons.

Creating the body container

The `<body>` container (also called, rather redundantly, the `.content` container) is usually the largest section of the page. It contains mostly information, such as articles or product and service descriptions. It, too, goes inside the main container.

To add a `<body>` container, follow these steps:

1. **Go to** `index.html` **and add the following content tags just beneath the** `.sidebar1` **tags, like this:**

```
<body>
<div class="container">

    <div class="header">

    <!-- end .header --></div>

    <div class="sidebar1">

    <!-- end .sidebar1 --></div>

    <div class="content">

    <!-- end .content --></div>

<!-- end .container --></div>

</body>
```

2. **Go to** `chapter7.css` **and enter this style directly below** `.sidebar1` **style:**

```
.content {
    padding: 10px 0;
    width: 75%;
    background: #333333;
    float: left;
}
```

Here's the other side of your floating columns: The `float` and `width` properties make sure the content container takes up the other 75 percent of the page, and that it too adjusts to the size of the page. You're almost done creating the containers. Your documents should look Listings 7-1 and 7-2.

Listing 7-1:   HTML selectors setting up page containers

```
<!DOCTYPE html PUBLIC "-//WAPFORUM//DTD XHTML Mobile 1.0//EN" "http://www.
           wapforum.org/DTD/xhtml-mobile10.dtd">
<html xmlns="http://www.w3.org/1999/xhtml">

<head>
<meta http-equiv="Content-Type" content="text/html; charset=utf-8" />
<title>My Mobile-Friendly Stie</title>
<link href="chapter7.css" rel="stylesheet" type="text/css" />
<meta name="HandheldFriendly" content="True" />
</head>

<body>
<div class="container">

   <div class="header">
```

(continued)

Listing 7-1 *(continued)*

```
    <!-- end .header --></div>

    <div class="sidebar1">

    <!-- end .sidebar1 --></div>

    <div class="content">

    <!-- end .content --></div>

    <!-- end .container --></div>

</body>
</html>
```

Listing 7-2:   CSS creating container styles

```
@charset "utf-8";

.container {
    width: 100%;
    max-width: 800px;
    min-width: 320px;
    background-color: #666;
    margin: 0 auto;
}

.header {
    background: #666666;
}

.sidebar1 {
    float: left;
    width: 25%;
    background: #666666;
    padding-bottom: 10px;
}

.content {
    padding: 10px 0;
    width: 75%;
    background: #333333;
    float: left;
}
```

Creating the footer

Like headers and sidebars, footers often hold information or links that remain constant from page to page. In this case, you add an e-mail link and a phone-dialer link, making it easy for your visitors to contact you from your website. They (and, with all those happy visitors, you) will be happy you did.

To create a footer, follow these steps:

1. **In** `index.html`, **add the following** `footer` **tags:**

```
<body>
   <div class="container">

      <div class="header">

      <!-- end .header --></div>

      <div class="sidebar1">

      <!-- end .sidebar1 --></div>

      <div class="content">

      <!-- end .content --></div>

      <div class="footer">

      <!-- end .footer --></div>

   <!-- end .container --></div>

</body>
```

2. **Go to** `chapter7.css` **and enter the following style:**

```
.footer {
   padding: 10px 0;
   background: #666666;
   position: relative;
   clear: both;
}
```

Great! Now you've got all four of your pages sections defined. Were you to test the page in a browser now, it wouldn't be much, as demonstrated in Figure 7-5, to look at. Just some empty boxes. Like any respectable web page, it needs content!

A footer typically runs the full width along the bottom of the page, with nothing — no columns or any other element — on either site. So to make sure the footer is pushed to the bottom, we used `position: relative;`. This simply makes the footer's position "relative" to the other containers, meaning it will adjust its position accordingly. The `clear: both;` property "clears" both sides of the footer; no other content or container can reside on "both" sides of the footer.

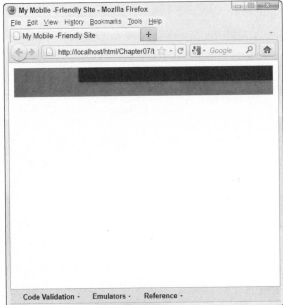

Figure 7-5:
Your mobile
page so far.

Using CSS to Format Text

XHTML contains a default set of tags, such as `<h1>`, `<h2>`, and so on, for headings, and the `<p>` tag for standard paragraphs, or body text. You can use CSS styles to modify the default tags or create all new text tags. Remember that many mobile devices don't support a lot of CSS formatting and don't react well when you deviate from the basics. So, to keep things as simple as possible, this operation — formatting text — is one of those areas where you don't want to get too fancy; more is often too much.

Keeping that in mind while you're creating text styles for mobile devices, it's generally a good idea to use and modify XHTML's built-in tags with CSS styles, rather than create all new ones — which is a somewhat common practice when designing for the big screen. (And to think — it just wasn't that long ago when everybody thought laptop monitors were too small.)

As you design your pages, remember that browsers read and format HTML pages from the top-left down. For that reason, most designers place all their text-formatting styles at the top of the CSS file, making sure that they all get read into memory *before* the browser comes across any text blocks that need them. (Remember, also, that you can further modify text, or override styles, within the respective container styles, all of which you learn how to do a little later in this chapter.)

Body text is, of course, the standard paragraph text in your document — you know, the *copy*, or the text that doesn't usually require any other special formatting, as do headings, lists, captions, and so on.

The following steps define the base font styles for your website:

1. **Go to the top of** `chapter7.css`, **insert a blank line after the character set declaration (the first line), and then enter the following** `body` **style:**

```
body {
    font: 100%/1.4 Verdana, Arial, Helvetica, sans-serif;
    background: #666666;
    margin: 0;
    padding: 0;
    color: #333333;
}
```

The `body` style property, `font: 100%/1.4 Verdana, Arial, Helvetica, sans-serif;`, sets the base typeface for the document. Written this way, this property declaration actually gives the browser a few fallbacks, in case the user's system doesn't have the desired font installed. (Mobile devices are not likely to have Veranda at all. I am just using it here to demonstrate this point.) The browser starts with, or tries to find and use, the first typeface — in this case, Veranda. It checks the user's device for that font first. If that font isn't available (installed on the user's handheld), it goes to the next font, and then the next, and so on. You should always list your fonts in the preferred order. Here, for example, you really want the page to use Veranda, but that's not always possible, so the next best font is Arial, and then Helvetica, and finally sans-serif, the default font that every device has.

Most of the properties, except for the `padding` and `font` declarations, speak for themselves. `Padding` is the space, measured in pixels, around the elements formatted with this style. The `100%/1.4` property in the `font` declaration tells the browser to display the text at 100 percent of the body, or default <p>, text size; and to set the space between the lines of text, to 1.4, or 1$\frac{4}{10}$ the text size. This will make more sense after you enter some text.

2. **Enter a blank line and enter the following style:**

```
ul, ol, dl {
    padding: 0;
    margin: 0;
}
```

This style simply tells the browser not to put a margin or any padding around any ordered, <ol>, unordered, <ul>, or definition, <dl>, lists you add to the document. You'll see how this works when you create the list for your menu.

3. Insert a blank line beneath the list style and enter the following style:

```
h1, h2, h3, h4, h5, h6, p {
    margin-top: 0;
    padding-right: 5px;
    padding-left: 15px;
    color: #CCC;
    text-align: left; }
```

Okay. Now you're probably wondering why you would set the margins and padding to zero in the `.content` style and then turn around and add a 15-pixel left and right padding to all the headings and paragraph text here. The short answer is that this is part of the "cascading" effect in *Cascading Style Sheets.* Your class styles start with the most basic formatting, and then you can use tag selectors and compound selectors to make specific formatting changes. I know this is getting complicated. But it will make more sense as you apply additional styles to the individual containers.

For now, though — so you can see what you've done so far — you add some text to the `.content` container in the next step.

4. Go to `index.html` **and insert the following tags and text between the** `.content` **container tags:**

```
<div class="content">
<h1>Welcome to MySite</h1>
<p>Introduce yourself here.</p>
<!-- end .content --></div>
```

TIP

If you're using Dreamweaver, you can get an idea how your pages will look at various screen sizes with that program's Multiscreen option, as shown in Figure 7-6. (Multiscreen is an option on the toolbar.)

If you're not using Dreamweaver, simply open `index.html` in a web browser, making sure you save it and `chapter7.css` first. (Depending on the editor you're using, you may have to close these documents in the editor first, which is another reason I prefer a source code editor, such as UltraEdit. Most source code editors have options for testing pages in one or more browsers.)

As you can see, XHTML's default top-level heading, <h1>, is far too big — especially for the smaller screen handheld devices. There are a number of ways to fix this, including simply using the next level heading tag, <h2>. But that only fixes the problem in this one instance and sort of defeats the purpose of using an external style sheet.

Now that you know the heading doesn't fit well, you can create a compound style to correct it. Because this compound style modifies an existing container, it should go beneath the class styles that set up the containers.

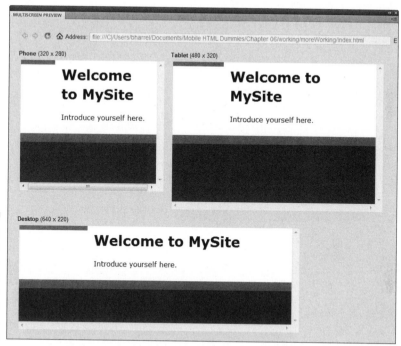

Figure 7-6:
Your page so
far in Dream-
weaver's
Multi-
screen
view.

5. **In** `chapter7.css`, **insert a blank line below the** `footer` **class style and enter the following compound style:**

```
.container .content h1 {
    font-size: medium;
}
```

If you test your page now, the heading should fit much better. While you're here creating styles to modify container text, you should add another compound style to recolor the sidebar text. The sidebar has a dark gray background, so a lighter color would look better (and be easier to read) than black. How about light gray?

6. **Insert a blank line and enter the following compound style:**

```
.container .sidebar1 p {
    font-family: Arial, Helvetica, sans-serif;
    color: #999;
    font-size: xx-small;
    text-align: center;
    line-height: 15px; }
```

Designing Menus and Navigation

By providing a menu in the left sidebar, you make finding information all that much easier for your mobile users. Like menus designed for computer screens, menus designed for handheld devices work better when they're easily identified as links. One technique for making menu items or buttons identifiable is to design them so that they provide feedback. You can, for example, tell links and buttons to change color — making them appear highlighted — when the user selects or tabs to them.

Making buttons and text links hot

If you've done any web page design at all, then you're familiar with the standard `<a href>` tag for creating *hyperlinks*. A hyperlink (sometimes called simply a *link*; some designers make a distinction between the two, reserving *hyperlink* for clickable text and *link* for clickable graphics) makes a button, graphic, or string of text "hot" — that is, clickable. For example, each item in this design's menu list contains a set of `<a href></a>` tags. In this example, you can make each list item link to any page or URL on the Internet by replacing the pound symbol (#) with a valid URL. (Note that the pound symbols are placeholders I added to the code to allow me to isolate and demonstrate how to create links. Were you creating this menu normally, it's not necessary to first create each menu item with a placeholder, and then come back and replace the placeholder with a URL. I did it this way so I could bend your ear on how to create links.)

```
<li><a href="http://www.
    myblog.com">Blog</a></li>
```

The `</a>` tag closes the hyperlink, and the element between `<a href>` and `</a>`, in this case the word `Blog`, becomes the actual clickable hyperlink. You can also turn images into hyperlinks with this method, which I show you a little later in the chapter.

There are two other highly useful hyperlinks: `mailto` and `tel`. The first, `mailto`, allows you to create clickable (or hot selectable links on mobile devices) e-mail links. When a user selects an object configured with `mailto`, her browser interacts with her computer's default mail client (usually Outlook in Windows or Mail in Mac OS X) to send an e-mail to the address specified in the hyperlink. For example, if you click the following `mailto` hyperlink on a Windows machine . . .

```
<a href="mailto:bill@
    williamharrel.com">bill@
    williamharrel.com</a>
```

. . . you launch Outlook's New message window, with the e-mail address, *bill@william harrel.com*, in the To: field. All the user has to do is type in the subject, compose a message, and click Send.

Extremely useful on cellphones, the `tel` tag creates a link that, when clicked, automatically dials the number configured in the hyperlink. This tag's configuration is very similar to `mailto`:

```
<a href="tel:555-555-555">555-555-5555</a>
```

To the user, these two hyperlinks look like any other text link.

bill@williamharrel.com · 555-555-5555

Yet another tried-and-tested mechanism for identifying text as a link is to underline it. As you create your menu in the sidebar and your e-mail and telephone links in the footer, you'll use both CSS methods to format the navigation links on the home page.

There are many ways to use style sheets to create menus. The method I show you here is one of the easiest; it also creates one of the more plain-looking menus. Plain and simple is good, though, especially in mobile site design. These menus don't fly out, explode, jiggle, or breakdance. Instead, they get the job done — by providing your users with an effective way to get around *without* making them wait for a bunch of fancy graphics to download.

Creating the menu list

One way you can create your menu items is with a simple HTML unordered list, which uses the `<ul>` and `<li>` tags. And, this is surely one of those situations where showing works much better than telling. So I'll stop talking so you can just do it.

To create a menu list, follow these steps:

1. **Go to the** `<div class="sidebar1">` **tag in** `index.html` **and enter the following list tags and text between the** `<div>` **tags, like this:**

```
<div class="sidebar1">
   <ul class="nav">
      <li><a href="#">Blog</a></li>
      <li><a href="#">Services</a></li>
      <li><a href="#">About Us</a></li>
      <li><a href="#">Contact Us</a></li>
   </ul>
<!-- end .sidebar1 --></div>
```

By the way, the pound symbols (#) in the previous code are placeholders that I added to make this easier for you. Instead of adding the pound symbols and replacing them later, as I have you do in moment, normally, when you type this list, you would usually just type the URLs the menu items link to, rather than the pound signs. I did it this way to emphasize how a menu like this works. Were you to add these links with Dreamweaver, for example, Dreamweaver would not insert these symbols. Instead, it would expect you to type the URLs to which the menu items link. This should make perfect sense to you in a moment.

Both HTML and XHTML support unordered and ordered lists (ordered lists, `<ol>`, are numbered lists). The `<ul>` tag sets up, or starts, the list. The `<li></li>` tag pairs define the separate list items, and the `</ul>` tag indicates the end of the list.

Notice that the opening `<ul>` tag calls to a class named "nav". Here, you can see a tag selector in action. The tag, `<div class="nav">`, tells the browser: Create an unordered list and use the `"nav"` class to format it.

2. **Go to** `chapter7.css` **and insert a blank line beneath the** `.container` `.sidebar` `p` **style (below the closing curly bracket), and insert the following styles:**

```css
ul.nav {
    list-style: none;
    border-top: 1px solid #666;
    margin-bottom: 15px;
}

ul.nav li {
    border-bottom: 1px solid #666;
}

ul.nav a, ul.nav a:visited {
    padding: 5px 5px 5px 15px;
    display: block;
    text-decoration: none;
    background: #666666;
    color: #CCCCCC;
}

ul.nav a:hover, ul.nav a:active, ul.nav a:focus {
    background: #999999;
    color: #FFF;
}
```

On the surface these styles look complicated. All they do is turn your unordered list into buttons. (*All*, he says.) If you look them over from that perspective, most of the style properties will make sense. The last two selectors, which control the appearance of the buttons during user interactivity, require some explanation:

✔ `ul.nav a, ul.nav a:visited` controls how the menu item appears after the user has visited this link. In other words, if the user has already visited the link, the text appears in a different color. (Not all mobile devices, however, support this option. When manufacturers and browser publishers drop features to reserve resources, it's small nuances like this that they leave out.)

✔ `ul.nav a:hover, ul.nav a:active, ul.nav a:focus` controls how the button appears when it's hovered over or, on mobile devices, *active*. In this example, when the user navigates to a menu item, the text and the background change colors, indicating which button is currently active, or about to get selected (clicked). This is the equivalent to a *rollover* on standard computers — you know, when a user hovers the mouse cursor over a button. As written, this style works for standard computer browsers and mobiles browsers.

If you test your page now, your menu will look more like a menu, and each menu item highlights when you hover over it, as shown in Figure 7-7. On a standard computer, you can see the rollover effects by hovering your mouse pointer over the menu items. Your mobile users can't hover, of course, but each button will highlight when they touch it or tab to it with navigation keys on their handheld devices.

Figure 7-7:
Highlighted
menu item.

Creating the footer links

Two important parts of this site's navigation scheme are the e-mail and telephone links in the footer. To create these, you use the `mailto` and `tel` tags discussed in the accompanying sidebar ("Making buttons and text links hot"). Then you create a compound style to change the footer link's text color to match the text color in the sidebar.

To create the footer links, follow these steps:

1. **Go to** `index.html` **and insert the following tags and text between footer container tags:**

```
<p><a href="mailto:bill@williamharrel.com">yourEmail@yourDomain.com</a> -
      <a href="tel:555-555.5555">555-555.5555</a></p>
```

2. **Go to** `chapter1.css` **and place the following compound style beneath the** `.container .content h1 style`:

```
.container .footer p a {
    font-size: small;
    color: #CCC;
}
```

Adding an Image to Your Layout

To top off your layout, you should add a banner image across the top of the page. The header container is designed to adjust to an image of any height; to keep the header in proportion with the rest of the layout, however, it probably shouldn't go over about 70 pixels high. The header image can also be any length — up to the maximum page size of 800 pixels, that is. However, I wouldn't make it any larger than about 320 pixels. You really don't want your visitors scrolling to see the banner. From a user's perspective, that's pretty annoying — not to mention that it usually greatly diminishes the effectiveness of the banner. You can use the `logo.jpg` image file that you downloaded from this book's companion website. The steps look like this:

1. **Go to** `chapter7.css` **and add the following style, above the first container style:**

```
a img {
    border: none;
}
```

This style, of course, simply makes sure that if you make the image hot, the browser won't display an image around it.

2. **Go to** `index.html` **and enter the following text and tags between the header container tags:**

```
<a href="index.html" class="header"><img src="images/logo.jpg" alt="Return
    to Home Page" /></a>
```

A common design technique is to link a logo or banner image to the site's home page so the user, no matter where he is in the site, can always get back to the top of the site by clicking the banner. The tag, `<a href="index.html" class="header">`, makes the banner image a clickable button that loads `index.html`, and the `alt="Return to Home Page"` property appears as a hover or selected tooltip-like message informing the user of the link's destination.

The completed `index.html` file and `chapter7.css` file appear in Listings 7-3 and 7-4.

Listing 7-3:   The complete `index.html` file

```
<!DOCTYPE html PUBLIC "-//WAPFORUM//DTD XHTML Mobile 1.0//EN" "http://www.
          wapforum.org/DTD/xhtml-mobile10.dtd">
<html xmlns="http://www.w3.org/1999/xhtml">

<head>
<meta http-equiv="Content-Type" content="text/html; charset=utf-8" />
<title>My Mobile -Friendly Site</title>
<link href="chapter7.css" rel="stylesheet" type="text/css" media="screen" />
<meta name="HandheldFriendly" content="True" />
</head>

<body>

<div class="container">

  <div class="header">
   <a href="index.html" class="header"><img src="images/logo.jpg" alt="Return
          to Home Page" /></a>
  <!-- end .header --></div>

  <div class="sidebar1">
    <ul class="nav">
       <li><a href="#">Blog</a></li>
       <li><a href="#">Services</a></li>
       <li><a href="#">About Us</a></li>
       <li><a href="#">Contact Us</a></li>
  <!-- end .sidebar1 --></div>

  <div class="content">
    <h1>Welcome to MySite</h1>
    <p>Introduce yourself here.</p>
  <!-- end .content --></div>

  <div class="footer">
    <p><a href="mailto:bill@williamharrel.com"> yourEmail@yourDomain.com</a> -
          <a href="tel:555-555.5555">555-555.5555</a></p>
  <!-- end .footer --></div>
<!-- end .container --></div>

</body>
</html>
```

Listing 7-4: The completed `chapter7.css` file

```
@charset "utf-8";
/* CSS Document */

body {
    font: 100%/1.4 Verdana, Arial, Helvetica, sans-serif;
    background: #666666;
    margin: 0;
    padding: 0;
    color: #333333;
}

ul, ol, dl {
    padding: 0;
    margin: 0;
}

h1, h2, h3, h4, h5, h6, p {
    margin-top: 0;
    padding-right: 5px;
    padding-left: 15px;
    color: #CCC;
    text-align: left;
}

.container {
    width: 100%;
    max-width: 800px;
    min-width: 320px;
    background: #666;
    margin: 0 auto;
}

.header {
    background: #666;
}

.sidebar1 {
    float: left;
    width: 25%;
    background: #666666;
    padding-bottom: 10px;
}

.content {
    padding: 10px 0;
    width: 75%;
            background: #333333;
    float: left;
}
```

```
.footer {
   padding: 10px 0;
   background: #666666;
   position: relative;
   clear: both;
}

.container .content h1 {
   font-size: medium;
}

.container .footer p a {
   font-size: small;
   color: #CCC;
}

.container .sidebar1 p {
   font-family: Arial, Helvetica, sans-serif;
   color: #999;
   font-size: xx-small;
   text-align: center;
   line-height: 15px;
}

ul.nav {
   list-style: none;
   border-top: 1px solid #666;
   margin-bottom: 15px;
}

ul.nav li {
   border-bottom: 1px solid #666; .
}

ul.nav a, ul.nav a:visited {
   padding: 5px 5px 5px 15px;
   display: block;
   text-decoration: none;
   background: #666666;
   color: #CCCCCC;
}

ul.nav a:hover, ul.nav a:active, ul.nav a:focus {
   background: #999999;
   color: #FFF;
}

a img {
   border: none;
}
```

Chapter 8

Using Templates

1 f you've been using a computer for more than ten minutes, you know what a template is, right? Microsoft Word, for example, comes with templates for creating everything from casual letters to legal briefs. Typically, a *template* is an empty document shell with a set of premade styles, or *style sheets*, that specify formatting of the content.

Although XHTML templates are similar in concept, they differ greatly in practice. For example, unlike your typical Word template (which you open, add content to, and then save as a document file), XHTML templates — especially those formatted with CSS — often consist of several different files. It's not uncommon, for instance, for one web page to reference two or more CSS files. Web pages can also rely on several different document files to make up the various sections — headers, sidebars, footers, body, and so on — of a single page.

In this chapter we look at creating the basic structure of a website with templates. There are many approaches to structuring websites with templates — ranging from simple static and reusable one-size-fits-all HTML files to full-blown modular sites where each page consists of several different files, known as *includes*.

As with many aspects of web design, using includes in your website requires that you go beyond basic HTML and CSS coding and do a little programming — but the results are well worth the effort. So, in this chapter, we do just that — reach beyond basic HTML and CSS coding — and show you how to create a PHP server-side template structure.

Understanding Why Pros Rely on Templates

Have you ever come across a website where every link you followed took you to a different-looking page with an all new color scheme and navigational layout? I have. Each new page is like visiting a different country. Worse, each new page requires visitors to reacquaint themselves with the layout and figure out how to get around and find information. Above all else — especially on mobile sites — your site should be designed to make content easy to find. One way to make that happen is to maintain a consistent "look and feel" throughout the site. Although the content itself may be different, the overall style, the *look and feel*, of the site itself should remain consistent throughout the site.

Designing and adhering to a structure is one of many ways templates help you create professional-looking websites. Before looking at the practice of creating and using templates, let's take a brief look at why professional designers rely on them — how templates can save you time and money and help you create and maintain professional-looking sites:

✔ **Controlling consistency:** Okay. So does it seem like I'm harping? Hey, I'm not talking about merely making every page look similar because it looks nice. Not at all. Think about the way you use a website. As you scan the home page, your brain is filing away information about how the content is organized: What do the menus across the top or along the side do? Do they have submenus? Are there navigational links at the bottom of the page that match the overall menu structure? How do I contact these people?

On well-designed sites, this structure does not change. After spending just a few minutes on your site, the user should be able to change gears and intuitively know how to get to where she wants to go next.

✔ **Easier updating:** One of the tremendous advantages of the Internet is that web content, unlike printed material, is (or should be) easily updated. Many websites change daily, even hourly, by the minute, or within seconds. If it weren't for well-designed templates, this constant, event-driven updating would not be possible. The people who update the content on these sites deal only with content, seldom giving thought to how it's formatted and presented. If they had to concern themselves with the tasks that templates handle, their jobs and the results (all that lightning-fast content) would be immensely more complicated to pull off, more time-consuming, and a lot less consistent.

✔ **Easier expansion:** You never know when the scope of a website project might change. On several occasions, I've had clients come to me with proposed changes to their sites — a new product line, a shopping cart, and so on — that instantly transformed a small, easy-to-manage website into a huge, work-intensive enterprise. At times like this, you'll bless yourself for having taken the time and spent the effort to design even the simplest site around a sound template system, instead of just tossing a few pages together and moving on to the next project.

✔ **Avoiding errors:** A basic truism in any design environment is that the more editing you do, the more opportunities there are for introducing errors into your project. Say your site has 25 pages, and you need to make the same change to all 25 of them. That's 25 opportunities to make a mistake. Templates, external CSSs, includes — all of these tools help you avoid errors. (The counter side is, of course, if you make an error on a template asset, your error will show up on all 25 pages. But then, it's also much easier to correct the error if that happens.)

✔ **Saving time and money:** When it comes down to it, isn't doing the best possible job as quickly and as efficiently as possible always at the top of the list of concerns? Most websites require a commitment over the long haul. I maintain and update sites today that I designed and published nearly 20 years ago. Taking the time to think through, plan, and execute the structure of your site might sometimes seem like superfluous work and a waste of time — and, at times, you might have trouble convincing the client that the few extra design hours are necessary. Taking short-cuts can often put you on dark, winding, difficult-to-navigate roads or take you to dead ends where all you can do is turn around and go back the way you came. A sound template structure can save your valuable time. As a designer, your time really is your most important asset.

Using premade third-party templates

One of the huge advantages of using templates is that there are so many premade, third-party professionally designed templates available. A simple Google search for *web templates* brings up so many hits that you could grow old looking at them all. Many are free or so inexpensive that, in the overall scheme of a web design project, they may as well be free.

There are many third-party template sites on the web, and they do quite well. Why? Because, rather than start completely from scratch (which is time-consuming), many professional designers prefer to use the templates sold at these sites. Take sites like `TemplateMonster.com`, for example (shown in the figure). Sites like these have hundreds of well-designed HTML templates at reasonable prices. All you have to do is swap out the canned content with your own, make whatever design changes you want, and — bam! — you have a professionally designed website in a fraction of the time it would have taken if you started from scratch. (Chapter 20 provides a list of ten great resources for finding third-party web templates.)

(continued)

(continued)

You might be wondering about the possibility of somebody else using the same template and your site looking too much like your competition's site. First of all, that's highly unlikely — in all the years I've been designing websites, I've never seen that happen. Besides, it's very easy to make color, font, and other design and layout changes to these templates; they allow you the flexibility to make them uniquely your own.

Which brings us to a very important consideration when selecting a third-party template:

Make sure it is well documented. In fact, try to get a look at the documentation *before* you purchase the template. If you can't do that, try to get a return agreement that allows you to change your mind if the documentation isn't sufficient to allow you to make changes without a lot of trial and error. The point, after all, is to *save* time, right?

Working with Dreamweaver Templates

Design programs such as Dreamweaver come with many nice-looking templates. Premade templates not only save gobs of time, but they also provide beginners with a great way to learn how to construct HTML pages and the accompanying CSS files. The templates that come with Dreamweaver are quite flexible and easy to adapt to your needs. In addition, there are hundreds of premade, third-party templates designed especially for modifying in Dreamweaver. (See the sidebar, "Using premade third-party templates.")

Many programs that aren't built for web design — such as Microsoft Word, PowerPoint, and Excel — allow you to save your documents as HTML or some other web format. Here's a word to the wise: *Do not* try to use one of these programs as a web design tool. Word, for example, creates extremely "dirty" code — so full of extraneous stuff that Dreamweaver has a special import feature designed solely to "clean up" files that have been saved to HTML in Word. Trust me: Word is not a web design program. Period.

Even when I do code much of a site by hand, I almost always start by setting up and modifying the basic framework of one of Dreamweaver's templates. Why? Because this a great way to get the structure in place — such as the page and container layout, markup language type, CSS files, and so on — while saving an hour or two in the process. Sure, you *can* do all this by hand (and you'll have to if you don't have Dreamweaver or a source code editor that does all this preliminary work for you), but why do more work and spend more time on something when you don't have to? (I use a dishwasher, too!)

Dreamweaver's New Document dialog box

If you're new to web design, Dreamweaver's New Document dialog box, shown in Figure 8-1, might seem a little daunting — there's a lot of stuff there. From another perspective, though, you can use it to set up your template and CSS files, and then take a look at the source code to see how certain page features are accomplished. Let's have Dreamweaver create a layout for us, and then look at how it put our page together. Just follow these steps:

Layout preview   DocType

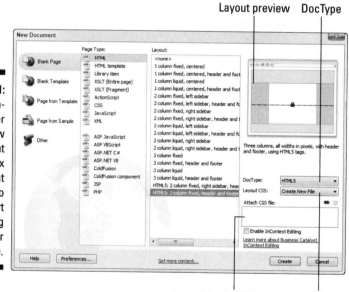

Figure 8-1:
The Dreamweaver New Document dialog box is a great place to start creating your template.

Attach CSS file   Layout CSS

1. **Click the File menu and choose New.**

   As you can see, Dreamweaver allows you to create all kinds of files, including HTML, CSS, JavaScript, and PHP, which are the four types of files we use in this chapter (and the remainder of this book).

2. In the Page Type column, choose HTML, and then, in the Layout column, choose 2 Column Liquid, Left Sidebar, Header and Footer.

The small preview on the right (shown in Figure 8-2) shows you the layout — the header across the top, the footer across the bottom, and the sidebar and the body area to the right of the sidebar. In all, there are four containers (five, if you count the page itself). The percentage symbol on the body container indicates that the width of the two vertical containers, the sidebar and content containers, are *liquid* — which means the columns are self-adjusting; they resize themselves according to the size of the browser window — while the other columns remain *fixed*, or the same size, regardless; they don't adjust with the browser window.

Figure 8-2:
This preview shows you the container layout of your selections.

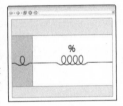

3. Click the DocType flyout and choose XHTML 1.0 Transitional.

You may have noticed that there is an XHTML Mobile 1.0 *doctype* (doctypes are discussed in Chapters 2 and 7). My experience is that it's too strict and doesn't allow some CSS formatting to display on newer devices. So, I prefer controlling formatting with CSS styles, rather than Dreamweaver's mobile doctype.

4. Click the Layout CSS drop-down and choose Create New File.

Notice that there is also a Link To Existing File option, which you could use if you were creating a new page template for an existing site that already had CSS style sheets. In new sites (as you'll see in a moment), the Create New File option starts a new external CSS file.

5. Click Create.

6. Dreamweaver suggests a name for the CSS file based on the layout you chose.

I'm not crazy about this naming scheme, so I simply rename the file here. As you'll see in a minute, the external CSS file that Dreamweaver creates contains all the necessary tags to format these containers and their content (the text and graphics inside them).

When you complete these five simple steps, you have, in effect, performed several tasks that would have taken you quite a bit of time to do manually. In just a few short minutes, Dreamweaver took care of the following tasks:

- ✔ Created an HTML page with all the necessary coding to lay out your header, sidebar, body, and footer containers.

- ✔ Created all the necessary CSS selectors to format the text within these containers. (Granted, the formatting probably won't be exactly what you want, but it's much easier to change the tags than to create them.)

- ✔ Created a sidebar with a menu of rollover-like buttons. All we have to do is change the button text and create the links.

- ✔ Created an external CSS style sheet with all the basic formatting tags in place, as well as extensive commenting to guide you through editing the styles to suit your needs.

- ✔ Created "placeholder" content that provides you with a visual reference to the page's overall appearance.

- ✔ But wait, there's more! If you're new to all this, it performed a whole bunch of functions you would have had to research and experiment with to get this far. Instead, you already have working mock-up to learn from.

The completed template files

As shown in Figure 8-3, Dreamweaver creates a somewhat basic page. (One thing I'm not wild about is the color schemes the designers at Adobe chose for these layouts, but they're easily changed.) The placeholder text inside each of the containers describes aspects of the layout and provides suggestions for modifying the formatting and content. Notice also in the Code view the `<div class=>` tags. These set up the containers themselves, as discussed in Chapter 7.

Technically, in Dreamweaver-speak, this is not what Dreamweaver calls a "template." (Dreamweaver templates themselves are different animals.) Instead, what you have is two files: the page file itself and a file with the `.css` extension. For our purposes, this is the start for your template. From here, you would start replacing the placeholder content — the logo, the menu labels and links, the header and footer content — with your own content, and then save the file. Making all of these changes is discussed in Chapter 7.

When you've replaced all the content and saved the file, this becomes your template. The only thing that changes from page to page is the content in the `.content` container. You simply open the page, save it with a different name, and create your body content.

Figure 8-3:
Dreamweaver creates a basic "blank" page and creates an accompanying CSS file — everything you need for starting your site has been created.

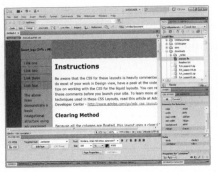 

Look over the HTML file and the CSS file and examine how the containers are created, as well as how the text is formatted. Were you to create your template by hand, this is the basic structure you would use to set up your columns and other containers. Notice that the CSS file is heavily annotated with comments describing what each style does and how, as well as several suggestions for changing the styles. Figure 8-4 shows a website created by modifying this Dreamweaver-created template.

Figure 8-4:
Right: Example of a Dreamweaver-generated template. Left: The same template adapted to a mobile site.

 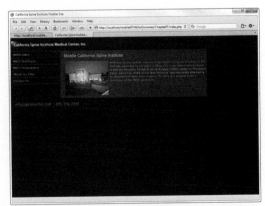

Choosing the Right Template Structure

There are many ways to approach setting up a website template system. In this section, we'll look at two of the most common: creating a static template file you reuse for each new page, and creating a dynamic template system by assembling pages consisting of multiple parts. Both have their advantages and disadvantages.

Creating a static template file

This approach, creating one file with all the necessary elements and using it for each new page in your site, works best for smaller sites. The primary drawback to this approach is that if you need to make changes to any of the elements that make up the template file, each page that uses the template file will also need to be changed.

This is not as bad as it sounds. If you use Dreamweaver or a source code editor such as UltraEdit, these programs have search-and-replace features that allow you to find and replace text and code across multiple — even thousands — of files at once. You just have to be very careful about how you construct your search-and-replace criteria. In other words, be very sure the change is constructed properly before you click Replace All.

The website in Figure 8-4 is a good example of a static template file. The site consists of only five pages, and only the .content container changes from page to page. The way I approach designing this type of template is to design the home page first, and then use it (or a copy of it) as the template file.

Creating modular template files

The technical term for what I call *modular* is *includes*. Includes are pieces, or modules, of pages. For example, take a look at Figure 8-5. Yes, I know this looks like the same page from Figure 8-4 — and, essentially, it is. However, it's created (or you could say "assembled") differently: Instead of one HTML file, it consists of three PHP files; the sidebar and the footer are includes.

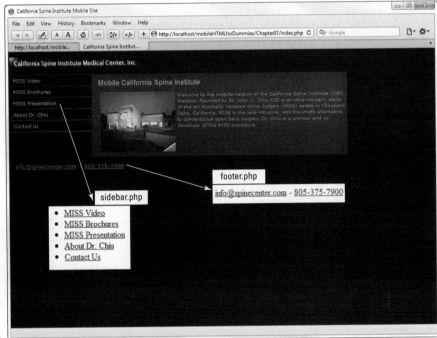

Figure 8-5:
A modular
web page
created as a
collection of
includes.

You may be wondering why the header is not also an include. If you think about it, this section of the page is already modular because it consists only of the company logo, a single graphics file. If the company ever changes its logo, changing the header in this case is simply a matter of editing the graphic. If, however, this header consisted of (say) a menu that spans the top of the page, then it would be prudent to create an include for the header. The accompanying sidebar offers a quick look at creating includes in Dreamweaver.

So why should you construct your pages this way? You probably already know the answer. If (down the road) you need to change or expand the menu, or change the footer information, all you need to change are the includes. The changes would automatically affect every page in the site using this template — even if your site consisted of a million or so pages!

Frankly, the only seamless way to do this is with server-side includes, for a number of very good reasons. There are ways to use JavaScript to create includes, but because not all mobile devices support JavaScript, it doesn't make much sense to use them. Especially when you consider that with the server-side method, which is so easy to use, it doesn't matter what technology your site visitor's devices support.

So, with that said, remember: To use this type of template, the server on which you host your mobile site must support PHP. Most hosting companies' servers do. Although there are some other technologies you can use for this purpose, such as Microsoft Server's Active Server Pages (ASP), PHP is by far the most widely used and supported.)

Creating includes with Dreamweaver's Library (Assets) technology

If you use Dreamweaver, it has a built-in feature for creating includes; it's called *Library*. Unique to Dreamweaver, the Library consists of "assets" you can use and reuse in your pages. Library assets have a .lbi file extension and are saved in the Library subdirectory. This technology uses CSS selectors and, in addition to being quite easy to use, it also works very well — as long as (of course) the users' mobile devices support CSS. Here's how to use it:

1. **Begin by creating the content you want in the include, including the links and special formatting not handled by your style sheets.**

   (That's right! You can format your includes with same CSS files used to format the rest of the document!) For example, the content for the footer include in our medical center site would look like this:

   ```
   <p><a href="mailto:info@spinecenter.com">info@spinecenter.com</a> - <a href="
       tel:805-377-7900">805-375-7900</a></p>
   ```

   Exactly as you would format it were you inserting it into your main document, right?

2. **Go to Dreamweaver's Assets panel (next to the Files panel, unless you've changed Dreamweaver's default workspace) and click the Library icon (it looks like an open book).**

3. **Click the New Library Item button in the lower-right corner of the panel, and then name the new Library asset.**

4. **Copy the content you created for this asset, code and all.**

5. **Click the Edit button in the lower-right corner of the Assets panel.**

6. **If Dreamweaver is not already in Split view, click Split in the upper-left corner of the document window, and then paste the content at the bottom of the existing code.**

   There — you have a new asset you can deploy to your heart's content. To use the Library item, follow these steps:

7. **Place your cursor in the document where you want the include.**

8. **Click the Insert button at the bottom of the Assets panel.**

   And there you go! As long as the users' devices support CSS, your new include will work. (If the users' devices don't support CSS, you should be directing them away from this page anyway.)

Server-side includes

As mentioned, letting the server do this work is really the only foolproof approach. Besides, when you're creating content for handhelds, it's always a good idea to hand off as much of the processing as possible, so as not to stress out the devices' overworked little brains.

Creating and deploying server-side includes is a two-step process. First, you create the content and save it, and then you reference the content file in your document. Let's do that now:

1. **Begin a new blank text document.**

   Except for links and any overriding formatting, you can format your include content from the same CSS files used by the main content page. In fact, your include doesn't need any additional code, such as `<html>`,`<head>`, `<body>`, and so on. If you created your new page with Dreamweaver, go ahead and delete everything on the page.

2. **Create the content for your include on the blank page.**

3. **Save the include file with a** `.php` **extension.**

   If you were creating a sidebar include, for example, you could name it `sidebar.php`.

4. **Go to the spot in the code of your main document file where you want to insert the include, and then type the following code:**

   ```
   <?php include("includes/filename.php"); ?>
   ```

The example given here assumes that you've created a subdirectory for your includes named `includes` — which is a good idea, especially if your site has several includes. Where you place the code, of course, depends on the layout of your page. In the medical-center page we've been working on, you would place the include code between the container `<div class>` tags, as shown in Listing 8-1.

Listing 8-1: Deploying sidebar and footer includes in main web page

```
<body>

<div class="container">
    <div class="header"><a href="index.html" target="_self"><img src="images/
            logo.png" alt="Logo" name="Home Page" width="320" height="32"
            vspace="10" align="center" id="Insert_logo" style="background:
            000000; display:block;" /></a>
    <!-- end .header --></div>

    <div class="sidebar1">
       <!--#include file="includes/sidebar.php" -->
    <!-- end .sidebar1 --></div>
```

```
<div class="content">
    <h1>Mobile California Spine Institute </h1>
    <p><img src="images/CSIeveninga.jpg" alt="CSI" width="175" height="136"
            hspace="5" align="left" />Welcome to the mobiile version of the
            California Spine Institute (CSI) Website. Founded by Dr. John C.
            Chiu, CSI is an ultra-modern, state-of-the-art Minimally Invasive
            Spine Surgery (MISS) center in Thousand Oaks, California.  MISS
            is the less-intrusive, less-traumatic alternative to conventional
            open back surgery. Dr. Chiu is a pioneer and co-developer of the
            MISS procedure. <br /></p>
<!--end .content --></div>

<div class="footer">
    <?php include("includes/footer.php"); ?>
<!--end .footer --></div>

<!-- end .container --></div>
</body>
</html>
```

Variations on your template theme

This system, although it will work nicely with most mobile sites, is not a one-size-fits-all solution. (Is anything?) Depending on the complexity of your site, you may need more than one template and more than one set of includes. Many sites have various departments, and each of those might have slightly different menu and page structures. Then, too, you may need to present the same content in several different languages.

The point is that this template system will get you started. And it's designed to expand easily.

Part III
Enhancing Your Site with Advanced Interactivity and Multimedia

In this part . . .

This part looks at taking your mobile websites beyond the basics of simple navigational buttons. It starts by introducing you to interactive HTML forms. After that you look at using multimedia — images, digital video, and Flash — in your sites, starting with a discussion of media file formats. (Which are the best formats and why and how to load them into and format them on your pages?)

This part ends with a discussion of new technologies, such as HTML5, CSS3, and WebKit extensions. Mastering these can save you lots of time. Time is, after all, money!

Chapter 9

Designing Mobile Forms

*B*ack at the start of the Information Age, as the personal computer was just being introduced as a household appliance, prognosticators had all kinds of predictions of how these devices — and the Internet — would change our lives. One prediction was that by now we'd all be taking advantage of the paperless office. The forests would finally get a break when we all stopped using so much paper. As it turned out, the talking heads missed the mark completely.

The advent of the PC has had an opposite effect. The world uses more paper than ever — mostly contributable to proliferation of computers and personal printers. What we did see, though, was a shift in the way we use and process forms. Although we use forms more than ever, most of them are electronic. We submit them online, rather than fill them out by hand and fax or snail-mail them.

Nobody likes filling out forms. Yet our lives are full of them. Most websites have at least one form of one type or another, ranging from simple "Contact Us" forms to login forms that provide access to blogs or online accounts. So, like it or not, when you choose to become a web designer, you've automatically taken on the role of form designer.

Web forms are one of the most common breaking points on the Internet. Few things turn off a mobile site user — sending them scurrying off to your competitor's site — quicker than a poorly designed, difficult to use, or malfunctioning web form. If your forms are too long, hard to understand, or don't work the first time the user clicks "Submit," the likelihood is very high that you've lost a potential customer.

In this chapter, you get a closer look at designing web forms. You start with an introduction to all the available form parts, or elements. Then I show you how to create a simple Contact Us e-mail form that gathers basic pieces of information about your user, such as name, e-mail address, and a comment.

You have several elements — such as checkboxes, radio-button groups, selection lists (menus), and several others — at your disposal. Matching components to data type can be critical to effectiveness of your forms.

Understanding XHTML Forms

An XHTML form gathers information the user submits on a web page and then does something with that data. What the form does with the information depends on what you tell it to do. The form can e-mail the data somewhere, save it to text file or database, or simply send the information to another web page and display it.

XHTML has about ten or so built-in form elements, and you can use CSS to format them to your liking. (See the sidebar "Formatting form labels and elements with CSS.") XHTML itself, however, does not have the ability to do anything with the form or form data. For that you'll need either a client-side (usually JavaScript) or server-side (usually PHP) script. Because you are creating forms for mobile devices, you should use PHP for processing your form data whenever possible. Why? Because not all handhelds can run JavaScript, and it's always a good idea to let the server carry the load when you're working with mobile devices. It's cleaner, more reliable, and doesn't make the handheld's processor do any unnecessary work.

Basic form construction

You can create forms that take up an entire page, or your forms can be part of a larger page. The form itself — the form body and all of the form elements — reside within the `<form></form>` tag pair. The form elements in Figure 9-1, for example, are created by placing the form field and button tags between the `<form></form>` tags shown in Listing 9-1.

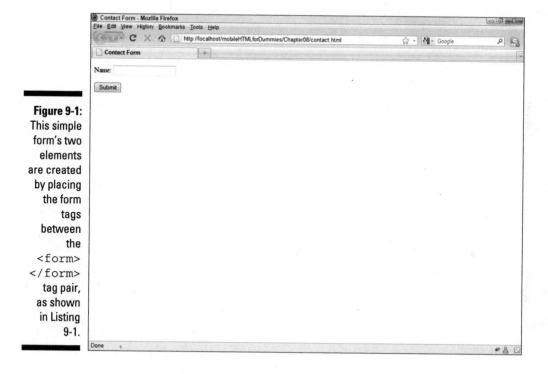

Figure 9-1:
This simple
form's two
elements
are created
by placing
the form
tags
between
the
`<form>`
`</form>`
tag pair,
as shown
in Listing
9-1.

Listing 9-1:   Example of using the `<form></form>` tag pair.

```
<body>
<form id="form1" name="form1" method="post" action="">
    <p><label for="name">Name</label>
    <input type="text" name="name" id="name" /></p>
    <p><input type="submit" name="submit" id="submit" value="Submit" /></p>
</form>
</body>
```

You can start your form anywhere on the page you want. Figure 9-2 shows a form in the right column. The designer accomplished this by placing the form tags inside the `rightColumn1` selector. (See Listing 9-2.)

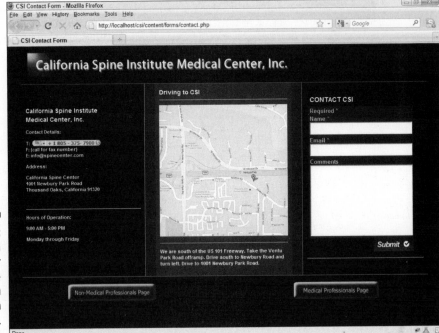

Figure 9-2:
You can
create your
form any-
where you
want on
the page.

Listing 9-2: The form appears on the page wherever you place the first of the `<form></form` tag pair

```
<div id="rightColumn1">
   <h2>Contact CSI</h2>
   <h3>Required*</h3>
<div id="contact">
   <form class="Dark_Default" id="contact" name="contact" method="post"
        action="<?php echo $_SERVER["PHP_SELF"]; ?>">
```

Before you start adding your form elements, the form tags look like this:

```
<form id="contact" name="contact" method="post" action="">
</form>
```

The following is a description of each these form properties and what they do:

✔ **form id** gives the form a unique ID, which is important for a few reasons. First, you can have more than one form or form area on a page. Each form would need its own ID. Depending on your application, you might also use this ID for referencing the form in your scripts, and you could use it for referencing in your style sheets.

✔ **name** serves a similar function as form ID, except that you would use it for referencing in CGI and Perl scripts, which are not in as wide use today as they once were. Even so, many web hosting companies use CGI in their default from-processing scripts; it's a form of server-side scripting.

✔ **method** tells the browser how to submit the data. There are two options: GET and POST. GET appends the data to the end of a URL and is typically used for database searches, and POST is typically used for changing values in a database, sending the data in an e-mail, or uploading files to a server.

✔ **action** is used to specify the name of the script or PHP page that processes the form data. You can see how this works in the "Creating a Contact Form" section, later in this chapter.

Dreamweaver is very adept at creating forms. You'll find each of the form elements on the Forms submenu of the Insert menu. When you choose one of them, Dreamweaver steps you through a wizard-like set of dialog boxes where you define the element attributes. When you finish, the program creates all the required tags to create the element.

Form elements

If you've spent more than a couple of minutes on the Internet, you've probably encountered all ten-or-so XHTML form elements. Each element is designed to handle specific kinds of data, and deploying them strategically not only makes filling out the form easier for your users but it can also help you control how the user enters data. How data — the formatting and the actual wording and punctuation — is submitted can often be crucial to certain data-collection applications. Figure 9-3 shows each of the different form types, which are described in the next few sections.

Figure 9-3:
XHTML form
element
types.

[Figure 9-3 shows a browser window titled "Contact Form - Mozilla Firefox" displaying various XHTML form element types including Text Field, Text Area ("Type your comment here"), Check Box items, Checkbox Item 1, Checkbox Item 2, Checkbox Item 3, Select List, Radio Button items, Field Set with Field Set 1 and Field Set 2, and a Submit button.]

Text field

Sometimes called a *text box*, the *text field* is the most common form element. Text fields allow users to type one line of text, usually in response to the field label, which is typically displayed to the left of or above the field. Use text fields for names, phone numbers, e-mail addresses, and so on. Text fields use the `<input type>` tag and are set up like this:

```
<input type="text" name="First Name" id="firstName" tabindex="1" />
```

You can create an accompanying label for the field with the `<label>` tag. For example, to place a label in front of the field, your code would look like this:

```
<label for="firstName">First Name:</label> <input type="text" name="firstName"
         id="firstName" tabindex="1" />
```

To place the label above the field, simply place a line break `<br />` before the text field or the paragraph `<p> </p>` pair around it.

Notice that `<input>` does not have a corresponding closing `</input>` tag. Many of the tags used in XHTML derive from earlier HTML versions. Unlike XHTML, HTML did not require closing tags. The slash (/) at the end of the tag closes the tag. In fact, you can use this syntax to close almost any XHTML tag, such as the line break tag, `<br />`, for example.

You can also control other attributes of your text fields, such as these:

- ✔ **size:** This controls the length (in characters) of your text field. To make the field 32 characters long, for example, you would use `size="32"`. (This does not restrict the length of the text string the user can type into the field. It simply controls the display size of the field. You can control the length of the text string with the next tag.)

- ✔ **maxlength:** Use this attribute to set the maximum number of characters the user can type into the field. The attribute `maxlength="100"` limits the number of possible characters to 100.

- ✔ **value:** Use this attribute to create a default text string for the text field, or what data the field will hold if the user doesn't fill in the field. Say, for instance, most of people filling out your form are from the United States, you could fill out this field for them with the `value` tag, like this: `value="United States"`, as shown in Figure 9-4. The user can override the default value by replacing the existing text. Listing 9-3 shows how to use the `value` property in your code.

You can use the text field element to create a password field, as shown in Figure 9-4, by changing the input type to *password* (`<input type="password">`), as shown in Listing 9-3. Password fields display asterisks, rather than text, when the user types in the field. Use the *value* attribute to set the password, like this: `value="mypassword"`. You'll need some scripts, though, to make this field do anything other than display asterisks.

```
1   <!DOCTYPE html PUBLIC "-//W3C//DTD XHTML 1.0
    Transitional//EN"
    "http://www.w3.org/TR/xhtml1/DTD/xhtml1-transit
    ional.dtd">
2   <html xmlns="http://www.w3.org/1999/xhtml">
3   <head>
4   <meta http-equiv="Content-Type" content=
    "text/html; charset=utf-8" />
5   <title>Untitled Document</title>
6   </head>
7
8   <body>
9   <form id="form1" name="form1" method="post"
    action="">
10    <p>
11      <label for="country">Country:</label>
12      <input name="country" type="text" id=
    "country" value="United States" />
13    </p>
14    <p>
15      <label for="pwd">Password:</label>
16      :
17      <input name="pwd" type="password" id="pwd"
    value="mypassword" />
18    </p>
19  </form>
20  </body>
21  </html>
```

Country: United States

Password : ••••••••••

Figure 9-4: Example of default value for a text field and a password field.

Listing 9-3: Setting up the initial field `value` and creating a `password` field

```
<form id="form1" name="form1" method="post" action="">
    <p><label for="country">Country:</label>
    <input name="country" type="text" id="country" value="United States" /></p>
    <p><label for="pwd">Password</label>
    <input name="pwd" type="password" id="pwd" value="mypassword" /></p>
</form>
```

Text area

The `Text Area` form element is often used for comment boxes on forms. Within reason, you can make them as big as you want and they can accept as many characters as you want. Text area uses the `<textarea></textarea>` tag pair and the typical text area code would look like this:

```
<label for="comment">Text Area: </label><textarea name="comment" id="comment"
            cols="50" rows="10" tabindex"2" >Type your comment here</textarea>
```

Notice that this code sets the comment box to 50 columns and 10 rows. Columns are the equivalent to characters, and rows are lines of text. To display default text in a text area box, you don't need the `value` attribute. There is no limit to the amount of text the user can enter. If she enters more lines of text than the number of defined rows, the text area box automatically adds a scroll bar to the right of the box. (Keep this in mind when adding text areas to your forms. If you don't want long, rambling comments submitted with your forms, consider not using text areas.)

Select (list or menu)

Many forms provide lists of options for users to choose from. The `select` form element allows you to create lists as either drop-down menus or as display lists. Lists can display the entire list, or a partial list with a scroll bar that exposes the remainder of the list values, as shown in Figure 9-5.

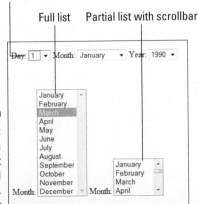
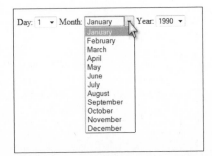

Figure 9-5: Examples of select menus and lists.

Making navigation easier with tabindex

Have you ever noticed that you can move from field to field on web forms with the Tab key? On a well-designed form, pressing the Tab key should move your cursor logically from one field to the next. On not-so-well-designed forms, pressing the Tab key moves the cursor erratically through the form. The difference between the two forms is that the designer of the well-designed form took the time to insert the `tabindex` property in the form element tags. For example, say the first field on your form is `First Name` and the second field is `Last Name`. After the user types in the `First Name` field, pressing the Tab key should move the cursor to the `Last Name` field. To set this up, use the `tabindex` property in each of your fields, like this:

```
<label for="firstName">First Name:</label> <input type="text" name="firstName"
    id="firstName" tabindex="1" />
<label for="lastName">First Name:</label> <input type="text" name="lastName"
    id="lastName" tabindex="2" />
```

Using a tabbing order is especially important on mobile websites. Many mobile devices, especially older smartphones and feature phones, navigate web pages with keys or selection wheels. This is the equivalent to using the Tab key on standard computers. An improperly implemented Tab order can quickly frustrate mobile users. Each browser behaves differently when you don't identify the Tab order. Without it, you often can't predict where the cursor might go next.

Select menus and lists use the `<select></select>` tag pair, and the list options are placed between the `<option></option>` tag pair, like this.

```
<select name="month">
    <option value="1">January</option>
    <option value="2">February</option>
    <option value="3">March</option>
    <option value="4">April</option>
    <option value="5">May</option>
    <option value="6">June</option>
    <option value="7">July</option>
    <option value="8">August</option>
    <option value="9">September</option>
    <option value="10">October</option>
    <option value="11">November</option>
    <option value="12">December</option>
</select>
```

The value between the quotation marks is the value this list submits, and the value between the tags is what the user sees. The example just given sets up a drop-down menu. To change from a drop-down to a display list, you simply add the `size` attribute to the select tag, like this:

```
<select name="month" size="4">
   <option value="1">January</option>
   <option value="2">February</option>
   <option value="3">March</option>
   <option value="4">April</option>
   <option value="5">May</option>
   <option value="6">June</option>
   <option value="7">July</option>
   <option value="8">August</option>
   <option value="9">September</option>
   <option value="10">October</option>
   <option value="11">November</option>
   <option value="12">December</option>
</select>
```

The preceding code would create a display list with the first four options displayed, and the remaining options are scrollable. To display the entire list, simply set the size value to number of options. In the above example, the size value would be 12.

Drop-down lists or display lists?

There are several very good reasons for using select lists over text fields. Forcing the user to choose from a list controls how the data gets submitted — and there are all kinds of applications where controlling what the form sends is beneficial. Say, for instance, you're collecting addresses in a database. Forcing the user to choose his state from a list ensures that you don't get a few thousand variations of *Mississippi* in your database. Using lists to control how dates are sent also saves you from having to sort out umpteen date format versions.

I'm sure you get the idea. There are thousands of ways users can mangle your data collection. Yet another benefit of select lists is that the value sent by the form can be different from what the user selects. Why is this beneficial? Let me give you an example; then, I'm sure, many more reasons will occur to you: Say your company collects customer information based on regions: Southeast, Midwest, and so on. Would you rather your user decides which state falls into what region, or would you rather he or she chooses a state and you — or you select list — decides which region the state is in? For your data collection purposes, North Carolina might be in the Southeast. The person filling out the form may not see it that way. Or maybe you just want to present the user with the names of months, but want them submitted as numbers.

Finally, should you use drop-downs or display lists? This depends on your application and how you want your form to look, of course. If your lists are very long, such as countries or states, for example, the drop-down menu or partial display list saves gobs of screen space — and frankly, they're much more attractive and professional-looking. A rule of thumb I use is: two or three list options go in a display list; more than three go in a drop-down.

TIP

If you use Dreamweaver, the program installs several common select lists in the Snippets panel. To use the preceding month select list, for example, you simply place your cursor where you want the list in your document, open the Snippets panel (click the Window menu and choose Snippets), navigate to the Form Elements, Drop-Down Menus subfolder, select the list you want and then click the Insert button at the bottom of the panel. You can also save select lists in the Snippets panel. The first time I created a states drop-down menu, for instance, I saved it as a snippet. I won't be typing those 50 states again!

You can also set a default value for your lists — you know, a preferred value that is automatically selected if the user doesn't select anything, such as (say) the highest priced widget you're selling in a shopping cart application, by adding the `selected` attribute to the option tag:

```
<option value="3" selected="selected">March</option>
```

Checkbox

The checkbox simply allows the user to switch a value on or off. You've seen this hundreds of times, especially when buying something online or agreeing to software terms and conditions. The checkbox has two states — checked or unchecked — but you can assign a value to a checked box (such as, say, "agreed") to clarify what the checked state is intended to mean.

Checkbox uses the `input` tag:

```
<input type="checkbox" name="agree" id="agree" value="Agreed" />
   <label for="agree">I agree <br />
   </label>
```

In the above example, if the checkbox is checked, the form sends the value `"Agreed"`. Without the value attribute, the value sent would be `"checked"`. As with the text field element, you can also use the `<label>` tag to place a label above, in front of, behind, or below the checkbox. You can change the initial value from `unchecked` to `checked` by placing the `checked` attribute in the `input` tag, like this:

```
<input type="checkbox" name="agree" id="agree" value="Agreed" checked="checked"
       />
```

Checkbox groups

Checkbox groups allow you to create groups of related options the user can select from, as shown in Figure 9-6. All of the checkboxes have the same name but different IDs and values. The purpose is to collect related data on the same topic. You could use a checkbox group, for example, on a medical-history form where you would want users to make multiple selections on the question. In other words, checkbox groups allow users more than one selection per group.

The code for a checkbox group looks like this:

```
<label>
<input type="checkbox" name="CheckboxGroup1" value="apples" id="CheckboxGroup1_0"
            />
   Apples</label>
   <br />
<label>
<input type="checkbox" name="CheckboxGroup1" value="oranges"
             id="CheckboxGroup1_1" />
   Oranges</label>
   <br />
<label>
<input type="checkbox" name="CheckboxGroup1" value="bananas"
             id="CheckboxGroup1_2" />
   Bananas</label>
```

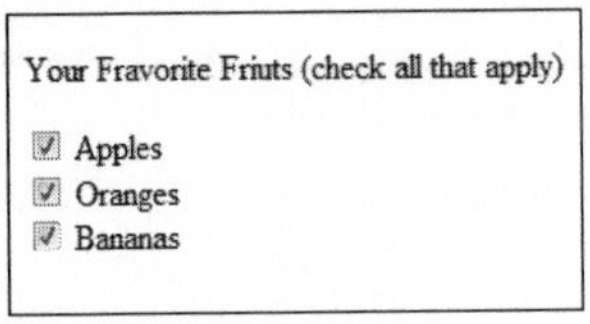

Figure 9-6:
Example of
checkbox
group with
multiple
selections

Your Fravorite Friuts (check all that apply)

☑ Apples
☑ Oranges
☑ Bananas

Radio buttons

Radio buttons are designed to work in groups. Use them when you want to limit the user's choices to just one. Say, for example, you're shopping cart form asks for a hat size. Using a radio button group, shown in Figure 9-7, ensures that you get only one hat size.

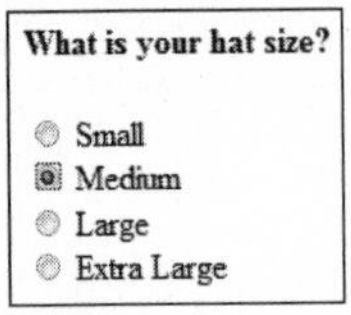

Figure 9-7:
Radio but-
ton groups
allow only
one selec-
tion per
group.

What is your hat size?

◉ Small
◉ Medium
◉ Large
◉ Extra Large

Radio buttons use the `<input>` tag with the `"radio"` attribute. All buttons in the group have the same name, but each button has a different ID and value, as follows:

```
<label>
   <input type="radio" name="hatSize" value="small" id="hatSize_0" />
   Small</label>
   <br />
<label>
   <input type="radio" name="hatSize" value="medium" id="hatSize_1" />
   Medium</label>
   <br />
<label>
   <input type="radio" name="hatSize" value="large" id="hatSize_2" />
   Large</label>
   <br />
<label>
   <input type="radio" name="hatSize" value="xLarge" id="hatSize_3" />
   Extra Large</label>
```

You can set the default — or option that is automatically selected if the user fails to check one — radio button with the `checked` attribute, as follows:

```
<input type="radio" name="hatSize" value="xLarge" id="hatSize_3"
                checked="checked" />
```

Fieldset

A *fieldset* is a set of fields grouped under one heading (or *legend*), as shown in Figure 9-8. Being part of a fieldset doesn't really affect how the fields and other elements in the set return data. Instead, the fieldset arranges and presents fields in a manner helpful to the user or the person filling out the form.

Fieldset
bounding
box   Legend

Figure 9-8:
Example of
a fieldset.

Formatting form labels and elements with CSS

By default, all of the labels use the body, or `<p>` formatting CSS rule, and the form fields themselves have their own formatting — black text on a white background. Usually, this is fine. However, good design often requires that your form pages match the other pages in your site. Or perhaps you're placing a form on an existing page that isn't white with black text, as shown in the figure on the left. In these situations, you can create a set of CSS rules specifically for your form elements.

The black labels in the example are unreadable, and the contrast between white form fields on the dark background is far too stark. You can correct this by creating and formatting containers for the form fields and selectors for the form labels and form text. To change the labels, you can create a selector specific to the form labels themselves, like this:

```
#form1 .labels label {
    font-family: Arial, Helvetica, sans-serif;
    font-size: 14px;
    font-weight: bold;
}
```

This selector targets all text between the `<form id="form1"></form>` tags that is formatted with the `<label></label>` tags — in this case the `"Name:"` and `"Comments:"` labels. To format the fields themselves, specifically the field backgrounds and text the user types into the fields, you can create a selector with the desired formatting and then apply it to the form fields. Here is an example:

```
.fields {
    background: #666;
    font-size:12px;
    color: #CCC
}
```

Now, when you apply this selector to the form elements, using the `class` attribute, like this:

```
<textarea name="comment" cols="45" rows="5" class="fields" id="comment"
        tabindex="2">Type your comment here.</textarea>
```

you get reformatted form fields that look much nicer on your dark page, as shown in the figure on the right.

You can use this technique on all of your form elements. It will also change the appearance of select drop-down menus and lists. You can also use CSS to position your form elements and labels on the page, just as you would position any other object, as discussed in Chapter 7.

Fieldsets use the `<fieldset></fieldset>` tag pair, as shown below:

```
<fieldset>
   <legend>Tell Us About Yourself</legend>
   <label for="name">Name:</label>
   <input type="text" name="name" id="name" tabindex="1" />
   <p>
   <label for="city">City:</label>
   <input type="text" name="city" id="city" tabindex="2" />
   </p>
   <p>
   <label for="phone">Phone:</label>
   <input type="text" name="phone" id="phone" tabindex="3" />
   </p>
</fieldset>
```

Buttons

XHTML supports a few different types of buttons — but the two used most often are Submit and Reset. XHTML buttons on their own — without programming — don't really do anything. (An exception is the Reset button; it will clear form fields without additional programming.) Sure, you can click them and the button will display a simulated "depressed" or clicked state, but that's it. The button won't actually submit the user's data, not until you apply some code to tell the button what to do with the data. Making buttons work is discussed in the "Creating a Contact Form" section, later in this chapter.

You create buttons with the `<input>` tag, like this:

```
<input type="submit" name="submit" id="submit" value="Submit" tabindex="4" />
```

You can create a Reset button by setting the `type` attribute to "reset", as follows:

```
<input name="reset" type="reset" value="Reset" tabindex="6" />
```

Reset, of course, clears the form fields, allowing the user to start with an empty form.

The button's label, or caption — the text on the button itself — comes from the `value` attribute. Buttons are unique from all other form elements in that you can also use graphics files, or images, such as small GIF, PNG, or JPEG files as buttons. This allows you to create stylized custom buttons in your forms, rather than the default button images. For more on this, see the sidebar, "Creating and using custom buttons."

As I said, buttons — just like every other form element — are pretty much worthless until you write some code to handle submitting the form, which is described in the next section.

Creating a Contact Form

The process for creating a form that e-mails the form data to a specific e-mail address, no matter how long the form or how many elements it has, is primarily the same. The steps in the process are as follows:

1. **Create the HTML page and basic formatting.** You can use either standard HTML or XHTML formatting or use CSS style sheets, as discussed in the sidebar, "Formatting form labels and elements with CSS."

2. Create all of your form elements and apply formatting as desired.

3. **Create the scripts to process the form.** You can use either JavaScript client-side scripts or server-side PHP scripts. Whenever possible, you should use server-side scripts. Forms are not the types of files that should require multiple copies of the same HTML page for various handheld devices. If you use JavaScript, not all handhelds can use the form, and you'll need a separate server-side form those devices, anyway.

You can find the files and example code for the following exercise at this book's companion website.

Setting up the form XHTML file

XHTML form tags are pretty basic — and, except for the up-and-coming HTML5 tags on the horizon, haven't changed much in a while. You really don't need any special treatment to display form elements on mobile devices. With that in mind, start a new HTML file and save it as `contact.html`. Then add the code in Listing 9-4.

Listing 9-4:   XHTML form tags

```
<!DOCTYPE html PUBLIC "-//W3C//DTD XHTML 1.0 Transitional//EN" "http://www.
            w3.org/TR/xhtml1/DTD/xhtml1-transitional.dtd">
<html xmlns="http://www.w3.org/1999/xhtml">
<head>
<meta http-equiv="Content-Type" content="text/html; charset=utf-8" />
<title>Contact Form</title>                                              →6

</head>
<body>

   <h1>Tell Us About Yourself</h1>

   <form id="contact" name="contact" method="post" action=" ">          →13
```

```
        <p>                                                              →14
            <label>First Name:<br />
                <input type="text" name="firstName" id="firstName" tabindex="1" />
            </label>
        </p>                                                              →18
        <p>                                                              →19
            <label>Last Name:<br />
                <input type="text" name="lastName" id="lastName" tabindex="2" />
            </label>
        </p>
        <p>
            <label>Email:
                <br />
                <input type="text" name="email" id="email" tabindex="3" />
            </label>
        </p>
        <p>
            <label>Comments:<br />
                <textarea name="comments" id="comments" cols="45" rows="5"
                    tabindex="4"></textarea>
            </label>
        </p>
        <p>
            <input type="submit" name="submit" id="submit" value="Submit"
                tabindex="5" /> <input name="reset" type="reset" value="Reset"
                tabindex="6" />
        </p>                                                              →38

    </form>                                                              →40

</body>
</html>
```

Some notes about Listing 9-1:

✔ **Line 6:** If you want to format your form legends, labels, and other form elements with CSS, you can also enter a link to the CSS file. (You can use the `chapter9.css` file on this book's companion website. If you want to use `chapter9.css`, the code to do so would look like this (insert it directly below the `<title></title>` tag pair):

```
<link href="pathToFile/chapter9.css" rel="stylesheet" type="text/css" />
```

✔ **Line 13 and Line 40:** The rest of the form elements go between these `<form>` tags. Later, you'll come back and fill in the action attribute to tell the server how to process the form.

✔ **Lines 14-18:** This is the first form field. The `tabindex` attribute on the next line might seem superfluous (this is, after all, the first field), but don't leave it out. Without it, the user won't be able to tab to the second field.

✔ **Lines 19-38:** The rest of the form elements.

Scripting your form

There are oh so many ways to script a form so that it submits the form data to an e-mail and sends it. On mobile sites, though, the only foolproof method is server-side scripts, such as PHP. Even then, there are many ways and many different scripts to accomplish this. For example, most hosting companies have at least one form mail-processing script on their servers. The drawback to many of these, though, is that your forms often have to meet a certain criteria, or have mandatory fields, or restrict your design freedom in some other way.

When all is said and done, the script should do these three things:

✔ Collect and process all of the data fields.

✔ E-mail the data in an easy-to read format.

✔ Inform the user that the appropriate form has been sent.

Constructing the PHP script

The title for this section is a bit of misnomer. I wouldn't suggest that you attempt to write your own PHP script (though you can, of course, if you're an experienced PHP programmer — but why?). The good news is that there are hundreds of PHP mail form scripts available on the Internet. There's no way you should have to reinvent that wheel — unless you *really* want to, that is.

What I like about the script I give you here is that it gathers and sends your form data regardless of the number of elements in your form, and it doesn't care what you name your fields. No matter what you throw at it, it processes the data, e-mails the data, and sends the user to a confirmation page, where you can include any text and images you want to tell the user the form has been processed.

You can find the script at this book's companion website.

In order for this procedure to work, your server needs to support PHP and be set up to send e-mail from PHP scripts. If your site is hosted on a server that supports PHP, most likely, it is set up properly to process this script.

To set up your script, follow these steps:

1. **Download the file** `sendresults.php` **and open the file in Dreamweaver or a source code editor.**

   Here is the script:

```php
<?php
//------------------------Set these paramaters------------------------

// Subject of email sent to you.
$subject = 'Results from Contact form';

// Your email address. This is where the form information will be sent.
$emailadd = 'your@emailaddress.com';

// Where to redirect after form is processed.
$url = 'http://www.williamharrel.com/mobileHTML/confirmation.html';

// Makes all fields required. If set to '1' no field cannot be empty. If
         set to '0' any or all fields can be empty.
$req = '0';

// ------------------------Do not edit below this
         line------------------------
$text = "Results from form:\n\n";
$space = ' ';
$line = '
';
foreach ($_POST as $key => $value)
{
if ($req == '1')
{
if ($value == '')
{echo "$key is empty";die;}
}
$j = strlen($key);
if ($j >= 20)
{echo "Name of form element $key cannot be longer than 20 characters";die;}
$j = 20 - $j;
for ($i = 1; $i <= $j; $i++)
{$space .= ' ';}
$value = str_replace('\n', "$line", $value);
$conc = "{$key}:$space{$value}$line";
$text .= $conc;
$space = ' ';
}
mail($emailadd, $subject, $text, 'From: '.$emailadd.'');
echo '<META HTTP-EQUIV=Refresh CONTENT="0; URL='.$url.'">';
?>
```

In order for this script to work properly for you, you need to make three easy changes, as laid out in the next steps:

2. **Find this line near the top of the script and change the current e-mail address to the address where you want the form data sent:**

```
$emailadd = 'your@emailaddress.com';
```

3. **Find this line, directly below the line in the previous step, and change the URL to the URL of the site where you will be uploading this script:**

```
$url = 'http://yourdomain.com/subDirectory/confirmation.html';
```

We will create the file `confirmation.html` in a moment. It will be a simple HTML file with one sentence telling the user that the form data has been sent. Simply supply the URL where you will be uploading the file.

4. **Find the following line in the script, which is directly below the line in the previous step, and change the value according the following instructions:**

```
$req = '0';
```

This line sets the fields in the form to required. In other words, with the current value of `'0'`, all fields must be filled in or, when the user clicks Submit, she will get an error telling her the fields she missed are empty. If any fields are left blank, the form will not submit. If you don't want all the fields to be required, set the value to `'1'`. (This particular approach is all-or-nothing. Creating a form where only certain fields are mandatory would require some much more elaborate PHP programming.)

5. **Save the file and upload it to your hosting server.**

Creating the confirmation page

Have you ever submitted an Internet form only to have it sit there and churn for a minute, and then simply display the same form you submitted? This leaves you wondering whether your form got submitted. A much better approach is redirecting the user to a confirmation page informing her that the data has been sent.

Although you can construct (or find) elaborate PHP scripts that display the data the user submitted, or scripts that allow the user to review the data and change it before submitting it, or a script simply displays a message confirming that the data has been received. To create the confirmation page, start a new HTML page and save it as `confirmation.html`. Then add the code in Listing 9-5.

Listing 9-5:   The confirmation page

```
<!DOCTYPE html PUBLIC "-//W3C//DTD XHTML 1.0 Transitional//EN" "http://www.
        w3.org/TR/xhtml1/DTD/xhtml1-transitional.dtd">
<html xmlns="http://www.w3.org/1999/xhtml">
<head>
<meta http-equiv="Content-Type" content="text/html; charset=utf-8" />
<title>Form Submission Successful</title>
</head>

<body>

<h2>Your Information has been Received. Thank You! </h2>

</body>
</html>
```

All we have left is to tell the form how to find the PHP script.

Making the form work

To make the form work all you need to do is fill in the `action` attribute with the path and filename to your PHP script. To do so, follow these steps:

1. **Open** `contact.html`.

2. **Go to the** `<form id=>` **tag and type the path and filename to** `send results.php` **between the action attribute quotation marks.**

   Depending on where you uploaded `sendresults.php`, type the path and filename between the quotation marks in the `actions` attribute. If `contact.html` and `sendresults.php` reside in the directory, your `<form>` tag will look like this:

   ```
   <form id="contact" name="contact" method="post" action="sendresults.php"/>
   ```

   Some designers keep all their scripts in a separate folder named `"scripts"` or `"php"`. If you have a lot of scripts, this is a good practice. If you saved `sendresults.php` to a subdirectory, your `<form>` tab should look like this:

   ```
   <form id="contact" name="contact" method="post" action="subdirectory/
           sendresults.php"/>
   ```

3. **Save** `contact.php` **and upload it to your hosting server.**

That's all there is to it. You should be able to fill out the form and submit it. The data should be sent to the e-mail address you used in `sendresults. php`. Also, you should be able to click the Reset button to clear the form contents, and when you submit the form, you should be redirected to `confirmation.html` as shown in Figure 9-9.

Figure 9-9:
The user receives this confirmation that the form has been sent.

> **Your Information has been Received. Thank You!**

If you use Dreamweaver, you can fill in the `actions` attribute by selecting the form or the `form` tag and then filling in the PHP script path and filename in the Action field in the Properties panel (sometimes called the Properties Inspector). Also, you can enter each of the form elements from the Form submenu on the Insert menu, which brings up wizard-like dialog boxes for creating each element.

Creating and using custom buttons

Some form applications call for using custom buttons, or non-XHTML buttons from graphics files. You can use any web-supported graphics format, such PNG, JPEG, or GIF created in Photoshop, Illustrator, Fireworks, or any other graphics program — and you can use nearly any graphic file as a custom button. To deploy the custom button, use the `src` attribute with the path and filename that lead to the image file, as follows:

```
<input name="Submit" type="image"
   value="Submit" src="images/dw.png"
   alt="Submit" />
```

Chapter 10

Working with Images, Videos, and Flash Movies

....

In This Chapter

▶ Understanding basic web image technology

▶ Encoding digital video for the Web

▶ Embedding images and videos into web pages

▶ Analyzing using Flash in mobile web pages

▶ Embedding Flash movies in web pages

....

Mobile web users enjoy multimedia — images, digital video, and Flash — just as much as every other Internet user. What they don't enjoy, however, is waiting for gruelingly slow multimedia files that take too long to download, or, even worse, downloaded files that don't work well or don't work at all. As a mobile web designer, it's your job to make users' multimedia experience on your site as pleasant as possible.

When working with media files — especially media files on mobile devices — this is seldom simply a matter of loading the file into a web page and moving onto the next task. Media files designed to appear on computers usually need optimizing for playback in web pages — and, to reemphasize, this is especially true when loading them into mobile web pages.

In this chapter you learn how to place multimedia files into web pages, which in itself is easy enough — you simply write the necessary code to point to and load the files into the pages. You also learn to optimize your multimedia files, so that visitors to your site don't have to wait too long to view and interact with your media files.

Using Graphics and Images on Mobile Sites

Graphics and images? There's a difference? Well, for the sake of this discussion, yes. Technically, graphics are *graphics*. But when discussing computer-generated graphics, we often make this distinction to discuss the two different types of computer graphics: *vector* and *bitmap*. Vector drawings, such as those generated by Adobe Illustrator or other "draw" type programs are often referred to as *graphics*, and bitmap graphics, such as those generated by Photoshop and other "paint" type image editors, are often referred to as images.

Vector versus bitmap

The differences between vector and bitmap image formats are vast, but as the two formats relate to web design, there are only a couple of things you need to know:

✔ Unless your site is designed in HTML5, you can't use vector images in your website. You must convert them to bitmaps.

✔ Vector images are drawn mathematically and bitmap images are composed of thousands — even millions — of tiny "bitmapped" dots. This difference — how these two formats are rendered — is critical to how you use images on the Internet.

An exception to vector graphics supported in web browsers is Scalable Vector Graphics (SVG). SVG graphics are created with XML and, although they are supported in non-HTML5 desktop browsers, they are not widely supported yet by mobile browsers. My prediction is that HTML5 vector graphics will become the norm for using vector images in mobile browsers. HTML5 is discussed in Chapter 11.

Vector drawings — more than what meets the eye

The advantage of vector-based drawings is that they are drawn mathematically. Because they are created through calculations, they can be resized without causing any degradation in the quality of the graphic. In addition, unlike bitmaps, vector file formats are very small, and they remain small, no matter how large you resize the drawing. Typically, vector file formats are Illustrator's AI and EPS (Postscript) formats. To use them in web pages, until HTML5, you had to convert them to a bitmapped format, such as JPEG. HTML5 supports a vector similar to Scalable Vector Graphics (SVG). HTML5 vector graphics support is literally a game changer for web graphics. Using vector graphics in your web pages is discussed in Chapter 11.

Bitmap images — what you see is what you get

Bitmap images are made up of patterns of strategically arranged dots. This is the critical difference between them and vector drawings. Because vector graphics are drawn mathematically and are easily scaled without degrading the graphic, they're said to be *device-independent* (or, sometimes, *resolution-independent*), meaning that they adapt their resolution regardless of the device on which they are displayed or reproduced. When displayed on computer monitors, for example, they appear at 72 dpi. When printed on printing presses, they can print at 300 dpi and beyond — even if you double, triple, or quadruple the image size.

Bitmap images are *device-dependent*, meaning that they maintain the *resolution*, or *dots per inch* (dpi), of the *device they were created on*. If, for example, you scan an image at 72 dpi, the data — the dots that make up the image — make up the entire image. That's it — there's no way to add any more data (or dots) to the image. When you resize them, you change the dpi. In other words, if you increase the size of a 72-dpi image, you reduce the resolution because you increase the space between the dots. This can cause jagged edges, or "jaggies," as shown in Figure 10-1.

Figure 10-1:
Figure 10-1:
Increasing
the size
of bitmap
images
stretches
the distance
between the
bitmapped
dots,
degrading
the
quality of
the image.

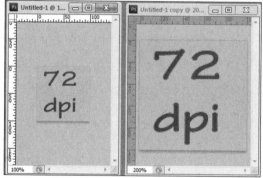

Display resolutions

Until recently, all computer monitors and nearly all handhelds displayed at 72 dpi. The new HD (High Definition) devices display at 96 dpi. If you produce images at higher resolutions, the data used to create the higher resolution — even though it must be downloaded, is ignored (or discarded). Therefore, creating images at resolutions higher than 72 (or 96) dpi doesn't actually increase the quality of your images. Instead, all you accomplish is creating larger file sizes that your mobile users' devices must download before the images can be displayed.

Color (or bit) depth

Another important consideration in balancing image quality and file size is *color*, or *bit*, depth. An image's bit depth measures the number of colors it can contain, as shown in Table 10-1.

Table 10-1	The Number of Possible Colors for Each Bit Depth
Bit Depth	**Possible Colors**
4-bit	16 colors
8-bit	256 color
16-bit	Thousands of colors
24-bit	Millions of colors

Adjusting the color depth on graphics that don't require high bit-depth settings can reduce file size significantly.

Deploying images with HTML

When you have your image file set up and saved at the right size, resolution, and color depth, you can import it into your web page with the `<img src>` tag, which, when you insert the code in the page or a CSS container (see Chapter 7), tells the browser where to load the image on the page. The `<img src>` tag also tells the browser where on the server to find the image file. In the following code, the browser knows to look in the `images` subdirectory of the root directory of the website:

```
<img src="images/logo.png" />
```

You can also modify the image display size with your code, as described under the section, "Image display size," later in this chapter, but usually it's a good idea to load images on web pages at a one-to-one display size. In other words, create your images at the size you need them, using your graphics software. Why? Well, enlarging them can degrade the image quality, unless you create them at higher resolution than 72 dpi. When creating images for mobile sites, however, you can start with an image large enough for devices with larger screens, and then scale it down for smaller-screen devices. This works fine, as long as your file size is not too big to begin with.

Image file size

So what is the right file size for an image destined to appear on a mobile device? The best answer is: as small as possible, without overly degrading the overall image quality. For simple graphics like logos and buttons, keeping the files under 10 kilobytes (KB) is fairly simple. Photographs are another story. Also, different devices and different networks are able to handle larger files better than others.

Mobile users visiting your site on a Wi-Fi connection, for example, can tolerate much larger files sizes than users on the cell 3G network, and users on 4G networks can handle larger images than those on 3G networks, and so on. I try to keep my photographs under 30KB, but that's not always possible — especially when the image takes up all or most of the screen.

Image display size

An image's display size is, of course, the number of pixels it takes up on the screen. You can control the display size on the page with the `width` and `height` attributes. These attributes are entered as pixels, like this:

```
<img src="images/logo.png" width="100" height="100" />
```

If you leave these attributes off, the image appears at its original size.

Making an image a clickable link

You can make an image hot, or a clickable link, by surrounding it with the `<a href>` tags, like this:

```
<a href="http://www.domain.com/page.html"<img src="images/logo.png" width="100"
          height="100" /></a>
```

Internet Explorer and some other browsers place an unsightly blue line around images when you place them inside link tags. You can get rid of the border with the `border="0"` attribute inside the `<img>` tag. However, you can get rid of the border on all images by placing the following selector in your CSS file:

```
a img {
border: none;
}
```

Using Digital Video in Mobile Web Pages

Delivering digital videos to web pages can prove particularly tricky, primarily because the video files are so big. Still, when deployed properly, video clips can be both highly entertaining and instructional. Similar to images (discussed in the previous section of this chapter), before you embed videos in a web page, you should make sure that not only the video itself, but also the video file is optimized for viewing on mobile devices.

Understanding digital video files

Unlike standard computers, most handhelds support a somewhat limited number of video file formats. In fact, many are limited to 3GPP and MPEG4. So, to play it safe, you really should choose between these two formats:

- **3GPP:** 3GPP (Third Generation Partnership Project) is file format designed for streaming playback over 3G telephone networks. Most 3G capable mobile phones support the playback and recording of video in 3GPP format. Other popular video formats, such AVI and MOV (QuickTime) can be converted to 3GPP (which has a .3gp file extension) with popular video-file converters such as Adobe Media Encoder (which comes with several Adobe products, such as Flash and Photoshop). This format is quite similar in features to MPEG4.

- **MPEG4:** Other than Adobe's FLV (Flash Video) format, MPEG4 (Moving Picture Experts Group 4), or MP4, is probably the most common video format on the Internet. It's highly versatile and does a great job of compressing video to make the files small enough to stream and play back in low-bandwidth environments.

Embedding, downloading, and playing digital videos

How well a video downloads and plays in web pages, especially mobile web pages, depends on a number of related factors, including:

- Frames per second (FPS) or frame rate
- Display size (or frame size)
- Compression
- Sound resampling (or compression)
- Streaming

Balancing these aspects of a digital video can be crucial to how well it plays over the Internet, especially over the mobile web on handheld devices. Let's take a brief look at each of them.

Frames per second (FPS)

One way to look at digital video is a as a series of slightly different images that appear in rapid succession to simulate movement. Each of those images is a *frame*, and the simulation of movement often depends on how many frames appear per second. The measurement is, in fact, frames per second, or FPS.

If you look at each frame as a separate image, you can see how this setting can greatly affect the file size. Removing frames removes images — a lot of data — but removing too many frames can make a video play jerkily.

You can use a media encoder, such as Adobe Media Encoder, to reduce the number of frames per second in your videos.

Generally, the process of making media files smaller, whether it's dropping frames, reducing the display size, or compression, entails removing data. Removing data can reduce quality. When the data has been removed, you can't put it back in or reverse the process — the damage is done. So, you should, whenever possible, make these changes to copies of your media file. You can't go backward. Adobe Media Encoder creates a separate encoded file, leaving the original unaltered.

Display size

Often referred to *frame size,* display size operates similarly to images, discussed earlier in this chapter, and greatly affects the video's file size. You can set your video to various display sizes by creating different versions of the video, or separate files. Although it's tempting to resample them to full screen size of the target device, keep in mind that the larger the display size, the larger the file size. Formatting a video to (say) the full display size of an iPad creates a huge file, and you'd probably need a really good media server and more-than-decent bandwidth to stream that much data to a mobile device.

Unlike images, resizing the display size is not simply a matter of opening the video in a program like Photoshop and instantly change the height and width. Instead, changing the display size of a digital video requires *resampling* or *encoding* the file in some kind of video converter or encoder program.

You can also use a video-editing program, such as iMovie or Adobe Premier, but encoders and converters tend to do the work faster. Another advantage of video converters or encoders is that most of them allow you to encode multiple files in batches, rather than having to set up each video one at time. In Figure 10-2, for example, I have several files queued up to encode one after the other. I can either take a nap or continue working while the videos encode in the background.

Media encoding programs, such as Adobe Media Encoder, which come free with several popular Adobe programs, such as Flash, Premier, and Photoshop, allow you to make multiple format changes — frame width, frame height, format, sound compression, cropping, and many other settings — to your video files at once, as shown in Figure 10-3.

Compression

Of all the ways to make video files smaller, compression removes the most data, making the file smaller — doing the most to make the file downloadable over the Internet. It can also, when applied too heavily, greatly degrade the video's quality.

As discussed in the section on working with images earlier in this chapter, there are two types of compression: *lossy* and *lossless*. Usually, when resampling video, lossy compression is required. Lossless compression doesn't remove enough data to affect file size much at all. Both MPEG4 and 3GPP do a very good job at compressing video without drastically degrading quality, as long as you don't go too far.

Compression occurs by applying somewhat sophisticated formulas to the data in the files. Most encoders, rather than forcing you to understand the formulas, allow you to choose a percentage of compression, or different quality levels, such as Maximum, High, Good, and Low. My experience with video compression settings in encoding or video-editing programs is that you usually have to experiment with the settings to find the right balance between quality and file size, at least until you get familiar with the program. Some programs come with presets for Internet streaming, and often these work fine. But not all digital video is the same, so using the same compression setting on all videos doesn't always work out.

Figure 10-2:
Media encoders such as Adobe Media Encoder allow you to process multiple video files in batches.

Cropping

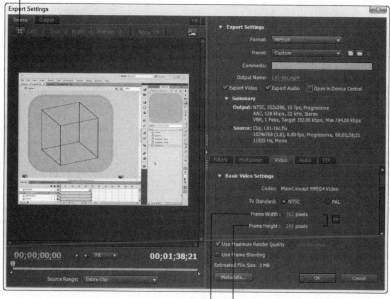

Figure 10-3:
Using a
media
encoder
to specify
settings and
make format
changes
before
encoding
the file.

Frame width Frame height

Sound resampling (compression)

Nearly every video file has a soundtrack. In fact, when you open the video file
in a video-editing program, you not only see the soundtrack separately but
you can also edit it separately.

Changing the sound settings in a video can also help greatly in reducing the
file size. A good media encoder, such as Adobe Media Encoder, will let you
set the sound compression and quality settings during the encoding setup
process. The three main settings to change are described here:

✔ **Sample rate:** An audio file's sample rate is measured in *kilohertz* (kHz).
  Let's not get all geeky here about what this means. Just be aware that a
  higher kHz increases sound quality and file size. A lower kHz does the
  opposite. A good, safe setting for digital video in web pages is 44 kHz.

✔ **Sample type:** This setting specifies sound quality as *bits per second* (bps).
  Again, the higher the bps, the higher the sound quality and larger the file
  size, and vice versa. A good setting for web pages is 128 bps or 16 Kbps.

✔ **Mono versus stereo:** Yes, nowadays computers do a pretty good job of playing stereo music and other types of stereo audio files. But keep in mind that not all files need two channels. Sound effects — such as mouse clicks, glass breaking, whatever — don't benefit from playing in stereo. Use a stereo setting only when the content of the file calls for stereo. Mono files are much smaller. Most mobile devices don't do stereo (except over headphones when the user is listening to music), and the ones that do don't do it justice.

It's tempting to go all-out and make the soundtracks of your videos extravagant masterpieces, but let's face it: Many computers, especially laptops, don't have the sound systems to take full advantage of all that data. And there's certainly no good reason to force your mobile users to download all that extra sound data — unless, of course, the sound and the sound quality are an extremely necessary part to the overall message of the video (say, when a user is comparison-shopping for music equipment).

Streaming

Rather than a form of video file compression or manipulation prior to deploying a video on the web, *streaming* is a process for delivering video files from the server to the end user's device. What streaming does is open a video channel, or stream, between the server and the device where, in addition to delivering the video, the two endpoints send information back and forth about the video download.

The primary objective behind streaming is twofold: First to eliminate the need for the end-user to wait for the entire video to download before it starts playing, and to ensure a smooth, uninterrupted playback of the video while it downloads.

Essentially, there are two types of video streaming: *video streaming* itself, which requires a video (or media) streaming server, and *progressive streaming*, which does not. Progressive streaming occurs between the video file and the player — the software on the device that plays the video. There is no media server involved. Support for progressive streaming must be encoded into the video file.

Perhaps the most developed form of progressive streaming is Adobe's extension of later versions of Flash Player and Flash Video file formats into file types such as FLV and SWF. Flash Player can also stream MP4 and 3GP files, but the files need to be embedded in a Flash movie in order for Flash Player to stream them. Because many mobile devices don't support Flash, this is not always the best approach.

Video streaming requires a media server set up for the purpose, known as (of course) a *streaming server*. A classic example of a media server is YouTube. When users play videos embedded in web pages displayed on computers, YouTube videos are streamed to Flash Player, but YouTube also has also delivery methods for devices that don't support Flash.

Many hosting companies offer media servers as part of their hosting service. Some charge for it, and some don't. Often, using a media server requires special treatment of the video files — not only in your web page code, but also in the server and the video files themselves. Because all this can vary widely from hosting service to hosting service, it's not really something I can go into here. If your hosting company offers a streaming service, it should also provide instructions on how to use that service, including specifications for the code and treatment of the video files.

If this sounds like a lot of work, well, if you use long, high-quality videos in your mobile web pages, it's worth the effort. Your videos will work much better and your users will appreciate it.

Deploying digital videos in web pages

YouTube offers an easy and effective way to deploy videos in your websites — without a high learning curve. If your video is small and short enough to play smoothly without a media server, you can insert it in your web pages with the `<embed></embed>` tag pair, like this:

```
<embed src="video/filename.3gp"></embed>
```

You can control the size of the video with the height and width attributes, like this:

```
<embed src="video/filename.3gp" width="352" height="288"></embed>
```

Also, you can set the video to start automatically, as follows:

```
<embed src="video/filename.3gp" width="352" height="288" autostart="true"></embed>
```

If you don't want the video to play automatically, set `autostart` to `"false"`. This configuration will display the video and play it wherever you insert this code on your page or CSS container, as discussed in Chapter 7. You should save the movie as 3GP; otherwise, to display the video with a set of playback controls, you'll need some assistance, such as some kind of plug-in or player, (which is another reason why Flash and/or YouTube is so popular among designers — because it's so easy to deploy).

Figure 10-4 shows the results of the code just given when inserted into a web page viewed with the iPhone 3.0 user agent (user agents are discussed in Chapters 4 and 5).

Video track

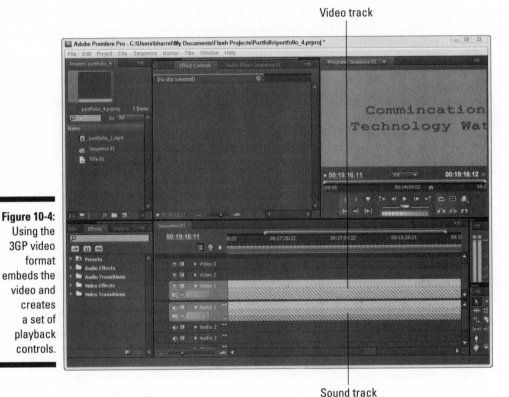

Sound track

Understanding Flash on Mobile Devices

Adobe Flash is a huge part of the Internet. In fact, as I write this, Flash Player is installed on more Internet-capable devices than any other software — even for mobile devices, despite Apple's refusal to allow it on their handhelds. When most people think of Flash, they think of animation, but Flash does so much more. Flash Video (FLV) is the prevailing method for delivering digital video content. Many of the fancy animated buttons and menus you see on web pages are made with Flash, and Flash is the driving force behind Internet applications such as online courses, surveys, and many other data-driven applications.

Flash on mobile devices, however, has been a mixed bag. The implantation has been spotty and problematic; one reason is that Flash applications and Flash Player tend to be memory hogs. In addition, up until recently, processors and memory allocations for mobile devices have been relatively underpowered and small.

Adobe responded to this problem initially by releasing a smaller, less capable version of Flash Player called *Flash Lite* specifically for mobile devices. As I write this, Flash Lite has spawned seven versions and a separate player for iPhone OS — and the many different handhelds in use today use different versions.

iPhone OS is for developing iPhone apps with Flash, not for developing web content for iPhones.

Before taking a brief look at these different versions and how they affect designing Flash applications for web pages, I should point out that much of the discussion of digital video in the previous section is also relevant to Flash content. Flash movie quality and file sizes are also managed by controlling display size, compression, frames per second, and sound resampling; Flash also benefits greatly from being deployed on media servers.

Flash Lite

Flash Lite is deployed on hundreds of thousands of mobile devices. There have been seven major releases of Flash Lite. To understand what each version supports, you have to know a little about the history of Flash — or at least the history of the programming language behind Flash, ActionScript. Since the introduction of Flash, there have been three major releases of ActionScript: ActionScript 1.0, ActionScript 2.0, and ActionScript 3.0. Each overhaul of ActionScript has greatly increased the power of the application, as well as what Flash designers and developers can do with Flash.

Flash Lite 1.0 and 1.1 are subsets of ActionScript 1.0, meaning that they support stripped-down sets of ActionScript functions. Flash 2.0 and 2.1 are subset of ActionScript 2.0, meaning that they support stripped-down sets of ActionScript 2.0 functions. Flash Lite 3.0 is a subset of ActionScript 3.0, the latest version of ActionScript in wide use today. Flash Lite 4.0 is an upgrade to Flash 3.0. It adds multi-touch functionality and is based on the most current full version of Flash Player, Flash Player 10.

None of these versions can do everything Flash Player can do — and in the case of Flash Lite 4.0, it does — things (such as multi-touch on computers) that the current version of Flash Player can't do. When you're creating or deploying Flash content for mobile devices that use Flash Lite, you can, as part of creating your different class versions of your website, create sub-classes for Flash content. Granted, this is a lot of work, and most designers don't do this.

The best place to find out which devices support which versions of Flash is Adobe Device Central, discussed in Chapter 4. You can sort Device Central's mobile device database by which Flash Lite versions the devices support, as shown in Figure 10-5.

Figure 10-5:
Adobe's
Device
Central
allows
you to sort
devices by
which Flash
Player they
support.

Flash Player 10

The latest and greatest version of Flash Player is version 10.x. Many of the newest smartphones and tablets on the market today have abandoned Flash Lite for the full-blown version of Flash Player. Faster processors and more memory, of course, are the reasons why manufacturers can build full Flash support into their devices. And as I write this, the first round of dual-processor devices is hitting market; they'll play Flash content much faster and better than ever was possible on mobile devices. This is great news for Flash designers and web designers alike.

For example, the page in Figure 10-6 has three Flash movies embedded in it: the main movie itself — which allows users to view different versions of the movie based on language — and the two buttons. Although embedding Flash content into a website can be a fairly easy and straightforward process, many Flash movies benefit from using JavaScript instructions to control their behavior and appearance, which I discuss in a moment.

Deploying Flash movies in web pages

Most designers use either Flash Professional or Dreamweaver to embed Flash content into websites. Why? Well, because there are a lot of possible variables that control aspects of how the movie plays, and both these programs are good at covering all the bases.

For example, both Dreamweaver and Flash include JavaScript instructions that check the user's Flash Player version to make sure the version she has is compatible with the movie. If it's not, it offers the user the option of downloading and installing the latest version of Flash Player (Granted, this isn't necessary right now on many mobile devices, but we are already seeing tablets and other handhelds that use Flash Player 10 and have the ability to update it through the browser.).

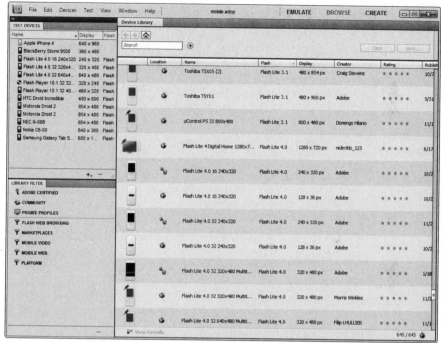

Figure 10-6:
Three Flash movies embedded in a web page.

Flash movies also benefit from using the `<object>` tag with parameters to control various aspects of how the movie plays — such as movie quality, background color, whether to allow the movie to play full-screen, and several other options. (The `object` element supplies the browser with information to load and render objects that are not native to the browser, such as Flash movies and digital videos.) Again, all this is not necessary simply to play the movie in the web page, but it all serves a valuable purpose.

However, playing Flash Movies in web pages does usually require some JavaScript. It's usually a good idea to let either Flash Professional or Dreamweaver generate those scripts automatically, so you really should use one of these programs to embed your Flash movies in your pages for you.

Switching content for non-Flash devices

Okay, so what about the mobile users who come to your site with handhelds that don't support Flash at all, namely iPhones, iPods, and iPads? Here are two methods for providing those users with alternate content. The first method simply replaces the Flash content (such as banners and menus) with a static image. The second method sends iPhone, iPod, and iPad users to an alternative page.

Providing alternate content

If you want to go the PHP route, then you need to rename your files with a `.php` extension rather than `.html` so that the server pipes the request through the PHP engine.

You may not need to serve up separate pages — if the Flash content is only part of the page and not the entire page or site, then you can add fallback images/content like this:

```
<object
type="application/x-shockwave-flash" data="../flash/ banner.swf"
width="600" height="66">
<param name="movie" value="../flash/banner.swf"/>
<param name="loop" value="false"/>
<param name="wmode" value="transparent"/>
<img class="bordered" src= "./images/banner.jpg" width="600" height="66"
            alt="some suitable text"/>
</object>
```

If Flash isn't available, then the image is shown; if images are disabled, then the alternative text is shown.

Redirecting Apple handhelds

You'll want to add this near the top of the `<head>` section so that the redirect happens immediately and the user doesn't load any unnecessary content. I put it just below the content-type `<meta>` tag, and above the `<title>` tag.

```
[HTML]<script type="text/javascript">
if(navigator.userAgent.match(/iP(od|hone)/i)
{
location.href='http://www.yourdomain.com/iPhone/index.html';
}
</script>[/HTML]
```

Also, you'll have to add that same code snippet to each of your pages — so, on your other nonmobile pages, you'll need to redirect the iPhone users to `/iPhone/index.html`. Why? Well, if people are getting to your site via search engines, they won't always arrive on the home page.

Chapter 11

Getting to Know HTML5 and CSS3

*M*ost of the millions of smartphones, iPads, and other tablets sold over the past few years support HTML5 and CSS3. As a result — as more time passes and they only get more pervasive — the lives of web designers get easier. Eventually we'll all be designing to these new standards and won't have to worry about which devices support what.

I've read several claims that HTML5 will do away with third-party animations, such as Flash, as well as JavaScript and PHP, and all we'll need is HTML5 and CSS3. But I'm not so sure that the people making these claims understand these technologies as web design tools. Flash is a lot more than just a simple animation program for creating animated menus, fades, rollovers and the like — and JavaScript and PHP do a lot more than format pages. HTML5 doesn't come close to creating the applications that developers can engineer with client-side and server-side programming.

However, HTML5 and CSS3 are still pretty great. They eliminate the need to jump over to third-party applications for simple stuff — such as drop shadows and rounded corners on boxes and containers — in Photoshop. In short, the new standards are pretty sophisticated, and surely will save us all some time, as well as make web page files smaller, but they don't eliminate the need for programming, application development and animation programs, and graphics editors.

With that said, this chapter takes an in-depth look at the HTML5 and CSS3, and the most interesting and useful new features.

Discovering HTML5's Latest and Greatest Features

So, you may be asking yourself, if there's a new way of doing things — HTML5 — on the horizon, why am I learning the old way (HTML4)? Welcome to the world of computer design: It obsolesces even while you watch, and in that way it's no different from any other 21st-century technology profession. Just as doctors and teachers need to stay abreast of the latest and greatest technologies in their fields, web page designers (successful ones, that is) must keep up with the changes in their industry. The good news is that, usually, the changes are good and, in the long run, they save you time and money. Right now though, as I write this, web designers — especially mobile web designers — cannot get by if they rely solely on HTML5 and CSS3. These technologies, like mobile web technology in general, are not quite ready for prime time. Although they are *becoming* widely supported, not enough mobile devices support them yet to allow you to ignore the older technologies.

So, just what's new in HTML5?

Although the changes in HTML5 are huge, it's fairly easy to categorize them — the features I want to talk about, anyway — into six basic areas, as follows:

✔ **Structure:** In Chapter 7, I show you how to use the `<div>` tag to section off your page into containers — you know, headers, footers, menu (or navigation) areas, and so on. HTML5 has many of these common sections built in. As you'll see in a moment, this can be very handy.

✔ **Vector graphics:** As discussed in Chapter 10, until HTML5, not all browsers supported vector, or Illustrator-type drawing graphics. Also, the bitmaps displayed in pre-HTML5 web pages don't support runtime modifications — changes to the graphic on the fly or as the page loads. To compensate, web designers have used Flash or Microsoft Silverlight to create this functionality. Although learning to create vector graphics with code can be challenging, you can now draw directly on the page with HTML5.

An exception to using vector graphics in non-HTML5 browsers is Scalable Vector Graphics (SVG). Because SVG requires a downloadable plugin to display in the most widely used browser — Internet Explorer — most designers don't use it. Besides, it's not yet widely supported on mobile devices.

✔ **Multimedia:** Designers have been using audio and video in web pages for some time now — but because these elements aren't native to earlier HTML versions, they've had to fall back on third-party applications to help deploy sound and movement. Though these features are still under development, eventually they'll make multimedia easier to deploy in websites.

✔ **Enhanced form elements:** As discussed in Chapter 9, without programming validation into your form fields, getting users to enter data in specific formats is troublesome. HTML5 has a slew of new form field types that can help you control how users enter data into your forms.

✔ **Better font usage:** Font usage has always been somewhat awkward on the Web. Until now, you just kind of called out your preferred fonts and hoped for the best. The new browsers allow you to include font files with your web pages — to ensure that the correct font gets displayed in the browser.

✔ **Other new features:** The Web has been around for a while now, and we've relied on browser cookies to save user information for specific sites. HTML5's local data storage allows sites to save much more data, and much more useful information about the users' sessions on your sites. Also, wouldn't it be nice if your users could drag and drop elements on your pages — say, when they're moving files onto a page for uploading to your servers? (You can do that now, but only with extensive scripting.) HTML5 allows you to create drag-and-drop functionality on your pages. And finally, imagine how helpful it would be to determine where in the world a user was when visiting your site. HTML5's new Geolocation feature will help get that information for you.

Using the HTML5 doctype

To take advantage of HTML5, you must use the correct doctype. (In Chapter 1, I show you the importance of using the right doctype to make sure the browser knows how to format your pages properly.) The HTML5 doctype looks like this:

```
<!DOCTYPE HTML>
```

It doesn't get much easier than that! Out of all this new information, this tidbit should be the easiest to remember, right? This new doctype also eliminates the need for the URLs and `<html xmlns>` statements in the `<head></head>` area of the page. However, you should still add the `Content-Type` and `charset` statement, as follows:

```
<meta http-equiv="Content-Type" content="text/html; charset=utf-8" />
```

You can find the complete W3C HTML5 vocabulary reference, which includes the entire HTML5 standard and tags, at this URL: `http://dev.w3.org/html5/spec/Overview.html`.

The reference at this URL is the Editor's draft and is constantly changing. It's huge, and not exactly a page-turner, but it is a comprehensive reference to the new markup language standard.

Getting acquainted with the new container tags

Technically referred to as *semantic elements,* the new container (or section) tags make it easier (and much more logical) to section off your pages. HTML5 has a new tag for just about every type of page section you would normally create. Here are the most significant new tags (the tag names kind of speak for themselves):

<header>:This element is used to define the heading areas for the sections on your page. You can also use it to create header sections. Headers, as demonstrated in Chapter 7, usually span the entire top of the page, or at least some part of the top of the page.

<section>: This element creates the generic sections of a page, usually the content areas. For example, in Chapter 7, I show you how to create a <div> tag named *content* to hold the main body section of the page. The <section> tag would be a good substitute in HTML5 pages. The <section> areas can also have <header> sections, though it's not mandatory.

<article>: The <article> element is used to define an independent item on the page that can be distributed on its own. According to the W3C, "The <article> tag specifies independent, self-contained content. An article should make sense on its own and it should be possible to distribute it independently from the rest of the site." Some examples they provide are forum posts, newspaper articles, blog posts, and user comments.

<footer>: This new element defines a footer for some part of a page. This tag does not have to be placed at the end of a page, article, or section, but, to me, it wouldn't really be a footer otherwise. In Chapter 7, I show you how to create a footer with a <div> tag. In this chapter, I show you how to create a footer with the <footer> tag.

<nav>: Can you guess what this one does? This is the container for the main navigation links, or menu, on your page. According to the W3C, this element is not intended for use with all link groups and should be reserved for major navigation blocks. For example, if you have a <footer> element that has navigation links, the standard does not require that you include these links in a <nav> element. The <footer> element stands on its own.

<aside>: Use this new element to create sidebars or some other content that is somewhat separate from the content around it. A good example is an advertising block. In Chapter 7, I show you how to create a sidebar with a <div> tag. In HTML5, you would use the <nav> tag.

<hgroup>: Sometimes, a page, article, or section may have more than one heading, such as a title and a subtitle. Take a look at Figure 11-1 for an example. In the figure, the drop shadow on "Article Heading," the rounded corners on the menu box, and the date element were all done without graphics files. The "Company and Heading" and "Subtitle or tagline" at the top of the page were created with the <hgroup> element, using an <h1> tag for the main title and an <h2> tag for the subtitle.

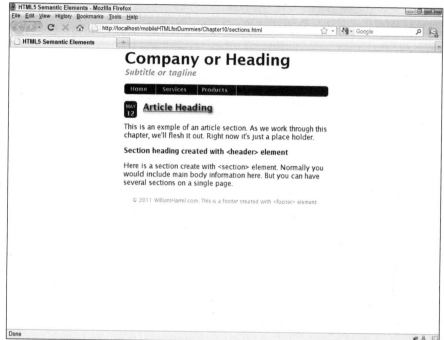

Figure 11-1:
A page
created
with HTML5
semantic
elements
and format-
ted with
CSS3.

Using the new semantic elements

Using the new container tags is much easier than creating CSS containers
and then calling them out in your HTML code. To use these new tags, simply
insert the tags in your code. In this section on HTML5 we create the sections
of the page shown in Figure 11-1; and then later in this chapter, in the CSS3
section, we'll format it.

Start by creating the HTML5 page and add the code in Listing 11-1.

Listing 11-1:   HTML5 semantic elements

```
<!DOCTYPE HTML>                                                        →1
<html>
<head>
4...<meta http-equiv="Content-Type" content="text/html; charset=utf-8">
5...<title>HTML5 Semantic Elements</title>
6...</head>
7...
8...<body>
9...<header>
10...   <hgroup>
11...      <h1>Company  or Heading</h1>
```

(continued)

Listing 11-1 *(continued)*

```
12...     <h2>Subtitle or tagline</h2>
13...   </hgroup>
14...</header>
15...</body>
</html>                                                          →16
17...
<nav>                                                            →18
19...  <ul>
20...    <li><a href="#">Home</a></li>
21...    <li><a href="#">Services</a></li>
22...    <li><a href="#">Products</a></li>
23...  </ul>
</nav>                                                           →24
25...
<article>                                                        →26
27...  <header>
28...    <h1>Article Heading</a></h1>
29...  </header>
30...  <p>This is an example of an article section. As we work through this
          chapter, we'll flesh it out. Right now it's just a place holder.</
          p>
31...  <section>
32...    <header>
33...    <h1>Section heading created with &lt;header&gt; element</h1>
34...    </header>
35...    <p>Here is a section create with &lt;section&gt; element. Normally
            you would include main body information here. But you can have
            several sections on a single page.</p>
35...  </section>
</article>                                                       →36
37...
38...<footer>
39...  <p>&copy; 2011 WilliamHarrel.com. This is a footer created with
          &lt;footer&gt; element.</p>
40...</footer>
```

Here are some notes about Listing 11-1:

- ✔ **Lines 1–16:** This code creates the page and the `<hgroup>` heading at the top of the page.

    If you use Dreamweaver (CS5 or later) you can choose HTML5 from the Doctype drop-down in the New Document dialog box. Also, when you use the HTML5 doctype, Dreamweaver's Code Hinting will suggest code entries for HTML5.

- ✔ **Lines 18–24:** The navigation section and menu list. The pound signs (#) are just placeholders. You can use whatever URLs you want — and whatever text you want throughout this document, for that matter.

- **Lines 26–36:** The `<article>` section. Notice the `<` and `>` around the words *header* and *section*. This is actually the code required to display the greater-than (>) and less-than (<) symbols on the page. Unless it's entered this way, the browser thinks the symbols are part of the markup.

  Your resulting page should look like Figure 11-2.

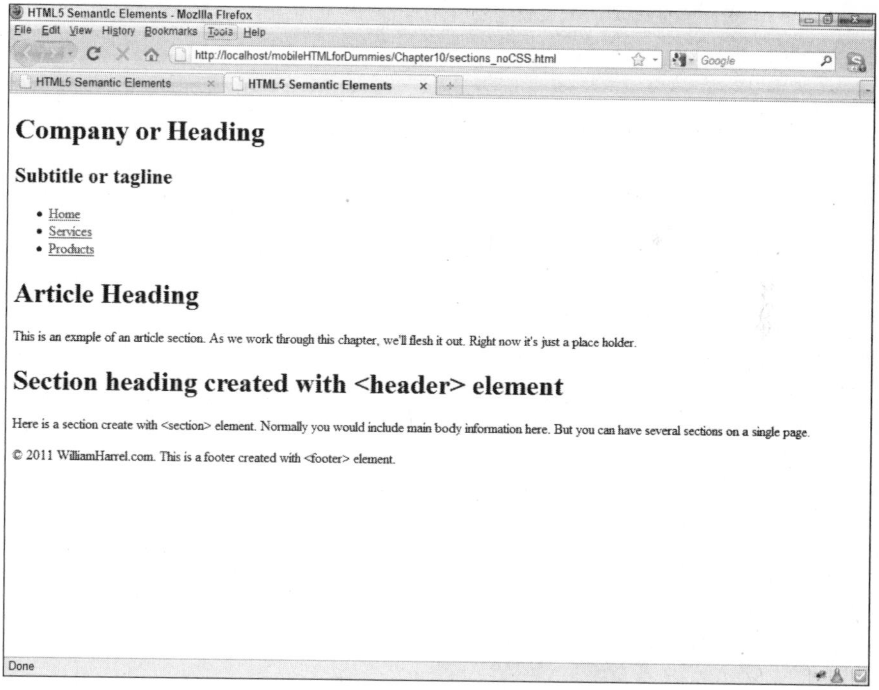
HTML5 Semantic Elements - Mozilla Firefox
File Edit View History Bookmarks Tools Help
http://localhost/mobileHTMLforDummies/Chapter10/sections_noCSS.html
Google
HTML5 Semantic Elements
HTML5 Semantic Elements
Company or Heading
Subtitle or tagline
Home
Services
Products
Article Heading
This is an exmple of an article section. As we work through this chapter, we'll flesh it out. Right now it's just a place holder.
Section heading created with <header> element
Here is a section create with <section> element. Normally you would include main body information here. But you can have several sections on a single page.
© 2011 WilliamHarrel.com. This is a footer created with <footer> element.
Done

Figure 11-2: The web page created from the HTML5 code.

Drawing vector graphics

HTML5 supports SVG — created at runtime, or dynamically, with the `<canvas>` tag. (Vector graphics are discussed in Chapter 10.)The drawings are achieved with either the `<canvas>` tag and some intrinsic JavaScript drawing prowess (a bit beyond the scope of this book). You can also use the `<svg>` tag and an xmlns reference to `w3c.org`, as shown in Figure 11-3. But this still requires some programming skills and some dedication. I've had a hard enough time drawing with high-priced graphics editors, let alone trying to do it with code. (If you're interested in drawing with JavaScript, I suggest you check out *JavaScript and AJAX For Dummies* by Andy Harris.

 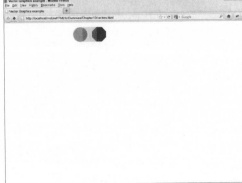

Figure 11-3:
Example
of drawing
an SVG 2D
graphic with
code.

If you're up to the task, there are many things you can do with this feature, including creating interfaces where users can create their own drawings by entering parameters, such as chart data and other preprogrammed information. The sky, as they say, is the limit. For example, check out the drawing of the cat in Figure 11-4. Impressive, huh? So is the code that draws it!

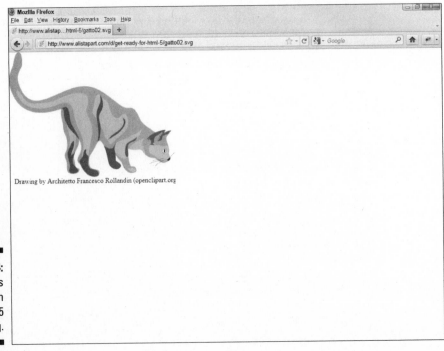

Drawing by Architetto Francesco Rollandin (openclipart.org)

Figure 11-4:
This cat was
drawn with
the HTML5
<svg> tag.

HTML5 multimedia tags

In Chapter 10, I show you how to use <embed> to display video on your pages. I also suggest that you use YouTube or some other video delivery service as a media server. The current implementation of HTML 5 across the various browsers does not inspire me to change that recommendation. The current browser implementation for this part of the HTML5 standards is spotty at best.

There are two new HTML5 multimedia tags in HTML5: <video> for embedding digital video and <audio> for embedding audio. The problem is that the different browser publishers can't seem to settle on, or agree to, which video formats to support.

Digital video

The W3C originally intended to use the free, open-standard OGG container format. But some browser publishers have issues with it. As of today (Spring 2011), only a few browsers— Firefox, Chrome, and Opera are the most notable — support the format. Eventually, all this drama will get worked out, and when it does, the OGG format (or whatever format or formats are finally agreed upon) should work as demonstrated in the following exercise. To follow along, you'll need to download a video in the OGG format from this book's companion website.

Create a new web page and add the code in Listing 11-2.

Listing 11-2:   HTML5 semantic elements

```
<!DOCTYPE HTML>
<html>
<head>
<meta http-equiv="Content-Type" content="text/html; charset=utf-8">
<title>HTML5 Video Example</title>
</head>
<body>
<section>
   <header>
      <h1>Video Header</h1>
   </header>
   <p>
      <video src="big_buck_bunny.ogg" width="320" height="200" controls
             autoplay>
      </video>
   </p>
</section>
</body>
</html>
```

Your finished page should look like Figure 11-5.

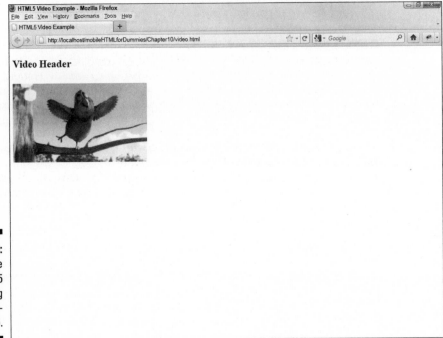

Figure 11-5:
Example
of HTML5
<video> tag
and result-
ing video.

YouTube has jumped on the bandwagon and provided an HTML5 alternative to its current Flash Player implementation. Overall, it works much better than trying to find a video format that will play in all browsers with the HTML5 <video> tag. You can sign up to use YouTube's HTML5 solution at www.you tube.com/html5 (provided you already have a YouTube account).

Digital audio

As is the case of video, discussed in the previous subsection, getting sound files to play across all the different browsers at HTML5's current (Spring 2011) implementation status is tricky, if not impossible. And the reason is the same, as well: some sluggishness (and perhaps disagreements) over the supported format standards.

With that said, you would embed audio files in HTML5 pages in a manner almost identical to the one you would use to embed video. Instead of using the <video> tag, however, you use the <audio> tag, like this:

```
<audio src ="audiofile.ogg" controls"> You can place whatever caption text you
                want here. </audio>
```

HTML5 forms

HTML forms have been around for some time. (pre-HTML5 forms are discussed in Chapter 8) And, until HTML5, they haven't changed much. Most of the common forms' functionality — primarily validation per field type, submission, and so on — usually comes from some form of scripting, either client-side JavaScript or server-side PHP. Many of the new form field types in HTML5 are designed to eliminate all that programming, and that's great news!

The bad news is that so far most browsers have not implemented most or any of these forms features. So far (as I write this) only Opera, shown in Figure 11-6, has made any significant headway in implementing these new features. As you can see in the figure, when these new features are in wide use, they'll be pretty nifty.

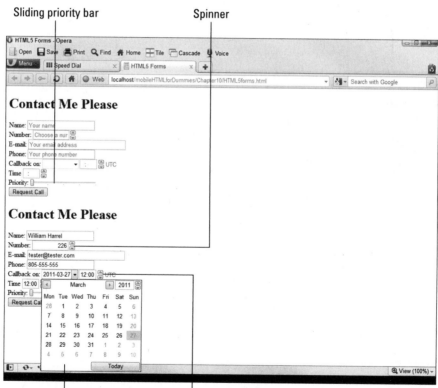

Figure 11-6:
Example
of some
HTML5
form fields
in Opera.
Notice the
Calendar
widget and
the sliding
priority bar.

These new elements could benefit both you the designer and the user in that they can help control how the user enters data. In some applications, as discussed in Chapter 9, how you receive data can be crucial. Just how useful these new elements will become really depends on how well they are implemented by browser developers and mobile device manufacturers. Right now that remains to be seen. Here's an overview of some of the more promising HTML5 elements:

- **Number:** The `number` element confines the field to numeric input. Depending on how it's implemented, you can define a few different attributes to specify how the field behaves. For example, this element supports a `step` value that forces the user to enter values that change according to the `step` criteria. A `step="2"` attribute, for example, forces the input increments to jump by 2, such as *2, 4, 6, 8* and so on. `Number` also supports `min` and `max` attributes that confine the input to a range of values. If you use, say, `min="0"` and `max="10"` attributes, for instance, the user cannot enter values outside of the 0-10 range. Some browsers will also display a "spinner," which is a set of up- and down arrows that, when clicked, ascends or descends the value automatically, as shown in Figure 11-6. In this case, if you use `step`, `min`, and `max` in combination with the spinner, clicking the arrows would adjust the number according to the values set in the attributes. If you were to use the 0-10 step-by-2 values I use in this paragraph, for example, the spinner would advance the number by *2* and stop at *10*.

- **Url:** This element is for entering web addresses. It doesn't have any particular formatting. For mobile devices, though, (when implemented properly) it brings up special keyboard configurations for typing URLs. Some mobile devices already do this on standard, non-HTML5 form fields — when they can discern that the field is for entering URLs, usually when your typing in the mobile browser's Address field.

- **Email:** This element, when implemented properly, configures the user's mobile keyboard for typing e-mail addresses — providing easier access to the @ symbol — and checks to make sure the input is a valid e-mail address.

- **Date:** When supported, this element, shown in Figure 11-7, provides an interactive calendar, allowing the user to enter a date by selecting it from the calendar. A huge benefit of this is that it allows you to control how the user enters the data without having to script the validation.

- **Time:** This element displays a small time field and a spinner (up- and down arrows) where the user can either type in the time or use the spinner. In either case — when the browser supports it — `time` allows you to control how the time data is received from the user.

You can also combine the `date` and `time` elements, as shown in the "Callback on" line in Figure 11-6. The code looks like this:

```
<label for="contact_callback">Callback on:</label>
<input type="datetime" id="contact_callback"><br />
```

✔ **Range:** This element, as shown in the "Priority" line in Figure 11-6, allows users to enter data — in browsers that support it — with a slider. The range element is similar to the number (discussed previously) in that it supports the step, max and min attributes.

Here are some other new elements worth mentioning, with names that, after the preceding discussion, speak for themselves:

✔ color

✔ datetime-local

✔ month

✔ number

✔ search

✔ tel

✔ time

✔ week

Deploying HTML5 form elements

For the most part, the code construction for the new elements is much like using form elements in previous versions of HTML, as discussed in Chapter 9. The primary difference is that now there are several more elements and they bring with them some new attributes. The code for the form in Figure 11-6 is shown in Listing 11-3.

Listing 11-3: HTML5 forms

```
<!DOCTYPE HTML>
<html>
<head>
<meta http-equiv="Content-Type" content="text/html; charset=utf-8">
<title>HTML5 Forms</title>
<link href="forms.css" rel="stylesheet" type="text/css">
</head>

<section>
   <header>
      <h1>Contact Me Please</h1>
   </header>
   <p><form>
      <label for="contact_name">Name:</label>
      <input id="contact_name" width="150" placeholder="Your name" autofocus
            ><br />
      <label for="contact_email">E-mail:</label>
      <input type="email" id="contact_email" placeholder="Your email
            address"><br />
```

(continued)

Listing 11-3 *(continued)*

```
        <label for="contact_phone">Phone:</label>
        <input type="tel" id="contact_phone" placeholder="Your phone number"><br
            />
        <label for="contact_callback">Callback on:</label>
        <input type="datetime" id="contact?callback"><br />
        <label for="time">Time</label>
        <input type="time" id="time" width="100" ><br />
        <label for="contact_priority">Priority:</label>
        <input type=range min="1" max="5" value="1"><br />
        (input type="submit" v alue="Request Call">
    </form></p>
</section>
```

Additional form features

In addition to the new form elements, HTML5 also has two new useful form field features. The first is `autofocus`, which tells the browser to automatically give focus — or make active — a particular form field when the page is rendered. Previous versions of HTML required JavaScript to do this. The second feature is the `placeholder` attribute, which allows the designer to define the text that appears in a field when its empty. Examples of `autofocus` and `placeholder` are shown in Figure 11-7.

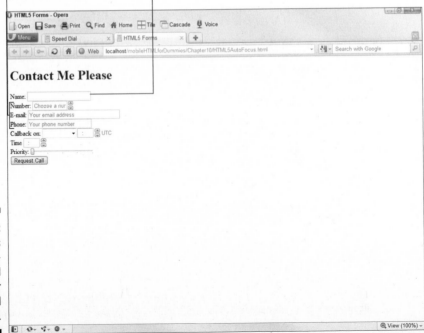

Autofocus ensures the first field is ready to receive input

Text placeholders

Figure 11-7: Examples of the auto-focus and placeholder form field attributes.

Embedding fonts

Font embedding in PDFs, Flash SWFs, and several other types of documents has been around for quite some time. It is new, however, to browser technology (technically, this is a new browser feature and not necessarily restricted to HTML5). With font embedding, the idea is that the font travels with the page file, in this case the HTML file. Usually, font embedding entails enclosing the font file inside the document file. In this case, though, you simply save the font file on the server with the HTML file and call it out in your code, just as you would as an image or video file.

Font files are not small files. And your mobile users will have to download a separate file for each font you use, or each font style you use, such as normal, bold, and italic. So you should use this feature sparingly and not load your mobile pages up with a bunch of embedded fonts.

About font files

Technically, many font files are "licensed," meaning that it's illegal to distribute them. Saving them on a server and allowing users to download them is tantamount to distributing the file. So, to save yourself some grief, use open source formats. You can find them at several places on the Internet, such as Google Web Fonts, at www.google.com/webfonts.

Also, not all browsers support all font formats. Most support TrueType, or TTF fonts, or OTF, which is a free version of TTF. Internet Explorer uses a format of its own with an EOT format.

To make sure all browsers get fonts, you should embed and upload a couple of different versions. You can find a utility for converting fonts for Internet Explorer at www.microsoft.com/typography/weft.mspx.

How to embed fonts

Fonts are actually embedded in your style sheets, rather than the HTML file, as shown in Listing 11-4. When you have them called out in the style sheet, you can use them as you normally do, as discussed in Chapter 6.

Listing 11-4: Embedded fonts

```
@charset "utf-8";
/* CSS Document */

@font-face {
    font-family: "Tahoma";
    src: url(Tahoma.otf;
}
@font-face {
```

(continued)

Listing 11-4 *(continued)*

```
    font-family: "Tahoma";
    src: url ("Tahoma.eot");
}

h1 {
    font-family: Tahoma;
    font-size: 200%
}

h1 {
    font-family: Tahoma;
    font-size: 100%
}
```

To embed and use fonts, follow these steps:

1. **Create a subdirectory in the local root directory of the site — I call mine** fonts.

2. **Call out the fonts in the CSS file as shown in Listing 11-4.**

   Place the font designations near the top of the CSS file, so that they start downloading right away. The @ symbol starts a new CSS element. Make sure you include the path in the url attribute property.

3. **Add the fonts to style selectors as shown in Listing 11-4.**

4. **Format you text as you normally would.**

When users who don't have these fonts on their Internet devices visit your site, the fonts will download and the browser will use them to format the text. Keep in mind, though, that users who come to your site with handhelds that don't have modern browsers can't take advantage of this technology. You'll want to use this feature only for the devices in your class profiles, as discussed in Chapter 5, for the newer smartphone and tablet devices.

Other notable HTML5 features

HTML5 brings a lot of new features to the designer's tool belt. Some are more notable than others. Three in particular that I find interesting: drag-and-drop, local storage, and geolocation. Here's a brief overview of each one:

✔ **Drag-and-drop:** On non-HTML5 pages, to implement drag and drop in any application on the web requires sophisticated PHP or JavaScript. If you've used Google Docs (or some other online application that allows you to upload files), the application allows you to drag files from your desktop, Windows Explorer, or the Mac's Finder and drop them onto a designated spot in the browser window. Some sites deploy Flash to accomplish this; HTML5, when implemented fully, will allow you to pull it off without special programming or Flash.

✔ **Local storage:** Google Docs offers a good example of an application for this feature. The local storage option, when implemented in the browser and built in to your code, automatically saves these documents (online spreadsheets, word-processor documents, presentations, and other file formats, shown in Figure 11-8) on the user's machine. The user can then make changes to the document while offline, and the browser will synchronize the documents when it senses an Internet connection. Currently, with applications such as Google Docs, the user must manually save the document and upload it manually. The file is completely replaced.

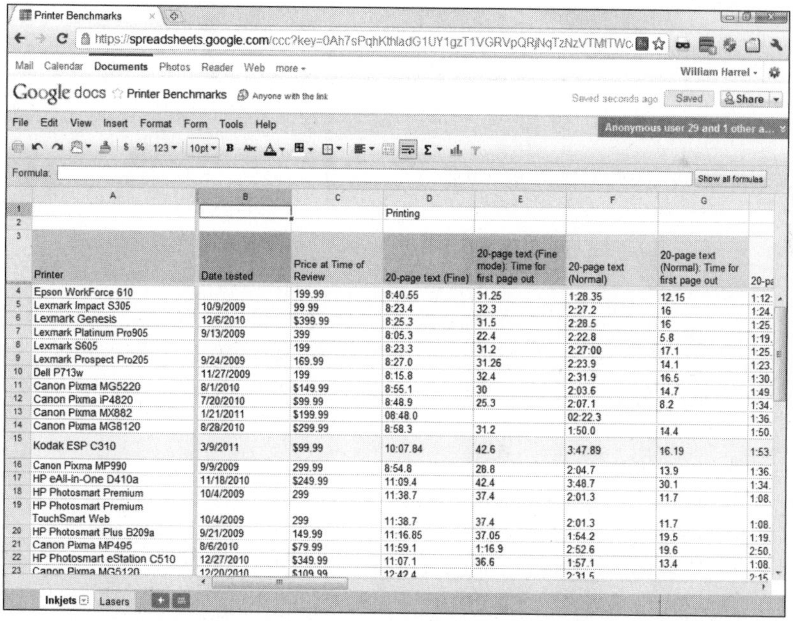

Figure 11-8:
This online spreadsheet is one type of application that can take advantage of HTML5 local storage.

Printer	Date tested	Price at Time of Review	20-page text (Fine)	20-page text (Fine mode): Time for first page out	20-page text (Normal)	20-page text (Normal): Time for first page out	20-pa...
Epson WorkForce 610		199.99	8:40.55	31.25	1:28.35	12.15	1:12
Lexmark Impact S305	10/9/2009	99.99	8:23.4	32.3	2:27.2	16	1:24
Lexmark Genesis	12/6/2010	$399.99	8:25.3	31.5	2:28.5	16	1:25
Lexmark Platinum Pro905	9/13/2009	399	8:05.3	22.4	2:22.8	5.8	1:19
Lexmark S605		199	8:23.3	31.2	2:27:00	17.1	1:25
Lexmark Prospect Pro205	9/24/2009	169.99	8:27.0	31.26	2:23.9	14.1	1:23
Dell P713w	11/27/2009	199	8:15.8	32.4	2:31.9	16.5	1:30
Canon Pixma MG5220	8/1/2010	$149.99	8:55.1	30	2:03.6	14.7	1:49
Canon Pixma iP4820	7/20/2010	$99.99	8:48.9	25.3	2:07.1	8.2	1:34
Canon Pixma MX882	1/21/2011	$199.99	08:48.0		02:22.3		1:36
Canon Pixma MG8120	8/28/2010	$299.99	8:58.3	31.2	1:50.0	14.4	1:50
Kodak ESP C310	3/9/2011	$99.99	10:07.84	42.6	3:47.89	16.19	1:53
Canon Pixma MP990	9/9/2009	299.99	8:54.8	28.8	2:04.7	13.9	1:36
HP eAll-in-One D410a	11/18/2010	$249.99	11:09.4	42.4	3:48.7	30.1	1:34
HP Photosmart Premium	10/4/2009	299	11:38.7	37.4	2:01.3	11.7	1:08
HP Photosmart Premium TouchSmart Web	10/4/2009	299	11:38.7	37.4	2:01.3	11.7	1:08
HP Photosmart Plus B209a	9/21/2009	149.99	11:16.85	37.05	1:54.2	19.5	1:19
Canon Pixma MP495	8/6/2010	$79.99	11:59.1	1:16.9	2:52.6	19.6	2:50
HP Photosmart eStation C510	12/27/2010	$349.99	11:07.1	36.6	1:57.1	13.4	1:08
Canon Pixma MG5120	12/20/2010	$109.99	12:42.4		2:31.5		2:15

Twenty-nine separate *Computer Shopper* reviewers update and add information to the spreadsheet in Figure 11-8. HTML5's local storage feature automatically saves the spreadsheet to the each user's local machine, allowing them to work on it offline, and then synchronizes changes when the reviewers go back online.

✔ **Geolocation:** This option uses the GPS feature found in many of today's handhelds to determine the location of the user. This, as you can imagine, has many applications — such as determining location for help filling out shopping cart forms, getting quotes based on location, and searches for local services. I've been to mobile sites with this feature (scripted, though, not HTML5). All of them ask permission to locate me — very important, for obvious reasons. Some of these sites, such as the Staples mobile site, can locate me right down to the address of the building I was browsing from. This is a bit disconcerting, but a great timesaver — and it can help alleviate some mobile users' frustration when they're filling out forms.

Examining the Most Useful CSS3 Enhancements

As discussed in the previous section, HTML5 is supported rather unevenly across all the popular browsers. The situation is, as I write this, similar with CSS3, and, as with HTML5, the results from using the new rules and selectors differ from browser to browser. Eventually, and not in the too distant future, all of this will level out and we'll get more predictable result from using the new standards. CSS3 — when implemented well — significantly widens the formatting options in HTML documents. In this section, I look at some of the more promising options and how to use them.

The list of CSS3 options — rules, selectors, tags, and so on — is rather extensive. You can find volumes of information about the development of CSS3, as well as the latest news, updates, and changes, on the CSS.info blog, at `www.css3.info`. The entire standard itself, the most extensive documentation, is on the W3C site (see Figure 11-9) at `www.w3.org/Style/CSS/current-work.en.html`.

Again, the new formatting options are extensive. I had trouble deciding which few to highlight here. I suggest you take a look at the W3C site to find others that you might find useful.

Figure 11-9:
The W3C's page on CSS formatting standards, including CSS3.

The W3C also has an extensive tutorial site. It describes all HTML and CSS elements and attributes, complete with great examples. You can easily find information on any version of HTML or CSS with the Search option in the upper-right corner of the page, or from the W3C Tutorial menu in the left column. To find HTML5 info, for example, simply search for *HTML5*. The CSS tutorials pages, shown in Figure 11-10, start at www.w3schools.com/w3c/w3c_css.asp.

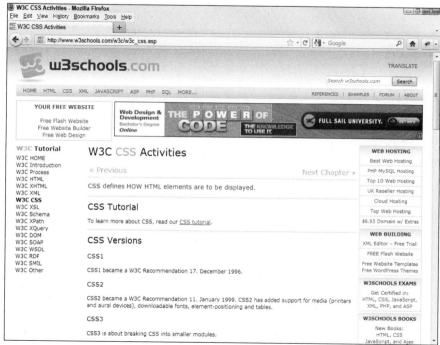

Figure 11-10:
The W3Schools website provides extensive tutorials and examples on how to use HTML5 and CSS3.

Although the list of new elements supported in CSS3 is somewhat extensive, not all of the new features are groundbreaking. The following list discusses the features I think are the most useful:

- **Special effects:** CSS3 has a slew of new effects attributes that really can eliminate the need to use graphics applications in many cases. Especially interesting are the border-radius (rounded box and container corners), box-shadow (container drop shadows), and text-shadow (text drop shadows).

- **Multicolumn:** This one is huge. Similar to word processors and page layout programs, such as Adobe Indesign, this selector will allow you to "flow" text over several columns. When you edit text in the first column, for example, the text behind it will automatically flow, or reflow, to reflect the changes. Multicolumn also has several other useful options, discussed a little later in this chapter.

✔ **Other useful features:** A couple of other interesting CSS3 features include support for some new color spaces, such as RGBA (Red, Green, Blue, Alpha), HSL (Hue, Saturation, Lightness), and HSLA (Hue, Saturation, Lightness, Alpha). No longer will we be confined to the colors in the RGB (Red, Green, Blue) color space, providing a wider range of available colors. HTML5 will also support *media queries*, which allow you to create styles for specific screens or viewing areas. In other words, you can create styles based on the display sizes of various devices; the browser will, in turn, format the page to that screen size, so sometimes you won't have to create multiple versions of the same site. The browser actually queries the device for its current display size.

Using the New CSS3 Features

Take a look at the page in Figure 11-11. Notice the drop shadow around the footer box, the menu bar and on the text in the "Company or Heading" and "Article Heading" text strings. Also take note of the rounded corners on the menu bar and the little box containing the date. Prior to CSS3, every one of these effects required that you create a graphic in an external program. I did all of these (and several other effects) with CSS3.

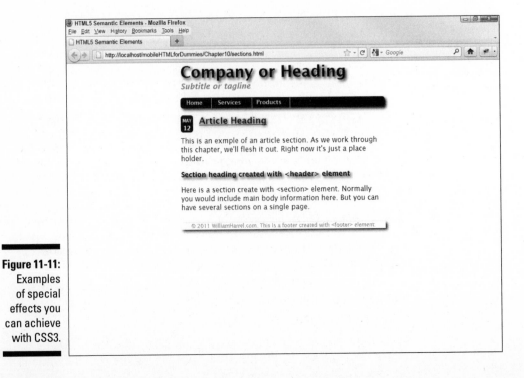

Figure 11-11:
Examples of special effects you can achieve with CSS3.

For the most part, using the new CSS effects is the same as using the old ones, as discussed in Chapters 2 and 6. You just have to know about them and what properties they support, and, of course how to enter the properties in your selectors. With that said, let's do a couple of them.

✔ **Box shadows:** Box shadows (box-shadow) create drop shadows around your CSS boxes or containers, giving them a 3D appearance. Drop shadows are not only attractive, when used correctly and not overdone, but they can also break up the monotony of a page — by subtly sectioning it off. The only way to get drop shadows on your web pages before HTML5 was by embedding background images or drawing them with JavaScript, which is no small feat.

To create the drop shadow for the menu bar in Figure 11-11, you would use the box-shadow property in your CSS selector, like this:

```
box-shadow: 4px 4px 5px #333;
```

From left to right, the box-shadow properties are

- The length of the horizontal offset, or the size of the shadow horizontally

- The length of the vertical offset, or the size of the shadow on the designated side of the box

- The blur radius of the shadow

Positive values for the first two properties put the shadow to the right and bottom of the element. Negative values put the shadow on the left and top. So, the settings we have used here add a shadow to the menu bar offset 4 pixels to the right and at the bottom, with a 5-pixel blur. The last property is the color of the drop shadow. In this case, it's gray.

✔ **Text shadows:** Text shadows work like, and have the same properties as, box shadows. The difference is they use text-shadow rather than box-shadow, and the text itself has the drop shadow, rather than the container the text is in. To create the drop shadow on the text "Article Heading" in Figure 11-11, the code would look like this:

```
text-shadow: 2px 2px 5px #333;
```

From left to right, the text-shadow properties are

- The length of the horizontal offset, or the size of the shadow horizontally

- The length of the vertical offset, or the size of the shadow on the designated side of the text

- The blur radius of the shadow

Positive values for the first two properties put the shadow to the right and bottom of the text. Negative values put the shadow on the left and top. So, the settings we have used here add a shadow to the text offset 2 pixels to the right and at the bottom, with a 5-pixel blur. The last property is the color of the drop shadow. In this case, it's gray.

The text in the header container at the top of the page has a stronger shadow. The property for it looks like this:

```
text-shadow: 4px 4px 5px #333;
```

✔ **Rounded corners:** Rounded corners, as shown on the menu bar and date box in Figure 11-11, rounds the corners of the boxes, giving them a softer, finished appearance. You create rounded corners with the `border-radius` property. However, it's not quite that straightforward. As I write this, not all browsers handle this option the same way. To get it to work in some browsers, you must add a browser prefix to the property. For example, to get this effect to work with WebKit browsers (the default browser on iPhones, iPads, iPods, and most Android devices, you would write the property like this:

```
webkit-border-radius: 6px;
```

The property, of course, sets the size of the rounded corners, in pixels. To set rounded corners in Firefox Mobile, Chrome Mobile, and other Mozilla-based browsers, you would use the `-moz-` extension:

```
moz-border-radius: 6px;
```

Opera browsers, including Opera Mobile, use the `-o-` extension.

```
o-border-radius: 6px;
```

There is a slew of new effects in CSS3, far more than I could list and go over in a single chapter. In the meantime, here is a list of some nifty effects:

`background`: This one is not new, but now it supports multiple backgrounds.

`background-clip`: You can use this one crop your backgrounds so that they don't extend into the border.

`background-origin`: This one is used to determine how the `background-position` of a background in a certain box is calculated.

`background-size`: This one speaks for itself, doesn't it?

`border-image`: This one — that's right — allows you to use an image as a border.

`border-color`: This one isn't new, but now you can use gradients.

`opacity`: This option controls an object's or container background's transparency.

`outline-offset`: When used in conjunction with `outline`, this option allows you to outline a container and then offset the outline by a specified number of pixels.

`resize`: This one, as I've heard young people say, is way cool. It allows you to create user-resizable `textarea` fields, as shown in Figure 11-12.

`text-overflow`: In text boxes that contain more text than they are big enough to display, this option allows you to create a visual indication (or *hint),* such as an ellipsis, telling the user the box contains more text.

`word-wrap`: This option allows you to break words to create better looking columns of text.

Figure 11-12:
Example of
a textarea
field resized
with the
CSS3 resize
selector.

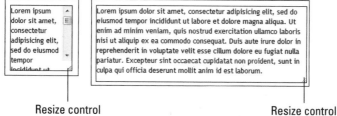

Resize control   Resize control

Using multicolumns

This feature, technically known as *multicolumn layout,* lets you create multiple columns of text without having to create separate containers for each column. Similar to word processors and page layout programs, the text "flows" from column to column. What this means: The browser knows that the columns are one text string instead of separate text strings — one for each column, as shown in Figure 11-13.

This really is a great, long-awaited feature. As I write this, multicolumn layouts are not fully implemented; you have to use browser extensions.

Did you notice that broken-teeth effect in the first line of the second column? This is, of course, the result of setting the text to full-justify with the `text-align: justify` option. CSS3 provides a number of options for adjusting letter spacing to fix this. (You can also use `word-wrap` to break long words to offset this unsightly effect.) Or you can opt not to justify the text in columns. If, however, you prefer justified columns (which does look better for certain types of documents), you can find information on adjusting letter spacing, `word-wrap` and several other helpful features at W3.org, at `www.w3.org/TR/2011/WD-css3-text-20110215/`.

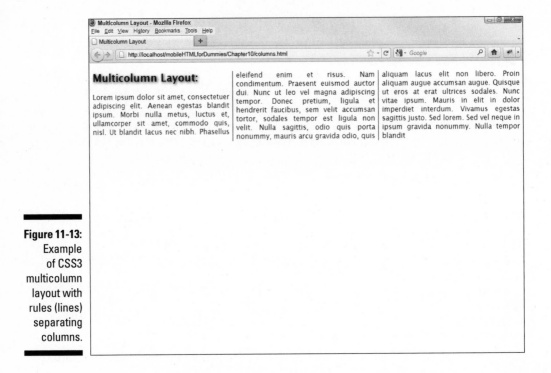

Figure 11-13:
Example
of CSS3
multicolumn
layout with
rules (lines)
separating
columns.

Setting up multiple columns

Multicolumn layout is not, as I write this, fully implemented, but most browsers have adopted it. So, you can use it with web extensions. With that in mind, let's set up the three-column layout that appears in Figure 11-13. Just follow these steps:

1. **Start a new HTML5 document with the HTML5 doctype, like this:**

```
<!DOCTYPE HTML>
<html>
<head>
<meta http-equiv="Content-Type" content="text/html; charset=utf-8">
<title>Multicolumn Layout</title>
<link href="multi.css" rel="stylesheet" type="text/css">
</head>

<body>
</body>
</html>
```

2. **Save the document as** `multi.html`.

3. **Start a new CSS document, as follows, and then save it as** `multi.css`:

```
@charset "utf-8";
/* CSS Document */


* {
    font-family: Lucida Sans, Arial, Helvetica, sans-serif;
}
```

4. **Find a block of text as long as or longer than the three text columns in Figure 11-13 and copy it to the system Clipboard.**

5. **In** `multi.html`**, between the** `<body></body>` **tags, set up the following container framework:**

```
<section>
   <header>
      <p><h1></h1></p>
   </header>
      <p></p>
</section>
```

6. **Between the** `<h1></h1>` **tags, type whatever heading you want.**

7. **Paste the text on the Clipboard between the second set of** `<p></p>` **tags.**

8. **In** `multi.css`**, beneath the font selector statement, insert the following selectors and properties:**

```
header > h1 {
    font-size: 200%:
    font-weight: bold;
    color: #000;
    text-shadow: 2px 2px 5px #333;
}

section {
    -moz-column-count: 3;
    -webkit-column-count: 3;
}
```

This example sets up a three-column layout for most mobile devices, such as all Apple handhelds, Androids, and any other devices that use WebKit- or Mozilla-based browsers. The list of devices that do so is extensive and growing. As I write this, Opera and Internet Explorer do not support this part of CSS3.

 Multicolumn layout for handhelds is limited. Internet Explorer, as of early spring 2011, for example, doesn't support HTML5 or CSS3 multicolumn layouts. You can create multicolumns on these devices with CSS2 `<div>` containers, as described in Chapters 2 and 7, and the JavaScript solution by the folks at cvwdesign.com at `www.cvwdesign.com/txp/article/360/multi-column-layout-with-css3-and-some-javascript`.

Formatting multicolumn layouts

To control column gaps (the space between columns) and place rules (the vertical lines between the columns), you can use CSS3 attributes with browser extensions, as demonstrated in the following steps:

1. **In the** `section` **selector in** `multi.css` **(created in the previous section), insert the following properties and browser extensions:**

   ```
   -moz-column-gap: 1em;
   -webkit-column-gap: 1em;
   ```

   The column gaps are measured in ems. An *em* is a unit of measurement in typography. It defines the proportion of the letter width and height with respect to the point size of the current font. In this case, the column is 1 em.

2. **To enter the rule (line) between the columns, insert these properties in the** `section` **selector:**

   ```
   -moz-column-rule: 1px solid black;
   -webkit-column-rule: 1px solid black;
   ```

3. **To justify the columns, insert this property in the** `section` **selector:**

   ```
   text-align: justify;
   ```

   After you save your two files and open `multi.css` in a WebKit or Mozilla browser, your page should have three columns with rules separating them. If not, double-check your code. It should look like the examples in Listings 11-5 and 11-6.

Listing 11-5: Multicolumn HTML5 page

```
<!DOCTYPE HTML>
<html>
<head>
<meta http-equiv="Content-Type" content="text/html; charset=utf-8">
<title>Multicolumn Layout</title>
<link href="multi.css" rel="stylesheet" type="text/css">
</head>

<body>
   <section>
      <header>
         <p><h1>Multicolumn Layout:</h1></p>
      </header>
```

```
            <p>Lorem ipsum dolor sit amet, consectetuer adipiscing elit. Aenean
                egestas blandit ipsum. Morbi nulla metus, luctus et, ullamcorper
                sit amet, commodo quis, nisl. Ut blandit lacus nec nibh. Phasellus
                eleifend enim et risus. Nam condementum. Praesent euismod auctor
                dui. Nun cut leo vel magna adipscing tempor. Donec pretium, ligula
                et hendrerit faucibus, sem velit accumsan tortor, sodales tempo
                rest ligula non velit. Nulla sagittis, odio quis porta nonummy,
                mauris arcu gravid odio, quis aliquam lacus elit non libero. Proin
                aliquam augue accumsan augue. Quisque ut eros at erat ultrices
                sodales. Nunc vitae ipsum. Mauris in elit in dolor imperdiet
                interdum. Vivamus egestas sagittis justo. Sed lorem. Sed vel neque
                in ipsum gravid nonum my. Nulla tempor blandit </p>
        </section>
    </body>
</html>
```

Listing 11-6:   Multicolumn CSS3 page

```css
@charset "utf-8";
/* CSS Document */

* {
    font-family: Lucida Sans, Arial, Helvetica, sans-serif;
}

header > h1 {
    font-size: 200%;
    font-weight: bold;
    color: #000;
    text-shadow: 2px 2px 5px #333;
}

section {{
    -moz-column-count: 3;
    -moz-column-gap: 1em;
    -moz-column-rule: 1px solid black;
    -webkit-column-count: 3;

    -webkit-column-gap: 1em;
    -webkit-column-rule: 1px solid black;
    text-align:justify
}
```

The `text-align` property is not new to CSS3. You can use it with non-CSS3 and non-HTML5 pages.

Other interesting CSS3 features

CSS3 also includes many other useful new features — enough to fill an entire book and then some. Here are a couple I plucked out of the list that I think are worth mentioning:

- ✔ **New color spaces:** CSS3 lets you define colors from a few new color models, including support for new color values, such as HSL (Hue, Saturation, Lightness) and two color values with alpha properties — RGBA (Red, Green, Blue, Alpha) and HSLA (Hue, Saturation, Lightness, Alpha). *Alpha* measures opacity, or transparency. You can see an in-depth discussion of CSS3 color spaces on the W3C website at `http://www.w3.org/TR/css3-color`.

- ✔ **Media queries:** Media queries allow you to define different styles for different devices based on their viewport, or display size. The device is queried for its current display size; the browser chooses the appropriate selectors. For example, you can provide specific styles for devices with a viewport of less than or equal to 480 pixels (such as some iPhones).

Chapter 12

Understanding Mobile WebKit Extensions and Other Mobile-Specific Options

As mobile devices become more powerful and as browser publishers develop their own extensions — such as Apple's WebKit extensions — the number of design options increases, as does the degree of complexity. Fortunately — as is usually the case with emerging technologies — specific protocols and products begin to break through at some point, separating themselves from the pack and eventually become the accepted way of doing things. Photoshop's domination in the image editing field and Dreamweaver's sturdy foothold in the web design market are good examples.

Open-source WebKit-based mobile browsers are becoming widespread in the mobile device market. Even devices that don't come with WebKit browsers installed are beginning to include support for WebKit extensions. As I write this, Microsoft has begun to include support for WebKit extensions in Mobile Windows 7 Internet Explorer. The point is that WebKit is becoming a force to contend with in mobile web design. With that in mind, this chapter takes an in-depth look at some of the WebKit extensions supported in mobile browsers and how to use them. Although I certainly can't show you how to use all WebKit extensions, the concepts in this chapter — how to deploy the extensions — apply to most of them and will give a general idea of how to use them in your mobile web pages.

This chapter also shows you how to use some HTML and CSS features designed specifically for handhelds, such as the `viewport` option, as well as some mobile-specific options for making sure your sites are displayed in full-screen mode and other specified resolutions. Although many of these options started as WebKit extensions on iPhones, iPads, and iPods, they are now widely supported across several mobile browsers.

What Are WebKit Extensions?

Perhaps few technologies have done more for standardizing mobile web development than WebKit extensions. WebKit started life as a browser engine consisting of enhanced HTML and JavaScript components, originally developed by Apple. But now WebKit is *open source:* the code is available to virtually anybody who wants to modify and adapt it however they need to. WebKit-based mobile browsers are the default browsers on many of the newer smartphones and tablets, including all Apple handhelds, Android smartphones and tablets, and several other devices.

WebKit *extensions* are HTML, CSS, and JavaScript enhancements that provide web designers with several design options otherwise unavailable through standard HTML markup and CSS styles. Many of the WebKit extensions, however, are also available — or soon will be — in HTML5 and CSS3, depending on the mobile browser and the device.

Not all options available to WebKit-based browsers are exclusive to those browsers. The `viewport` feature, for instance — which allows you to control the display size of your website on mobile devices — is a prime example. Also, some of the orientation (portrait versus landscape) options, that originated on Apple (mobile Safari) phones now also work on many non-Apple handhelds. With that in mind, `viewport` and orientation options are designed specifically for handhelds. After all, most desktop and notebook computer users are not constantly switching the orientation of their monitors. Right?

The `viewport` extension is just one example of how the publishers of non-WebKit browsers have taken a WebKit-extension concept and adapted it to their browser. Each browser has adapted different concepts, and which ones varies among browsers. Also, each update of a non-WebKit browser introduces new features, some WebKit-inspired, some not, making defining which browsers have adapted what features a bit of a moving target.

Viewport

Because mobile devices display sites at so many varying sizes and resolutions, it's difficult to control how your web pages look from device to device.

One helpful method is to use the `viewport` meta tag to control several display options, such as the page's height and width, how much a user can zoom in and out on a page, or whether the user is allowed to zoom in or out at all. As you create your various mobile profiles and different sets of mobile pages, you can use this option to better control how HTML and CSS display on various devices.

Like most other meta tags, `viewport` uses the `name` and `content` attributes, like this:

```
<meta name="viewport" content="width=320, height=240 user-scalable=yes" />
```

To control the user zoom, or scale, levels, use `initial-scale`, `maximum-scale`, and `minimum-scale` attributes, as follows:

```
<meta name="viewport" content="width=320, height=240 user-scalable=yes, initial-
        scale=1.5, maximum-scale=3.0, minimum scale=1.0" />
```

When you use `viewport` with CSS styles that define your overall page width and various CSS container sizes set to percentages, as discussed in Chapter 7, you can force your content to fit on various screen sizes without having to create separate style sheets for each device class, as shown in Figure 12-1.

Figure 12-1: Example of page forced to fit the screen with viewport.

You can also use the `viewport` property `device-width` to automatically force the web page to fill the width of the screen. However, this option, which doesn't control the page display height, can sometimes provide undesirable results, especially if you don't want your users to have to scroll on specific pages. If, for example, you wanted the page to fill the width of the screen and disallow scaling, you use the following `viewport` meta tag and attributes:

```
<meta name="viewport" content="width=device-width user-scalable=no" />
```

The `device-width` attribute forces the page to display at the full width of the device's screen. The `scalable=no` attribute disallows resizing. This ensures that the page always displays at the desired width, no matter how the user tries to change it.

Working with device orientation

Most of the new smartphones and all of the new tablets support portrait (upright) and landscape (sideways) *orientations*. If you have one of these smartphones, or have played around with one, you may have noticed that when you turn the device sideways, web pages don't always resize to the new orientation, instead giving you results similar to Figure 12-2. This happens because many devices don't automatically (or adequately) compensate for the change in screen size that results from rotating the handheld.

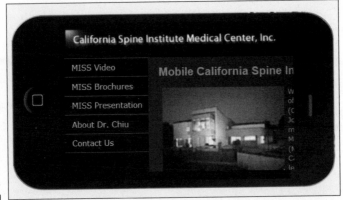

Figure 12-2: Example of mismatched screen redraw after changing phone orientation.

WebKit-based browsers and some others support built-in functions and events to detect when the device orientation has changed and redraw the screen to compensate. The two most common of these functions are as follows:

✔ The `window.orientation` event reports the current screen orientation, using the following values:

> *0* is *portrait mode,* or when the user holds the device upright.

> *90* is *rotated left,* or when the user turns the handheld counter clockwise.

> *–90* is *rotated right,* or when the user turns the device clockwise.

> *180* is *upside down,* or when the user flips the phone 180 degrees. This one is not supported on all devices. Earlier iPhones, for example, do not use it. (Please note that as I write this, not all mobile browsers support this option.)

✔ The `orientationchange` event fires each time the user rotates the device 90 degrees.

On their own, these two options don't do much. When used in conjunction with CSS and JavaScript, though, they're quite handy and can save you a lot of time — by eliminating the need to create multiple class profiles for different screen sizes. In effect, there are three parts of the process and three corresponding files to be created: the HTML page, the external CSS file, and the JavaScript file. You can find these files at this book's companion website.

Setting up the rotatable page

Setting up the rotatable page is quite similar to setting up any other mobile web page. The only real difference is that you use the `viewport` meta tag (discussed earlier in this chapter) to set the initial and maximum page scale. In order for the page orientation scripts to work properly, the initial zoom level and maximum zoom level must be the same, usually *1.0*.

To set up a rotatable page, create a new HTML page and insert the code from Listing 12-1. Save the file as `index.html`.

Listing 12-1:   HTML code for the device orientation project

```
<!DOCTYPE html PUBLIC "-//W3C??DTD HXTML 1.0 Transitional//EN" "http://www.
            w3.org/TR/xhtml1/DTD/xhtml1-transitional.dtd"?>
<html xmlsn="http:/www.w3.org/1999/xhtml">

<head>

<meta http-equiv="Content-Type" content="text/html; charset=utf-8" />
<meta name="viewport" content-"width=device=width; initial-scasle=1.0; maximum-
            scale=1.0;">        →7
<link href="smartphone.css" rel="stylesheet" type="text/css" />
<title>Detecting and Changing Handheld Orientation </title>
<script type="text/javascript" src="orientScreen.js"></script>           →10
<script type="text/javascript">
     window.addEventListener("load", function() { setTimeout(loaded, 100) },
            false);

     function loaded() {
        document.getElementById("page_background").style.visibility = "visible";
        window.scrollTo(0, 1);
     }
</script>                                                                 →18

</head>

<body onorientationchange="updateOrientation();">                         →22
```

(continued)

Listing 12-1 *(continued)*

```
<div id="page_background">                                          →24
    <div id="page_ccw">
        <h2>The handheld is landscape - counter clockwise</h2>
    </div>
    <div id="page_cw">
        <h2>The handheld is landscape - clockwise</h2>
    </div>
    <div id="page_portrait">
        <h2>The handheld is in portrait mode</h2>
    </div>
    <div id="page_upsideDown">
        <h2>The handheld is upside down.</h2>
    </div>
</div>                                                               →37

</body>
</html>
```

Some notes about the code in Listing 12-1:

- ✔ **Line 7:** The `maximum-scale=1.0` attribute in the `viewport` meta tag prohibits user scaling. Without this attribute, if the user scales the page, when she rotates the page, it maintains the scaled display size, which is not the effect you want to achieve with this procedure.

- ✔ **Lines 10–18:** These lines tell the browser about the external JavaScript file and when and how to use it. This script primarily references and interacts with an external JavaScript named `orientScreen.js`. Then it tells the external script when to kick in. Check out the event listener in the third line. This "listens" for a change in the handheld's orientation; when it detects a change, it fires a function named `loaded` — which in turn tells the external script to display the CSS selector that's appropriate for the device's orientation. A look at the external script (in the section, "Creating the JavaScript," later in this chapter) should make all of this clearer.

  In this and other scripts in this section you use the `document.get ElementById` method to identify and call to the appropriate CSS selector. In this example, the CSS `page_background` selector contains the content — the background — you want to display. This is the standard method for deploying selectors in your JavaScripts.

- ✔ **Line 22:** The `onorientationchange="updateOrientation()";` attribute in the `<body>` tag consists of two parts: `onorientation change` is a variation of the `orientationchange` event, which references the `updateOrientation()` function in the JavaScript that you create a little later in this process.

> ✔ **Lines 24–37:** This code controls what the user sees each time she rotates the device. As you can see, there is an entry for each orientation, identified by CSS <div> container selectors. In other words, there is different content for each orientation.

There's a little more work to do on this page — a JavaScript that references an external script and tells the browser how and when to fire it, which we create a little later in this process

Creating the external CSS file

The CSS file for this application consists of several typeface configuration tag selectors, discussed in Chapters 2 and 6, ID selectors for the four orientations, as well as class selectors for each of for orientations. The different types of selectors are also discussed in Chapters 2 and 6. In addition to these selectors, four more class selectors are referenced and controlled from the JavaScript — which makes all this magic happen. I realize this sounds a bit complicated, but it will all come together as we move through this procedure.

Let's start by creating the tag selectors. You don't need all these selectors to complete this particular exercise — the resulting page consists of only <h2> text strings. I have set this up as if you were creating an entire, full-featured web page or site. All these selectors would be necessary in your external CSS file to format multiple pages with various types of text blocks and strings. In other words, you could use this style sheet to create a mobile website with rotatable, self-adjusting content.

Create a new CSS file, save it as `smartphone.css`, enter the tag selectors from Listing 12-2, and then save this file in the same directory as `index.html`.

Listing 12-2: External CSS file for the device orientation project

```
html, body, form, fieldset, p, div, h1, h2, h3, h4, h5, h6{          →1
   margin:0;
   padding:0;
   -webkit-text-size-adjust:none;
   color: #000;
   }

body{
   font-size: 100%;
   }

ul, li, ol, dl, dd, dt{
   list-style:none;
   padding:0;
   margin:0;
```

(continued)

Listing 12-2 *(continued)*

```css
    }

a{
    text-decoration:none;
    }

body{
    background:#999;
    font-family: Arial;
    color:#F00;
    }

p{
    font-size:12px;
    padding-bottom:8px;
    color: #F00;
    }

a{
    color:#333;
    text-decoration:none;
    }

h1{
    display:block;
    width:112px;
    height:41px;
    text-indent:-5000px;
    }
#page_background{
    padding-top:100px;
    background:#000 url(images/page_background.gif) repeat-x;
    overflow:auto;
    }

#page_ccw,
#page_cw,
#page_portrait,
#page_upsideDown{
    display:none;
    }
.display_portrait,
.display_upsideDown{
    width:device-width;
    }
..display_ccw,
.display_cw{
    width:device-width;
```

→44
→45

→49

→51

→56
→57

```
    }                                                          →64

.display_ccw #page_ccw,                                        →66
.display_cw #page_cw,
.display_portrait #page_portrait,
.display_upsideDown #page_upsideDown{
    display:block;
    }                                                          →71
```

Some notes about Listing 12-2:

- **Lines 1–44:** Again, all these selectors do is format the various text strings on the site pages. Notice, however, the third property in the first selector. This is an example of a WebKit extension, as indicated by the `-webkit-` prefix. This particular extension tells the browser not to adjust the font size. In other words, the font will remain the same size no matter what size the display switches to after the device's orientation changes.

- **Lines 45–49:** This selector creates the only content on this page, as shown in Figure 12-3. To add additional content, you would simply create other selectors. Notice that I have inserted a repeating background image. This is the gradient background behind the text in Figure 12-3.

You can create backgrounds from images in single containers, entire pages, or even table cells with this method. To create an image background, for example, you would simply add the `background` property to the main, or top (the container holding all of the other containers), selector. In Dreamweaver, you can add an image background to an entire page from the Page Properties dialog box, accessed from the Modify menu: Simply type the image's file path and filename in the Background Image field.

Figure 12-3:
Creating a gradient behind text was by repeating a simple graphic inside the `page_` `back` `ground` container.

✔ **Lines 51–56:** These other four selectors are the four different orientation selectors — one for each of the four possible handheld orientations. Notice that they are grouped together, as designated by the commas, and that their only property is `display:none`. By default, none of them is displayed. The orientation of the device and the JavaScript determine which selector is displayed when.

✔ **Lines 57–64:** The first four selectors here are what the JavaScript uses to control which content is displayed according to the orientation of the device. Notice that the two portrait selectors — upright and upside down — are grouped because they're the same display size, as are the two landscape selectors. The `width:device-width` property tells the browser to size the page to fit the screen. This allows you to use the same page and style sheet for multiple devices.

✔ **Lines 66–71:** The next set of selectors associates the class selectors with the ID selectors. When you see the JavaScript in the next subsection, this will make more sense. This entire section of selectors is designed to display the appropriate ID selector, according to the detected orientation.

Creating the JavaScript

Now that you have the HTML page and CSS file created, it's time to write a small JavaScript to make it all come together: Start a new flat text file, save it as `orientScreen.js` in the same directory as your HTML file, and then enter the JavaScript code shown in Listing 12-3.

Listing 12-3:   JavaScript file for the device orientation project

```
window.onload = function initialLoad(){
    updateOrientation();
}

function updateOrientation(){
    var contentType = "display_";
    switch(window.orientation){
        case 0:
        contentType += "portrait";
        break;

        case -90:
        contentType += "cw";
        break;

        case 90:
        contentType += "ccw";
        break;

        case 180:
        contentType += "upsideDown";
```

```
        break;
    }
    document.getElementById("page_background").setAttribute("class", contentType);
}
```

If you place these three files — the HTML, the CSS, and the JavaScript — side by side, you can see how they interact with each other. For example, the `onorientationchange="updateOrientation();"` in the `<body>` tag of your HTML page refers, or fires, the `updateOrientation` function in your JavaScript file. The `var` (variable) and `case` statements in the `update Orientation` function references the selectors at the bottom of your external style sheet, the ones that define each of the four `<div>` containers in your HTML file. The completed application should look like Figure 12-4, depending on the orientation of the device.

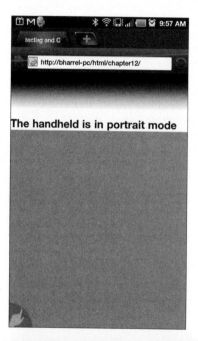

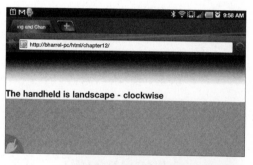

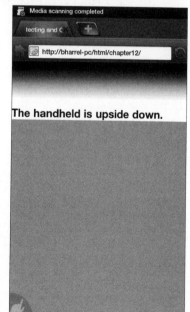

Figure 12-4: The handheld displays a different selector for each orientation.

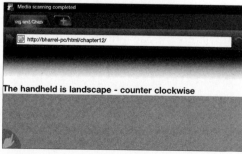

For a more detailed of how JavaScript works with your CSS and HTML files, see Chapters 3 and 13.

Creating Artwork with WebKit Extensions

WebKit has a variety of extensions for 2D and 3D drawing and animation effects, including (but in no way limited to) drop-shadows, rounded box corners, transitions, animations, and radial and linear gradients. (For examples of drop shadows and rounded corners, see Chapter 11.) In this section, you create a gradient background, a box that transitions from one color to another and an animation using CSS WebKit extensions.

As with many WebKit extensions, extensive options are available for controlling the appearance of gradients and other effects. There's no way to remember them all (at least I can't remember them). You can find extensive information at Apple's Safari development site, including all supported CSS rules and properties, at `http://developer.apple.com/library/safari`. For information on everything WebKit, including several developers' tools, visit the WebKit Open Source site at `http://webkit.org`. Keep in mind, though, that not all WebKit extensions are supported on all devices, and some are supported only in standard computer browsers.

Creating a WebKit gradient

Whipping up a gradient with WebKit provides a good idea of how to use WebKit CSS extensions to create other special effects, such as transitions and animations. Many of these and other WebKit effects are created similarly, with often only the function name and properties being different. These types of CSS attributes accept functions as properties, or parameters. Many WebKit extensions are functions. In several object-oriented programming (OOP) languages, functions are written in the following format (for a more detailed discussion of functions, see Chapter 3):

```
functionName(function arguments, parameters or properties)
```

WebKit functions are written similarly. The information inside the parentheses defines, or sets the parameters for, the function. In the following selector, for example, `-webkit-gradient` is the function; the data inside the parentheses defines the placement, size, and colors of the gradient:

```
body {
background-image:  -webkit-gradient(
   linear,
   right bottom,
   left top,
   color-stop(0.13, rgb(131,234,200)),
   color-stop(0.57, rgb(158,255,240)),
   color-stop(0.79, rgb(190,255,255))
);
}
```

From top to bottom, the attributes for the gradient, shown in Figure 12-5, define the gradient, as described in Table 12-1:

You can also create gradients and other special effects in Mozilla-based browsers, such as the Firefox mobile browser, with Mozilla extensions, which can find at the Mozilla Developer site located at

```
https://developer.mozilla.org/en/css_reference/mozilla_extensions
```

The gradient just given, as written for Mozilla browsers, would look like this:

```
-moz-linear-gradient (
   Center bottom
   rgb(131,234,200) 13%,
   rgb(158,255,240) 57%,
   rgb(190,255,255) 79%
)
```

Table 12-1	Gradient Attributes
Property	*Effect*
`linear`	Sets the property of the table.
`right bottom`	Sets the direction of the right color of the gradient. You can also use `left` to make the gradient flow in a different direction.
`left top`	Sets the direction of the left color of the gradient. You can also use `right` to make the gradient flow in a different direction.
`color-stop(0.13, rgb(131,234,200))`	Sets where the color stops and RGB color values.
`color-stop(0.57, rgb(158,255,240))`	Sets where the color stops and RGB color values.
`color-stop(0.79, rgb(190,255,255))`	Sets where the color stops and RGB color values.

Notice the `color-stop` statements. The first values set where a color stops (and the next one starts) based on percentages of the page's display width. In other words, the second `color-stop` statement stops the second color 57 percent of the way from the left side of the page, and the third statement stops at 79 percent of the page. The RGB color definitions are *nested* inside the color density properties, or parenthesis inside parenthesis. Sometimes, depending on the complexity of your gradient (or other type of effect), you'll need to nest multiple properties inside other properties, as in the following example, where I have nested several color options in the same argument:

```
background: -webkit-gradient(radial, 50% -50, 0, 50% 0, 300, from(#676767),
            to(black)) black;
```

If you adjust the first `color-stop` values (that is, the 0.13, 0.57, and 0.79 values), you'll get a better feel for how these settings affect the gradient. These numbers simply tell the browser where to start changing the colors in the gradient. The browser itself actually draws the gradient, using these numbers (and the RGB values) as references. (See Figure 12-5.)

If you're familiar with programming, these complex arguments are common. You can find more information on programming in general in Chapters 3 and 13.

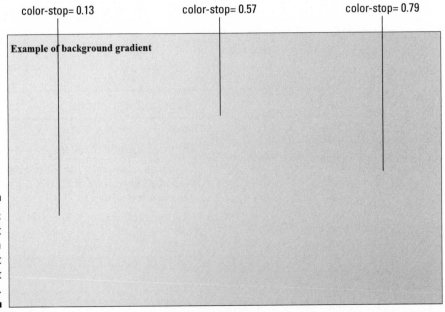

Figure 12-5:
A gradient drawn with the WebKit gradient extension.

Creating a WebKit transition

A *transition*, of course, is an effect that goes — or *transitions* — from one state to another. If you've ever created, say, a PowerPoint slide show, perhaps you have created transitions, such as fades or wipes, between slides. One of the more common transitions affects is the *fade*, where an object — or the entire screen — gradually appears or disappears. (Figure 12-6 should give you a general idea.) You can create transitions that fade into portions of the page, or a single `<div>` section or create a transition that covers the entire page.

Figure 12-6:
Example of
a graphic
box tran-
sitioning
from white
to black on
a mobile
device
screen.

Creating a WebKit transition consists of three parts — the HTML page; the CSS, and the JavaScript. In this example, because there is so little of it (and this is not typically the kind of effect you'd create across multiple pages), we'll put the CSS in the head of the HTML file. In fact, for this example, you create the entire page, all three parts — HTML, CSS, and JavaScript — in the same file. (See Listing 12-4.)

Like most pages that hold effects created with WebKit extensions and JavaScript, there's nothing special about the HTML pages that contain WebKit transitions. You set them up just as you would any other mobile web page. In this case, start a new web page, save it as `transitions.html`, and then enter the code in Listing 12-4.

Listing 12-4: **WebKit transition file**

```
<!DOCTYPE html PUBLIC "-//W3C//DTD XHTML 1.0 Transitional//EN" "http://www.
            w3.org/TR/xhtml1/DTD/xhtml1-transitional.dtd">
<html xmlns="http://www.w3.org/1999/xhtml">
<head>
<meta http-equiv="Content-Type" content="text/html; charset=utf-8" />
<title>Transition</title>
<style>                                                              →6

#box {
   width: device-width;
   height: 480px;
   background-color: black;
   color: #FFF;
   font-size:50px;
   font-style:italic;
   padding-top:180px;
   padding-left:170px;
   -webkit-transition: opacity 3s;
}                                                                   →18

.transition {                                                       →20
   opacity: 0;
}                                                                   →22

</style>
<script type="text/javascript">                                     →25
function show() {
   var box = document.getElementById("box");
   box.className = (box.className=="transition text goes here") ? "" :
             "transition text goes here";
   box.innerHTML = box.className;
}
</script>                                                            →31

</head>

<body>
   <h2>Transition</h2>                                              →36
      <input type="button" onclick="show()" value="Transition" />
   <div id="box">
   </div>                                                           →39
</body>
</html>
```

Some notes about Listing 12-4:

✔ **Lines 36–39:** This is the HTML to set up the button the user will use to initiate the animation and creates a `<div>` container for the animation, which we create with the CSS and a very simple JavaScript. Notice the property `onclick="show()"`, this calls to a function in the JavaScript named *show*, which you'll see in a moment.

✔ **Lines 6–18:** The CSS. Aside from the extension that actually tells the browser to create the animation, setting up the CSS is identical to setting up any other selector. The transition itself is created with the `-webkit-transition-` extension, like this:

```
-webkit-transition: properties;
```

There are several possible properties available for setting the duration of the fade, delays, and several special effects: CSS values, such as `linear`, `ease-in`, `ease-out`, and many others that are not necessarily specific to only the transition extension. You can get a list of CSS property functions and what they do at `developer.apple.com`. Click the "CSS Property Functions" link.

Keep in mind that not all extensions are available on all mobile devices.

The most commonly used properties for controlling transitions are `name`, `duration`, `timing`, and `delay`.

You can write this and other WebKit extension functions in two ways, as I've done here, placing all the attributes on the same line or in the same statement, or writing them as separate extensions (which I show you in the next statement, like this:

```
-webkit-transition-property: opacity;
-webkit-transition-duration: 3s;
-webkit-transition-timing-function: ease-in;
```

Writing them on the same line requires a specific syntax — the attributes must be written in a certain order. Writing them as separate extensions, because this doesn't require a specific order, can sometimes be easier. For more information on this and using the WebKit transform extension in general, check out the "CSS Animation" page at the following URL: `www.webkit.org/blog/138/css-animation/`.

Notice that when setting up internal styles — styles inside the HTML file — the CSS code goes between the `<style></style>` tag pair, which is markedly different from how you set up external style sheets, discussed in Chapters 2 and 7.

Most of these properties set up the size and shape of the graphic box and the text inside. The `-webkit-transition` statement tells the browser how to blend the transition as an `opacity`, which is the transition's *property,* and sets the transition duration to three seconds. (Yes, I know that programming terminology, the way the different terms change based on how the code is written, is confusing. I find that deploying the code without getting hung up on what the different parts are called helpful — unless, of course, you're taking a programming course and learning the terms is crucial to your grade . . . .)

✔ **Lines 20–22:** This selector sets the opacity value to 0. In other words, the opacity value is 100 percent transparent. It will transition to completely transparent. Were you to use a value of *.50,* for instance, the box would transition to 50-percent transparent.

✔ **Lines 25–31:** The JavaScript. This simple JavaScript to animate the transition is fired by the `onclick` attribute of the button tag. It fires a function named `show`, which references the `#box` CSS selector through a `var` (variable) statement. (For more on variables, see Chapter 3.)

This script merely animates the transition according to the parameters set in the CSS. It also creates the text `"transition text goes here"` in the `box.className = (box.className=="transition text goes here") ? "" : "transition text goes here";` statement and formats it based on the CSS.

The `innerHTML` property modifies the document's HTML on the fly. It changes the page's content without refreshing the entire page, making the page redraw quicker and thereby seem more responsive. This property, when used with `getElementById` in your JavaScript code, refers to an HTML element and changes its contents.

When you've entered in Listing 12-4, save and test your page. The box should fade off the page, as should the text in the box. (Well, the text doesn't actually *do* anything. It just seems to fade away as the box fades to white.) Clicking the button again should cause the box to fade back onto the page.

Creating a WebKit Animation

Many people on the Internet claim that WebKit extensions and HTML5 (discussed in Chapter 10) will eliminate the need for Flash and other types of animation software. Although it's true that some of these enhancements might eliminate the need for external programs for some of the simplest animations and other effects, what you can do with WebKit extensions is limited. Flash and other web special-effects tools are in no big danger from this quarter.

With that said, what you *can* do with WebKit extensions is pretty nifty, and — since WebKit extensions are native and often hardware-accelerated — animations and other affects you build with them display and perform much faster than those you create with external utilities and embed in your web pages. So the animations you create with the WebKit extension -webkit-animation are not only fun to create but they also initiate quickly and run smoothly. After all, there are no bulky external files to download; the animation is achieved with a few lines of code and the browser does the rest.

This animation consists of three parts, the HTML page tags, the CSS, and the JavaScript. To make the process easier to demonstrate, we'll place all the code in the HTML file (see Listing 12-5). When you finish, you'll have created an animation that moves a dynamically drawn box on a square path around the screen, as shown in Figure 12-7.

The one key difference in the HTML for this animation and the transition animation in the previous section is that this one initiates, or *fires*, the animation from the <body> tag, similar to the device orientation script in the "Working with device orientation" subsection earlier. In other words, the animation starts automatically, rather than requiring the user to click a button.

You can use this technique to fire nearly any other JavaScript automatically, so that the script executes without user interactivity. For example, if you wanted to create a transition that runs automatically, simply fire the script using the following method, rather than associating it to a button.

Start a new web page and enter the code in Listing 12-5. Save it as animation.html.

Figure 12-7:
Example of
animation
moving on a
four-corner
square path.

Listing 12-5:   WebKit animation file

```
<!DOCTYPE html PUBLIC "-//W3C//DTD XHTML 1.0 Transitional//EN" "http://www.
            w3.org/TR/xhtml1/DTD/xhtml1-transitional.dtd">
<html xmlns="http://www.w3.org/1999/xhtml">

<head>
<meta http-equiv="Content-Type" content="text/html; charset=utf-8" />
<title>Animation</title>

<style>                                                         →8
#box {
   width: 200px;
   height: 200px;
   background-color: black;
   position: absolute;
   top: 0px;
   left: 0px;
}

.squarePath {                                                   →18
   -webkit-animation-name: squarePath;
   -webkit-animation-duration: 8s;
   -webkit-animation-timing-function: ease-in-out;
   -webkit-animation-iteration-count: infinite;
}
@-webkit-keyframes squarePath {
   from {
      top: 0px;
      left: 0px;
   }

   25% {
      top: 0px;
      left: 200px;
   }

   50% {
   top: 200px;
   left: 200px;
   }

   75% {
      top: 200px;
      left: 0px;
   }

   100% {
      top: 0px;
      left: 0px;
   }
```

(continued)

Listing 12-5 *(continued)*

```
}                                                                    →49

</style>                                                             →51

<script type="text/javascript">                                     →53
    function move() {
        document.getElementById("box").className = "squarePath";
    }
</script>                                                            →57

</head>

<body onload="move()">                                              →61


    <div id="box">
    </div>


</body>
</html>
```

Some notes about Listing 12-5:

✔ **Line 61:** Notice the `onload="move()"` property in the opening `<body>` tag. This fires a function in the JavaScript named `move`, as you'll see a little later in this exercise.

✔ **Lines 8–51:** The CSS. As discussed in the previous section about CSS transitions, `-webkit-animation` has several property definitions, such as `-webkit-animation-name`, `-webkit-animation-duration`, and so on. Each one allows you to set a separate property of the extension.

The first selector, `#box`, of course, creates the dynamically drawn graphic box. The next selector, `squarePath`, starts the animation. Notice that there is a separate property statement for several aspects of the animation, such as the animation name (referenced in the script), the duration, the timing (see the sidebar, "Understanding animation timing"), and the iteration-count, or the number of times to run the animation. In this case, the `infinite` value sets the animation to run indefinitely. It never stops — until the user navigates away from the page.

Many WebKit extensions support the same property definitions. In the previous transition animation, in the "Creating a WebKit transition" section earlier in this chapter, you can also use these (and other) properties to control the behavior of the transition.

✔ **Lines 18–49:** This code sets up the square path of the animation. The `@-webkit-keyframes` extension starts the animation and references the `squarePath` selector. If you're familiar with animation and video software, then you know that a *keyframe* stores information about an animated object, or initiates a change in the animated object's property. In this case, each direction change on the square path is the equivalent to a keyframe.

This is more of a metaphorical keyframe, though, than an actual keyframe in the traditional sense. In all there are five keyframes — the original, or starting, position (from), and the four positions where the animation changes direction, designated by *25%, 50%, 75%* and *100%* selectors.

I say *metaphorical* because when you're working in an animation program such as Flash, you actually design your animation over a timeline, or a span of frames. You create keyframes along the timeline. When setting up an animation in a web page like this, the timeline is simulated, as are the keyframes.

The square moves 200 pixels right, makes a turn and goes down 200 pixels, makes another turn, moves right 200 pixels, and then turns again and returns to its starting position. There are five selectors because there are five destinations — including returning the box to its original position.

✔ **Lines 53–57:** The JavaScript for this animation consists of one function with two lines of code. It simply gets the #box selector and references the squarePath selector. The browser does the rest.

When you've finished typing in Listing 12-5, save and test your page. The square box should move in a square pattern to four points on the screen — right, down, left, up — and then repeat the process continuously until you navigate away from the page. You can use this code to animate any object drawn with WebKit extensions or JavaScript.

Understanding animation timing

Animation timing controls how and when an animation moves. In animation and video software, for example, animation is usually controlled over a span of time broken into frames. Animation sequences are usually rated in frames per second (FPS). (For more on animation and FPS, see Chapter 10.) In addition to FPS, most animation programs, such as Flash, let you further control how animations behave with *timing* settings, such as *ease-in, ease-out, ease-in-out,* and a few others.

These timing settings provide some additional effects to the animation. An *ease,* for example, is a gradual stall or slowing. In other words, when an animated object eases *in,* it slows to a fraction of the overall speed of the animation, making it seem as though it has slowed down, or *eases,* significantly when it starts. Then it catches up and moves at its normal speed. *Ease-out,* of course, reverses the effect, slowing down the animation at the end of the sequence. *Ease-in-out* stalls the animation on both ends. For examples of eases and other animation settings, see this book's companion website.

The animation we create in this section has four paths — one for each side of the square path it moves along. In this case, the ease-in-out occurs on all four paths, or sides. On a linear, one-path animation, the ease effect occurs only once — or, in the case of ease-in-out, once at the beginning (in) and once at the end (out) of the animation.

Part IV
Building Real-World Applications

The 5th Wave   By Rich Tennant

"David will be adding rich, dynamic audio to my slide transitions."

In this part . . .

This part covers sophisticated web applications, such as automating with JavaScript, and creating a JavaScript quiz application that keeps track of the user's answers and tallies the score. You learn how to make your site search-engine-friendly, so that people can find your site, and how to create a search engine for your site, so your users can find information on your site. You also learn how to create a mobile shopping cart, or e-commerce, interface.

Chapter 13

Automating Your Sites with JavaScript

*F*or mobile devices, JavaScript can be a real workhorse. It can tell you when the browser looking at your website is a mobile device — and automatically change what appears on the screen, either by changing the URL or changing the CSS. Likewise, JavaScript can determine the screen size of the device — is it a pretty big one, like a tablet, or is it a small one that shares space with a keyboard on a mobile phone? Knowing the size of the screen helps determine the format of the materials you're presenting.

That's not all that JavaScript can do. Little chores such as form validation — and specialized new elements in HTML5 such as `<canvas>` — rely heavily on JavaScript. Searches and calculations are possible because JavaScript can compare outcomes with strings and numbers to find matches (or non-matches) and take care of the details for you.

This chapter explains how to create web pages using JavaScript that can distinguish between different browsers. If your page detects a mobile device, it can reformat the page for a smaller screen; otherwise, it displays the page for a general computer screen. In this way, your page can serve uses with different viewing devices.

Who's Looking?

One of the first things you want JavaScript to determine is whether the browser that's looking at your website is mobile or non-mobile. Is the device using a big viewing area or a little one? If the viewing area is on a mobile device, JavaScript can help by switching the viewed materials.

In order to find the user's device and browser, you can use the Document Object Model (DOM). The DOM holds the `navigator` property, which itself has several different properties, one of which is the `userAgent` (discussed in Chapter 5). The `userAgent` has its own properties and methods as well, but by itself it provides information about whether the screen is for a mobile or non-mobile device.

For our purposes here, a *property* is any characteristic found in the DOM, and a *method* is a function that does something — such as find out what kind of browser is looking at your page.

By examining the contents of the `navigator.userAgent`, you can detect just what kind of device and browser are looking at your page. The first step, then, is to write some JavaScript that displays what kind of device the user is using.

Finding the basics

To get started in tracking down the specific device looking at your page, start with a simple little JavaScript program that prints out the details for you. Open a new HTML page in your favorite HTML document editor or text editor, add the script in Listing 13-1, and then save the file as `basicSniff.html`.

Listing 13-1:   The basic sniffer script

```
<!DOCTYPE HTML>
<html>
<head>
<script type = "text/javascript">
var sniffer=new Object();                                    →5
sniffer.agentNow=navigator.userAgent;                        →6
document.write(sniffer.agentNow);
</script>
<meta http-equiv="Content-Type" content="text/html; charset=UTF-8">
<title>JS Work</title>
</head>
<body>
</body>
</html>
```

Some notes about the code in Listing 13-1:

✔ **Line 5:** The script first places an `Object` instance in a variable named `sniffer`. Objects are "things" that you can use in a program. Your car is an object with seats, a steering wheel, and a brake (properties); and things that it does — drives, stops, heats, and cools (methods). To make an object "come alive," you place it in a variable. You do that by *assigning* it to a variable, such as `sniffer`, by using the equal sign (=) operator. When you've done that, `sniffer` has all of the properties and methods of the object.

✔ **Line 6:** The property `agentNow` is added to `sniffer` and assigned the value of `navigator.userAgent`. This process changes the value of `navigator.userAgent` into the agent currently viewing the page to `sniffer.agentNow`.

Test the file on your computer, using any browser, and you see something like the following:

```
Mozilla/5.0 (Macintosh; U; Intel Mac OS X 10.6; en-US; rv:1.9.2.16)
        Gecko/20110319 Firefox/3.6.16
```

These results are what you'll see on a Macintosh using a Firefox browser. If you test the same web page on an iPhone, you see something like Figure 13-1.

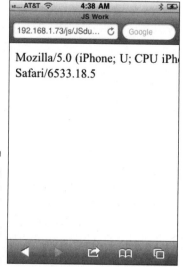

These results provide useful information, but all you really need to find out is whether the page is being viewed by an iPhone. (As they stand, the results are an example of *too much information*.) This is a good start, then, but we need to add more to narrow down our findings.

On the trail of iPhone

In looking further into `navigator.userAgent`, we find that it has several properties and methods we can use. (Remember that a method is a feature of an object that *does something*.) First of all, it has a method that changes all the information to lowercase text. That can be handy so we don't have to use inter-case searches (iPhone uses *inter-case* letters — capitals in the middle of the word). Second, `userAgent` has a `search` method that examines its own contents to find the string (text) you're trying to find. If it finds the search string, it returns a positive number; if not, it returns a negative number. So all you have to find is whether the returned value is 0 or greater. (Even 0 is greater than −1!) The following lines take care of the search:

```
var agentNow=navigator.userAgent.toLowerCase();
agentNow.search("iphone");
```

If the resulting value is true, it can return a lot of different positive numbers. (My iPhone returned 13.) However, all you want to know is whether the returned value is greater than −1. So you can write your search statement to return a value of *true* or *false* (called a Boolean), in which a value of 0 or greater would signify true, as follows:

```
agentNow.search("iphone")>=0;
```

Another way of writing that last line would be to use the `sniffer` object again and store the results in an iPhone property of `sniffer`. In such a case, you've added the property `"iphone"` to `sniffer`. The value of `sniffer.iphone` is either true or false. It's true if the agent is greater than or equal to 0. Otherwise it is false.

```
sniffer.iphone=(agentNow.search("iphone")>=0);
```

Now you can use `sniffer.iphone` to find whether the agent is an iPhone. To do so, open a new HTML page in your favorite HTML document editor or text editor, add the script in Listing 13-2, and then save the file as `sniff Apple.html`.

Listing 13-2: Sniffing out iPhones

```
<!DOCTYPE HTML>
<html>
<head>
<script type = "text/javascript">
    var sniffer=new Object();
    var agentNow=navigator.userAgent.toLowerCase();
    sniffer.iphone=(agentNow.search("iphone")>=0);
    document.write(sniffer.iphone);
</script>
<meta http-equiv="Content-Type" content="text/html; charset=UTF-8">
```

```
<title>iPhone Sniffer</title>
</head>
<body>
</body>
</html>
```

If you test this file on your computer with any browser, you'll see the word
False on the screen. Test it on an iPhone, however, and you'll get the word
True. (If you don't have an iPhone, don't worry. The next section shows you
how to test any mobile device.)

Finding any mobile device

Now you've seen how to find an iPhone. That's great, but what about the
devices like Androids, Blackberrys, or any other mobile thingamajig that
people use? Finding these devices is just like finding the iPhone, but instead
of listing the name "iPhone" you put in another name, such as "Android".

The reason for using an object is that you can load up an object with as
many properties and methods as you want. So, when you want to add other
objects to the list of devices that you're looking for, you simply use a loop to
go through the object to see whether any of the elements is true. A special
loop structure iterates (loops) through an object and reveals the values of its
properties. Objects are set up like a bag full of different things, each with a
number that can be addressed. For instance, we can look at sniffer as
follows;

```
sniffer[0];
sniffer[1];
sniffer[2];
sniffer[3];
```

That list is the same as writing this:

```
sniffer.iphone;
sniffer.android
sniffer.blackberry;
sniffer.series60;
```

Each has a value; at any time, we can add more types of mobile devices
(properties) to the sniffer object. Over time, you may add lots of different
properties, but not to worry. By using the for..in loop, you can find all of
an object's properties and their values. Here's the basic format:

```
for(var myVariable in myProperty)
{
    document.write(myProperty[myVariable]);
}
```

Using `document.write()` is just a way to send the value to the screen. You can put the value in a variable or other data storage.

Returning to the example using the `sniffer` object, when `true` is located, you know that one of the mobile devices you've defined in the object has been found. The following shows the code where the variable named `mobile` is used to find each property in the `sniffer` object:

```
for(var mobile in sniffer)
{
    document.write(sniffer[mobile]);
    document.write("<br/>");
}
```

Each `sniffer[mobile]` is either `true` or `false`, just as you saw with `sniffer.iphone`. If you place the names of several different devices in the `sniffer` object, you'll see a list of `true` and `false` output text on the screen. To see how to set up the program, open a new HTML page, enter the script in Listing 13-3, and save the file as `sniffType.html`.

Listing 13-3: Sniffing out any mobile device

```
<!DOCTYPE HTML>
<html>
<head>
<script type = "text/javascript">
    var sniffer=new Object();
    var agentNow=navigator.userAgent.toLowerCase();
    sniffer.android=(agentNow.search("android")>=0);
    sniffer.series60=(agentNow.search("series60")>=0);
    sniffer.iphone=(agentNow.search("iphone")>=0);
    sniffer.blackberry=(agentNow.search("blackberry")>=0);
    sniffer.windowsce=(agentNow.search("windows ce")>=0);
    for(var mobile in sniffer)
    {
        document.write(sniffer[mobile]);
        document.write("<br/>");
    }
</script>
<meta http-equiv="Content-Type" content="text/html; charset=UTF-8">
<title>Mobile Sniffer</title>
</head>
<body>
</body>
</html>
```

If you test this file on your computer with any browser, you'll see the word `false` appear several times on the screen. Test it on an iPhone, however, and the word `false` will appear several times — along with a single instance of the word `true`. (Figure 13-2 shows how the output looks on an iPhone.)

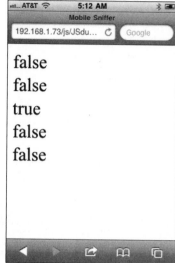

Figure 13-2:
Display of
different
object
elements.

Keep in mind that the purpose is to determine whether *any* mobile device is at your site. The more types of mobile agents you can identify, the better your site can handle mobile visitors.

If a new mobile device becomes available, just add it to the list. For example, add this and all `"gizmo"` mobile devices are located:

```
sniffer.gizmo=(agentNow.search("gizmo")>=0);
```

Of course, the real question remains — so what? What can you do if you identify a mobile device. The next few sections take a look at the options available to you.

Making Changes for Mobile Devices

People tend to format web pages for the screen they happen to have. At different times, the "standard" for screen size changes — it used to be 800 by 600 pixels, and then it changed to 1024 by 768, and it will change again. In the meantime, though, the devices used to read web pages get smaller. Ideally, if the user has a desktop or laptop computer, the web page appears in the "full-size" and if a mobile device, in "mobile-size." In this section, you'll see how to have multiple sets of web pages. The default size is full-size and if JavaScript detects a mobile device, it changes it to mobile-size.

Jumping to a mobile page

Now that you can see how to detect viewing by a mobile device, you may want to add a special page that optimizes mobile viewing. To see how to create a special mobile-viewing page, start with a regular web page and view it on both your computer and a mobile device. If the page looks good on both, you don't have to create a separate page for mobile devices. Sometimes, however, what looks just right on a computer screen just looks wrong on a mobile device.

To get started, take a look at the JavaScript in the following snippet:

```
<script type = "text/javascript">
   var sniffer=new Object();
   var agentNow=navigator.userAgent.toLowerCase();
   sniffer.android=(agentNow.search("android")>=0);
   sniffer.series60=(agentNow.search("series60")>=0);
   sniffer.iphone=(agentNow.search("iphone")>=0);
   sniffer.blackberry=(agentNow.search("blackberry")>=0);
   sniffer.windowsce=(agentNow.search("windows ce")>=0);

   for(var mobile in sniffer)
   {
   if(sniffer[mobile])                                              →12
   {
    window.location = "MobileSize.html";
   }
   }
</script>
```

As you can see, the first part is the mobile device detection code worked out in the previous section.

Line 12 determines whether there's a mobile device. If a mobile device is being used, the value of `sniffer[mobile]` will be `true`. When a mobile device is detected, the JavaScript code `window.location` redirects the user to a special page for mobile device viewing — `"MobileSize.html";`. The following steps provide an example of how to do create dual pages for different user agents:

1. **Create a PNG " anchor logo" about 200 pixels wide and 245 pixels high and save it as** `anchor.png`.

2. **With the same graphic, change the size to 40 by 49 pixels, and save it as** `anchorMobile.png`.

3. **Open a new HTML page in your favorite HTML document editor or text editor.**

4. **Add the script in Listing 13-4 and save the file as** `FullSizeSwitch.html` **in the same directory as your graphic images:**

Listing 13-4:   Creating dual pages for different user agents

```html
<!DOCTYPE HTML>
<html>
<head>
<script type = "text/javascript">
   var sniffer=new Object();
   var agentNow=navigator.userAgent.toLowerCase();
   sniffer.android=(agentNow.search("android")>=0);
   sniffer.series60=(agentNow.search("series60")>=0);
   sniffer.iphone=(agentNow.search("iphone")>=0);
   sniffer.blackberry=(agentNow.search("blackberry")>=0);
   sniffer.windowsce=(agentNow.search("windows ce")>=0);

   for(var mobile in sniffer)
   {
    if(sniffer[mobile])
    {
     window.location = "MobileSize.html";
    }
   }
</script>
<meta http-equiv="Content-Type" content="text/html; charset=UTF-8">
<title>Two Size Full</title>
</head>
<body>
<img src="anchor.png" width="200" height="245" alt="anchor" style="float: left">
<H1 style="color:blue; font-family:'Arial Black', Gadget, sans-serif">The Blue
            Anchor Inn</H1>
<header style="font-family:Verdana, Geneva, sans-serif;font-style:italic;
            font-size:16px; margin-left:220px; margin-right:300px"> A place
            where you can drop your anchor and relax with good food and good
            friends. Founded in 1844 it served as a Civil War port for Union
            gunboats, monitors and full sail ships of the line. In World Wars
            I and II, American troops disembarked to the African and European
            theaters of war from this port. During Prohibition, the Inn was
            used as a place of transfer for smuggled rum from Cuba and whiskey
            from Canada. Presidents Roosevelt, Kennedy and Nixon have been our
            guests. </header><p>
<p><p>
<h3>Open daily for Lunch and Dinner:</h3>
<h4>
Monday-Thursday: 11:30am-10:00pm<br>
Friday-Saturday: 11:30-Midnight<br>
Sunday: 1:pm -10:00pm
</h4>
<ul>
<li>Fish </li>
<li>Lobster</li>
<li>Crab</li>
<li>Clams </li>
</ul>
</body>
</html>
```

5. **Test the file on your computer with any browser.**

Figure 13-3 shows what should appear on a typical computer screen. If you test the exact same page on a mobile device (without the JavaScript code to send it to another file), Figure 13-4 shows what appears:

Figure 13-3:
Full-page
display.

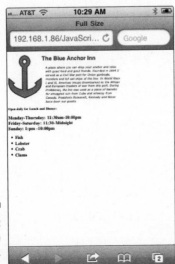

Figure 13-4:
Mobile
display.

Here you can clearly see the name of the inn and the anchor logo, but the historical text is unreadable and the notice of hours is difficult to read as well. Fortunately, the page can be redesigned with a mobile device in mind. One solution is to use the script in Listing 13-5. Open a new HTML page, add the script in Listing 13-5, and then save it as `MobileSize.html`.

Listing 13-5: Script for switching to a mobile device

```
<!DOCTYPE HTML>
<html>
<head>
<meta http-equiv="Content-Type" content="text/html; charset=UTF-8">
<title>Mobile Size</title>
</head>
<body>
<img src="anchorMobile.png" width="40" height="49" alt="little Anchor"
         align="left">
<H1 style="color:blue; font-family:'Arial Black', Gadget, sans-serif">The Blue
         Anchor Inn</H1>
<header style="font-family:Verdana, Geneva, sans-serif;font-style:italic; font-
         size:32px; margin-left:10px; margin-right:20px"> A place where you
         can drop your anchor and relax with good food and good friends.
         Founded in 1844, it served as a Civil War port for Union gunboats,
         monitors, and full-sail ships of the line. In World Wars I and II,
         American troops disembarked to the African and European theaters
         of war from this port. During Prohibition, the Inn was used as
         a place of transfer for smuggled rum from Cuba and whiskey from
         Canada. Presidents Roosevelt, Kennedy, and Nixon have been our
         guests. </header>
<p><p><p>
<h3 style="color:blue; font-size:48px">Open daily for Lunch and Dinner:</h3>
<section style="font-family:Verdana, Geneva, sans-serif;font-style:bold; font-
         size:24px; margin-left:10px; margin-right:20px"> Monday-Thursday:
         11:30am-10:00pm<br>
 Friday-Saturday: 11:30-Midnight<br>
 Sunday: 1:pm -10:00pm
 <ul>
  <li>Fish </li>
  <li>Lobster</li>
  <li>Crab</li>
  <li>Clams </li>
 </ul>
</section>
</body>
</html>
```

Several differences can be seen in Listings 13-4 and 13-5:

- Image size from 200 x 245 to 40 x 49
- In the `<header>` container, the font size changed from 16px to 32 px
- The margins (left/right) change from 220/300px to 10/20px
- H3 changed from default to a blue color and font size of 48px
- Default body font changed to 24px sans serif font with a 10/20px margin

Now load the HTML file named `FullSize.html` on your mobile device using any mobile browser. The loaded page on the browser should switch automatically to `MobileSize.html` — with the results shown in Figure 13-5.

Figure 13-5:
The
improved
mobile
display.

As you can see in Figure 13-5, the page is much different. The graphic logo has been reduced to a little icon, the full content of the header materials is visible, and the information about the hours appears with a big blue header, followed by a clear display of open times and main dishes. All the important material can be seen at a glance without making the user fumble around resizing the screen.

The important point is that mobile pages often require content different from what appears on a full-size computer screen. You don't want to ask the user to choose which file to view; so you just let JavaScript do the work in deciding whether the page selects material for a big or mobile screen.

Don't change the page — change the style sheet

Instead of creating two different HTML pages for computer and mobile device screens, you can change the style sheets using a single page. Because development takes place on a computer and not a mobile device, the default style sheet is developed for computer screens. With two (or more) style sheets, you can build sheets for different kinds of screens, as discussed in Chapter 5.

One of the ironies of mobile and computer screens is that mobile screens require *larger* fonts for a default rendering that users can see without enlarging the view area by stretching the screen with their thumbs and fingers. (I use *both* thumbs — now you know where the expression, "all thumbs" comes from.) If your website can be viewed without forcing the user to enlarge the mobile screen, you're more likely to have happy mobile viewers.

Mobile and computer screen style sheets

For this exercise, I use two different style sheets to make a simple point — computer and mobile device screens need different size fonts. I start with a typical computer page viewed on a mobile phone and show what a different style sheet does for the visibility of the page on the mobile screen. In Figure 13-6, you can barely make out the text on the left, even though it's very clear on a standard computer screen. On the right, however — using a different style sheet — the body text is quite clear, as is the header.

Figure 13-6:
The same page on a mobile phone with different style sheets.

The important feature about Figure 13-6 is that a *single* web page generated both views. Further, we can reuse a big hunk of the JavaScript created to find mobile devices and just use a single `document.write()` statement to make the switch. However, before looking at the main page, you need two style sheets. To make these sheets, first open a new CSS page in your favorite HTML document editor or text editor. (Note that HTML document editors typically have an option to create CSS files.) Enter the script in Listing 13-6 and save it as `standard.css`. Then open another CSS page, enter the script in Listing 13-7, and save the file as `styleMobile.css`.

Listing 13-6: Standard style sheet

```
@charset "UTF-8";
/* CSS Document */

body {
    background-color: #dcdcdc;
    font-family: Arial, Helvetica, sans-serif;
    font-size: 14px;
    color: #cc0000;
}


h1 {
    font-family:"Arial Black", Gadget, sans-serif;
    color:#00f;
    margin-left:40px;
}
```

As you can see, the body font in Listing 13-6 is a hefty 14 pixels, and the head-line uses the h1 element. This will be easy to see on a computer screen — but as you can see in Figure 13-6, it's hardly visible on a mobile device.

Listing 13-7: Mobile device style sheet

```
@charset "UTF-8";
body {
    background-color: #0000cc;
    font-family: Arial, Helvetica, sans-serif;
    font-size: 48px;
    color: #00ff00;
}

h1 {
    font-family:"Arial Black", Gadget, sans-serif;
    color:#FF0;
    margin-left:20px;
    font-size:72px;
    text-align:center;
}
```

In Listing 13-7, the body font is enlarged to 48 pixels, and though that may seem extreme, the resulting text is easily visible on a mobile device without screen enlargement. To emphasize the differences, the colors are changed and the h1 is centered, as well as being pumped up to 72 pixels.

Making the switch

Now that you have two different external style sheets, all you have to do is to switch them when viewed by a mobile device. As you may recall, the tag to install an external style sheet is,

```
<link rel="stylesheet" type="text/css" href="sty.css">
```

If you place two links to two different style sheets in the same header, the page uses only the last style sheet link. In other words, it cancels the first style sheet.

So all you have to do is to add a second link tag *only if the script detects a mobile device.* The way to do that is to use the DOM statement, `document. write()` and write the second style sheet dynamically. The following script incorporates the JavaScript for detecting a mobile device and adds the second link for you. To create a web page that switches style sheets, open a new HTML page in your favorite HTML document editor or text editor, enter the script in Listing 13-8, and save the file as `styleSwitch.html`.

Listing 13-8:   Switching style sheets automatically

```
<!DOCTYPE HTML>
<html>
<head>
<link rel="stylesheet" type="text/css" href="standard.css">
<script type = "text/javascript">
   var sniffer=new Object();
   var agentNow=navigator.userAgent.toLowerCase();
   sniffer.android=(agentNow.search("android")>=0);
   sniffer.series60=(agentNow.search("series60")>=0);
   sniffer.iphone=(agentNow.search("iphone")>=0);
   sniffer.blackberry=(agentNow.search("blackberry")>=0);
   sniffer.windowsce=(agentNow.search("windows ce")>=0);

   for(var mobile in sniffer)
   {
     if(sniffer[mobile])
     {
      document.write('<link rel="stylesheet" type="text/css" href="styleMobile.
           css">');
     break;
     }
   }

</script>
<meta http-equiv="Content-Type" content="text/html; charset=UTF-8">
<title>Style sheet swap</title>
</head>
<body>
<h1>Style H1</h1>
This is standard size text.
</body>
</html>
```

You can load `styleSwitch.html` on d a server and view it using any mobile browser. Also, test the script on your computer. You'll see the default style, and it looks fine on a computer screen. With this program, you can make your page look right on either mobile or standard computer screens.

Validate Your Forms, Please

Form validation is used in password-protected sites as well as just about every application using data input from HTML that goes into a database. For example, suppose you want to only allow registered users into your site (and they pay you for the privilege!). You need to validate their entry.

Using an HTML `<form>` element, you can build a web page where a user types in a username and a password before being allowed to enter. The JavaScript checks *both* entries and decides whether the request is valid.

Using the DOM with forms

Because JavaScript deals with DOM objects, you have to understand the relationship between the form object and the DOM. In the code, the name of the form includes the name applied to the `<form>` element and names applied to the different input elements. (Forms are discussed in detail in Chapter 9.) Consider the following HTML snippet:

```
<form name="validate" onsubmit="return vaidationFunction()" >
<input type="text" name="userName">
```

In DOM-talk, the reference would be this:

```
document.forms["validate"]["userName"].value;
```

The `.value` property is whatever the user puts in the text input form. The first bracketed value (`validate`) is the name of the form, and the second bracketed value (`username`) is the name of the input element. It may look funny at first, but it's very logical; when you've become accustomed to the format, it makes perfect sense.

Note that the statement `document.forms[...` uses the plural *forms*; not *form*. You'll save hours of frustration if you remember this!

Next you take the values entered into the forms and place them in variables. The variables are compared with valid usernames and passwords, and then they're also placed in variables. For example, this statement compares the lowercase value of uname with the string `"tycoon"`, and if the values are the same a `true` value is placed into the variable unb as a Boolean value:

```
var unb=(uname.toLowerCase()=="tycoon");
```

(Remember, Boolean is just a fancy way of saying *true* or *false*.) If both the Boolean variables (one for username and one for password) are true; then the form validates. To compare two values, JavaScript uses the logical AND

(&&) operator. For instance this statement places a `true` value into the `success` variable only if *both* variables are `true`:

```
var success=unb && pwv;
```

Then you can enter a conditional statement to evaluate whether the user should be allowed access.

HTML and JavaScript validation together

Now you're set to create a validation form. The web page provides valuable finance information (`"Buy low. Sell high."`) to users who successfully enter the correct username and password. To get started, open a new HTML page in your favorite HTML document editor or text editor, enter the script in Listing 13-9, and then save the file as `Validate.html`.

Listing 13-9: Validating forms

```
<!DOCTYPE HTML>
<html>
<style type="text/css">
h1 {
    color:blue;
    font-size:48px;
    text-align:center;
}
body {
    margin-left:20px;
    font-family:Verdana, Geneva, sans-serif;
    font-size:24px;
    color:#C60;
    background-color:#FC0;
}
</style>
<script type="text/javascript">
function vaidationFunction()
{
    var uname=document.forms["validate"]["userName"].value;
    var pw=document.forms["validate"]["secret"].value;
    var unb=(uname.toLowerCase()=="tycoon");
    var pwv=(pw.toLowerCase()=="money");
    var success=unb && pwv;
    if(success)
    {
        alert("Big tip!->Buy low. Sell high.");
    }
    else
    {
```

(continued)

Listing 13-9 *(continued)*

```
        alert("Please check your user name and password.");
    }
}
</script>
<head>
<meta http-equiv="Content-Type" content="text/html; charset=UTF-8">
<title>Password Validation</title>
</head>
<body>
<h1>Valuable financial advice for logged in users!</h1>
Enter User Name:
<form name="validate" onsubmit="return vaidationFunction()" >
  <input type="text" name="userName">
  <br/>
  Enter Password:<br/>
  <input type="password" name="secret">
  <br/>
  <input type="submit" value="Validate" name="sub">
</form>
</body>
</html>
```

Now load the HTML file named `Validate.html` on your mobile device, using any mobile browser. Figure 13-7 shows what you'll see. The style sheet enlarges the text for mobile users — but as soon as the user taps the data entry boxes (input forms), the images become very large — huge, in fact, as shown in Figure 13-7. Here the text has to be large enough for the mobile user to see immediately what action is required, but also small enough that when the device zooms in on the data input, it can still be read. The 24-pixel fonts were a compromise, but as you can see they couldn't very well have been much smaller or larger. The Validate button is just visible initially, but once data entry begins, it's is clearly visible; so no attempt to change its size seemed needed.

Figure 13-7:
Three
steps in the
validation
process.

Chapter 14

Creating a Mobile Quiz

• •

• •

Among other interesting and exciting features, JavaScript brings interactivity to your websites. It allows you to develop sites beyond the pretty face provided by HTML and CSS. JavaScript allows you to make that pretty face talented — to make your good-looking web pages dance and sing, even breakdance. In addition to providing your web creations interesting animation options, you can also create JavaScript applications that make decisions based on user input — applications such as, say, an interactive quiz.

Suppose you're teaching JavaScript, and you want to put together an online quiz to test your students on JavaScript concepts and terms on their mobile devices. In this way, while they're waiting in line, put on hold, or sitting at the bus stop, they can review and test themselves on JavaScript terms and concepts. Over time, you can update your quiz, adding new material — either by expanding it with additional questions or substituting all new ones for existing questions.

This chapter looks at the processes and techniques you will use to become a master quiz builder! As with most big projects, it's often good to break a full-blown web application down into different tasks, defining each one and tackling each of them individually. That is, you want to reduce this somewhat complex process to a series of logical steps. In this case, the main parts of creating an online quiz consist of three different technologies: HTML, CSS, and JavaScript.

Furthermore, the quiz itself will consist of different phases, or operations. These operations are not the exclusive domain of a single technology. You may have to use two or more of the technologies together for the different phases. This chapter shows you how to construct the various phases and combine them into a single application.

Understanding Multiphase Application Development

Each type of web application has its own set of phases, sometimes known as *operations* or *routines*. An online quiz, for example, would consist of the following phases:

- ✔ **User input:** That's a geeky way of saying that the quiz-taker needs a way to enter answers to the questions in the quiz.

- ✔ **Data storage:** When the answers have been entered, you need a way of storing them. For this quiz, the storage is temporary so you don't have to worry about trying to write the answers to a permanent storage technology, such as a database or even a local hard drive. All storage is done in memory, saving the user's answers so that the application can tally and score the quiz.

- ✔ **Quiz evaluation:** The quiz-taker will want to know how well she did on the quiz. (Of course after you've spent time creating the quiz *you'll get 100 percent!*) The last phase of the application is scoring and presenting the user with the results.

For the quiz to be comprehensive (and useful), these routines must be combined into one seamless application. Let's start by examining the different operational parts and which technologies each phase requires.

The User Interface

An application's user interface (UI) represents the part of the program where a user interacts with the web page. In this case, the UI is the part where the user actually *takes* the quiz. So, first you should determine which technologies provide what options to help create the user the UI. HTML, for example, provides the necessary form fields, in this case text boxes, radio buttons, and checkboxes. Forms and form fields are discussed in detail in Chapter 9.

The important thing to keep in mind when developing for mobile environments is that the relative sizes of the UI will change as soon as the user begins to thumb the viewing window to a larger size. By defining the CSS relative to the form where the UI elements are viewed, you can optimize the relative sizes. So if you're going to resize the text, be sure to define it in the form tags as well as in the body element.

Whatever you do, remember that your UI will look different on a mobile device than it will on the screen where you develop it. So be sure to pay attention to the relative sizes of the input elements — text input, radio button input, and checkbox input — as well as the size of the fonts.

The text box

When designing a quiz for a mobile device, you're probably not going to have much display area for essay questions (and nobody likes them anyway). Besides, long multiword and multisentence answers would be incredibly difficult to score with JavaScript.

You *could* include a big essay area using the `<textarea>` tag, discussed in Chapter 9, but that would not leave much room for other questions. So, we won't create any essay questions for this quiz. However, you do have room for short answers, such as one-word answers. JavaScript has lots of different named parts, defined with terms your students should know. So, you could quiz your students on their knowledge of JavaScript terms and concepts. Let's do that!

For example, one question you might ask could be: "What elements are used for temporary storage in JavaScript?"

The answer is *variables*.

To hold this information until time to place it into a JavaScript variable, you use an HTML `text input`, or *text field*, form element. Text fields (also known as *text boxes*) and other form elements are discussed in Chapter 9. An example of a text field is shown in Figure 14-1.

With some mobile devices, such as the iPhone shown in Figure 14-1, as soon as you tap on the input box, the text box enlarges and the keyboard appears. When the Done button is tapped, the keyboard disappears, and the user can resize the screen by stretching it with finger and thumb — a process known as multi-touch.

Figure 14-1:
Text input
box, text
field.

The radio button

Another handy tool for creating quizzes is the *radio button*, also discussed in
Chapter 9. Use the radio button when you want only one correct response
in a list of two or more possible responses. For example, `True/False` questions are the kind of *mutually exclusive* choice that radio buttons are good
for. If you tap one button, the other buttons' statuses become *unchecked*. For
example, Figure 14-2 shows a radio button group consisting of three political
orientations. If any one button is tapped (checked), the other two buttons'
statuses become unchecked.

If you're creating a questionnaire to gather user demographics, respondents
are often reluctant to fill out several text boxes. (We used to use pen and
paper for this. Humans have become so spoiled!) Radio buttons make it easier
for them to respond, and you're more likely to get the information you're
seeking!

The checkbox

The third UI component in our JavaScript quiz is the *checkbox*, discussed in
Chapter 9. Like radio buttons, checkboxes gather user responses through
predefined choices. However, unlike radio buttons, checkboxes are not mutually exclusive. Users can check as many responses as they want for any single
question. For example, in designing an online store, a developer might want

to include options for gift wrapping, expedited shipping, and receiving a pro-
motional newsletter from the company. A user might want all, some, or none
of those options, and checkboxes make it possible (and easy) to choose the
desired selections. Figure 14-3 shows an example of where a checkbox might
come in handy:

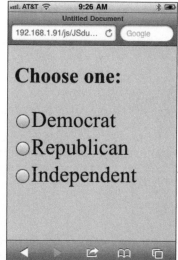

Figure 14-2:
A radio but-
ton group
with three
possible
answers.

Figure 14-3:
Checkboxes
allow users
to make
more than
one selec-
tion.

Data Storage

The concept of *data storage* often conjures up images of server-side programming and really complex stuff. Not here. Whenever you use a form in HTML, you are likely to store data. Most HTML tags have a name and a value. When users enter information into a form, they place the data that they have entered into a temporary storage area, a field. JavaScript can access that stored information and do something with it. In this section, you will see how different kinds of forms store data and how that data can be retrieved.

Basic data storage in forms

In order to understand data storage in forms, we need to look at the Document Object Model (DOM), discussed in Chapter 3. To express the DOM in code, we have to envision an outline. At the top of the outline is the *document* — a fancy name for "web page." So all references to the page in DOM-talk is:

```
document
```

That's pretty easy to remember. What's in the document (page) is then attached to the document by dots (periods). Thus, your typical DOM statement looks something list this:

```
document.myForm.myInput.value
```

That DOM statement in an outline looks like the following:

    I. My web page (document)

      a. My form (form element)

      i. My input (text, radio button, text box)

        1. Value (contents) of element to the immediate left.

Now, you're ready to write a little HTML script with all of the ingredients. To do so, open a new HTML page with your favorite HTML document editor or text editor, add the script in Listing 14-1 and save it as `DataStorage.html`.

Listing 14-1:   HTML data storage script

```
<!DOCTYPE HTML>
<html>
<head>
<script type="text/javascript">
function showDOM()
{
```

```
      alert(document.myForm.myInput.value);
}
</script>
<style type="text/css">
/*BEC0CA,A99570,8B7155,6C4A36,491E42 */
body {
    font-family:Verdana, Geneva, sans-serif;
    color:#491E42;
    background-color:#BEC0CA;
}
form {
    font-size:24px;
}
</style>

<meta http-equiv="Content-Type" content="text/html; charset=UTF-8">
<title>Data in Elements</title>
</head>
<body>
<form name="myForm">
Enter text:<br/>
  <input type="text" name="myInput"><p/>
  <input type="submit" value = "Click Me" onClick="showDOM()">
</form>
</body>
</html>
```

If you test this file on your mobile device using any browser, you will see
something like Figure 14-4.

Figure 14-4:
DOM
statement
with stored
value.

In reviewing the DOM statement, you can see that the `alert()` function displays whatever is typed into the text box:

```
document.myForm.myInput.value
```

That's because the contents of the text input box named `myInput` is within the form container named `myForm`, all of which reside on the web page (document.)

Think of the little dots as being *links in a chain* — those little beaded chains used on key chains. The DOM statement is just a way of taking whatever is stored in the form elements and doing something with it — for example, displaying it with a JavaScript function.

Storing and retrieving data in radio buttons

Dealing with radio buttons is a little trickier than text. With radio buttons, you have to provide a value attribute and you have to check to see whether or not the radio button has been selected. or "checked." It's best to start off with some simple code here:

```
Choose favorite:<br/>type of pet:<br/>
  <input type="radio" name="zapRadio" value="cats">Cats<br/>
  <input type="radio" name="zapRadio" value="dogs">Dogs<br/>
  <input type="radio" name="zapRadio" value="birds">Birds<br/>
```

First of all, a string, numeric, or Boolean is assigned to the value attribute of each radio button. In the preceding list, `cats`, `dogs`, and `birds` have been assigned to the radio button values. Second, each radio button can either be in a state of `checked` or `unchecked`. Third, all of the names in each radio input element in a group *must be identical*.

Storing values in radio buttons

Storing a value in a radio button requires only that you assign a value to the `value` attribute. The user chooses a value by clicking one of the buttons, which is *very easy*. On the screen, the radio buttons will look like Figure 14-5.

Take a look at Figure 14-5 and ask yourself, *How do I get the value of the clicked radio button?*" You cannot use the DOM statement, because all of the radio buttons have the *same name*:

```
document.formName.zapRadio.value
```

Further, you must specify only that a radio button that has been selected. This requires a two-step process.

1. Determine whether the button has been selected (checked) or not.

2. Get the value of the selected button.

Figure 14-5:
Radio but-
tons store
whether a
button is
checked or
unchecked.

One of the secrets of radio button names is that although a group must all have the same name, each of the names is given a number. (This is exactly the way array elements work.) Here's another way to look at the DOM for the three buttons:

```
document.formName.zapRadio[0].checked;
document.formName.zapRadio[1].checked;
document.formName.zapRadio[2].checked;
```

The DOM statements can be either True or False. Because only one of the buttons in the group can be checked at any one time, only one can be True. So, the next trick is determining which button is checked.

Computers hate to waste any integers, and so arrays and array-like elements in the DOM begin with 0 instead of 1. Like arrays, you can find the length of a form or input groups like radio buttons by checking the length attribute. If your highest-numbered radio button is myRadio[8], the length will be 9 because even though the array ends at 8, numbered from 0 to 8, the total number of elements is 9.

Looping through radio buttons

In order to find which radio button is checked and the value of that radio button, JavaScript uses a loop. A loop is simply a repeated operation like asking, *Are we there yet?* When we arrive, we announce, *"We're here!"* and the question is no longer asked. However, we now need to ask, *Where are we?* The "value" of the location is where we have stopped — *We're at the zoo!*

The loop format in JavaScript keeps asking, *Is this one checked?* When the loop finds the checked radio button, it then asks, *What's the value?* In DOM, the queries are written as follows:

```
True? document.formName.zapRadio[XX].checked;
Value? document.formName.zapRadio[XX].value;
```

The XX represents an unknown value.

The `for` loop has a beginning value that will be set to 0 because the radio button array begins with 0. The number of radio buttons in the group determines how many times the loop will run — each "run" is called an *iteration*. We will use a variable the length of the radio button group that we can get from the name of the group (`zapRadio`).

```
var radioSize=document.myForm.zapRadio.length;
```

Next, using the `radioSize` variable, we will begin the `for` loop with a variable that holds the value of the current iteration and declares the loop's starting point:

```
for(var fl=0;fl<radioSize;fl++)
{
```

The first line declares, "*Start the loop with a variable (fl) set to 0. Then, check to see if it is smaller than the length of the button group (radioSize) and then increment (increase) the next iteration by 1 (fl++).*"

Each time the loop iterates, it checks to whether the radio button is checked using the code:

```
if(document.myForm.zapRadio[fl].checked)
{
```

Remember that the button is either going to be checked or not, and replies with either `True` (checked) or `False` (not checked). If it detects a `True` response, it then announces that the button is checked. In this case, an `alert()` function will do the trick:

```
alert(document.myForm.zapRadio[fl].value);
```

That's all there is to it. We can now make a little program that finds which pet a user prefers. To do so, open a new HTML page on your favorite HTML document editor or text editor, add the script in Listing 14-2, and then save the file as `ChoiceDataStorage.html`.

Listing 14-2: Using radio buttons

```
<!DOCTYPE HTML>
<html>
<head>
<script type="text/javascript">
function showDOM()
{
var radioSize=document.myForm.zapRadio.length;
    for(var fl=0;fl<radioSize;fl++)
    {
        if(document.myForm.zapRadio[fl].checked)
        {
            alert(document.myForm.zapRadio[fl].value);
        }
    }
}
</script>
<style type="text/css">
body {
    font-family:Verdana, Geneva, sans-serif;
    color:#491E42;
    background-color:#BEC0CA;
}
form {
    font-size:24px;
}
</style>

<meta http-equiv="Content-Type" content="text/html; charset=UTF-8">
<title>Data in Elements</title>
</head>
<body>
<form name="myForm">
Choose favorite<br/>type of pet:<br/>
  <input type="radio" name="zapRadio" value="cats">Cats<br/>
  <input type="radio" name="zapRadio" value="dogs">Dogs<br/>
  <input type="radio" name="zapRadio" value="birds">Birds<br/>
  <input type="submit" value = "Click Me" onClick="showDOM()">
</form>
</body>
</html>
```

Test the file on your mobile device using any browser. Figure 14-6 shows what you will see.

Radio buttons are a little more challenging to get information from than are text input forms, but keep in mind that they're a lot easier for the user. As a general rule, *the easier it is for the user, the more difficult it is for the developer.*

Figure 14-6:
Retrieving
information
from data
stored in
radio
buttons.

Storing and retrieving data in checkboxes

Working with checkboxes is very similar to working with radio buttons, with
one important exception: In a checkbox group, you can make more than
a single selection. You can name checkboxes either as array-type group-
ings like radio buttons or you can treat them as independent selections.
Much of the information of the previous section on radio buttons applies to
checkboxes — we can skip some of the preliminaries. However, you'll see an
important difference in that each checkbox in this example has a different
name as shown in the following DOM representations:

```
document.codeForm.checkH.value;
document.codeForm.checkC.value;
document.codeForm.checkJ.value;
document.codeForm.checkP.value;
document.codeForm.checkA.value;
```

All of the checkboxes belong to the same form (`codeForm`), but each has a
unique name. However, we still need to determine whether a checkbox has
been checked or not. Further, instead of simply sending out the name of a
single selection, we will send out all of those that have been checked. To do
that, each checked value is placed into a variable and then concatenated
(joined) to any other checked checkbox in the variable. The following snippet
shows the process:

```
if(document.codeForm.checkC.checked)
{
    mycode += " " + document.codeForm.checkC.value;
}
```

Using the variable `mycode` with the compound operator `+=`, the program can store all of the different selections separated by a blank space (" "). Okay, you should be all set to create a checkbox operation. To do so, open a new HTML page on your favorite HTML document editor or text editor, add the script in Listing 14-3, and save the file as `CheckboxDataStorage.html`.

Listing 14-3:   Using checkboxes

```html
<!DOCTYPE HTML>
<html>
<head>
<script type="text/javascript">
function checkPlease()
{
   var mycode=" ";
   if(document.codeForm.checkH.checked)
   {
      mycode +=document.codeForm.checkH.value;
   }

   if(document.codeForm.checkC.checked)
   {
      mycode += " " + document.codeForm.checkC.value;
   }

   if(document.codeForm.checkJ.checked)
   {
      mycode += " " +document.codeForm.checkJ.value;
   }

   if(document.codeForm.checkP.checked)
   {
      mycode += " " +document.codeForm.checkP.value;
   }

   if(document.codeForm.checkA.checked)
   {
      mycode += " " +document.codeForm.checkA.value;
   }
   alert(mycode);
}
</script>
<style type="text/css">
body {
   font-family:Verdana, Geneva, sans-serif;
   color:#3C4631;
   background-color:#EAE9C0;
}
form {
   font-size:24px;
}
```

(continued)

Listing 14-3 *(continued)*

```
</style>

<meta http-equiv="Content-Type" content="text/html; charset=UTF-8">
<title>Checkbox Data</title>
</head>
<body>
<form name="codeForm">
 Which internet coding
<br/>
do you use?<br/>
  <input type="checkbox" name="checkH" value="html5">
  HTML5<br/>
  <input type="checkbox" name="checkC" value="css3">
  CSS3<br/>
  <input type="checkbox" name="checkJ" value="javascript">
  JavaScript<br/>
   <input type="checkbox" name="checkP" value="php">
  PHP<br/>
   <input type="checkbox" name="checkA" value="actionscript">
  ActionScript<br/>
  <input type="submit" value = "Click Me" onClick="checkPlease()">
</form>
</body>
</html>
```

Test the file on your computer or mobile device using any browser. Figure 14-7 shows the checkboxes with the multiple checks and the alert window with the different selections:

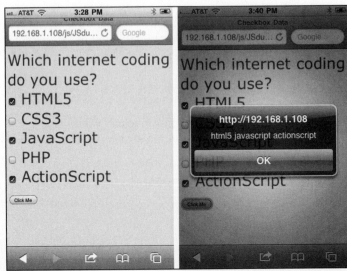

Figure 14-7:
Multiple selections and the selections display.

Now that you can see how to collect and retrieve data with a number of different HTML forms, you're in a position to create something you can use on your mobile device. As noted at the beginning of the chapter, you'll be making your very own JavaScript Quiz.

The JavaScript Quiz Project

In order to do this project, you may want to periodically review how data are stored and retrieved with the different kinds of form inputs and how they can be addressed in DOM format. Everything you need to know, you can find in the previous sections in this chapter.

In order to focus on the different parts of the project, I divided it into three parts: the CSS for the UI, the HTML for collecting and storing data, and the JavaScript for retrieving and displaying data. The project uses separate files for the CSS and JavaScript used by the HTML file. So, be sure to place all of the three files in the same directory.

CSS for a JavaScript quiz

For the artistically challenged among us, the problem of getting a good set of colors can be daunting. Fortunately, help is at hand. Digital artists from all over the world use Adobe Kuler (`http://kuler.adobe.com`). It's free, it's online, and it's easy to use. To get started, go to Kuler and in the Search window, enter the term *Java Script* (two words). Because someone has saved a color combination with the name *Java Script*, you will get a color scheme with compatible colors. With more than half a million color combinations, you will find most search terms have something in the ballpark that you want. When you get the Java Script color combination, you will find the following hexadecimal color values:

```
FFC30D,4F3817,FFFF95,E89840,B8B86A
```

Using a color descriptions for each hexadecimal value, open a new CSS page with your favorite editor, add the code in Listing 14-4, and save the file as `js.css`.

Listing 14-4:   CSS for the JavaScript Quiz

```css
@charset "UTF-8";
/* CSS Document
Orange-Yellow FFC30D, Brown 4F3817, Cream FFFF95,
Lt Burnt OrangeE89840, Light Rusted green B8B86A*/
body
{
    background-color:#FFFF95;
    font-family:Verdana, Geneva, sans-serif;
    color:#4F3817;
    font-size:24px;
}
form
{
    font-size:24px;
}
h1
{
    font-size:62px;
    background-color:#4F3817;
    color:#B8B86A;
    text-align:center;
    padding-bottom:6px;
}

#notice
{
    background-color:#E89840;
}
```

The CSS is similar to other style sheets created in this chapter and elsewhere in this book. For the quiz, a special `#notice` ID is added so that certain terms can be highlighted. In this case, a negative selection requires highlighting.

The HTML UI and storage module

The heart of the quiz for a mobile device is in the HTML. The quiz includes one text form, two radio button forms, and a checkbox form. These forms can all temporarily store data. The submit button form calls a JavaScript program to gather the data and generate a score to be presented to the user. To create the HTML page, open a new HTML page in your favorite editor, add the script in Listing 14-5, and then save the file as `JSquiz.html` in the same directory as the `js.css` file.

Listing 14-5:   HTML for the JavaScript Quiz

```
<!DOCTYPE HTML>
<html>
<head>
<!-- //Java Script
//Orange-Yellow FFC30D, Brown 4F3817, CreamFFFF95,                →5
//Lt Burnt OrangeE89840, Light Rested green B8B86A                →6
-->
<script src="jsquiz.js"></script>                                →8
<link rel="stylesheet" type="text/css" href="js.css" />
<meta http-equiv="Content-Type" content="text/html; charset=UTF-8">
<title>JavaScript Quiz</title>
</head>
<body>
<h1>JavaScript Quiz</h1>
<form name="jsquiz">
  1. What is the name of the structure used to defer execution of a script?
  <input type="text" name="defer">
  <p/>
  2. JavaScript requires a statement of data type for variables.<br/>
  <input type="radio" name="wtype" value ="true">
  True    
  <input type="radio" name="wtype" value ="false">
  False
  <p/>
  3. What is used to launch a function? (Check all that are correct.)<br/>
  <input type="checkbox" name="launch">                          →26
  a. Tag name<br/>
  <input type="checkbox" name="launch">
  b. Event<br/>
  <input type="checkbox" name="launch">
  c. Function call<br/>
  <input type="checkbox" name="launch">                          →32
  d. Form attribute
  <p/>
  4. Which of the following<span class="notice"> cannot </span>be
           accomplished with JavaScript?<br/>
  <input type="radio" name="uses" value ="turnpg">
  a. Go to different web page<br/>
  <input type="radio" name="uses" value ="alert">
  b. Display an alert message<br/>
  <input type="radio" name="uses" value ="db">
  c. Enter data into a database<br/>
  <input type="radio" name="uses" value ="validate">
  d. Validate data entry<br/>
  <input type="submit" name"done" value="Send in answers" onClick="evalNow()">
</form>
</body>
</html>
```

At this junction, do not test the page. It still needs its JavaScript. However, you should take note of some of the features that are slightly unique.

✔ **Lines 5–6:** The color combination descriptions are at the top of the page. This helps in visualizing the color palette you have to work with that is stored in the CSS module.

✔ **Line 8:** The JavaScript is in an external file and is invoked using the `<script>` tag.

✔ **Lines 26–32:** The checkbox input elements all have the same name (`"launch"`). That's because JavaScript is able to treat each as a separate numeric element just like radio buttons. The only difference is that with a radio button group, only a single choice is possible. That is not true with the checkbox.

Also note that the checkboxes do not include value attributes. Actually, none of the forms requires one, but they were added to the radio buttons in case you wanted to expand the scoring. (Of course, you can add values to the checkbox forms.)

All that the quiz needs now is an "engine" to calculate the quiz results. As you will see in the next section, it's not difficult at all.

The Quiz's JavaScript scoring engine

The final piece of the quiz puzzle is the external JavaScript file. As you will see, the JavaScript module is just a single large function (`evalNow`) that determines how many correct answers have been submitted.

To examine the whole quiz, you need to add the JavaScript module. To do so, open a new text page with your favorite editor, add the script in Listing 14-6 and save the file as `jsquiz.js` in the same folder with the `JSquiz.html` and `js.css` files.

Some document editors like Adobe Dreamweaver have JavaScript templates, but even a simple text editor will do the job.

Listing 14-6: JavaScript scoring engine for the JavaScript Quiz

```
// JavaScript Document
function evalNow()
{
    var score=0;
    var q1=document.jsquiz.defer.value;
    if(q1.toLowerCase() =="function")
    {
        score++;
    }
```

```
    var q2bC=document.jsquiz.wtype[1].checked;
    if(q2bC)
    {
        score++;
    }


    var q3bC=document.jsquiz.launch[1].checked;
    var q3cC=document.jsquiz.launch[2].checked;

    if(q3bC && q3cC)
    {
        score++;
    }

    var q4cC=document.jsquiz.uses[2].checked;

    if(q4cC)
    {
        score++;
    }
    alert("You have " + score + " correct responses.");
}
```

The quiz evaluation is set up to add one point for each correct answer. The value is added to a variable named `score`. The points are added using the ++ operator attached to the end of the scoring variable.

The value of the text box is first converted to a lowercase response. Then it is compared with the correct answer — `function`. No matter how the user enters the correct answer (*Function, FUNCTION,* or any other case combination), the scoring system can correctly evaluate it.

The checkboxes and radio buttons only have to be evaluated for whether they are checked or not. If the correct ones are checked, a point is added. In the case of the checkbox, two correct selections are required, and so it uses the following code:

```
var q3bC=document.jsquiz.launch[1].checked;
var q3cC=document.jsquiz.launch[2].checked;

if(q3bC && q3cC)
{
    score++;
}
```

The second and third choices are correct in the checkbox question, and so using the logical AND operator (`&&`) JavaScript makes sure that both have been selected. Note that the elements are identified by `launch[1]` and `launch[2]` to see whether the *second* and *third* checkboxes are checked — remember that `launch[0]` is the first checkbox.

When all of the answers are evaluated, the `score` variable is placed into a string statement within an `alert()` function to display the good (or bad) news to the user. Figure 14-8 shows how the quiz appears in a mobile device during and after the score is evaluated.

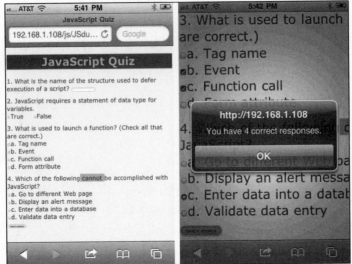

Figure 14-8: A competed mobile quiz with three different type of form field questions.

Chapter 15

Making Your Mobile Site Search-Engine Friendly

Search engines? What do they have to do with HTML and CSS? Considering that much of the process of getting your site found on the popular search engines depends on your markup code, making your site search-engine-friendly has a lot to do with your code.

Traditionally, one of the primary measures of a site's success is how much traffic — how many visitors, or *hits,* it gets. Despite all the money spent on radio, television, and magazine advertising, search engines — primarily Google — are the real forces that shape Internet traffic. If your site is successful, more people will find anvd navigate to your site through search engines than through any other medium.

And nowadays, hands down, the most successful search engine is Google. In fact, some researchers put Google's search engine market share as high as 72 percent, or more than 3 times the market share of all its competitors combined. So, it only makes sense when you optimize a site for search engines, that Google be your primary focus. Besides, in many cases, optimizing a site for Google also prepares that site for many other search engines.

This chapter examines some of the many ways to prepare your site and your code for getting it found on Google. You learn how search engines find and index sites, including what criteria — aside from paying for it — gets a site closer to the top of the search engine's list of sites. Believe it or not, just being the most pertinent, or being the closest match to the user's search terms, is not always good enough. Sometimes, it isn't even close to good enough.

You can do many things to enhance your site's standing on Google, such as creating efficient <meta> tags in the <head> section of your pages; using relevant page titles, headings, and subheads; the density, or how often, you use keywords in your copy; the placement of keywords on your pages; image alternative text; sitemaps; and many other techniques. This chapter examines the most effective search engine optimization (SEO) practices.

You Build It, but They Don't Come

During the many years I have been designing websites for clients, I have run into several people who believed that to achieve success on the Internet, all you have to do is build a nice-looking, informative website, and then sit back and wait to get rich. This reminds me of a famous line from a popular Kevin Costner baseball movie, _Field of Dreams_. A ghost in the movie tells the protagonist, Costner, who is contemplating building a baseball diamond in his corn field, "If you build it, they will come."

When it comes to generating website traffic, this attitude is extremely naïve. In one way or another, most websites are designed to perform some kind of marketing — even sites where the site itself is the product. Marketing is an arduous, ongoing, time-consuming task. Search engine optimization is a form of marketing and an important part of an overall marketing plan. As the site designer, the job of preparing a site for search engines often falls to you.

Understanding How Search Engines Find Websites

Frankly, the answer to the question, "How do search engines find websites?" is simple. You — the website designer, website owner, or SEO professional — tell the search engine about the site and where (the URL) to find it. It's how, or how well, you tell them about the site _in the pages themselves_ that determines where (the _position_) the site places (_ranks_) in the list.

Google, for example, has an intricate set of criteria it examines to determine where the site places on search results page. It scores the site based on several factors, factors calculated by examining and indexing the site. To do that, Google must first be told about the site and where to find it.

Registering your site

Although all search engines are slightly different, they can't examine and index your site until they know that it exists and where to find it. Google, for example, requires you to register the site. Registering your site is easy, as shown in Figure 15-1. Simply navigate to `google.com/addurl/?continue=/addurl`.

Over the years, this URL has changed several times. You can always find the current registration page by searching for *register site google*.

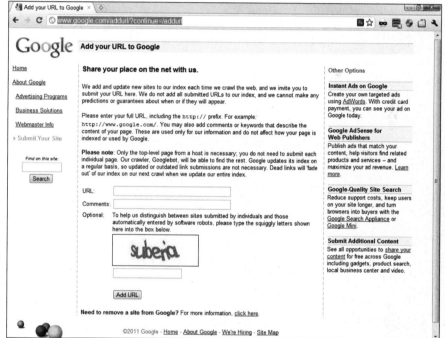

Figure 15-1: Google's site registration page.

Spiders, crawling, bots, robots, and other science fiction terms

As new technologies emerge, they bring with them their own unique set of often confusing (and sometimes amusing) terms. People who are unfamiliar with Internet search engine technology must surely scratch their heads at terms like *spiders, crawling* (or *web-crawling*), *bots,* and *robots.* Essentially, all these terms refer to primarily the same technology — the software that search engines like Google use to examine and index websites. No matter what you call them, these applications all do essentially the same thing: visit websites and collect and store information about them. They are often referred to as *spiders* because, metaphorically, they crawl around the Web.

Cold, hard clicks for cash

People often ask me how to get their sites positioned at the top or near the top of Google's search result pages. The answer is, "The only sure, tried, and tested method for assuring priority placement on Google and most other search engines is to pay for it."

When you look at a Google search results page, shown in the figure, notice the top three positions and the list of results down the right side of the page. These advertisers, who are subscribers to Google's AdSense program, paid for these positions. Or, better yet, they "bid" for them. The advertisers in the top positions bid the highest amount.

Top three results are
pay-per-click...

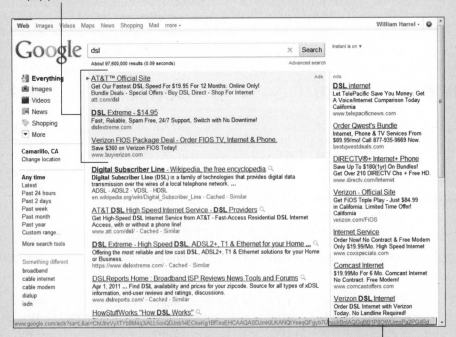

...as are all the
results on the right side

However, it isn't quite that simple. These advertisers don't actually get charged each time their listing gets displayed in one of the top positions. Instead, they pay only if the user clicks the listing and goes to the advertiser's website. In other words, they bid how much they are willing pay for the "click-through." In Internet-speak, this is a product known universally by the generic name of "pay-per-click" advertising.

Shortly after you tell Google about your site, it sends out its spiders to read and index your site. The indexing process consists of building lists— pages, page titles, headings, subheadings, `meta keywords`, `meta descriptions`, the text in the `alt` attribute properties of your images (discussed in Chapter 7), and several other places on the site, including *Sitemaps*.

After the spiders gather the information about your site, Google's server applications weigh, or *rank,* the data using Google's own proprietary algorithms. Other search engines use similar methods but different ranking criteria. Google, for example, leaves out articles (*a, an,* and *the*) and other "insignificant" words. Other search engines, such as AltaVista, do not. Where the words occur on the site, how often they occur, and so on, are all part of the ranking system. Words in page titles, subtitles, and `meta` tags, for example, are weighted more heavily than words in the main body, or copy.

So, the SEO techniques described in this chapter help place you at the top of the list in the free, or non-pay-per-click sections of search engine results pages. Sometimes, depending on your budget, you just have to settle for that.

Preparing Your Site for Search Engines

How you optimize your website for Google and other search sites really depends on how you intend to use the search engine. If you use the pay-per-click method described in the sidebar, "Cold, hard clicks for cash," the procedure is much different than if you don't. Paid advertising SEO is performed primarily from the search engine's SEO setup pages and is not really dependent on how you set up your pages. In fact, many companies pay SEO professionals to optimize pay-per-click services. Sometimes, depending on the product or service you're selling, the way you set up your keywords can play a huge role in how much money you spend. We're talking thousands of dollars. Paying somebody who understands how the various services work can be a wise investment.

SEO for free search engine placement, though, isn't as financially risky so you can afford to experiment. The techniques described in this section are pretty much tried and tested — not just by me, but by many web design and SEO professionals. Keep in mind that the order in which I arrange these techniques is critical. From first to last, I list them in the order Google weighs them. Keywords in page titles and other `meta` tags, for instance, rank higher than keywords in the body text, or the copy, of your site.

Optimizing with meta tags

As discussed in Chapters 2 and 7, you place meta tags in the <head> section of your HTML pages. In addition to using them to define Content-Type and the page's character set, you can also use them to create keywords and descriptions, which the search engines use to index your site. The three most important are <title>, <META NAME="keywords">, and <META NAME="description">.

Not only are the page title and description critical to how search engines index your site, but Google and some other sites also use this data to describe the site in the search results list. In Figure 15-2, for example, the data between the <title></title> and in the <META NAME="description"> tag are what Google uses for the site title and site description in the search results, respectively. (Notice the absence of pay-per-click listings. Nobody is competing for the use of my name as a keyword — so I don't have to pay to get to the top of the list!)

Description

Title

```
<html>
<script src="/Scripts/swfobject_modified.js" type="text/javascript"></script>
<head>
<title>William Harrel - Writing, Editing, Print and Website Design</title>
<meta http-equiv="Content-Style-Type" content="text/css">
<META http-equiv=Content-Type content="text/html; charset=iso-8859-1">
<META NAME="keywords" content="Web design; writing; writer; designer; editor; print media;
document design; flash; animation; technology writing; technical writer; world wide web design;
www design; brochures; marketing; multimedia; desktop publishing; blog design; Adobe Acrobat;
Photoshop; Indesign; Adobe; search engine optimization; William Harrel; Harrel; Bill Harrel;
William D Harrel;">
<META NAME="description" content="williamharrel.com, over 25 years experience writing, editing,
print media and website design">
<meta name="verify-v1" content="X55ZxwKHaFa15qOJgWI/eyNY4KXayqc/4mO2Oiexjrw=" />
<META NAME="ROBOTS" CONTENT="ALL">
<LINK HREF="style.css" TYPE="text/css" REL="stylesheet"><meta http-equiv="Content-Type" content=
"text/html; charset=windows-1251"><style type="text/css">
<!--
body {
    margin-left: 0px;
    margin-top: 0px;
    margin-right: 0px;
    margin-bottom: 0px;
}
-->
</style></head>

<body bgcolor="#616161">

<script type="text/javascript">
<!--
```

Figure 15-2: Google uses the <title> and meta description data for the page title and description in the search results list.

The all-important page title

Technically, the <title> is not a meta tag. But it and the other elements described in this section are the most critical to search engine ranking and indexing. I group them here for convenience and clarity.

In addition to naming the page in the browser title bar, as described in Chapter 6, the data between the <title></title> tags is critical to SEO.

Whenever possible, without getting carried away, you should try to squeeze as many keywords into it as possible. This really is a balancing act between making it all fit on the browser title bar, having the title make sense, and getting the keywords in. The title in Figure 15-2 works well, I think. (Even if I do say so myself.)

Also keep in mind that you can get a lot more data indexed and get multiple listings in the search engines if you give each page in the site a different title. For example, if you or your client provides multiple services, consider using a different page title — such as "Company Name–This Service," or "Company Name–That Service" — for each page. This is also true of descriptions, discussed next.

Some people are tempted to squeeze too many keywords into the title. Yes, the search engines weigh the title heavily, but they also weigh the other `meta` tags data almost as heavily. These are much more appropriate for shoe-horning in keywords.

Page descriptions

Page descriptions are important for a number of reasons other than providing data for search engines. Not only do the search engines use them for indexing keywords and describing the page in the search results list (shown in Figure 15-2), but also, if you don't use them, Google and some other search sites will use text from the body of the page itself.

Descriptions provide more space for your keywords than titles. Because some or all of the description shows up in the search list, as shown in Figure 15-3, your description should be a coherent sentence, or at least a series of coherent phrases.

Page descriptions use the `meta` tag with the `description` attribute, like this:

```
<META NAME="description" content="The California Spine Institute is the center
        for Minimally Invasive Spinal Surgery to help cure back pain,
        spinal stenosis, and many other forms of chronic back pain using
        the latest techniques in MISS including laser spine surgery,
        endoscopic back and neck surgery, and x Stop" />
```

You should give some thought to your descriptions. The preceding example isn't bad. It includes a lot of data without being too difficult to read or follow. (It's too long to fit in Google's description field, but that isn't unusual.) Think about all the keywords you want to use, as well as the message you want to convey, and combine them gracefully. Say, for example, your business serves only a specific geographic location. You could start your description with that information: "Serving the Southern California area for 15 years, we . . . ." See how much is accomplished with just a few words? In addition, *California* and *Southern California* are now part of your search terms, or keywords.

Figure 15-3:
Some or all
of the page
description
appears in
the search
results list
and over
the page
preview
thumbnail.

Keywords

Unlike titles and descriptions, the `keywords` meta data does not display in most search results pages. Because of this, you don't have to worry about phrasing or whether the entire tag makes sense. And you can use as many keywords as you want. However, not all search engines will use them all, so put the most important ones first.

The keyword `meta` tag uses the `keywords` attribute, and it is written as follows:

```
<META NAME="keywords" content="California, spine center, minimally invasive
          spinal surgery, spine surgery, laser spine surgery, x stop,
          endoscopic back surgery, endoscopic neck surgery" />
```

Neither keywords nor titles and descriptions are case sensitive, though you should use caps appropriately in the latter two for obvious reasons — they are displayed in the search results listing. There are, however, some basic formatting and other tenets you should follow to ensure maximum effectiveness, such as these:

- ✔ **Use commas** to separate each keyword or phrase.

- ✔ **Arrange terms correctly.** Using two- and three-word phrases is fine, but you should arrange them in the order a user would typically type them. *Technical writer,* for instance, should not appear in your keywords as *writer technical.* Experienced search engine users often use quotation marks to search for specific phrasing. When they search for "*web design,*" (including the quotation marks), for example, the search engine first looks for and then matches the term as it is written.

✔ **Use acronyms** and initials. If the field or product your site advertises has buzz acronyms and titles, such as *TV* for *television,* or *WWW* for the Web or Internet, include them in your keywords.

✔ **Use variations and alternate spellings** of your keywords. If you are an animator, you should use both *animator* and *animation.* It also doesn't hurt to use the plural versions of your keywords. Some words also have alternate spellings, and some English-speaking countries spell words differently; they often use different words altogether for the same thing. The British, for instance, spell *pajamas* as *pyjamas.* There are hundreds of these variations, though, and you can't use them all.

✔ **Use abbreviations** when it's common to do so. I'm certainly not advocating abbreviating everything. But for some services and products, it's quite common — even preferred. The use of *Dr.* for *doctor* comes to mind.

Keywords and site content

In addition to indexing and ranking the contents of your `<title>` and `<meta>` tags, Google and other search engines also index and weigh the actual page content, the text that your site visitors read (or at least you hope they read it). This data does not get as high a ranking as `meta` data, and — although you should be mindful that Google and other search engines glean and index keywords from the page text — in my opinion, you should balance this. Don't sacrifice clean, easy-to-read copy. In other words, do not compromise the message of the page because of your desire to use your keywords.

Also, keep in mind that the placement of your keywords is important. Keywords in headings and subheads rank higher than keywords in the body text paragraphs. Furthermore, the various search engines have different criteria, and you can't possibly meet the requirements of all of them — that is, not if you want to compose meaningful, professionally written copy.

Understanding and using keywords

After all the SEO finessing and manipulation is said and done, keywords are what search engines index. Without them, there is nothing for search engines to find and display on search results pages. Your most important keywords are what lead potential customers to your web pages. Keywords generate web traffic.

How Google reads and indexes a site

Google's spider, or robot, is commonly known as Googlebot. After the Google servers are made aware of a new site, usually Googlebot goes looking for the home for the site. In addition to reading and indexing the meta data and page text, Googlebot reads all the links on the page. It then follows the links (crawls) to those pages and reads and indexes them. If there are new links on these pages, it goes through the entire process again, then again, and so on.

This is the basic process by which Googlebot crawls the Web and gathers and indexes websites. This method enables Google to include all the pages on your site — as long as they are all part of an unbroken chain of links. In other words, as shown in the figure, all pages will be indexed as long as Googlebot can get to each of them, in one way or another, from the home page.

In the figure, for example, `index.html` is not directly linked to `map.html`. Googlebot, however, will learn the existence and whereabouts of `map.html` while reading and indexing `contactUs.html`. The spider simply continues to crawl from page to page to page until it runs out of links.

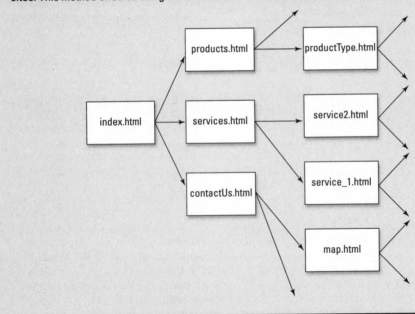

When using keywords in your copy, the two most important areas of consideration are

- ✔ **Placement:** Where the keywords are located is important, to varying degrees, with the major search engines.

- ✔ **Density:** How many keywords appear on the page makes a difference t o all the search engine algorithms. The choice of which keywords to target on each page is often critical — especially when using highly competitive keywords.

This brief discussion of using keywords in your web pages is meant as an overview. For a more detailed explanation of how search engines use keywords, see *Google AdWords For Dummies* by Howie Jacobson.

Keyword placement

Each major search engine has different criteria for ranking keywords in the *copy*, or main text, on your pages. Google, for example, doesn't seem to care where on the page — the top, middle, or bottom sections — the keywords are placed. Yahoo!, on the other hand, seems to place a premium on keywords placed closer to the top of the page. All search engines rank keywords used in headings and subheads slightly higher than when the same words are used in standard paragraphs. Also, words placed between bold (`<b></b>`) and italic (`<i></i>`) tags rank slightly higher.

Also, pay special attention to the text you place in your alternative (`alt`) attribute of your `<image>` tags, discussed in Chapter 6. Keep in mind, though, that most search engines index and rank the text in the `alt` attribute only when the image is hyperlinked. Otherwise, most search engines ignore the alternative text altogether.

In other words, the following `image` tag alternative text will get indexed and ranked:

```
<a href="index.html" target="_self"><img src="images/logo.png" alt="California
        Spine Institute" width="320" height="32" vspace="10" /></a>
```

And the `image` tag alternative text will not get indexed and ranked:

```
<img src="images/logo.png" alt="California Spine Institute" width="320"
        height="32" vspace="10" />
```

Keyword density

Each search engine uses different keyword density criteria. Some search engines permit heavier keyword numbers and density on the page, while others, such as Google, are much stricter in the density levels they allow. Google permits about a 2 percent keyword concentration per page; some others allow up to 5 percent. When you exceed these percentages, some search engines view it as a form of spamming. This can cause lower rankings or get those keywords ignored altogether.

For maximum benefit, the site's home page and other pages should each have a slightly different focus. This is especially important for highly competitive keywords — products or services with a high concentration or presence on the Internet. The keyword phrase *web design,* for example, is a highly competitive search term. In such cases, it's good practice not to focus on more than one keyword or phrase per page.

For less common search terms, you don't need to concentrate on a single keyword. With fewer sites targeting those search terms, the page can focus on more words and phrases, enabling the page to be found by different keyword combinations.

Okay. So what if there are pages on your site you don't want indexed and listed on Google? (There are many reasons you might not want a page indexed. Perhaps it's a members-only page, or perhaps you charge a fee for reading specific pages on your site.) To tell Googlebot *not* to index your page, simply insert the following code in your HTML page <head> section:

```
<META NAME="googlebot" content="noindex" />
```

After you optimize your pages for the search engines, you probably would like to know how effective the optimization is, right? There are number of free tools on the Internet. Some of them are quite good and rather informative — and best of all, easy to use. The SEO Analysis Tool at seoworkers.com/tools/report.html runs a complete check and provides a free report with several suggestions for optimization. If you're looking for the ultimate analyzer, though, check out Google's Webmaster Tools. You need a Google account to use it (it's free). Webmaster Tools analyzes your site, keeps track of your web traffic, and provides all kinds of useful information, such as which keywords are bringing you the most traffic, as shown in Figure 15-4.

Figure 15-4: Google's free Webmaster Tools are a suite of applications for analyzing and optimizing your search engine traffic.

Using Sitemaps to Submit Your Sites to Search Engines

You're probably thinking that this section talks about the sitemaps found on many websites that provide a list and link to all the pages within a specific site. But no, instead, this is a different type of sitemap. This *Sitemap* starts with a capital *S* and performs an entirely different function. This Sitemap informs Google and other search engines about the pages in your website. It provides information that the search engines can use for finding pages and listing information about the pages on search results pages.

Creating and using Sitemaps is beyond the scope of this book, but I wanted to make you aware of them. The information in this section is offered primarily to pique your interest.

Why Sitemaps?

Sitemaps perform a number of useful functions. Most importantly, they make sure that search engines know about all the pages in your site, or at least all the pages in the Sitemap. Also, they provide a great way to list information about pages that don't have body copy, such as digital video and Flash pages. For example, a Sitemap video entry can specify the video length (in minutes and seconds), subject, and audience rating (PG, R, and so on). An image entry can describe an image's subject matter, type, licensing information, and so on. Figure 15-5 shows an example of a video entry in a Sitemap from Google's Creating Sitemaps page.

Figure 15-5:
Example
of Video
Sitemap
entry in
an XML
Sitemap file.

```
<?xml version="1.0" encoding="UTF-8"?>
<urlset xmlns="http://www.sitemaps.org/schemas/sitemap/0.9"
        xmlns:image="http://www.sitemaps.org/schemas/sitemap-image/1.1"
        xmlns:video="http://www.sitemaps.org/schemas/sitemap-video/1.1">
  <url>
    <loc>http://www.example.com/foo.html</loc>
    <image:image>
        <image:loc>http://example.com/image.jpg</image:loc>
    </image:image>
    <video:video>
        <video:content_loc>http://www.example.com/video123.flv</video:content_loc>
        <video:player_loc allow_embed="yes" autoplay="ap=1">http://www.example.com/videoplayer.swf?video=123</video:player_loc>
        <video:thumbnail_loc>http://www.example.com/thumbs/123.jpg</video:thumbnail_loc>
        <video:title>Grilling steaks for summer</video:title>
        <video:description>Get perfectly done steaks every time</video:description>
    </video:video>
  </url>
</urlset>
```

Are you getting the idea? Sitemaps can also contain other useful information about your pages, such as the date a page was created, last updated, and when and how often you expect the page to change.

Creating your Sitemap

Google accepts Sitemaps in a few different formats. However, the accepted protocol for all search engines is XML. I actually use a program called Zoom Search Engine Indexer; it generates Sitemaps automatically after analyzing the site. I have not attempted to create one from scratch. As I write this, the Zoom Search Engine Indexer, shown in Figure 15-6, will create XML Sitemaps of up to 99 pages for free. (No, I don't use the free version. Many of my sites have well beyond that many pages.) Even then, I often have to open the XML file in Dreamweaver or UltraEdit and tweak some of the entries.

My point is this: Unless you have some experience working with XML, you might be better off using some sort of Sitemap generator. If you want to give the by-hand method a try, though, Google has some pretty extensive Help pages starting on its webmaster Central pages, starting at `google.com/support/webmasters/`.

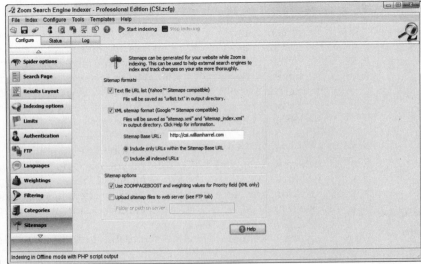

Figure 15-6:
The Zoom
Search
Engine
Indexer.

Chapter 16

Building a Mobile Search Page

*A*lthough menus and hyperlinks are great tools for helping your mobile users find and navigate your websites, at some point sites get much too big and contain far too much data to rely on simple navigation and inter-activity mechanisms. Besides, a simple one- or few-word menu entry doesn't always adequately describe the contents of a page. A page describing, say, a laser surgery procedure, for example, could include all kinds of terms that are not implied in a menu entry or a hyperlink text string.

Perhaps more than other computer users, mobile users tend to be in hurry. Providing them ways to find information on your mobile site as quickly as possible will make the site more successful and therefore more popular. Without question, one of the most useful tools for helping users find data on your site is a search page, or perhaps a search field on an existing page.

Generally, there are three approaches to creating search capabilities for a website:

✔ **Use a utility** that creates the searchable database and search and results pages for you. There are several of these available, and some, such as WrenSoft's Zoom Search Engine, are free or inexpensive.

✔ **Use a search engine API (application programming interface),** such as Google's Custom Search API or Yahoo's Search API. These utilities enable you to create a Google or a Yahoo! search engine that searches and displays results based solely on the sites and pages you define.

✔ **Create your own search engine from scratch,** including creating your own searchable database and search and results pages.

This chapter covers the first two options. First, I show you how to find and select the right search engine-building utility based on your needs. Then I show you how to use one of them, Zoom Search Engine, to create a search application for your site. This chapter also examines using the Google Custom Search API, which is by far the most popular technique for creating searchable websites. I show you how to sign up with Google to use the API, how to deploy it, and how to customize the search and results pages.

In my opinion, given the complexity and time involved in the third option, creating your search engine from scratch is not really a sensible approach. The other ready-made and easy-to-deploy options make creating an engine from scratch overcomplicated and unnecessary. Unless your client insists on her own custom-made search engine (and none of mine ever has), I wouldn't bother. Besides, it requires far too much programming and goes far beyond the scope of this book.

Making Your Site Searchable

Indexing consists of collecting keywords and phrases on the site and saving them in easily searched formats, such as flat text files, spreadsheets, or databases. In fact, this is what Google and most other search engines do. Their spiders and robots glean your pages and save the data in *ginormous* databases on their servers. To make your site searchable, you need to do essentially the same kind of indexing, though on a *much* smaller scale, of course.

Essentially, whether users search for your site from a search engine, such as Google (described in Chapter 15), or if they search the contents of your site locally, the data that makes up your site — the meta tags, content, image `alt` tags, PDFs, and so on — should be indexed. The alternative — scripts that search and organize individual page content on the fly — when the user clicks "Search," is far too inefficient and time-consuming to be effective unless the site is small — too small to need search capabilities! Instead, the search engine scripts search the index.

Finding and Using Search Engine Utilities

Calling the products I talk about "utilities" is probably a bit of a misnomer. They are, in effect, search engines. But when most people hear "search engine," they assume Google and Yahoo!. However, the programs that index and subsequently search and display results on websites locally (as opposed to searching for websites) are also known as search engines.

If you do a search for the term *search engine* you will come up with many online search engines and even online utilities that index and search individual websites. You have to comb through the search results to find programs that you install on your web server, programs that then index the site and provide search functionality. Several are available, and they have very different features. Many of them run on a limited number of web server platforms. PerlFect, for example, is a free search engine that runs only on Unix, Linux, and Windows NT, which leaves out a bunch of other possibilities. Others, such as Zoom Search Engine, claim to be free, but the free version leaves out a bunch of important search criteria, such as the capability to index PDFs and other important file formats.

Make sure the search engine you choose supports and does what you need it to. Over the next few pages, I walk you through the most important features and why they are worth considering.

Choosing your search engine

A few years ago, when I started including search engines on some of my larger websites, I looked long and hard. Yes, I kissed a few frogs before I found one that met my needs. What I learned from that experience is that not all search engines are created equal. Finding one that is reasonably priced, easy to use, and has enough flexibility to let me control how a search is processed — what is searched and how the results are displayed — is critical to creating highly useful search engines in a reasonable amount of time. This is especially important when defining search applications for mobile sites. Efficiency is critical.

With those criteria in mind, here are six things to consider when looking over the somewhat vast field of search engines:

- **Cost:** Considering that you can set up a Google or Yahoo! search of your site for free (or quite cheaply if your site represents a small business), it doesn't make sense to pay much for a search engine utility. Some utilities limit the number of pages you can search, what you can search, and even the number of searches allowed.

  Make sure that "free" doesn't include hefty upgrade fees to get exactly what you need. Also make sure that the purchase of a license doesn't limit you to using the software on just one website. Many products allow you to use the software as often as you want, which can save you a lot of money.

- **Types of documents indexed:** Another important consideration is what types of documents you can index. Some search engines, especially free and shareware solutions, only index HTML- and HTM-based documents. Make sure the software you choose indexes all the types of documents you use on your website, including PDFs, SWFs (Flash), XML, PHP, DOC (Microsoft Word), and so on. Also important is that the software provides an easy way to exclude directories and documents from indexing.

✔ **Ease of use:** Look over the documentation of the software you choose *before* purchasing it. Some software requires writing scripts and setting up SQL or MySQL databases, which can add greatly to the learning curve.

One of the several reasons why I chose Zoom Search Engine, for instance, is that it can be installed as a Dreamweaver extension and used inside Dreamweaver to index the site and deploy the search engine. It also creates its own databases. In addition, it enables me to index the site on my workstation and then upload the search application and database files. I find all of this very handy.

✔ **Platform:** Make sure the search engine software runs on the web server where your site is hosted. If the site's search and results pages require PHP, for example, make sure your server supports PHP.

Whenever possible, unless you expect only newer smartphone and tablet traffic, use a program that supports server-side code. This increases the number of devices that can use the search engine. Also, using a program that supports server-side code means that the mobile devices visiting your site don't have to do all the work. It's much quicker and more efficient to let the server process the application code, especially because this type of application can have as many as a few thousand lines of code! Chapter 6 has additional information on the benefits of server-side versus client-side scripting.

✔ **Support:** Be sure you understand the program's support terms. Some free and shareware programs provide only e-mail or FAQ and blog support. This is fine, but take a look at the FAQ or blog support pages and note how long it takes the software publisher's support staff to respond to support questions. If the application provides documentation, make sure you understand it. Also take a few minutes to see how difficult the program is to set up and use. How long does it take to create the search application and deploy it?

✔ **Customizable:** The software you choose should enable you to customize the search application in several ways. It should be easy, for example, to change the appearance of the search and results pages; you don't want your search pages to stick out like sore thumbs. They should look like they are part of the same website.

You should be able to modify what gets indexed in several ways, such as by document type or directory, and you should be able to exclude specific words and phrases. It is also handy to have the capability to apply *weighting,* or preferences, as to how much relevance is placed on specific parts of the documents you're indexing. You might want to give more weighting to page titles than to body text, for instance. For more on search engine weighting, see Chapter 15.

Creating a search application

You'd think that indexing and searching a site would be simply a matter of doing just that — indexing and searching the site, right? On most sites, there is usually data, even entire pages, that you don't want indexed. You will often want the data on one page to show up higher in your results list than the same data on another page. And, of course, you'll want your search and results pages to look as closely as possible to the rest of the pages on your site. It can be quite jarring for the user who has been surfing around on, say, black pages with white text to suddenly wind up on a page with a stark white background with black text!

In this section, I show you how to create a search application using the features available in Zoom Search Engine — not because I think you should use this application, but because it provides me with a backdrop to describe what is important when setting up search capabilities on your site. Few search engine utilities offer as many features as Zoom Search Engine. The Zoom Search Engine program is highly versatile and customizable, and provides every feature you'll need to create highly useful search engines.

I like Zoom Search Engine for several other reasons, too. It's inexpensive. The $99 Professional version indexes up to 200,000 pages with more than 500,000 unique keywords and phrases. It also supports search and results pages in PHP, JavaScript, ASP, ASP.NET, and CGI. In addition to HTML and HTM pages, it indexes just about every other kind of document, including PDFs, DOC (Microsoft Word), PowerPoint, and many others. It's easy to exclude documents and directories on all kinds of criteria. And it can be installed as a Dreamweaver extension, which was highly useful for me.

Another reason I like Zoom Search Engine is that it enables me to create Sitemaps for submission to Google and other search engines. See Chapter 15 for a discussion of Sitemaps.

You can choose whatever solution you want. However, no matter what program you choose, the concepts discussed in this section are important to the success of your search application. Figure 16-1 shows an example of the search and results pages I created with this utility.

Figure 16-1:
Example of PHP mobile search engine created with a search engine utility.

Choosing the search engine scripting language

You need to choose a programming language for your search engine, and your choices are dependent on the server your site is hosted on. Although many applications enable you to choose JavaScript for the search engine script language, unless you are designing a search engine that will run only on the latest mobile phones and tablets, you should choose another format. JavaScript, as discussed in Chapters 3, 13, and 14, is a client-side scripting language and doesn't run on several mobile devices. And, for that matter, not all mobile devices support all JavaScript commands and functions.

CGI, Perl, and PHP are the most common server-side languages. You can use any of them. However, of the three, PHP is the fastest, most common, and most widely used. Also, most PHP code is contained within the search and results pages themselves, so you don't have to worry about uploading and keeping track of separate script files and directories. ASP and ASP.NET are also server-side languages. These run primarily on Windows-based web servers. If your site is hosted on a Windows server, both languages are quite capable. Of the two, ASP.NET is newest and leanest.

Another reason not to use JavaScript for your search engine code is that the mobile device — more specifically, the mobile browser — must interpret and process the code. Servers are much faster at this than the average mobile device. Unlike many JavaScript applications, search engines can require quite a few lines of code, so speed is important.

Deciding what to index

One of the more convenient things about using a well-developed search engine utility like Zoom Search Engine is that it lets you choose which files to index without requiring you to write a lot of time-consuming code. The program writes the code for you. For example, in Figure 16-2, Zoom Search Engine indexes only the files indicated in the Scan Extensions list, and only the page elements displayed in the Indexing Options dialog box.

Another reason to use a search engine utility is that the code required to scan and index non-HTML pages, such as Flash SWFs and Acrobat PDFs, is very high-end. A good utility will create that code for you. I hate to keep harping, but creating a good search engine for your site from scratch requires a lot of programming savvy.

Deciding what to index consists of two parts: what URL or URLs to index, and which files to index. In most cases, you index only one URL, the address of the site for which you are creating a search engine. However, many utilities enable you to index and search several URLs, and you can use this built-in option to index subdomains, such as mobile.mysite.com.

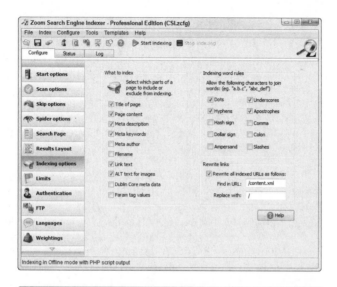

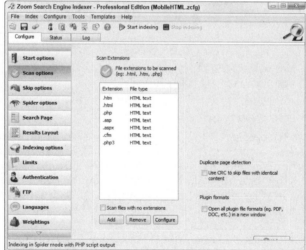

Figure 16-2:
Search engine utilities enable you to designate which files to scan easily, without having to research how to write the code.

Deciding what not to index

If there are parts of your site you don't want indexed and searched, a good utility program will let you exclude them in a few different ways. In addition to excluding content based on page and file names, Zoom Search Engine, for example, enables you to exclude specific words from the index. That's ideal if you don't want specific content to show up in your searches. An option to exclude words of a minimum number of letters is also helpful.

Designing the search and results pages

Designing the search and results pages consists of two phases: modifying the behavior of the pages and modifying their appearance. Behavior is controlled with code, the PHP or other scripting language that creates the search engine application; appearance is controlled with HTML and CSS. Behavioral concerns on the search page include what types of searches to allow, such as Boolean operators or wild cards; whether to allow the user additional options, such as matching any word in the search term or requiring all the words typed into the search field to be matched; the number of items to appear in the search results list, and so on.

The search page in Figure 16-3 shows a pretty good sampling of options designed to make the user's search more successful. The Zoom Search Engine dialog box gives you a pretty good example of the options worth considering, as well as a good idea of how complicated the scripts to accomplish all this would be if you tried to program the search application yourself.

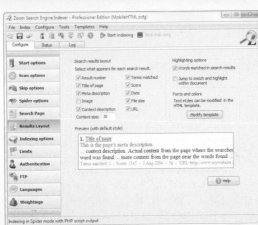

Figure 16-3:
Example of a search page with multiple search options and the search engine utility dialog box used to create the options.

Various search engine utilities have different approaches to controlling the appearance of search and results pages. What I like about the Zoom Search Engine approach is that you edit the HTML and CSS code in a template that the search application reads before creating the pages. With this approach, you are never actually editing the application pages — the pages containing all the intricate code — themselves. The search page for an application can have nearly 3,500 lines of complicated, integrated PHP script. (Each script depends on the integrity of the others.) You don't want to try to edit these pages on your own.

Designing the results page requires deciding what appears on the page and in the list entries themselves. Should you, for example, include the number of search results, the page titles, and meta descriptions in the results list items? Do you want the matched terms highlighted, the search relevance score, the date the pages in the list were created, the pages' URLs, and so on, displayed? Figure 16-4 shows a dialog box of the important results page items and an example of how the selected items will appear in the list entries.

Figure 16-4:
When designing a results page, you control which items are displayed on the page itself and in the search results list items.

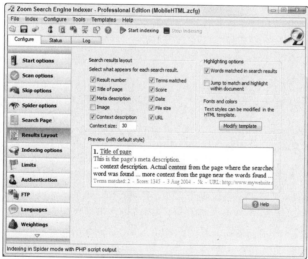

Weightings

Weighting is SearchEngineSpeak for *priority* or *rating.* (Also see Chapter 15 for more on weighting.) When you apply weightings to page elements or sections, such as page titles, meta descriptions, and so on, you're telling the search engine to prefer the keywords in those elements over the same keywords in other elements. It makes sense, doesn't it, to give a higher rating to keywords in the page title than keywords in the page body? Figure 16-5 shows a dialog box for applying weightings to various page elements. Notice also that the section on the right of the dialog box allows you to apply weighting by a word's position on the page. Keywords closer to the top can be weighted higher than keywords closer to the bottom.

Figure 16-5:
Apply
weightings
to specific
page ele-
ments so
keywords
indexed in
those ele-
ments take
precedence
over key-
words in
other page
elements.

Recommended, synonyms, custom meta fields, and more

Believe it or not, there is a whole bunch of search engine features not listed in this section — all designed so that you can provide a better search experience for your users. Here are a few more options to look out for when considering search engine utilities:

✔ **Recommended:** In addition to rating keywords, you can *recommend* them in the search results. In other words, when the user searches for a specific keyword, your search results page can list pages that you'd prefer they looked at first — even suggesting them as "recommended."

✔ **Synonyms:** This sort of speaks for itself, doesn't it? Creating synonym matches allows you to control display results even further.

✔ **Custom meta fields:** A feature that I find particularly helpful is the capability to create custom meta tags to control search results. This option provides another way to influence which pages get listed first in the search results.

Deploying a Google Search of Your Site

You may be wondering why you would want a Google search on your site. Wouldn't this actually provide search results for other sites on the Internet and take your users away from your site? The answer is, not if you don't want it to. Google, Yahoo!, Bing, and other major search engines provide APIs and services — usually free — that enable you to use their search engines to search only your site.

Google has two tools for setting up a search of your site. The one you should choose depends on your needs. Both products require an account at Google, which you can sign up for free. The two tools are

- ✔ **Google Standard Edition:** The Standard Edition is free, but, unless your site is for a nonprofit organization, university, or government agency, you have to allow Google to run ads on the results page. Some webmasters don't mind this. It's a free and easy way to get a search engine on your site. This option also enables you to make a little money through Google's AdSense program if visitors actually click the ads.

- ✔ **Google Site Search:** Google Site Search is Google's business search solution. Site Search, which, as I write this, starts at $100 annually for up to 20,000 searches. This is not bad, considering that this averages 1,667 searches per month. Your site would be getting respectable traffic if you have that many searches, especially on a mobile site. (Not all visitors will search the site.) The better it's designed, however, the fewer number of searches are necessary. The next tier, 50,000 searches, runs $250 annually. If the site has enough traffic to get more than 4,000 searches a month, neither you nor your client should mind paying less than $25 a month for a search engine, especially if the site is generating revenue!

Signing up for a Google search engine

If you don't use a Google product already, such as Gmail or YouTube, you can sign up for a free account at google.com. After you create your account, you start the process of creating your Google search engine at `www.google.com/intl/en/options/` (which displays the page shown in Figure 16-6).

Simply select the Custom Search option in the left column.

The Custom Search link brings up the Google Custom Search page, shown in Figure 16-7. Click the Create a Custom Search Engine button in the upper-right section of the page to move to the next phase in the process, where you can read about the benefits and features of the search engine product.

Custom Search option

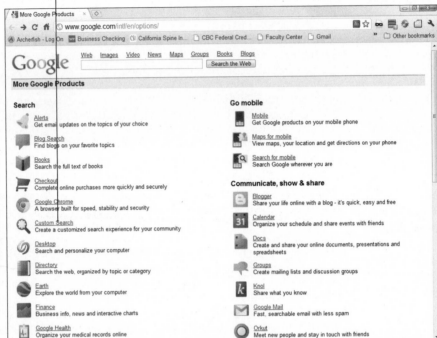

Figure 16-6:
Click the
Custom
Search link
to begin the
process of
creating
a Google
search
engine for
your site.

Setting up your search engine

Finally, you get to the page where you set up your search engine, shown in
Figure 16-8. The page has three sections: Describe Your Search Engine, Define
Your Search Engine, and Select an Edition. Here are five things to think about
as you fill in this form:

- **Name:** This field simply enables you to give a working name to the
  search engine. It is *not* used in the search and has nothing to do with
  how options appear in the search results list.

- **Description:** This field does not affect your search or the appearance of
  the search and results pages. Keep in mind that many people, especially
  designers, have many search engines. This field simply helps people
  keep track of their search engines.

- **Language:** You can create multiple versions of the same search engine
  in different languages by repeating this process for each language.

- **Sites to search:** This is where you put the URL for your website, or multiple
  URLs sites if you are searching more than one site. You can also control
  what gets searched here by providing specific subdirectories in your URLs.

✔ **Select an edition:** This is where you choose the type of account you want, the standard free search engine that displays ads on the page, or Site Search, which does not display ads and provides more customization options. If you choose the free version, you can upgrade later. Notice the Learn More button beneath the two edition options. Click it to see descriptions of both editions. In addition to the absence of ads, the Site Search version offers many more configuration options.

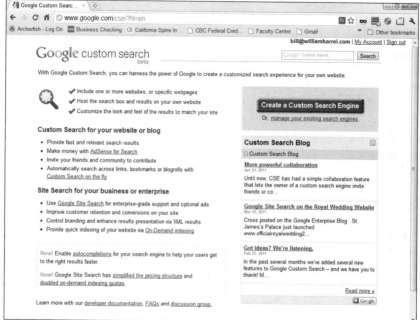

Figure 16-7:
This page describes the benefits of a Google Search engine with multiple links to pages describing various options.

Designing your search field and results pages

After you have filled out the form in Figure 16-8, agreed to the terms and conditions, and clicked Next, you'll be taken to the Try It Out page. From here, you pick a color scheme for your search field and results page. As I write this, six options are provided, as shown in Figure 16-9. Choose a scheme as close to your site as possible.

You can customize the scheme later using Google's CSS and JavaScript API option, described in the search engine's API documentation. This requires some well-developed JavaScript skills, however. If you want to try it, click the CSS and JavaScript link in the lower-right corner of the page.

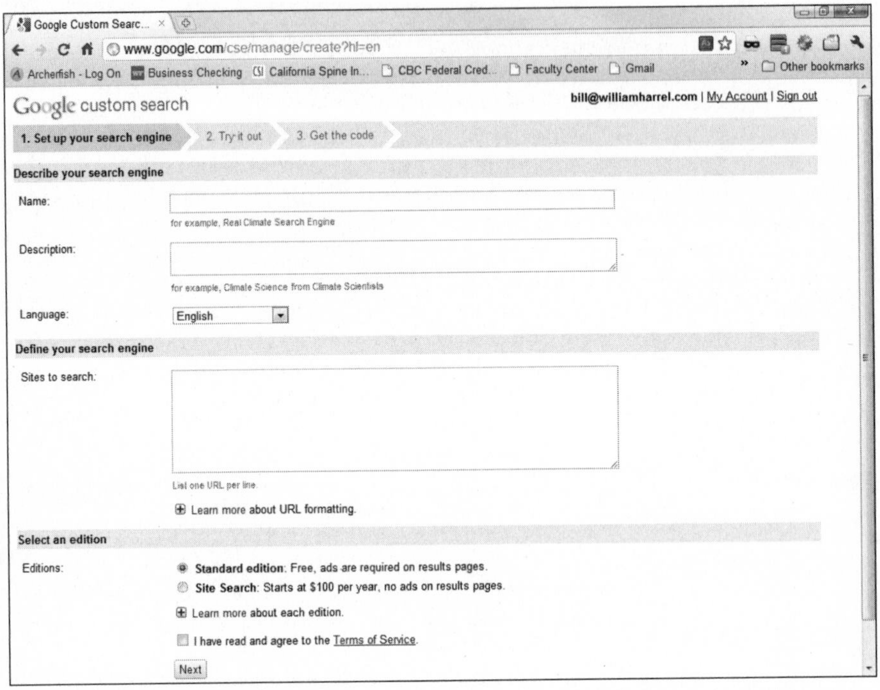

Figure 16-8:
Setting up
your new
search
engine.

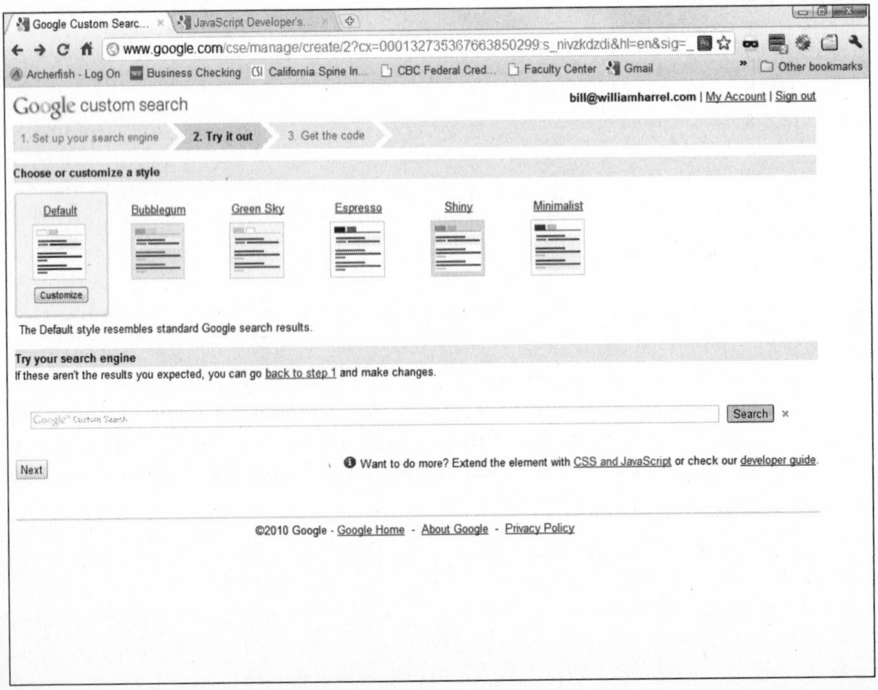

Figure 16-9:
Choose
a color
scheme and
try out your
new search
engine.

Trying out your search engine

You can see how each color scheme will display your search field results pages by selecting them, which automatically changes the appearance of the search field. To see how the results page will look, type a keyword or search term in the field and click Search. Figure 16-10 shows the results for the Minimalist theme.

Notice the ads at the top and along the right side of the page. I searched for the keyword *laser*. Notice that ads match my search term. As you can imagine, on a business site, displaying ads for possible competitors is not the ideal result. Eliminate the ads by signing up for the $100-per-year Site Search edition, rather than the Standard free edition.

Figure 16-10:
Example of
the search
results
page for the
Standard
edition
Google
search
engine.

Ads by Google	Ads by Google
Excel Laser Vision Lasik	**Beverly Hills Laser/Derm.**
www.exceleye.com Harvard-Trained Dr. Ferzaad Moosa Over 60,000+ Procedures Performed	Top Dermatologist in LA for Acne, Rosacea, Wrinkles, Skin Care
	www.90210derm.com
Top LASIK Doc	
www.laser-prk.com Cedars-Sinai/U.C.L.A. LASIK expert new 'LaserWave' technology	**Red Green Blue Lasers**
	From 375nm to 1064nm Free space and fiber coupled
Spine Center - California Spine Institute for Minimally Invasive ...	www.rgblase.com
The California Spine Institute is the center for Minimally Invasive Spinal Surgery to help cure back pain, spinal stenosis, and many other forms of chronic ...	
www.spinecenter.com/	**lasers**
	low-level Laser irradiation,safety, without side effects,long life-span
Low Energy, Non-Ablative Holmium Laser Thermodiskoplasty for ...	en.hnc.cn
A computerized finite element model of the herniated disc, pre and post laser thermodiskoplasty, developed for the purpose of demonstrating the amount of ...	
www.spinecenter.com/papers/aanos_ltd/page2.htm	**High Power Green Laser**
	50mw Green Laser $17.95 Free Shipping, Get Yours Now!
Percutaneous Microdecompressive Endoscopic Cervical Discectomy ...	www.shophde.com
Percutaneous Microdecompressive Endoscopic Cervical Discectomy with recently added application of Non-Ablative Lower Laser Energy (Laser Thermodiskoplasty) ...	
www.spinecenter.com/Abstracts/Abstracts%20archive/abs8.html	
California Spine Institute Medical Center, Inc. - California Spine ...	
... Zoom globalMissPres - Endoscopic Laser Spine Surgery assets/text/text.swf content/text/laserSpine true content/text/simple page/bg1.gif Zoom laserSpine ...	
www.spinecenter.com/assets/site.xml	
Dr. Chiu's Scientific Research Papers	
Low Energy, Non-Ablative Holmium Laser Thermodiskoplasty For ... Percutaneous Microdecompressive Endoscopic Cervical Discectomy with Laser Thermodiskoplasty ...	
www.spinecenter.com/Abstracts/Abstracts%20archive/abstracts.htm	
California Spine Institute Mobile Site	
His clinical interests include endoscopic spine surgery, tissue modulation technology (laser) and surgical informatics related to a "digital technological ...	
www.spinecenter.com/mobile1/about.html	
Material and Methods	
... decompressive endoscopic spinal discectomy with laser thermodiskoplasty, i.e., collagen	

If you use the Try Your Search Engine option to test the color scheme, to get back to the Try It Out page, click your browser's Back button. Once you have settled on a color scheme, click Next.

You can sign up for Google's AdSense product and enter into a revenue-sharing agreement with Google. That means each time a user clicks an ad on your results page, you make a little money. Each click pays only a few cents, based on the keyword or search term and how much the advertiser pays for the click-through. To find out more about AdSense and sign up, go to `https://google.com/adsense/`.

Deploying your Google search engine

Deploying your search engine is simply a matter of copying the code Google generates for you at the completion of this process. After you have chosen your color scheme, as described in the preceding section, and clicked Next, you are taken to the Get the Code page, shown in Figure 16-11.

Google custom search   bill@williamharrel.com | My Account | Sign out

| 1. Set up your search engine | 2. Try it out | **3. Get the code** |

To get code for other hosting options, adjust your settings on the Look and feel page.

Custom Search element code

Paste this code in the page where you'd like the Custom Search element to appear. **Note:** For the most cross-browser compatibility, it is recommended that your HTML pages use a supported doctype such as `<!DOCTYPE html>`. CSS hover effects require a supported doctype.

```
<div id="cse" style="width: 100%;">Loading</div>
<script src="//www.google.com/jsapi" type="text/javascript"></scrip
<script type="text/javascript">
  google.load('search', '1', {language : 'en', style : google.loade
  google.setOnLoadCallback(function() {
    var customSearchControl = new google.search.CustomSearchControl
    customSearchControl.setResultSetSize(google.search.Search.FILTE
    customSearchControl.draw('cse');
  }, true);
</script>
```

Congratulations, you've finished creating the search engine "California Spine Institute".

Next steps
Visit your search engine's control panel and customize it further in the following ways:

• Include more sites.
• Change the look and feel.
• Sign up to make money with Google AdSense.
• Create search refinements and promotions.

We've sent a confirmation email with this information to bill@williamharrel.com.

Figure 16-11:
To deploy the search engine, copy this code and paste it into your web page.

You can create a dedicated search page, as shown in Figure 16-12, or place the code in a `<div>` container, discussed in Chapters 2 and 7, to deploy the search to a section of an existing page.

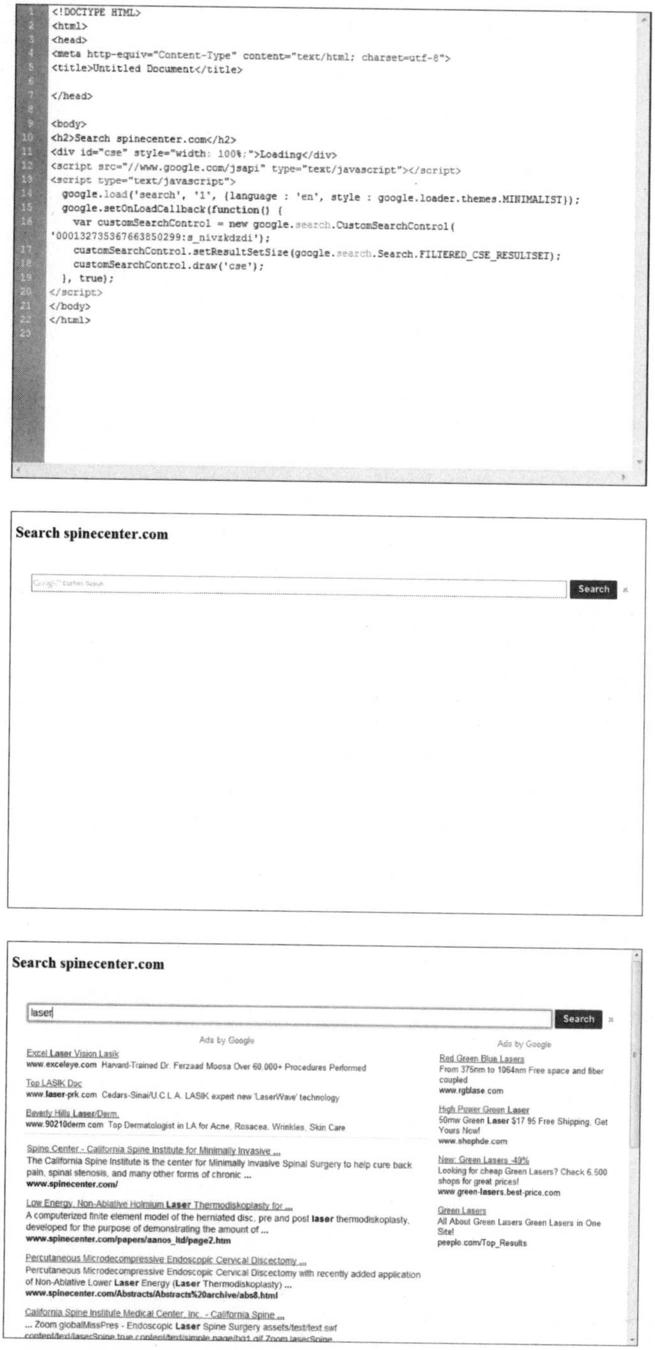

```
1   <!DOCTYPE HTML>
2   <html>
3   <head>
4   <meta http-equiv="Content-Type" content="text/html; charset=utf-8">
5   <title>Untitled Document</title>
6
7   </head>
8
9   <body>
10  <h2>Search spinecenter.com</h2>
11  <div id="cse" style="width: 100%;">Loading</div>
12  <script src="//www.google.com/jsapi" type="text/javascript"></script>
13  <script type="text/javascript">
14    google.load('search', '1', {language : 'en', style : google.loader.themes.MINIMALIST});
15    google.setOnLoadCallback(function() {
16      var customSearchControl = new google.search.CustomSearchControl(
        '000132735367663850299:s_nivzkdzdi');
17      customSearchControl.setResultSetSize(google.search.Search.FILTERED_CSE_RESULTSET);
18      customSearchControl.draw('cse');
19    }, true);
20  </script>
21  </body>
22  </html>
23
```

Search spinecenter.com

Search spinecenter.com

Figure 16-12: Example of a Google Custom Search engine: code view, search, and results pages.

Adding a Google search to an existing site template

After you have created your Google search engine, you may want to incorporate it into your site structure so the search engine pages look as closely as possible like the rest of your site. If you created a base template for your site, this really is pretty simple. It's just a matter of deciding where to place the code on the page, or inside which `<div>` container. Creating and using CSS selectors and containers is discussed in Chapters 2 and 7.

Google allows you to modify the appearance of the results list and to make many other changes at the core, or application, level of their code. But this really is a job for highly experienced programmers. If you're interested in modifying the appearance of your Google search engine's results list, check out `http://code.google.com/apis/customsearch/docs/js/cselement-devguide.html`.

You can place the Google search engine code anywhere you want on the page. The width will, within reason, automatically adapt and resize to the area you designate for it — except for the height, as shown in Figure 6-13. No matter where you put the code, users will have to scroll to see the search results. This is not uncommon on Google results pages, mobile or otherwise.

Web APIs and Ajax

Perhaps you noticed from the Help pages and page titles that Google's search engine API (application programming interface) is something called *Ajax*. Ajax (Asynchronous JavaScript and XML) is a design approach and a set of techniques for delivering an interactive, desktop–like user experience for web applications in browsers. Ajax achieves this by reloading only parts of pages, instead of the entire page, when responding to user input. Instead of whole-page refreshes, small amounts of data are exchanged with the server, rendering the application quickly usable. This is very useful on mobile devices.

Ajax is attractive to web designers because it provides responsive web applications without the need for extensive backend infrastructures. Users benefit from applications that have the familiar feel of desktop applications and provide expanded capabilities.

Ajax is emerging as an important technology for creating low-overhead applications, such as the Google Custom Search engine and Google Maps API (discussed in the next section of this chapter). You can find thousands of ready-made Ajax applications on the Internet, and several are designed for use inside Dreamweaver. For more information on Ajax, visit the W3Schools tutorial at `w3schools.com/ajax/default.asp`.

Figure 16-13:
Example of
the Google
search
engine
deployed in
a website
template.

Placing a Google Map on Your Website

Many types of businesses, especially retail establishments and service companies such as lawyers' and doctors' offices, benefit from providing maps and directions to their locations. Google Maps API makes deploying maps easy on computers and handhelds. Essentially, the process is as simple as copying the code into your template and plugging in the correct map coordinates. I show you how to do that in this section.

Getting the Google Maps API code

Google has several flavors of map APIs, including one for Flash and a few other platforms. The latest and greatest is Google Map JavaScript API V3, which is optimized for mobile devices. In addition to road maps, it supports satellite, aerial, and panoramic photo street views.

If you do a Google search for *Google Maps API,* you come up with several options, including earlier versions of the JavaScript API. The latest version, V3, runs in HTML5 and is simply an all-around better app for mobile devices. You can find the latest version of the map API at http://code.google.com/apis/maps/documentation/javascript/ (which brings up the page shown in Figure 16-14). Click the Tutorial link in step 2 in the How Do I Start section in the upper-right corner.

Tutorial link

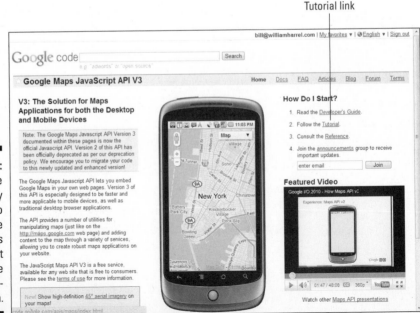

Figure 16-14: The gateway page to the Google Maps JavaScript API code and documentation.

Embedding the Google Maps API code

From the Google Maps JavaScript API V3 Tutorial page, you can either read and follow along with the step-by-step instructions, or copy the example document code into a blank web page and make the necessary changes. If you want to incorporate the map into your site template, the process becomes a little more complicated, but not much. Follow these steps to copy the code into a blank HTML page and modify it to display the location of your business or your client's place of business:

1. **On the Google Maps JavaScript API V3 Tutorial page, scroll down to display the code box shown in Figure 16-15.**

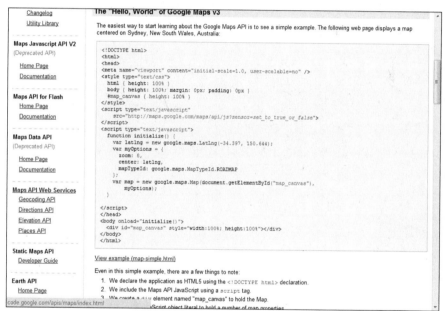

Figure 16-15: The Google Maps API code.

2. **Copy all the code in the box.**

3. **Start a blank HTML page and paste the code into the document.**

4. **Go to the line of code that reads:**

```
src="http://maps.google.com/maps/api/js?sensor=set_to_true_or_false"> and
        change set_to_true_or_false to true.
```

This tells the application to sense the user's current location, using the mobile device's built-in GPS. Setting it to `false` would, of course, tell the application not to sense the current location.

5. **Test the page.**

   By default, the map is set to an address in Sydney, Australia. The location is set by longitude and latitude in the line of code that reads:

   ```
   var latlng = new google.maps.LatLng(-34.397, 150.644);
   ```

   To set this to the location for your (or your client's) place of business, determine the location's longitude and latitude and change these values. You can change the zoom level by changing the `zoom:` option, which is the first line under `var myOptions`. The default value is *8*. Higher numbers zoom in and lower numbers zoom out.

There are many sites on the web for determining longitude and latitude. One that I find works well is iTouchMap.com. Simply go there (`http://itouch-map.com/latlong.html`), type in the business's address, and iTouchMap.com will give the coordinates. Note that some coordinates begin with minus signs (–). Be mindful of the minus (–) signs — they are critical to displaying the correct location.

Chapter 17

Creating a Mobile Shopping Cart

* *

In This Chapter

▶ Analyzing your shopping cart needs

▶ Handling payments, taxes, and shipping

▶ Understanding SSL certificates

▶ Understanding online e-commerce services

▶ Using a server-side shopping cart application

* *

Selling products and services on the Internet has become a multibillion-dollar industry. The number of users buying products on the Internet with their mobile devices is rising daily and may soon bypass the number of users making purchases from standard desktop computers and notebooks. The web applications that provide the interface for Internet shopping, or e-commerce, are called *shopping carts*.

If you've purchased anything on the Internet, you most likely used a shopping cart. In fact, some of largest, most successful companies in the world, such as Amazon and eBay, are, in essence, giant shopping carts. And these huge shopping carts all have mobile versions.

Designing a shopping cart specifically for handhelds — because of screen size and diverse device limitations — presents a unique set of challenges. For example, the code that drives the typical shopping cart is usually lengthy and somewhat processor-intensive, so you don't want to create a cart that processes most of the code on the mobile device itself. Also, shopping carts usually display many images of products, often several versions and sizes of images for each product — and usually many images on the same page. So you need to be especially careful of image file sizes and download times.

Shopping cart solutions come in many shapes and sizes, from numerous sources. However, as with search engines (discussed in Chapter 16), there are really only three methods for developing a shopping cart for your mobile site: using an online solution, such as MobiCart or Google Checkout; using a ready-made server-side shopping cart application, such as X-Cart or Zen Cart; or designing your own cart from scratch.

In this chapter we look at the first two options — using online shopping carts and using shopping cart software packages. The third option — designing the cart from scratch, or writing your own code — is, in my opinion, not a viable option; it would be a huge, time-consuming endeavor. With all the free and low-cost solutions available, taking on that hassle isn't really a sensible approach. Time is your most valuable resource; you want to avoid a huge waste of your company's (or your client's) money.

Shopping cart solutions literally come in all shapes and sizes. Before choosing one, you have several decisions to make, such as how well is the solution suited to selling *your* products or services? How many products do you have to sell? How often will you need to add and remove products? How will you collect your customer's money? How will you calculate and charge for shipping, sales tax, and so on.

And this is a bare-bones list. There are many other things to consider, so this chapter begins with a checklist of what you should consider *before* deciding on a solution and beginning to build your e-commerce site.

Deciding What You Need Your Shopping Cart to Do

Huh? You just want to sell products and collect money online? Isn't this much ado about nothing? I guarantee that after you read this section, you'll understand why decision-making and planning are critical to creating a successful shopping cart. Not only do your needs vary depending on what you're selling, but many other aspects of how the shopping cart behaves are crucial.

Most shopping carts, for instance, require services from and interaction with a few third-party resources. To calculate and charge for shipping, for example, your cart will need to interact with at least one shipping service's (UPS, FedEX, USPS) rate tables. If you want to charge credit cards in real time during a transaction, you'll need a credit card processor, such as PayPal or a merchant account with your bank. The e-commerce solution you choose will need to support these services — from the vendors you use for these services! If your client already does business with vendors for these services, your e-commerce solution should support her existing services. It's not always easy to talk a company into changing these mission-critical vendors, especially if they're happy with the ones they're already using.

So, as you can see, you have some planning and research to do.

Handling payments

No matter what you sell online, you need a way to process payments — some kind of merchant-account vendor to take the payment from the customer's credit card or bank account and put it into your bank account. There are literally hundreds of solutions available. Some are easy to sign up for and use; others require extensive credit histories and personal financial guarantees.

The payment process you choose will also have to be secure. How you handle security — making sure that your customers' private information isn't snatched during transit — depends on the payment solution you choose. This section examines choosing processors and securing payment.

 A primary reason why people shop on the Internet is that it's easy. Whatever payment solution you choose must be simple and immediate. I've seen people try to set up and operate e-commerce systems that require customers to send checks or an employee to get orders from e-mails and process credit cards. Unless you're selling immortality, many people will not continue this checkout process, or simply will not follow through by sending a check.

Payment processors

If your company or client already has a merchant account with a credit card processor, this vendor probably already has a secure online interface for taking payments. In these situations, you'll need to incorporate that solution into the shopping cart. Make sure the cart software or web application you choose either supports the merchant account interface or at least provides a method for handing off payment information to third-party processors and receiving the results to complete the transaction. Sometimes, depending on the software, including such a feature may require some minimal programming to create the bridge between the two applications. You should make sure that this process is well documented — and that you understand what is involved.

If you don't already have a merchant account, one of the most popular — and easiest to get, set up, and use — is PayPal. (If you've purchased anything at all from eBay, you're probably familiar with PayPal.) Aside from being easy to deploy, PayPal has some other good reasons for choosing it as your solution:

- ✔ **Trusted name recognition:** A clear benefit of using PayPal is that a good percentage of your customers are familiar with it and won't hesitate to enter their payment information.

- ✔ **No account required:** Unlike many other solutions, PayPal lets your customers pay without having an existing account or having to go through the hassle of setting up an account.

✔ **Versatile payment options:** PayPal allows your customers to use nearly every credit card available or have payments taken directly from their checking accounts. This arrangement ensures that you won't lose any sales due to type-of-payment limitations.

✔ **Seamless integration:** As shown in Figure 17-1, the handoff between the cart software and PayPal is nearly seamless — the customer doesn't have the jarring sensation of moving between the cart interface and the payment-processing interface.

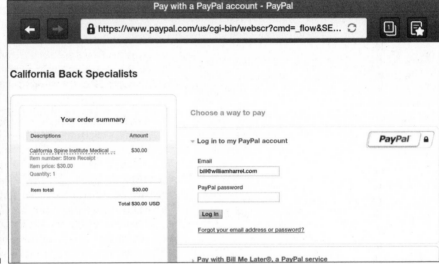

Figure 17-1:
PayPal integrates tightly with most shopping cart applications, passing information seamlessly between interfaces.

Security

No matter what payment solution you use, your customers' transactions should be processed over a secure, encrypted connection. Savvy Internet users know when the data they're entering on a website is protected from snooping. They know to look for indications from their favorite browser that a web page is "secure." Figure 17-2 shows a secure web page in a WebKit browser, as indicated by the lock and the `https` (opposed to `http`) portion of the URL in the address field.

If you use PayPal or some other payment processor, the payment portion of the transaction will be secured automatically. However, many of your customers will be looking for the indication of a secured transaction well *before* they get to the payment step in the process. On my sites, I always *secure all of the shopping cart pages*, so that when the user signs up for an account or enters any other personal data, that's encrypted, too.

Understanding Secure Socket Layer (SSL)

SSL is the industry-standard security mechanism for establishing and maintaining encrypted links between web servers and browsers. This "socket" ensures that all data passed between the web server and the browser is *encrypted*, or rearranged during transport so it can't be deciphered if it's intercepted.

To create an SSL socket for a website, the web server requires an SSL *certificate* for that website. SSL certificates are products you can purchase from several sources, including most web hosting companies. In addition, to allow web servers and browsers to pass encrypted data, they also verify for the user that the domain actually belongs to the owner of the SSL certificate and that the SSL issuer has verified the company's information.

The process of encrypting submitted data remains invisible to your customers. Instead, their browsers display an indicator to let them know they're using SSL-encrypted pages — most browsers display a lock icon somewhere in the browser window. When the user clicks the lock icon, the browser displays the SSL certificate, who owns it, the level of encryption (64-bit, 128-bit, or 256-bit). SSL certificates are issued to companies or individuals who have been verified by the Certification Authority, the entity issuing the certificate.

Typically an SSL certificate will contain your domain name, your company name, your address, your city, your state, and your country. It also contains the expiration date of the certificate and information about the Certification Authority issuing the certificate. When a browser connects to an SSL site, it retrieves the SSL certificate, checks its expiration date, checks to ensure (a) that the certificate has been issued by a trusted Certification Authority, and (b) that it's being used by the website for which it was issued. If any of this information doesn't jibe, the user is notified that the site is insecure.

Using an SSL adds a bit of expense to hosting a website. An SSL certificate requires a *static IP address* for the site using it, which costs a few dollars a month (usually less than $5) and the cost of the certificate itself, which runs between $50 to $150 per year, depending on the bit-level of the encryption and the certificate issuer. If you're selling products on your site or collecting user data, your customers and users will appreciate that you have thought about securing their data. Some users will not use your site if you don't.

When the SSL certificate is installed, you load your pages securely by calling to them with the HTTPS protocol, as with `https://mystore.mydomain.com` or `https://www.mydomain.com/mystore`.

Securing pages with the HTTPS protocol requires a *secure socket layer* (SSL). (In fact, you should consider using SSL whenever you ask users to enter personal data, such as addresses, phone numbers, and so on.) You can purchase an SSL for your website from your web hosting vendor. For more about this security measure, see the accompanying sidebar.

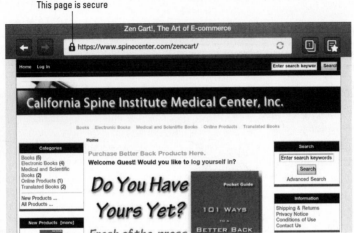

This page is secure

Figure 17-2:
This lock
and the
HTTPS
protocol
in the URL
indicate a
secure site.

What are you selling?

You'd be surprised at what people sell online. Furthermore, I am often amazed at what some people are willing to buy. No matter what you're selling, though, it probably fits into one of three categories: a shippable product, a downloadable product, or a service. Each type of product requires different behavior from your shopping cart.

Selling shippable products

This is by far the most prevalent type of product sold on the Internet. The range of products sold online is vast — everything from computer cables to boats and automobiles. To sell these types of products effectively, your shopping cart must support a number of features. The following list includes the most critical:

- **Images:** You may want to display images of your products, display several different views, or show the user some enlarged views, as in Figure 17-3. Not all shopping carts can do these things.

- **Shipping:** There are oh-so-many things to think about when it comes to shipping. Do you, for example want to offer free shipping, flat-rate shipping, or actual-cost shipping — based on which shipping companies' rates? Do you want to add handling fees? This list goes on and on. Before settling on a solution, you should know beforehand what these needs are, rather than try to adapt these polices to the e-commerce software you choose.

  If you're shipping oversize and/or heavy products such as furniture, remember that these types of items often need to be sent via freight, rather than via standard shipping. In such cases, you may need to contact the shipper to get a quote based on size, weight, and destination; these types of shipping quotes can't be provided automatically over the Internet. Your e-commerce solution must provide a way to give your customers shipping quotes after you get the shipping cost.

Figure 17-3:
Depending
on what
you're sell-
ing, your
customers
may want
to see
enlarged
or multiple
views of
your
products.

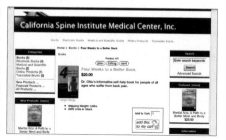 

Selling downloadable products

Downloadable products are, of course, software — which can include computer programs, artwork, documents, e-books, and so on. Basically, the
definition covers any type of computer file(s) you sell and then transfer from
your web servers to the customer's computer. These products do not require
shipping, but they do provide other challenges to your shopping cart application. Your e-commerce solution, for example, will have to provide the user
with secure access to the downloadable product, as shown in Figure 17-4.

It will also need to control access to the file. In other words, you don't want
to provide an uncontrolled link or URL that allows unlimited downloads —
unless, that is, you don't mind giving your products away. (Your client or
boss might mind!)

Selling services online

Hmmm . . . What kind of services would you sell online? Legal consultations?
Medical examinations? Believe it or not, some people sell these services
online and other people buy them. But I'm thinking more along the lines of,
say, online support contracts — or perhaps access to a specialty blog or
some other type of web content. Often these types of services have recurring
charges, such as monthly or annual fees.

If you're selling subscription-like services, you'll need an e-commerce solution
that supports this type of product — something along the lines of member-
ship fees or dues. Often these types of products are paid for automatically.
When the service expires or comes up for renewal, the shopping cart automatically "hits" the customer's credit card or bank account.

Download info

Access to the
downloadable product

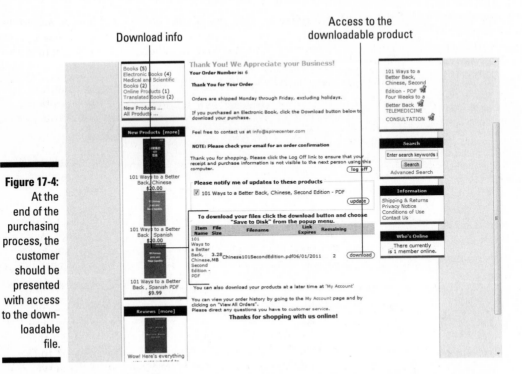

Figure 17-4:
At the
end of the
purchasing
process, the
customer
should be
presented
with access
to the down-
loadable
file.

Some payment processing solutions, such as PayPal, provide the capability
to charge a customer's account monthly, bimonthly, annually, and so on. The
trick here, though, is to get the payment information to flow back into the
e-commerce software. The point, of course, is to make sure the solution you
choose supports recurring charges *and* provides a way for your staff to easily
verify whether a customer's account is current or active.

For example, if you're selling support contracts, your support staff should be
able to do a quick check on the status of the customer's contract before continuing with the support call.

Deploying an Online Mobile E-Commerce Service

As mentioned at the beginning of this chapter, you have two basic choices
for creating an online store:

✔ **Use an online service:** This is typically the easiest and fastest way to get your shopping cart up and in business — but this solution is also typically the most limiting. It doesn't give you a lot of options for configuration and product presentation.

✔ **Use a server-side shopping cart software application:** This method usually provides a much richer feature set and configuration options, but these packages also tend to be considerably more complicated and time-consuming to set up and deploy.

This section examines finding and setting up an online mobile e-cart solution. The next section, "Creating a Server-Side Mobile Shopping Cart," discusses finding and setting up an e-commerce solution on your web server.

An online e-commerce solution is just that — a web application that allows you to list your products and sell them to people who visit your site. As I write this, these solutions are popping up all over the Internet. Some are free; some charge a small monthly or annual fee. Others charge a small percentage for each transaction, or sale.

A Google search for *mobile shopping carts* yields millions of results — far more than you can possibly review and analyze (and far more than I could possibly write about). Before you start looking at solutions, I suggest that you first read the section, "Deciding What You Need Your Shopping Cart to Do," earlier in this chapter. Know *what* you need before looking for the service to help you sell your products.

In addition to making the decisions covered by the information discussed earlier in this chapter, I also suggest that you consider the following:

✔ **Cost:** What will the service cost you? Is there a monthly or annual fee? Does the service charge a percentage of each sale? If the service is free, does *free* mean that you must allow the service to run ads on your mobile shopping cart pages?

✔ **Supported devices:** Which devices does the service support? Which technology does the service use to ensure compatibility? Server-side code? Apps (small programs the customer downloads and installs on her device)? JavaScript or some other client-side technology that limits which devices can use the online store?

✔ **Ease of use:** The primary reason for choosing an online service is ease of use and deployment. Make sure you understand what you're getting into *before* you get into it!

✔ **Integration with your site:** How well will the online service integrate with the rest of your website? Is it easy to come close to the your existing site's layout and color scheme? Will the customer be redirected to another website to make and complete the transaction? If so, how obvious is this location change?

When you set up a PC store nowadays, most online e-commerce services are designed to compensate for mobile devices in one of two ways:

- ✔ Mobile device users will see mobile versions of the site automatically.
- ✔ The site's CSS and HTML are designed to adjust the page automatically for viewing on handhelds.

With that handy amenity in mind, here's a short list of online e-commerce solutions that work well with mobile devices:

- ✔ **Yahoo Store:** Perhaps the most popular and largest service on the Internet, Yahoo Store offers a robust feature set and a fairly easy path to modifying your store interface to match your website. It has payment processing, shipping, inventory management, and order management modules built in. It also supports downloadable products and recurring payments. This solution, however, is also one of the most expensive. It runs about $36.00 per month and charges a 1.5 percent transaction fee on each sale. You can learn more about and sign up for Yahoo Store at `store.yahooo.com`.

- ✔ **Big Commerce:** A rapidly growing service, Big Commerce is highly customizable, and it allows you to upload several different images at several different sizes. It's also optimized for mobile WebKit browsers (discussed in Chapter 12). You can set up several chargeable options (such as engraving or embroidering), and it has several modules for selling on Facebook and other social networking sites. Big Commerce's pricing is tiered, based on the number of products in your store and web traffic. Prices run between $25 and $300 per month. You can learn more about and sign up for Big Commerce at `www.bigcommerce.com`.

- ✔ **MobiCart:** MobiCart is a different approach to creating a shopping cart. It relies the mobile-app concept for setting up a mobile online store. You create an online cart and your customers use your store to download an app from Apple's App Store or Google's Android Market. Granted, for customers making single, one-time purchases, this is not an ideal approach to selling online. However, for customers who order from your store regularly, this is a great way to provide them with a convenient way to place orders easily, no matter where they are or what they're doing. As I write this, MobiCart is free. You can find out more about MobiCart at `www.mobi-cart.com`.

Creating a Server-Side Mobile Shopping Cart

Although online mobile shopping cart services are quick and convenient — ideal for selling a few products on relatively slow to moderate sites, as discussed in the previous section, they have several drawbacks. Especially if you're selling a lot of products and your shopping cart gets a lot of traffic. My primary concerns about mobile solutions are that they can be expensive — the more you sell, the more they cost — and that they're not easily moved if you decide you need a different solution.

In this section, I walk you through installing, setting up, and deploying a server-side shopping cart. During this discussion, I use Zen Cart as a backdrop for the discussion. The reason I've chosen Zen Cart is that it supports all the features (and then some) discussed in the "Deciding What You Need Your Shopping Cart To Do" section earlier in this chapter. You can run Zen Cart on any server that supports PHP and MYSQL or CGI and MySQL, which the majority the web servers on the Internet do. It is easily moved to another web server. And it's free. The only costs you incur using Zen Cart are the payment processing charges from your credit card processor or merchant account.

Zen Cart is also written with self-adjusting HTML and CSS style sheets, meaning that you don't have to create separate carts for desktop computers and mobile devices, as shown in Figure 17-5. Because Zen Cart pages rely on CSS and HTML, you can easily configure them to match your existing website. You can learn more about Zen Cart and download it from `www.zencart.com`.

Many hosting services provide free shopping cart applications; many, in fact, provide Zen Cart. Before deciding on a solution, check with your hosting service to see what it has to offer. Make sure that the software it offers meets your needs. Keep in mind that in most cases you don't have to use the program that your hosting service provides. Solutions such as Zen Cart are relatively easy to install on any server.

Figure 17-5:
Zen Cart shopping cart displayed on desktop computer and mobile browser.

Installing and deploying the shopping cart

No matter which server-side shopping cart program you choose, the procedure for setting it up and launching it will consist of the these eight basic steps:

1. Create the database.

2. Install the software.

3. Configure the software.

4. Customize the interface.

5. Enter and configure your products.

6. Set up payment processing.

7. Set up shipping processing.

8. Deploy the shopping cart.

Each one of these general steps can entail several procedures, depending on what you're selling and how the software handles specific tasks.

For this demonstration of setting up and deploying a server-side shopping cart, I'm using the test server I've installed on my workstation. You can follow along and create your own shopping cart by installing XAMPP for Windows or XAMPP for Macintosh, as described in Chapter 4.

Creating the database

Any shopping cart program worth its salt creates its pages *dynamically*. In other words, rather than making *you* create multiple static pages for your products, checkout pages, and so on, the shopping cart creates HTML page content on the fly — as needed. To make this happen, the content is saved in a database. Server-side scripts, usually PHP, call to the database and request the content required for each specific page.

This method has many advantages over creating multiple pages for the shopping cart application. Typically, shopping carts are fluid — you frequently make changes to products, prices, specials, shipping and tax rates, as well as several other aspects of the cart. Saving and pulling the data from a database allows you or your client to make such changes without having to reconfigure existing pages and create new web pages. This method also ensures a much higher degree of accuracy and integrity; it eliminates the need to change multiple pages each time you make a product or price change.

Most shopping cart packages use MySQL database server; most Apache-based web servers — the predominant web server at most web hosting services — make MySQL available to their customers. The first step in setting up your shopping cart is creating an empty database to hold your product and other information. Typically, all you need to do is create the database and a user the shopping cart software can use to configure the database tables and populate the database.

Your hosting service should provide you with a URL for creating MySQL databases, similar to the page shown in Figure 17-6. (I'm using the XAMPP MySQL interface page. Undoubtedly, your hosting company's page will be different. But it should provide similar features — a way to create the database and a default database user.) To create your shopping cart database, follow these steps:

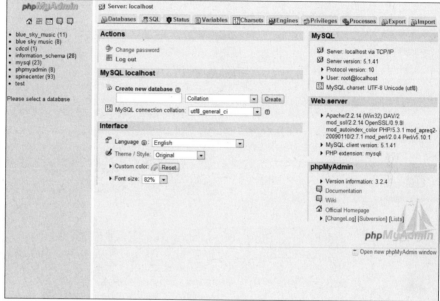

Figure 17-6:
The first step in setting up your shopping cart: Create an empty database.

1. **Go to the URL provided by your hosting company.**

2. **Type the name of your new database into the appropriate field.**

   In this case, I use the name of the shopping cart software, *zencart*. Shopping cart applications don't usually require special or custom databases; the default settings should do the job nicely.

3. **Click the appropriate button to create the database.**

   When the server has created the database, you should be presented with a page for configuring it. Your shopping cart software should do most of the configuration for you, after you create a user account and password in the database. On my test server, this is accomplished with the options on the Privileges tab. From there, clicking the Add a New User link brings up the page shown in Figure 17-7.

Figure 17-7:
Creating
a user
account for
the shop-
ping cart
software to
use to popu-
late your
database.

The figures in this section show the MySQL server interface pages on my workstation. These pages provide complete, unfettered access to the server. Most likely, the interface provided by your hosting company will not, for security reasons, provide you with this level of access. Therefore, most of these options will not be displayed, making creating a user account for your database much simpler, as shown in the Add a New User page at DreamHost in Figure 17-8. In fact, if you're setting up a database on your hosting service's server, I suggest you refer to the services support files for instructions on creating a database and a new user account.

4. **Type a username and password and click the appropriate button to save the changes.**

   If you're setting up your shopping cart on an XAMPP test server, be sure to click the Check All link in the Global Privileges section to provide all privileges to the new user account.

Installing the shopping cart software

It this situation, the word *installing* is bit of a misnomer. Few, if any, web hosting companies are going to let you actually *install* anything on their servers. Instead, you typically unzip the application on your workstation, upload the files to the web server, and then access the setup application via a URL.

Figure 17-8:
MySQL con-
figuration
pages for
your host-
ing service
make most
of the setup
decisions
for you.

If you're installing the shopping cart on a test server, you can simply unzip and copy the files to the subdirectory from which you'll be running that shopping cart. After that, you can browse to the URL and start setting up the software, as I've done if Figure 17-9. With Zen Cart, most of the initial setup entails connecting to the database and creating some basic records, such as company name, contact info, and the cart's administrator credentials.

Figure 17-9:
When
you've
uploaded
the shop-
ping cart
files to the
server,
you can
browse to
the URL for
the shop-
ping cart to
begin the
installation
process.

Hello. Thank you for loading Zen Cart™.

You are seeing this page for one or more reasons:

1. This is your **first time using Zen Cart™** and you haven't yet completed the normal Installation procedure. If this is the case for you, you will need to upload the "zc_install" folder using your FTP program, and then run zc_install/index.php via your browser (or reload this page to see a link to it).
2. Your /includes/configure.php and/or /admin/includes/configure.php file contains invalid *path information* and/or invalid *database-connection information*. If you recently edited your configure.php files for any reason, or maybe moved your site to a different folder or different server, then you'll need to review and update all your settings to the correct values for your server. See the Online FAQ and Tutorials area on the Zen Cart™ website for assistance.
3. Additional Details: includes/configure.php file contents invalid. ie: DIR_FS_CATALOG not valid or not set

To begin installation ...

1. The Installation Documentation can be read by clicking here: Documentation
2. You will need to upload the "zc_install" folder using your FTP program, and then run zc_install/index.php via your browser (or reload this page to see a link to it).
3. The Online FAQ and Tutorials area on the Zen Cart™ website will also be of value if you run into difficulties.

Copyright © 2003-2011 Zen Cart™

If you're installing a different shopping cart program, the setup pages and the procedure will, of course, be different. However, the information provided in the following steps — which choices to make and why, are relevant to any application that uses MySQL as the database and PHP for the scripts that access the database and create the application's web pages. You should have the setup instructions for the program you're installing on hand, though, in case the procedure is dramatically different or if you encounter differences in terminology.

The following steps walk you through the initial setup of Zen Cart on a test server. If you're not using Zen Cart, you can use them as guidelines for setting up the software you're using.

1. **Download the shopping software from the vendor's website.**

2. **Unzip (decompress) the files and copy them to the subdirectory from which you'll be running the shopping cart.**

   I've copied the files to a `Zencart` subdirectory on my test server. If you're installing your shopping cart on your web server, you can FTP them to the server with Dreamweaver or an FTP client such as FileZilla, which you can download for free at `http://filezilla-project.org/`.

3. **Browse to the initial setup page for the shopping cart.**

   The Zen Cart welcome page provides some information about the software and instructions for beginning the installation process. In this case, the instructions are to browse to `zc_install/index.php`, a URL located in subdirectory of the `zencart` directory, which brings up the setup Welcome page.

4. **Browse to `/Zencart/zc_install/index.php`.**

5. **Click the Continue button.**

6. **Select the radio button to agree to the license agreement and then click Continue.**

   Zen Cart performs a check of the system to make sure the server is running a compatible version of PHP, as shown in Figure 17-10. If the inspection detects any compatibilities on the server or that the required PHP features are not active, it will notify you on this page.

   XAMPP and other Apache servers are usually configured properly by default to run Zen Cart and most other PHP applications. If your web host does not run the necessary features by default, you'll need to contact them to find out how to enable them. If you're running a test server other than XAMPP, refer to that server's documentation for configuration information. Again, in most situations, this will not be necessary.

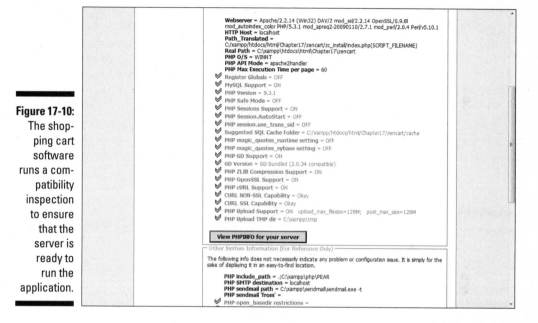

Figure 17-10:
The shop-
ping cart
software
runs a com-
patibility
inspection
to ensure
that the
server is
ready to
run the
application.

**7. If the inspection determines that your server is ready to run the shop-
ping cart, click Install.**

Step 7 brings up the Database Setup page. Although there are many
options on this page, all you really need to be concerned with is the
Database Information section, shown in Figure 17-11. Here's a description of these options and how you should fill them out:

- **Database Type:** Unless some other database software is running
  on the system in addition to MySQL (which there probably is not),
  this drop-down should have only one option — MySQL. In any
  case, you should choose MySQL.

- **Database Host:** The database host is the DNS name of the database. If you're installing your shopping cart on a remote hosting
  server, you should use the DNS name given to you by your hosting
  service. If you're installing on a test server on your workstation,
  use **localhost**.

- **Database Username:** This is the username you created when you
  set up the database in the "Creating the database" section, earlier
  in this chapter.

- **Database Password:** This is the password you created when you set
  up the database in the "Creating the database" section of this chapter.

- **Database Name:** This is name of the database you created when
  you set up the database in the "Creating the database" section, earlier in this chapter.

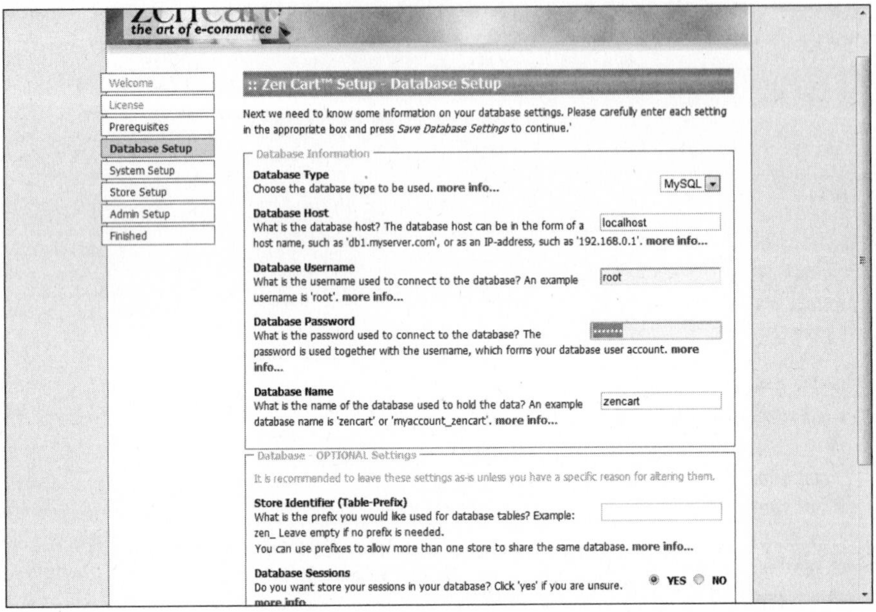

Figure 17-11:
Zen Cart's database configuration screen.

8. **Enter the appropriate information in the required fields and click Save Database Settings.**

   Step 8 displays the System Setup page. You can accept all the defaults on this page.

   If you're installing on a remote server, and you've purchased and installed an SSL certificate (as described in the sidebar, "Understanding Secure Socket Layer [SSL]," earlier in this chapter), you should click the "Enable SSL" and "Enable SSL in Admin Area" radio buttons at the bottom of the screen, and fill in the fields in the SSL Details section of this page, using the information provided by your hosting service.

9. **Click Save System Settings.**

Configuring your shopping cart

After you've installed the shopping cart software and configured the database, you'll need to configure your store. Clicking the Save System Settings button in Step 9 in the previous section brings up the Store Setup page shown in Figure 17-12. Here's a list of the options on this page:

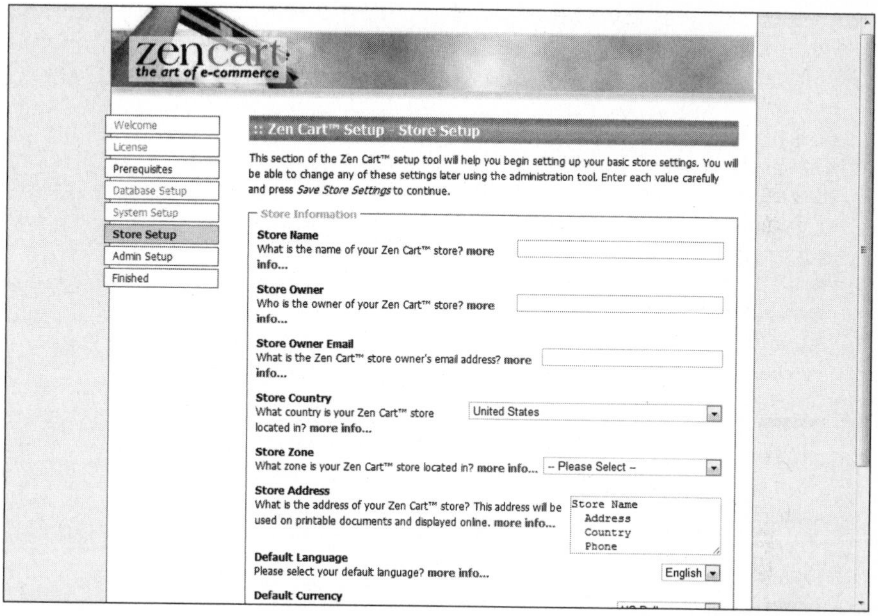

Figure 17-12:
Use this
page to
personalize
your online
store.

✔ **Store Name:** You can use this to name the store. This is the name that shows up in e-mails sent to your customers from the store. Use something descriptive, such as "My Company Online Store."

✔ **Store Owner:** The store owner is an individual or company who owns and operates the store.

✔ **Store Owner Email:** This the e-mail address of the owner of the store. Note that the shopping cart doesn't use this address to notify the store administrator of purchases and other events. That option is on the next screen.

✔ **Store Country:** Enter the country where the store is located.

✔ **Store Zone:** This is the location of the store. For stores located in the U.S.A., enter a state.

✔ **Store Address:** This is the physical address of the store.

✔ **Default Language:** Enter the language of the store (Zen Cart has several different language modules you can install later.)

✔ **Default Currency:** Enter the default currency for the store, or the currency with which you want to do transactions.

✔ **Store Demo:** Zen Cart comes with several example products that you can install to see how the store works. Use this option if you want to install them. You can easily delete them later.

Making your shopping cart secure

As the operator of an online store, you have a serious responsibility: Most shopping carts store customer information, including credit card numbers and other information — and it's your responsibility to see that this information is never compromised. Each shopping cart application has its own routine for securing shopping cart data. Zen Cart, for example, instructs you to delete the folder containing the installation files, `zc_install`. You should also follow the instructions on the Setup Finished page for making a couple of `configure.php` files read-only, which disallows intruders to change the application's configuration.

Also, the first time you try to go to the administration pages of the application, you'll see the warning shown here.

The program won't let you access the admin pages until you've secured them. Before moving on to customize the store and populate it with products, you'll need to click the "Help for renaming the admin folder can be found here" link and follow the instruction for securing the administration pages. It's fairly straightforward and simple.

To configure your store, follow these steps:

1. **Enter the desired information on the Store Setup page and click Save Store Settings.**

   This brings up the Administrator Account Setup. From here you configure the store administrator and username, password, and e-mail address. This is the e-mail address that the store uses when it sends notifications of purchases and other events.

   2. **Fill in the fields on the Administrator Account Setup page can click Save Admin Settings.**

      This concludes the setup process for the shopping cart. The next page, Setup – Finished, provides instructions for making your e-commerce site secure. You can go to the shopping cart by clicking the Click Here to Go to the Store button at the page.

Customizing your shopping cart's interface

If, like Zen Cart, your shopping cart uses CSS to format your pages, then modifying the cart's appearance to match your existing website should be fairly simple. All you'll need to do is locate the CSS files and change the code to suit your needs. Editing CSS style sheets is discussed in several chapters in this book, primarily Chapters 2 and 7.

Each shopping cart program will, of course, have slightly different options for modifying the appearance of the interface. Zen Cart encourages you to create a duplicate set of the default template and modify it. You can find instructions for doing this and many other appearance changes at `http://tutorials.zen-cart.com/index.php?category=4`.

Entering and configuring your products

Typically, entering products into a shopping cart database consists of creating product categories, adding product information (such as prices and descriptions), and creating the product images. Except for the creating and resizing the images, most of this is done from the shopping cart's *backend*, or admin pages, shown in Figure 17-13.

Creating product categories

Not all shopping carts require multiple categories — it depends, of course, on the number of products you're selling and whether they logically fall into different categories. In Zen Cart, you need at least one category. You can create it and other categories from the Categories page, which you can get to by clicking the Catalog menu and then choosing Categories/Products. From there, you click the New Category button, which brings up the New Category page shown in Figure 17-14. Simply fill in the simple form, naming the category and giving it a description. Then click Save. (You can also add a category image if you want. This is simply a matter of preference.)

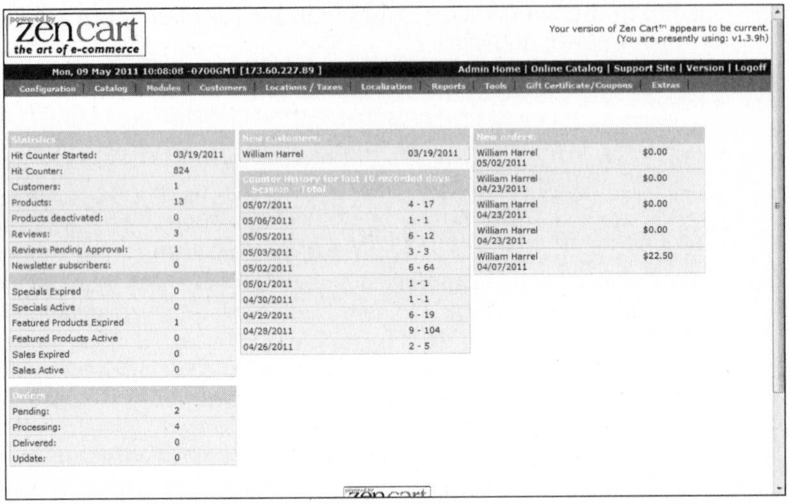

Figure 17-13:
The Zen Cart Admin interface, where you add products and control the behavior of your shopping cart.

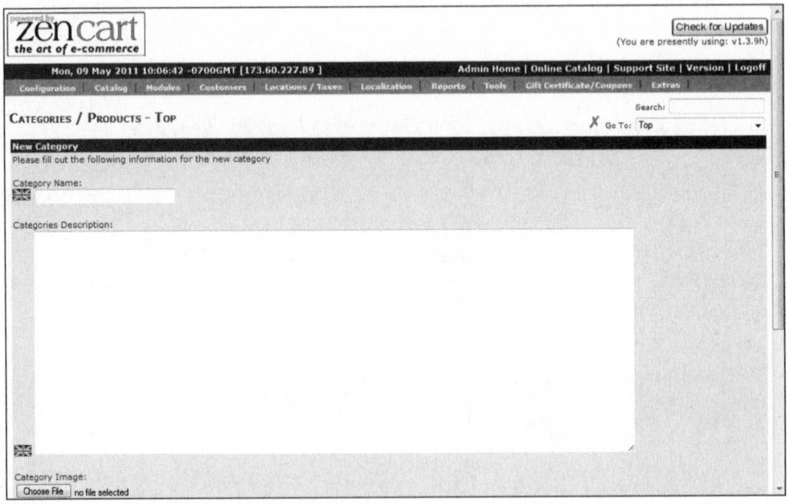

Figure 17-14:
Zen Cart's New Category page.

Creating product images

Each shopping cart application handles product images differently. Some, for example, require specific display sizes. Some support multiple images for the same product; others do not. Some have the ability to display the same image at different sizes. Zen Cart supports both options — multiple images and the capability to display the same images at multiple zoom levels.

Although programs like Zen Cart allow you to use the same image at multiple zoom levels, you'll want to be careful about this. For this feature to work properly — displaying the image well at all sizes — the image must be configured to the maximum display size. What this means is that the mobile device will have to download the entire file, no matter what size the image is on the page. On a page consisting of several product images, you could wind up downloading many huge files in order to display the product images at their *smallest* size, which can slow the download and display of the entire page significantly.

The options for configuring and using product images in Zen Cart are quite extensive; therefore, so is the information describing how to use them. In addition to the information provided here and in Chapter 10, which covers formatting media for the Web, you can find additional information for creating and deploying images in your shopping cart at `http://tutorials.zen-cart.com/index.php?article=58`.

Keep in mind, when configuring images for your shopping cart, that symmetry is important (as shown in Figure 17-15). Keep all your *thumbnails* — initial display images — the same size, so that your product pages don't look like collages of mismatched multisize images.

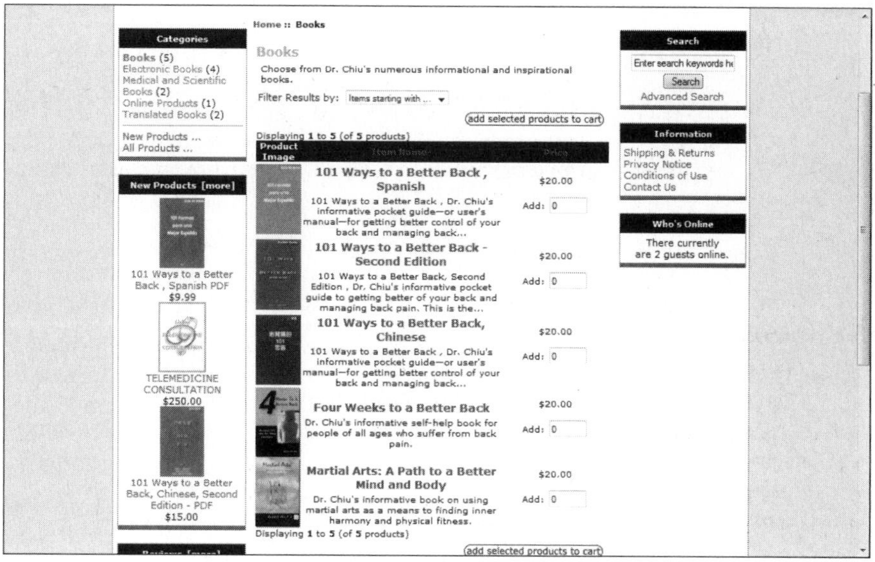

Figure 17-15: Keep all the thumbnail images in your shopping cart the same size, so that your page maintains its symmetry.

Adding products

When you've created your categories and created your images, you can start populating the database with your products. Again, each shopping cart application will handle this somewhat differently. Zen Cart lets you create your products all on one screen and select and upload your images at the same time.

Products are created from within a category. On the Category page, discussed in the "Creating product categories" section of this chapter, and shown in Figure 17-15, click the category in which you want to add a product, and then click the New Product button, which brings up the screen shown in Figure 17-16.

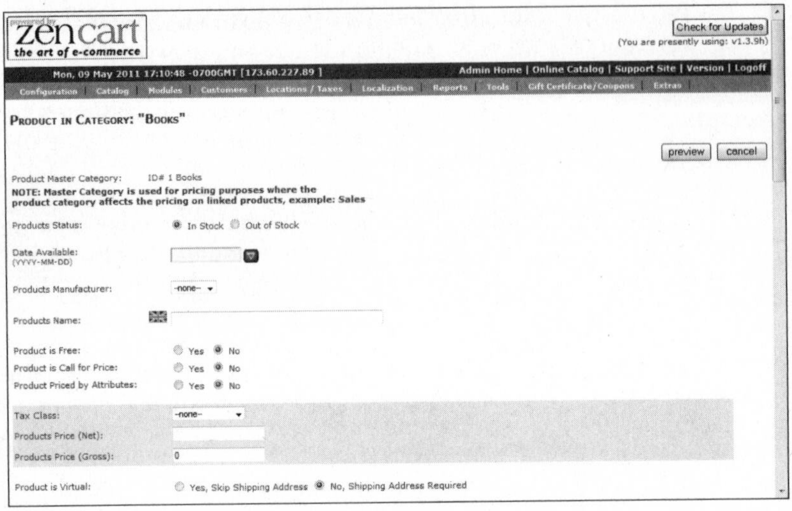

Figure 17-16:
Zen Cart's
Product in
Category
page, which
allows you
to enter and
configure
your
products.

How you fill out this page is critical to how your products are displayed. The following list describes each option and how to configure it:

- **In Stock/Out of Stock:** Zen Cart and other full-featured shopping carts allow you to control inventory. This option is part of that system. If you check Out of Stock, the product will show up as sold out on your product pages.

- **Date Available:** Use this option to control the date at which the product becomes visible in the shopping cart. This option also controls when a product appears in the New Product section of the shopping cart.

- **Product is Free/Product is Call for Price/Product is Priced by Attributes:** The first two options speak for themselves. The third, Product is Price by Attributes, allows another, more advanced section of the application to control pricing with several variables, such as whether the customer orders a downloadable or shippable version of the product.

- **Tax Class:** Zen Cart and other full-featured applications let you create multiple taxation scenarios, such as per state or region. Use this option to assign a specific tax class to the product.

- **Product Price (Net)/Product Price (gross):** These two options let you set two prices for the product, a single unit price and a bulk, or multiple-unit price.

- **Product is Virtual:** *Virtual products* are downloadable products. You don't, of course, need shipping addresses for downloadable products.

- **Always Free Shipping:** Use this option to control free shipping options.

- **Products Quantity Box Shows:** This option works with the Products Quantity page displayed further down the page. Use it to control whether your customers can see how many products you have in stock.

- **Product Qty Minimum/Product Qty Maximum/Product Qty Units/Product Qty Min/Unit Mix:** These options allow you to sell products in bulk, or lots. In other words, the customer must purchase specific quantities of the product. The way these options work together is somewhat detailed. You can get more information at `http://tutorials.zen-cart.com/index.php?article=37`.

- **Product Description:** This option kind of speaks for itself — but you should know that this field supports most standard HTML tags. Thus you can format the text as desired and create hyperlinks, lists, and any other text formatting features, as shown in Figure 17-17.

- **Products Quantity:** This is part of Zen Cart's inventory control system. In addition to keeping track of the number of units on hand, it also displays the current number in stock to the customer.

- **Products Model:** You can use this option to create or include a model number for the product.

- **Products Image:** Use this option to select the product image file. This option also uploads the image to the remote server and creates a link to the image so it's displayed properly.

- **Product URL:** Use this option to create a link to a product page to provide the customer with a more detailed description of the product. You can either create your product pages or link to the manufacturer's product pages.

- **Products Shipping Weight:** The shopping cart uses this option to calculate shipping costs, if you're using a shipping system based on product weight.

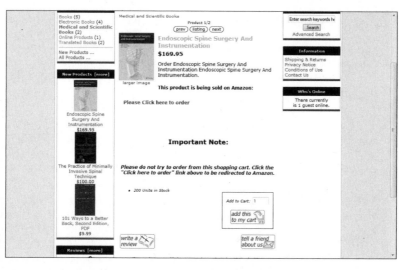

Figure 17-17: Example of using HTML tags to control the appearance and features of the product description.

Setting up payment processing

Online payment processing is a huge topic and there are many, many options, as discussed in the "Handling Payments" section earlier in this chapter. Zen Cart supports several popular payment processing options, including Authorize.Net and PayPal, which are two of the more widely used. Payment processing options are configured through the Payment module, which you can get to from the Modules menu. Instructions for installing each option are also on this page.

Setting up shipping processing

There are just about as many options for processing shipping as there are payment processors. Full-featured shopping carts let you create your own shipping parameters or use the shipping tables from major shippers, such as UPS, FedEx, and the U.S. Postal Service. Zen Cart lets you do both, as well as configure a separate "handling" charge. Or you can choose to charge either a flat rate or per-product rates. You can set up shipping parameters in the Shipping module, which you can get to from the Modules menu. When you get there, the options are pretty straightforward. If you want to interact with shipper's rate tables, you can find that information at http://tutorials.zen-cart.com/index.php?category=12.

Deploying the shopping cart

Finally! You've installed your shopping cart, configured the database, customized the interface, entered your products, set up payment and shipping processing — at last you can put your store online and rake in the dough. All you have to do to get it working is create a link to it from your website. If the site will run under a SSL certificate — as discussed in the sidebar, "Understanding Secure Socket Layer (SSL)" — you should use the https protocol in your hyperlink.

Also, you can get further exposure for your shopping cart by optimizing your pages for Google and other search engines, as discussed in Chapter 15.

If you've installed Zen Cart on a test server and want to move it to your web host's server, the information for doing that can be found at http://tutorials.zen-cart.com/index.php.

Part V
The Part of Tens

"Look at this, Mother! I customized the browser so I can navigate the Web the way I want to."

In this part . . .

This part provides links to a bunch of stuff you should find useful. Chapter 19 shows you where to find ten different mobile emulators, which are small applications that allow you to see what your site will look like on specific devices. Chapter 20 contains links to several sites that have multiple mobile web templates — some are free, some are for sale. In Chapter 21 you'll find links to ten widgets, which are small snippets of code you can use to create page elements, such as menus, Google Maps, 3D product viewers, and several other useful objects.

Chapter 18

Top Ten Mobile Emulators

Mobile emulators allow you to see a simulation of what your mobile site will look like on specific mobile devices. Although this in no way compares to viewing a site on an actual mobile device, they're the next best thing. After all, there's just no way (unless you work in a mobile phone store) to see how your site will display on all the different handhelds on the market.

You should try your site in as many mobile emulators as you can — or as many as you have time for. There are many mobile emulators on the Internet. Some are for specific types of mobile devices, such as iPhones or BlackBerry handhelds; and some allow you to switch between various mobile devices. Some are downloadable utilities you install on your computer, and some are online sites where you enter your mobile site's URL and view the results on a web page.

This chapter looks at some of the more popular and useful mobile emulators. You learn where to find these emulators and how to use them. Viewing your mobile sites in emulators allows you to make critical adjustments to your layout before publishing the site and making it available to the world.

Adobe Device Central

Perhaps the most comprehensive of all device emulators is Adobe's Device Central, shown in Figure 18-1. Device Central is a utility that comes with most of Adobe's popular design and media editing software, such as Flash, Dreamweaver, Photoshop, and Illustrator. You can't buy it as a standalone application (though it would be nice if you could).

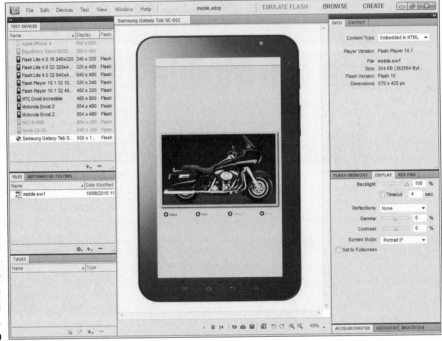

Figure 18-1:
Adobe
Device
Central
emulates
nearly every
mobile
device
available.

Device Central has the largest database of mobile devices, as far as emulators go, that I'm aware of, and the database is updated daily, not only by Adobe but also by Adobe users. Device Central also provides the most information and emulation options I've seen. Not only can you see how your pages look on specific devices but you can also get detailed descriptions of what technologies, such as HTML and CSS versions, each device supports, and oh so much more information.

For example, you can switch orientation back and forth, see how much memory your page or media uses (as shown in Figure 18-2), and even see simulations of how your site will look in various lighting situations, such as indoor, outdoor, and sunshine scenarios, as shown in Figure 18-3. Frankly, if you have this utility, you probably won't need to worry about going out on the Internet and finding others.

It really doesn't get much better than this. Device Central even shows how memory usage changes when you click links or load new pages.

Memory used by this movie

Figure 18-2:
Device
Central
depicts how
much mem-
ory a Flash
SWF file is
using.

Simulating lighting environments

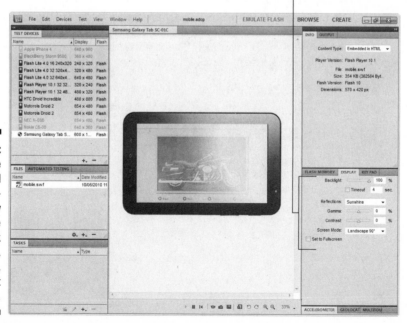

Figure 18-3:
Device
Central
can simu-
late how
your page
will look
indoors,
outdoors,
or in direct
sunshine.

Opera Mini Simulator

Opera Mini is a mobile version of the popular web browser, Opera. Many intermediate-to-advanced mobile users download this browser on their handhelds because it provides a slew of features not supported on the default browsers that come with several popular devices. It is also fast and supports most WebKit extensions (discussed in Chapter 12). You can find the Opera Mini Simulator at www.opera.com/mobile/demo.

Using the Opera Mini Simulator is easy. Simply browse to the preceding URL and enter the address for the mobile site you want to view in the address bar in the upper-right corner of the emulator. When your home page has loaded, you can also click links and menu items to see how the other pages in your site will display.

TestiPhone–iPhone Simulator

Many iPhone, iPod, and iPad simulators on the Internet are quite good. I've had good luck with TestiPhone, which displays content relatively accurately. You can get to TestiPhone at www.testiphone.com.

The one thing I've noticed — TestiPhone included — is that emulators seem to forget that Flash isn't supported on iPhones and other Apple handhelds. They play the Flash contents, anyway. Also, some iPhone emulators, unlike the Opera Mini Simulator in the previous section, ignore JavaScript; others ignore detect and switch scripts (discussed in Chapter 6). If the emulator you use does this, simply type the URL to the mobile version of the site.

Using TestiPhone, shown in Figure 18-4, is simply a matter of browsing to the preceding URL and typing the URL in the address bar at the top of the emulator. When your mobile home page has loaded, you can then test your other pages by clicking your menu and link items.

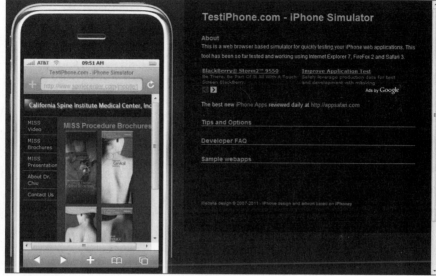

iPad Peek

The iPad Peek iPad emulator at `http://ipadpeek.com` is a great resource for seeing how your mobile pages will look on an iPad. These devices have fairly large screens, and often you don't need to compensate for them in your code. They don't, however, support Flash.

To use iPad Peek, shown in Figure 18-5, simply browse to `http://ipad-peek.com` and enter the mobile site you want to test in the address bar. When the home page loads, you can test the rest of your site by clicking menu items and other links. You can rotate the iPad emulator by clicking the iPad bevel, or the black area around the display area.

Bevel

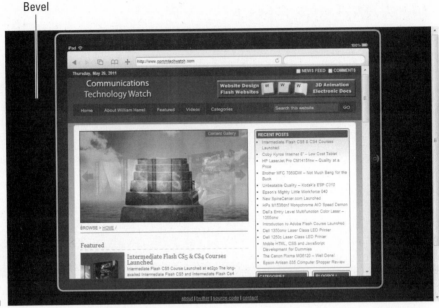

Figure 18-5:
To rotate
the iPad in
iPad Peek,
click any-
where on
the iPad's
bevel.

Android Emulator

For some reason, it's tough to find an Android Emulator, especially an online version. As I write this, all I could find is the emulator that comes with the Android Software Development Kit (SDK). Most operating systems (OS) have SDKs, which are usually distributed by the developers of the operating system. SDKs are designed to help you create apps for a particular OS.

The good news is that you don't have to download and install the Android SDK, which is a somewhat involved and complicated process, to get the emulator. The folks of Redmond Pie have extracted the emulator from the SDK and wrapped it into a standard Windows installation executable you can download and easily install on your Windows computer. You can find the Android Emulator install file and instructions for installing and using the emulator at `www.redmondpie.com/android-emulator-for-windows`.

Not all handheld platforms have good online emulators. It's hard to find, for example, good online emulators for BlackBerry and Android devices. In fact, I had trouble finding a good BlackBerry emulator at all, even download-able simulators. Most of them are device-specific, emulating only one type of BlackBerry handheld, such as the BlackBerry Storm. This is another great reason to look into comprehensive emulators, such as Adobe Device Central, discussed earlier in this chapter. Device Central allows you to test on emula-tors for most mobile devices, without scouring the Internet for OS-specific emulators.

DeviceAnywhere

DeviceAnywhere is an online subscription service for mobile app developers and site designers. The service allows you to purchase monthly subscription "packages" based primarily on manufacturers or OS. They also offer hourly rates. This service has a huge list of emulators, but it's not cheap. You really have to be a serious (and relatively successful) designer to make using a service like this cost-effective. But this type of service does provide highly accurate emulators.

Mobile Simulator

Mobile Simulator is a small, easy-to-use site that lets you see your site on a simulated BlackBerry Storm, iPhone, a small-screen Android, and a Nokia E72. I didn't find the iPhone simulator, compared to others, all that useful, but you can use this site to get a feel for how your sites will look on small-screen Droids and some BlackBerries. Unfortunately, though, you can't rotate this simulator. You can get to the Mobile Simulator at `http://mobile simulator.info/blackberry1.htm`.

To use the Mobile Simulator browse to the preceding URL and then type the mobile website address in the field to the left of the emulator. To switch between devices, simply click the device name to the left of the emulator. After the home page has loaded, you can test the other pages on the site by clicking menu items and other links.

User Agent Switcher

This Firefox add-on allows you to "spoof" specific user agents. I discuss user agents in Chapters 3, 4, 5, and 13. This add-on sort of emulates various mobile devices inside your Firefox browser. What it actually does is tell the web server that your browser is a designated user agent, such as, say, an iPhone, rather than a standard computer browser. You can find the User Agent Switcher add-on for Firefox at `https://addons.mozilla.org/en-US/firefox/addon/user-agent-switcher`.

After you install the add-on (choose Add-ons from the Firefox menu in Firefox 4.0), you can change the default user agent. To change the user agent in Firefox, simply click the Tools menu and choose Default User Agent, which opens a submenu of installed user agents. Choose the user agent you want and then press Ctrl+R to reload the page.

Firefox sends the new user agent string to the server, and the server sends pages designed for that user agent, depending on how you've developed your website — which is the topic of this book.

Additional user agents are developed for User Agent Switcher from time to time. You can find them and further information about using this add-on from the developer's Help pages at `http://chrispederick.com/work/user-agent-switcher/help`.

Apple's Safari also has a robust debugging and WebKit–extension checking feature that you can turn on by placing Safari in developer mode. The developer mode options are on the `Develop` menu. There is also a `User Agent` option on the `Develop` menu that emulates Apple's iOS for iPhones, iPads, and iPods.

Mobile Phone Emulator

The Mobile Phone Emulator allows you to test some devices unavailable on some other emulators, such as HTC and Samsung handhelds. It also allows you to enter a bunch of values not available in many emulators, such as screen resolution and OS type. You can find Mobile Phone Emulator at www. mobilephoneemulator.com.

To use the this emulator, you simply choose the device in the first drop-down under Cell Phone Terminal, and type the URL in the first field under Website to Simulate. This is not the most accurate emulator in the world, but what I like about it is that it sees and uses my detect-and-switch scripts.

Chapter 19

Top Ten Mobile Template Sites

. . . .

*O*ne of the most time-consuming parts of the mobile website design process is creating and laying out the initial design of the site — that is, coming up with the site's template. (Creating mobile web templates is discussed in Chapter 8.) Usually, getting the overall design, such as CSS containers, menus, buttons, and color scheme, entails quite a bit of trial and error. For me, this is often one of the more arduous parts of the process.

When you're designing for a client, sometimes you need to come up with a few different designs for the client's consideration. Even the most seasoned designers use third-party templates, especially when the client is not willing to pay you for your time to come up with a custom design for her site. In these situations, you can save time, and save your client money, by starting with a template.

One of the primary concerns of designers and clients alike have about using templates is that you run the risk of developing a site that looks too much like somebody else's. But I can tell you from years of experience that by the time you change the images and color scheme in a template, the chances of it looking like another site using the same template are slim to none. Besides, literally thousands of web templates are available on the Internet. It's highly unlikely that you or your client will choose one that many other companies or organizations have also chosen.

You can find many free mobile web templates on the Internet, and many templates that are relatively inexpensive. By inexpensive, I mean less than $100. When you consider how long it can take to come up with an original design, this really is a good deal.

In this chapter, I show you ten of the best mobile template websites, or template stores, available on the Internet. Also, I give you a few pointers for choosing templates. These sites are great places to choose from hundreds of well-designed templates with great documentation on customizing them and adding content. These sites can trim hours from the overall design and deployment process.

How to Choose a Web Template

Okay, you're thinking, *what can be so hard about choosing a template?* It's not *difficult,* per se; you just need to look before you leap when choosing a template. Which template can save you the most time and deliver the most efficient path to success? Choosing a template, for example, that you have to shoehorn in, manipulate, and make compromises to make your content fit is far less preferable to choosing a template that accommodates your content easily. Equally important is the template's documentation. It can be oh-so-helpful if the creator of the template provides adequate descriptions of how to modify the template and replace the boilerplate content.

Matching the template to your content

Check out the three sites in Figure 19-1. Obviously, these three templates are completely different styles and are suited for different types of content. Keep in mind that you'll be replacing what you see with your own images, icons, and text. You may also be changing the colors.

Figure 19-1: Mobile templates come in many different styles and accommodate different types of content.

One of the templates, for example, uses an image that completely fills the screen. One consists of only a logo, icons, and menu items. Another has a small banner across the top. All three convey different tones. When choosing a template for your site, you should consider all these objective technical issues as well as the more subjective design style and tone issues. Think about your content, including the sizes of your images, the amount of text your pages need, and whether your site is a serious business site or a frilly and fun site.

You get the idea, right?

Documentation

The drawback of many free templates is that they're not well documented. Not *all* fee-based templates have good documentation, either, but the larger template stores, such as TemplateMonster.com and Templates.com, require their designers to create good documentation on how to modify the template's appearance and replace the boilerplate content with your own content. Many of the template stores also have strong support pages describing how to edit the CSS, HTML, and the images included with the templates.

Granted, you can probably figure out how a template is constructed — especially after reading this book. But having this information provided for you can save you lots of time. If the sight has buttons and menus constructed from CSS styles, for example, how do you change the labels on the buttons?

Do yourself a favor, check out the site's help files, FAQs, and other support pages before you purchase or commit too much time to using a template. If possible, take a look at the documentation for the template and make sure you understand what's required to customize it and add your content.

Templates.com

Templates.com, shown in Figure 19-2, is a fairly large repository of web templates and all sorts of other products you can use in your web designs, such as clip art and 3D models. It offers templates for sale, and several free templates, including free mobile templates. The templates on Templates.com are all professionally designed and well documented.

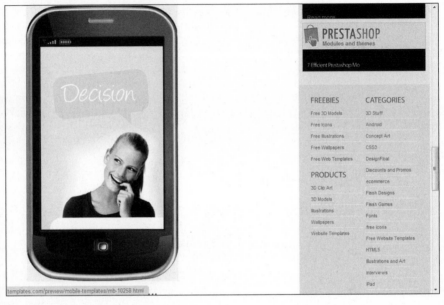

Figure 19-2:
Templates.
com
provides a
huge selec-
tion of web
templates,
including
mobile
templates.

TemplateMonster.com

Perhaps the largest template repository in the world, TemplateMonster.com, has hundreds of professionally designed mobile web templates, including many HTML5 mobile templates. The templates are categorized by business types, but you certainly are not locked into using a template designed for a specific business category.

Although there are several free templates, the average price for a mobile template is about $40. The templates are all very well documented and supported.

MoveToDotMobi

MoveToDotMobi, shown in Figure 19-3, offers around 40 (as of this writing) very well-designed mobile templates. The templates run about $90 each, and are designed to reformat according to the handheld's screen. Although the number of templates offered at this site is not big, the variety is good. You should be able to find one that meets the overall tone and theme of your site. You can find MoveToDotMobi at www.webdesignformobiledevices. com/html-ready-mobile-website-templates.php.

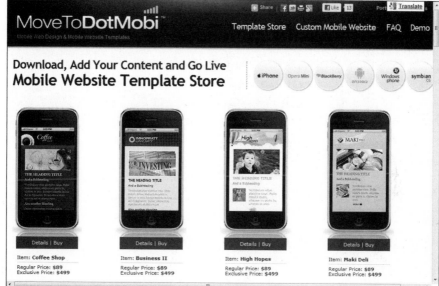

Figure 19-3: MoveTo DotMobi professionally designed mobile templates.

MEE Templates

MEE Templates, shown in Figure 19-4, has a growing number of very nice mobile templates and mobile blog templates. They run about $30 each and are available in a variety of different languages. The company also offers a 40 percent discount for freelancers and marketing firms, making them an even better bargain. The company's ads on the site claim you can have your site up in 20 minutes. I don't know about that, but customizing these templates and exchanging the boilerplate content for yours is very easy. You can find MEE Templates at www.meetemplates.com.

OSWD

OSWD provides about 2,000 free templates. Not all of them work well for handhelds, so you need to be selective. For example, don't choose a template with three or more columns for your mobile site. Nearly all the templates are designed with self-adjusting CSS that forces the pages to resize to the screen size of the device viewing the site. Again, the great thing about this site is the number of *free* templates. It also offers a good selection of premium, or for sale, templates. You can find OSWD at www.oswd.org.

mobiHybrid

Allwebco Design Corporation's mobiHybrid templates, shown in Figure 19-5, are PHP-based templates designed to work on all sizes of computer and hand-held screens. The server-side scripts serve up the appropriate pages according to the screen size of the device viewing the site. Because all the scripts are PHP, these templates should work well with nearly all mobile devices. Most of the templates run just over $20, which is a great bargain. You can find the templates at http://allwebcodesign.com/setup/mobi-templates.htm.

Figure 19-5: MobiHybrid templates are PHP sites designed to display on all device screens. The server-side scripts do all the work.

Perfectory

Perfectory is another huge repository of mobile web templates. Many of the templates offered here are also offered at other template stores, such as TemplateMonster.com, at about the same price. Mobile templates run about $40. You also find some templates here are not available at other sites. Many of these mobile templates are designed in HTML5 and CSS3, making them ideal for newer handhelds, but they may require some revising to work with all mobile devices. Perfectory's mobile templates are located at www. perfectory.com/category/mobile-templates.htm.

FreeTemplatesOnline

Despite this site's name, FreeTemplatesOnline (freetemplatesonline. com) provides a wide range of mobile web templates averaging about $40 each. I couldn't find many free mobile templates. However, this site does have a wide range of Zencart shopping cart templates, and some of them are quite good. (Zencart is discussed in Chapter 17.) Customizing Zencart's built-in template can be quite a chore. These shopping cart templates, which are priced between $130 and $150, are a quick and easy way to get your Zencart pages to meet your design needs.

bMobilized

This is not a template site. Instead, a mobile website conversion tool converts existing websites to mobile sites. All you do is enter the URL, and bMobilized (`bmobilized.com`) does the rest. (See Figure 19-6.) I tried this on several sites, and overall it works reasonably well. It doesn't create the fanciest sites I've seen, but what it does produce is acceptable — especially considering the technology and the speedy conversion.

If you subscribe to the site (which, at $19.99 per month, is a little steep), you get access to templates and other tools to help you customize the code bMobilized creates. You need to use it at least monthly to make it worth your while. But you can cancel at any time and keep the sites that bMobilized generated for you. I guess 20 bucks is not a huge amount to pay for a mobile site, and again, all things considered, the sites I generated with this tool were passable.

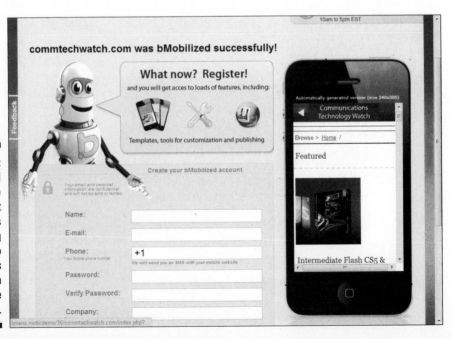

Figure 19-6: bMobilized is an online utility that converts existing websites to mobile sites quickly with acceptable results.

Chapter 20

Top Ten Mobile Widgets

Web app? Widget? What's the difference? If you search for one or the other on Google, you'll get results for both. For the sake of this chapter, the distinction is negligible. A *web app* or *widget* here is simply a snippet of code you paste into your web page to create a desired object, such as a menu, a button, an array of buttons, some type of media viewer, such as a 3D rotation viewer, and so on. There are hundreds of web apps and widgets on the Internet, and they do all sorts of things. For simplicity's sake, from here on, let's just call them *widgets*.

The advantage of widgets is that they save you from re-creating the wheel. Many page elements you might want to use in your web sites have already been developed and placed on the Internet — all you have do is copy the code into the appropriate location on your web pages, and then make some minor adjustments to get the widget to look an behave the way you want it to.

This chapter finds and describes ten of the most popular and useful widgets available. You can then use these widgets in your future projects.

Google Maps JavaScript API

This widget allows you to add a Google Map, shown in Figure 20-1, to your website. The latest version, V3, is designed to work with standard computers and mobile devices. For instructions on installing it in your website, see Chapter 16. You can get the code for this widget at `http://code.google.com/apis/maps/documentation/javascript/`.

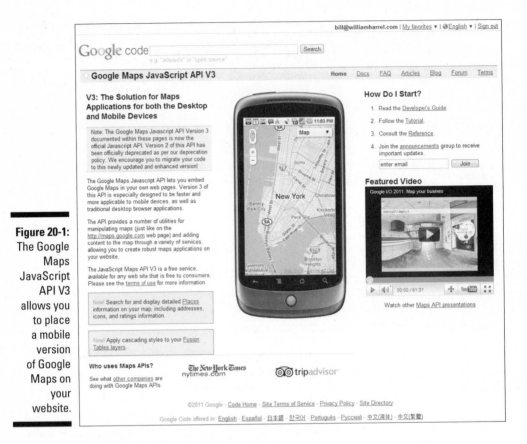

Figure 20-1:
The Google
Maps
JavaScript
API V3
allows you
to place
a mobile
version
of Google
Maps on
your
website.

JqueryUI Accordion Menu

An accordion menu creates collapsible sections on your page. The user can open the sections by clicking on the various section heads, as shown in Figure 20-2. There are several accordion widgets available on the web, as well as a Dreamweaver widget for creating them. You can find a good one at `http://jqueryui.com/demos/accordion/`.

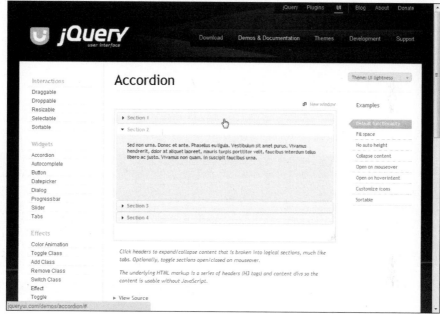

Figure 20-2: An accordion menu widget helps you create collapsible sections on your pages.

YouTube Video Bar Widget

The YouTube Video Bar widget lets you put a YouTube player on your web pages. Your visitors can then use it to play back YouTube content on your site. You can also use it in conjunction with the Video Search Control widget to allow users to search for YouTube content. This widget allows you to set parameters to control which YouTube content is searchable from your site. So, say for example you, your organization, or client has a YouTube channel. You can confine the searches to your channel. You can find information for installing these two widgets at `http://code.google.com/apis/you tube/getting_started.html#widgets`.

jQueryUI Tab Menu Widget

Similar to accordion menus, discussed earlier in this chapter, tab menus allow you to create tabbed sections on your pages for displaying content, as shown in Figure 20-3. There are several tab menu widgets on the Internet. One of the more complete and easiest to use is located at `http://jqueryui.com/demos/tabs`.

Figure 20-3:
Tab menu
widgets
allow your
users to
click tabs
to display
content.

Two-Column Widget

Creating two columns with CSS isn't as easy as it looks, so I created this
widget, shown in Figure 20-4. Everything you need — the HTML for the entire
page and the CSS — is here. All you need to do is copy the code, modify it
to meet your needs, and replace the boilerplate text with your own. You can
find this widget at `http://commtechwatch.com/?p=1058`.

You can find the code for this widget at this book's companion website.

jQuery Droppable Widget

This widget allows you to create a drag-and-drop widget. (See Figure 20-5.)
The user drags an object to another object and immediately gets feedback
that she has completed the task successfully. This is a great little widget for
creating simple match-up quizzes — you know, "Find the matching objects."
You can find this widget at `http://jqueryui.com/demos/droppable`.

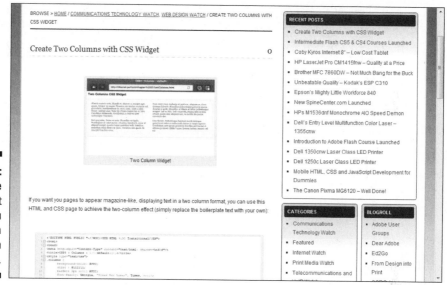

Figure 20-4:
This simple widget helps you create a two-column text page.

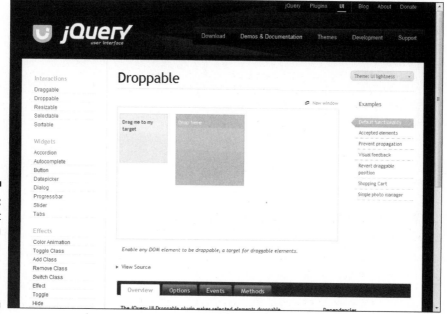

Figure 20-5:
This widget allows you to create a simple drag-and-drop application.

3D Rotation Viewer

This one will save you gobs of time. It supplies all the code you need to create a 3D product viewer, shown in Figure 20-6. The great thing about it is that smartphone and tablet users can use their fingers to rotate the 3D image. You can find an example of the widget at `www.uize.com/examples/3d-rotation-viewer.html`.

The instructions for creating the image and implementing the widget are at `www.uize.com/reference/Uize.Widget.Drag.html`.

Figure 20-6:
A nifty 3D image rotator — a great widget for creating a 3D product viewer.

HTML5 Video Player Widget

This widget requires Dreamweaver to implement, but it's a great way to include video in your mobile web pages. It doesn't use Flash, so it will work well with Apple devices. It also has a fallback to older technologies so that it will play on older devices and browsers that don't support HTML5. You can find this widget the Adobe Exchange at `www.adobe.com/cfusion/exchange/index.cfm?event=extensionDetail&extid=2294029`.

Rounded Corners, Gradients, and Drop Shadow Widget

HTML5's rounded corners, gradients, and drop shadows, discussed in Chapter 11, can often eliminate the need for creating these effects in a third-party graphics application. However, creating these effects can require research and trial error. This widget, shown in Figure 20-7, named by the author, Andrew Polhill, as simply CSS Widget, creates these effects for you. All you need to do is change the CSS and HTML code to meet your particular needs. You can find this widget and instructions for using it at `http://thatguynamedandy.com/blog/css-widget-rounded-corner-gradient-drop-shadow`.

Google Web Toolkit Button

This widget creates a standard HTML button without creating all of the typical accompanying form code — nowadays, buttons aren't used in websites just to send form information The widget allows you to create enabled and disabled buttons, as well as buttons with event listeners for initiating scripts. Event listeners are discussed in Chapter 3.

You can get this Google widget, shown in Figure 20-8, at `www.gwtapps.com/doc/html/com.google.gwt.user.client.ui.Button.html`.

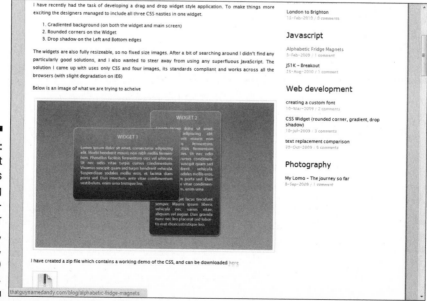

Figure 20-7: CSS Widget creates good-looking rounded-corner boxes, gradients, and drop shadows.

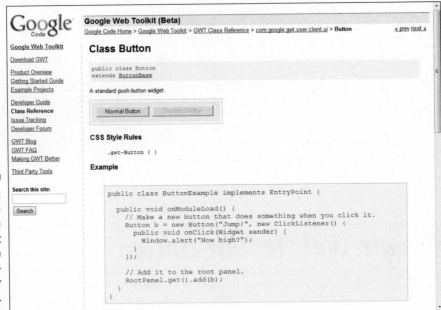

Figure 20-8:
You can use this Google widget to create simple buttons for your scripts.

Index

• F •

• G •

Apple & Macs

iPad For Dummies
978-0-470-58027-1

iPhone For Dummies,
4th Edition
978-0-470-87870-5

MacBook For Dummies, 3rd
Edition
978-0-470-76918-8

Mac OS X Snow Leopard For
Dummies
978-0-470-43543-4

Business

Bookkeeping For Dummies
978-0-7645-9848-7

Job Interviews
For Dummies,
3rd Edition
978-0-470-17748-8

Resumes For Dummies,
5th Edition
978-0-470-08037-5

Starting an
Online Business
For Dummies,
6th Edition
978-0-470-60210-2

Stock Investing
For Dummies,
3rd Edition
978-0-470-40114-9

Successful
Time Management
For Dummies
978-0-470-29034-7

Computer Hardware

BlackBerry
For Dummies,
4th Edition
978-0-470-60700-8

Computers For Seniors
For Dummies,
2nd Edition
978-0-470-53483-0

PCs For Dummies,
Windows
7 Edition
978-0-470-46542-4

Laptops For Dummies,
4th Edition
978-0-470-57829-2

Cooking & Entertaining

Cooking Basics
For Dummies,
3rd Edition
978-0-7645-7206-7

Wine For Dummies,
4th Edition
978-0-470-04579-4

Diet & Nutrition

Dieting For Dummies,
2nd Edition
978-0-7645-4149-0

Nutrition For Dummies,
4th Edition
978-0-471-79868-2

Weight Training
For Dummies,
3rd Edition
978-0-471-76845-6

Digital Photography

Digital SLR Cameras &
Photography For Dummies,
3rd Edition
978-0-470-46606-3

Photoshop Elements 8
For Dummies
978-0-470-52967-6

Gardening

Gardening Basics
For Dummies
978-0-470-03749-2

Organic Gardening
For Dummies,
2nd Edition
978-0-470-43067-5

Green/Sustainable

Raising Chickens
For Dummies
978-0-470-46544-8

Green Cleaning
For Dummies
978-0-470-39106-8

Health

Diabetes For Dummies,
3rd Edition
978-0-470-27086-8

Food Allergies
For Dummies
978-0-470-09584-3

Living Gluten-Free
For Dummies,
2nd Edition
978-0-470-58589-4

Hobbies/General

Chess For Dummies,
2nd Edition
978-0-7645-8404-6

Drawing
Cartoons & Comics
For Dummies
978-0-470-42683-8

Knitting For Dummies,
2nd Edition
978-0-470-28747-7

Organizing
For Dummies
978-0-7645-5300-4

Su Doku For Dummies
978-0-470-01892-7

Home Improvement

Home Maintenance
For Dummies,
2nd Edition
978-0-470-43063-7

Home Theater
For Dummies,
3rd Edition
978-0-470-41189-6

Living the
Country Lifestyle
All-in-One
For Dummies
978-0-470-43061-3

Solar Power Your Home
For Dummies,
2nd Edition
978-0-470-59678-4

Internet

Blogging For Dummies,
3rd Edition
978-0-470-61996-4

eBay For Dummies,
6th Edition
978-0-470-49741-8

Facebook For Dummies,
3rd Edition
978-0-470-87804-0

Web Marketing
For Dummies,
2nd Edition
978-0-470-37181-7

WordPress
For Dummies,
3rd Edition
978-0-470-59274-8

Language & Foreign Language

French For Dummies
978-0-7645-5193-2

Italian Phrases
For Dummies
978-0-7645-7203-6

Spanish For Dummies,
2nd Edition
978-0-470-87855-2

Spanish
For Dummies,
Audio Set
978-0-470-09585-0

Math & Science

Algebra I
For Dummies,
2nd Edition
978-0-470-55964-2

Biology For Dummies,
2nd Edition
978-0-470-59875-7

Calculus For Dummies
978-0-7645-2498-1

Chemistry For Dummies
978-0-7645-5430-8

Microsoft Office

Excel 2010 For Dummies
978-0-470-48953-6

Office 2010 All-in-One
For Dummies
978-0-470-49748-7

Office 2010 For Dummies,
Book + DVD Bundle
978-0-470-62698-6

Word 2010 For Dummies
978-0-470-48772-3

Music

Guitar For Dummies,
2nd Edition
978-0-7645-9904-0

iPod & iTunes For
Dummies, 8th Edition
978-0-470-87871-2

Piano Exercises
For Dummies
978-0-470-38765-8

Parenting & Education

Parenting For Dummies,
2nd Edition
978-0-7645-5418-6

Type 1 Diabetes
For Dummies
978-0-470-17811-9

Pets

Cats For Dummies,
2nd Edition
978-0-7645-5275-5

Dog Training For Dummies,
3rd Edition
978-0-470-60029-0

Puppies For Dummies,
2nd Edition
978-0-470-03717-1

Religion & Inspiration

The Bible For Dummies
978-0-7645-5296-0

Catholicism For Dummies
978-0-7645-5391-2

Women in the Bible
For Dummies
978-0-7645-8475-6

Self-Help & Relationship

Anger Management
For Dummies
978-0-470-03715-7

Overcoming Anxiety
For Dummies,
2nd Edition
978-0-470-57441-6

Sports

Baseball
For Dummies,
3rd Edition
978-0-7645-7537-2

Basketball
For Dummies,
2nd Edition
978-0-7645-5248-9

Golf For Dummies,
3rd Edition
978-0-471-76871-5

Web Development

Web Design
All-in-One
For Dummies
978-0-470-41796-6

Web Sites
Do-It-Yourself
For Dummies,
2nd Edition
978-0-470-56520-9

Windows 7

Windows 7
For Dummies
978-0-470-49743-2

Windows 7
For Dummies,
Book + DVD Bundle
978-0-470-52398-8

Windows 7 All-in-One
For Dummies
978-0-470-48763-1

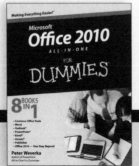

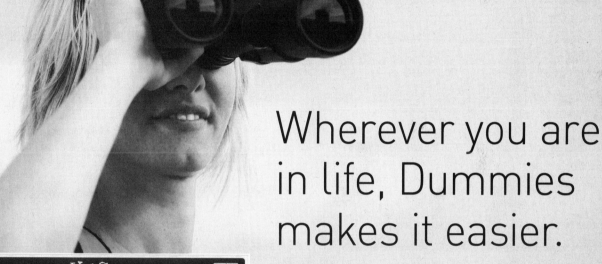

Wherever you are in life, Dummies makes it easier.

From fashion to Facebook®,
wine to Windows®, and everything in between,
Dummies makes it easier.

Visit us at Dummies.com

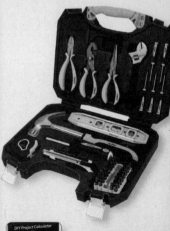